CHRISTMAS
around the world

CHRISTMAS
around the world

by
Emily Kelley

pictures by
Priscilla Kiedrowski

Carolrhoda Books · Minneapolis, Minnesota

To my family and the memory of my dad,
and especially to my Sam   —E.K.

For George and my mother, *God Jule!*
                                    —P.K.

Manufactured in the United States of America

LIBRARY OF CONGRESS CATALOGING-IN-PUBLICATION DATA

Kelley, Emily.
   Christmas around the world.

   (A Carolrhoda on my own book)
   Summary: Describes Christmas traditions in Mexico,
Iran, China, Sweden, Iraq, Spain, and Norway.
   1. Christmas — Juvenile literature.   [1. Christmas]
I. Kiedrowski, Priscilla, ill. II. Title. III. Series.
GT4985.5.K44 1986   394.2'68282   85-13260
ISBN 0-87614-249-8 (lib. bdg.)

1 2 3 4 5 6 7 8 9 10 94 93 92 91 90 89 88 87 86

Contents

Christmas is the celebration of the birth of Jesus Christ. Almost 2,000 years ago, a carpenter named Joseph and his wife, Mary, lived in Nazareth, a town in Palestine. Mary was about to have a child. Christians believe that an angel had come to Mary and told her she would give birth to the Son of God.

At that time, Palestine was ruled by the Romans. Their emperor had ordered that a list called a census be made of everyone in the Roman Empire. So Mary and Joseph had to go to Bethlehem to add their names to the census. When they arrived in the town, there was no room for them inside the inn. But one innkeeper allowed them to stay in the stable, where Mary gave birth to her son, Jesus. They made a bed for him in the animals' manger. Many shepherds came to see Jesus in the stable. They said angels in the sky had sung to them about this special baby. From far away, three wise men came to give him gifts.

Today, Christians around the world celebrate Christmas every December 25. In this book you will read about some of the world's most heartwarming Christmas customs. Some of these customs are ancient. Others are much newer. From country to country, people celebrate Christmas in many different ways. But one thing is certain. Christmas warmth and joy are the same for Christians everywhere.

In Mexico, Christmas is called
Navidad (nah-vee-DAHD).
The main celebration is
posadas (poe-SAH-dahs),
which means "inns."
For nine nights
friends gather together for a parade.
They carry small figures
of baby Jesus, Mary, and Joseph.
They carry lighted candles
and sing Christmas carols.

Each night one man
pretends to be Joseph.
He knocks on a house door.
The house stands for
a Bethlehem inn, or *posada*.
"Can Mary rest here?" he asks.
"No," he is told.
"The inn is full."
After first being turned away,
everyone is asked in for a party.
Posadas ends on Christmas Eve.
When Joseph knocks on the door,
he is told there is room
only in the stable.
Everyone comes inside right away.
They sing songs and say prayers.
The figure of baby Jesus
is put into a manger.

Then bells ring and whistles toot.

There is a big, happy party.

Afterward, everyone goes to church.

11

Each night of *posadas*,
children play the piñata
(peen-YAHT-uh) game.
A piñata is a jug.
It is often made in the shape
of an animal.
One piñata is filled with water.
Another is filled with confetti.
The best one is filled with toys,
candy, fruit, and gifts.
Now the piñatas are hung
above the children's heads.
One child is blindfolded,
given a stick,
and twirled around.
He swings with his stick.
Two misses, then—*Whack!*
He hits the piñata with water in it.
Everyone gets splashed.

Each child takes a turn
until the good piñata is broken.
Then everyone dives for the toys
and sweets.

13

Iran is where the three Wise Men
lived when Jesus was born.
It was called Persia back then.
When they heard of Jesus's birth,
they started out for Palestine.
They carried gifts for Jesus.
A bright star rose in the sky.
It led them to Bethlehem,
where they found Jesus in a manger.

14

Today Christians in Iran
call Christmas "Little Feast."
They begin a fast on December 1.
They eat no meat, eggs,
milk, or cheese.
It is a time for peace and prayer.
Little Feast begins
after church on December 25.
A favorite dish called *harasa*
(hah-RAH-sah) is eaten.
It is a chicken stew.
People in Iran do not give gifts
on Christmas Day.
But children always get new clothes.
They wear them proudly
at Christmastime.

In China, Christmas brings
a special glow.
The Christians light their houses
with beautiful paper lanterns.
Their Christmas trees are called
"trees of light."
They are decorated with paper chains,
paper flowers, and paper lanterns.

Santa Claus visits China too.
He is called Dun Che Lao Ren
(dwyn-chuh-lah-oh-run).
Children hang up muslin stockings.
They hope Dun Che Lao Ren will come
and fill them with presents.

In Sweden, Christmastime
begins on December 13.
This is St. Lucia Day.
St. Lucia was a brave young woman
who lived in the fourth century.
Many people then
didn't like Christians.
So the Christians
had to hide in dark tunnels.
St. Lucia carried food
to them every night.
She wore candles on her head
to light the way.

On St. Lucia Day, Swedes
celebrate the Festival of Light.
Long before sunrise,
the oldest girl in the family
dresses all in white.
She puts an evergreen wreath
with seven lighted candles
on her head.
She carries coffee and buns
to her family in their rooms.
On Christmas Eve,
the family has a special dinner.
They usually eat ham and fish.
Then everyone opens their gifts.
On Christmas Day,
they will go to church
and relax afterward.

In Iraq,
Christians celebrate Christmas
in a special way.
On Christmas Eve,
the family gathers together.
One of the children
reads about the birth of Jesus.
Others in the family
hold lighted candles.

After the reading,
a bonfire made of thorn bushes
is lit in the yard.
It means good luck for the coming year
if the thorns burn to ashes.
Everyone sings
while the fire burns.
When the fire dies,
everyone jumps over the ashes
three times.
Each person makes a wish.

On Christmas Day,
another bonfire is lit.
This one is in the churchyard.
Then the church service begins.
The bishop comes in.
He carries a figure of baby Jesus
on a red pillow.
After the service,

28

the bishop blesses one person
with a touch.
That person then touches
the person next to him or her.
Everyone touches
the next person in turn.
Finally everyone has felt
the "touch of peace" on Christmas Day.

In Spain, most people go
to church on Christmas morning.
They spend the rest of the day
with family and friends.
On Christmas night,
one country custom in Spain
goes like this.
Many people go to the village square.

Here they find the "urn of fate."
Everyone writes his or her name
on a slip of paper.
The papers are put into the urn.
Then someone draws the names out,
two at a time.
Each pair will be best friends
for the coming year.

One very old Spanish custom
is still celebrated in Cadiz, Spain.
It is called "swinging in the sun."
Swings are set up
in the center of town.
The children of Cadiz take turns
seeing who can swing the highest.
They try to lead the sun farther north
so that winter will change into spring.

Twelfth Night is very important
to many people in Spain.
Twelfth Night is on January 6,
12 nights after Christmas.
It was 12 nights after Jesus was born
that the Wise Men first visited him.
On this night, children put
barley in their shoes.
Then they put their shoes
in doorways and on balconies.

The barley is
for the Wise Men's camels.
In the morning,
the barley is gone.
The Wise Men have left candy and gifts
in its place.

Many Christmas customs in Norway
began long, long ago.
One favorite custom starts
at harvest time late in the fall.
The best wheat is saved.
At Christmastime
it is put on poles
made from tree branches.
These make nice perches
for the birds.

A large circle of snow
is cleared away beneath each pole.
Norwegians say the birds dance
in the circle between meals.
This works up their appetites.
Just before sunset on Christmas Eve,
the head of the household checks
on the wheat in the yard.
If many sparrows are eating,
it means a good year for growing crops.

On Christmas Eve,
the family has a big dinner.
After dinner, it is time
for opening presents.
Then all the brooms in the house
are hidden.
Long ago, Norwegians thought
that witches and naughty spirits
came out on Christmas Eve.

They didn't want the witches
riding their brooms.
The fire shovel and tongs
are also hidden so the naughty spirits
can't play with them.

Spruce logs are burned in the fireplace.
The hot sparks will keep
witches from
flying down the chimney
into the house.
Lights are left on all night
to keep evil spirits away.
One bright light is lit
in a window to welcome
any Christmas travelers.
On Christmas Day,
most families go to church.
They spend a quiet day together.
This is a time for remembering.
They remember the reason
for Christmas warmth and joy.
They remember the birth of Jesus
nearly 2,000 years ago.

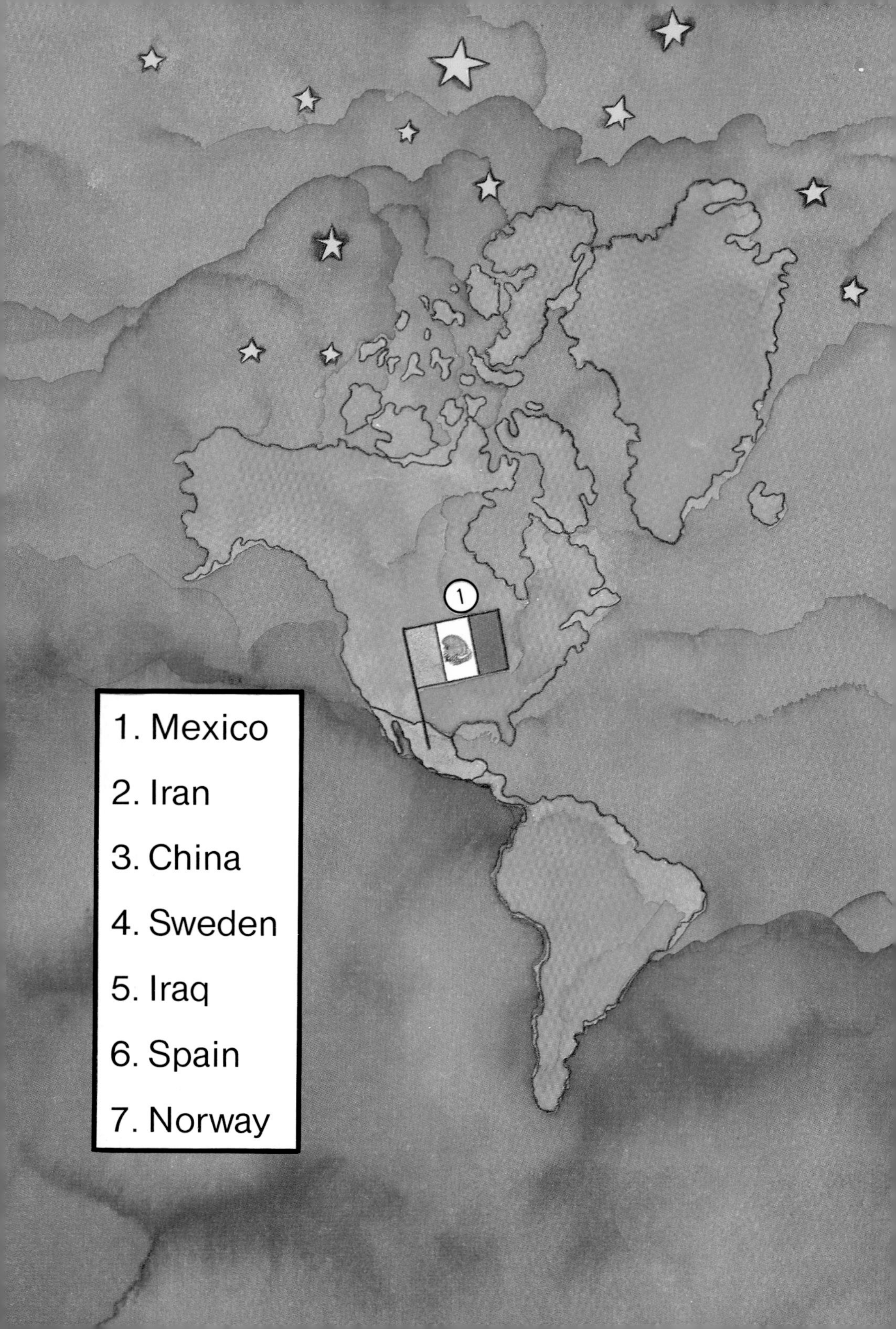

1. Mexico

2. Iran

3. China

4. Sweden

5. Iraq

6. Spain

7. Norway

Other Customs

Australia and New Zealand

Christmas comes in summertime in these countries. Families often celebrate by having a picnic at the beach!

Denmark

The people of Denmark have their big Christmas meal at midnight on Christmas Eve. For dessert they have a special rice pudding with one almond in it. Whoever gets the almond will have good luck in the coming year.

France

On Christmas Eve, French children put their shoes in front of the fireplace. They hope that *Père Noël* (Father Christmas) will fill them with presents.

Germany

Besides lights, tinsel, and ornaments, German families put spicy cakes called *Lebkuchen* on their Christmas trees. These tasty ornaments are made in many different shapes.

CHRISTMAS JOKES

Q: Why are a lion at the beach and Christmas alike?

A: Because the lion has sandy claws.

Q. Why does Santa Claus go down the chimney on Christmas Eve?

A: Because it soots him so well.

Q. What does Santa Claus like to do in his garden?

A: He likes to hoe, hoe, hoe.

A CHRISTMAS CRAFT

Using colored construction paper,
trace and cut out three bells
exactly the same size.
Fold each bell the long way
down the center. Glue the sides
of the bells together to form
a three-sided ornament.
Hang it on the tree
or use it as a centerpiece.

GRANDMA JO'S CHRISTMAS COOKIES

1 cup powdered sugar
1 cup granulated sugar
1 cup butter or margarine
1 cup vegetable oil
2 eggs
1 teaspoon vanilla
4 cups plus 4 heaping teaspoons all-purpose flour
1 teaspoon salt
1 teaspoon baking soda
1 teaspoon cream of tartar

1. Cream sugars, butter, and oil until light and fluffy.
2. Add eggs and vanilla and mix well.
3. Sift together dry ingredients and gradually stir into butter mixture.
4. Cover dough and refrigerate for one hour.
5. Preheat oven to 350°
6. Roll small pieces of dough into balls and place on ungreased cookie sheet.
7. Flatten each ball with the bottom of a glass that has been dipped in red or green sugar.
8. Bake for 10 minutes or until golden brown.

Makes 5 dozen

Glossary

barley (BAR-lee): a kind of grain

bishop (BIH-shup): A high-ranking church official

carpenter (CAR-pen-tur): a person who builds things out of wood

census (SEN-suss): an official count of the number of people living in a certain area

confetti (kun-FET-tee): tiny bits of colored paper that are thrown during celebrations

emperor (EM-per-er): the head ruler of an empire

fast: to go for a period of time without eating certain foods

harvest (HAR-vest): fruits, grains, and vegetables that are gathered when they are ripe

lantern (LAN-turn): a kind of light that can be carried easily

muslin (MUZZ-lin): a kind of cotton cloth

urn (ERN): a large vase

AMERICAN

SURNAMES

AMERICAN

SURNAMES

Elsdon C. Smith

CHILTON BOOK COMPANY

Philadelphia · *New York* · *London*

Published in Philadelphia by Chilton Book Company
and simultaneously in Ontario, Canada,
by Thomas Nelson & Sons Ltd.
ISBN   0-8019-5263-8
Library of Congress Catalog Card Number 71-85245
Designed by Harry Eaby
Manufactured in the United States of America by
Quinn & Boden Company, Inc., Rahway, N. J.

To My Wife Clare

CONTENTS

FOREWORD
ix

1
CLASSIFICATION OF SURNAMES

Rise of hereditary surnames—Names on the Mayflower—*Great American surnames—Names from Who's Who—Abbreviated names—Immigrant alterations—Four classes of surnames—Surnames from animals—Auxiliary words—Diverse origins of names—Attitude to foreign names—Change of names by immigrants—Jewish change of names—Summary of types of change—Common elements in American surnames indicating nationality—Surnames without vowels—Idem sonans—Spelling of names—Pronunciation—Names from words that have changed their meanings.* PAGE 1

2
SURNAMES FROM FATHER'S NAME
Patronymics

Patronymical elements: -ing, ap, O', Mc-, -son, -sen, De—Diminutive endings—Other relatives—Plain forms—From Christian names: William, John, Richard, Robert, Roger, Walter, Allan, Henry, Ralph, Saints' names, Charles, George, Gregor, Alexander, Anthony, Martin, Patrick, Lawrence, Christopher, Bennet—Old Testament names—New Testament names—More Bible names—Anglo-Saxon names—Patronymics from occupations—Germanic names—Pet forms—Lithuanian names—Dutch names—Slavic names—Scandinavian names—Irish names—Scottish names—Welsh names—Spanish names—French names—Italian names—Metronymics—Miscellaneous patronymics. PAGE 41

3
SURNAMES FROM OCCUPATION OR OFFICE

Overseers—Manor officials—Smith—Miller—Forester—Manor servants—Carter—Messenger—Shepard—City occupations—Names from land tilled—Taylor—

vii

CONTENTS

4
SURNAMES FROM DESCRIPTION OR ACTION
Nicknames

5
SURNAMES FROM PLACES

6
SURNAMES NOT PROPERLY
INCLUDED ELSEWHERE

FOREWORD

Preparing a book on American surnames with all their forms and different national derivations is not quite so difficult as trying to eliminate the oceans by dipping the water out with one hand, a teaspoonful at a time, but both tasks seem to be endless. One cannot logically compare the length of two infinities. American surnames is such an inclusive subject without easily definable limits that the study in one small volume must necessarily be of a somewhat erratic and indefinite nature. Emphasis has therefore been placed on the names which identify the most people.

The study of family names in every country leaves much to be desired although important studies have been made in Germany, Sweden, France, Belgium, Russia, Mexico, and England with lesser studies in other countries. Until the names in every country are analyzed in depth in much the same way as etymologists have done with words in the modern languages, which probably will not be accomplished for generations, final authoritative work on surnames cannot be completed in the United States. Some of the complexities are only hinted at here. All early forms and their use must be inspected and their locations carefully recorded.

The various dialectal pronunciations that sprung up and flourished in different parts of every country in Europe during the period surnames became fixed will have to be examined and studied thoroughly before the last word can be written on American surnames, and since so much knowledge has been lost which can never be retrieved, it is highly unlikely that the history of surnames will ever be compiled in a fully satisfactory manner.

Names reflect through their meanings the life of men in the Middle Ages. There is included in this work only that brief account of the activities of the people of the Middle Ages which had sufficient impact to affect the names used by the man's neighbors and acquaintances in speaking to or of him. The meaning of a surname is the meaning ascribed to the word at the time surnames were being adopted. Sometimes when alternate derivations are given it means that the name is derived from two separate sources. In other cases it denotes disagreement among authorities as to the correct translation of a word from a dead language. The meaning of a word may change, but the meaning of a particular surname is settled for all time.

Fewer surnames are seen along the business streets in America compared to European countries. Business in this country is done largely through giant corporations employing many people, whereas in European countries most of it is done by a myriad of those small shopkeepers whose names are listed on their signboards. Today the use of surnames in social intercourse is being replaced by the easy, familiar use of Christian names in everyday speech. And for purposes of exact identification they are now being supplemented by numbers. Almost everyone has a social security number, and anyone of substance who needs to be differentiated from others has a bank account number, credit card number, club number, auto license number, driver's license number, military service number, telephone number, and even a zip code number, together with a host of numbers separating him from others in various miscellaneous activities.

Besides their dictionary meanings, surnames as sounds convey to the modern mind the activities, history, and operation of our modern complex society. Without them the social and business structure called civilization would drop to a low level, almost come to a standstill. Numbers are not, and never will be, adequate substitutes for family names despite the turn to computers to relieve the tedious monotony of accumulating the vast quantity of records deemed necessary now. Surnames have secondary meanings, a connotation or mental description of the person,

Foreword

which we recognize without giving the matter thought. Numbers cannot well call to mind the personalities of their bearers.

In recent years the study of names has been found to be of significant value in anthropology, archaeology, biography, ethnology, folklore, genealogy, geography, history, lexicography, linguistics, literature, philology, psychology, religion, sociology, and related branches of learning. Through a knowledge of proper names, including nicknames, a deeper understanding of these subjects may be developed. At the present time a much more detailed investigation of names as they pertain to the above fields of learning is needed.

Names record accurately the intensity of a group's religious fervor. Primitive gods and their attributes are sometimes kept in the memory of man through names. In the study of the religious and social attributes of savage tribes that have no written records, an examination of their personal and place names provides valuable hints of their feelings, attitudes, and early customs. When kings are more important than priests, names reflect that fact. Much information, even concerning common people not important in political history, may be gleaned from the names they bore. The location of geographical features and boundaries can sometimes be reconstructed with the aid of personal names. Light on early and almost forgotten civilizations is disclosed by names. If it were not for the fact that all names were derived from words in common use, the nationality of many ancient peoples would be more of a puzzle than it is today. Names are helpful in deciphering ancient and forgotten languages. Personal names are almost the only source for knowledge of the Amorite language. Name-study supplements the knowledge of words and their use in communication. The correct usage of personal names helps smooth the way in present-day social intercourse.

Practically every combination of letters is a name of someone. Cartoonists know this when they try to name a character. Herb Williams came up with Tilp for a character thinking that he had a name never heard before. Four letters came in wanting to know where he had found the name, all from people named Tilp, each claiming to be the only Tilp in America.

A schoolteacher in Brooklyn was satisfied with her family name of Doody until a television program, "Howdy Doody," leaped into

FOREWORD

favor and her students quickly adopted the phrase very definitely having her in mind. A man named Woodruff Woodpecker complained to Walter Lanz, creator of the animated cartoon series on Woody Woodpecker, because people laughed at him upon observing the similarity of the name.

Conversely, Richard B. Gump, president of Gumps, the fabulous San Francisco Oriental store, has a sense of humor and the cartoon of Andy Gump by Sidney Smith and Gus Edson bothered him not at all. The cartoonists sent him a drawing of Andy Gump saying, "Hello, Cousin Dick," which he proudly displayed in his office. Another man, James Gump, changed to James Gale in protest against Andy Gump's actions. Sergeant Dick Tracy of the Chicago Police Department has had trouble because his name is the same as that of a celebrated cartoon detective created by Chester Gould. Although he has had some embarrassing moments because of the name, he says that it is an asset because "if you are a policeman with that name, people remember you."

That people today are swayed by names is a certitude that one cannot question. Even as the people of ancient and bygone civilizations looked with favor or disfavor upon names and the naming process as an expression of power from some indescribable force, so in this day and age man is pushed and torn by the mystical pressure of a name. Whether this predisposition is exercised more by sound than actual meaning or by some concealed interrelation than through a traceable connection is a question too intricate to solve here.

In political circles names are magic. In Ohio, Robert A. Taft, Jr., the grandson of the former President and Chief Justice William Howard Taft, son of Robert Alphonso Taft, who narrowly missed the Republican presidential nomination, and the nephew of Charles P. Taft, an active political leader, easily was elected representative-at-large from Ohio in 1962. Truly Taft is a magical name in America. The late "Boss" Crump of Tennessee was a bit cynical in the matter. He often bragged that he could get out a heavy vote for Judas Iscariot if he tried. "The name," he observed, "is familiar!"

Name voting, that is, voting for little-known persons because their name reveals their nationality to be the same as that of the voter, is a principle recognized by all master politicians. In 1968 both the Republican and the Democratic nominees had this idea in mind when picking their running mates. Governor Agnew is of Greek extraction and Senator Muskie's father was Polish. At the same time, a name indicating a racial block is a distinct handicap in a bailiwick where few of that nationality are voters. A name similar to the name of a former popular officeholder also garners many votes from unobservant citizens. A favorite political trick of unscrupulous opponents is to run others with the same or a similar name against a favorite to divide the vote.

When John F. Kennedy won election in 1952 to the Senate over the incumbent, Henry Cabot Lodge, an unknown John F. Kennedy, who ran the stockroom in the Gillette Safety Razor factory in South Boston, filed for State Treasurer. Without effort he won the primary nomination from two opponents. He issued no printed matter, attended few meetings, hoisted a banner only in his hometown, spent less than two hundred dollars, and then was elected successfully. Massachusetts voters are no more careless than the voters of other states.

Politicians have discovered that the use of their name or nickname in a clever rhyme strengthens them at election time. When Governor Nelson A. Rockefeller was wheeling and dealing in connection with the nomination for Presidency of the country, the terse couplet: "Who Else But Nelse?" was displayed. This emphasized the opinion of his followers that there was really no choice. Inez Robb, a national columnist, expressed her opinion that this "poem" would do a lot more for him in the long run than "Be Cocky with Rocky" or "I Beller for Rockefeller."

One of the most widespread campaign slogans and one that did a great deal for Dwight D. Eisenhower was "I Like Ike." To counteract it the Democrats could not come up with anything better than "I'm Madly for Adlai" for their candidate, Adlai Stevenson. This slogan, however, taught the electors how to pronounce the candidate's first name even though they might be unfamiliar with some of the more unusual Biblical names.

In the 1960 Kennedy-Nixon battle, the phrases, "Let's Stick with Dick" and "Come Back with Jack" were commonly heard. Even in view of the closeness of the race, "Come Back with Jack" might be said to be the better election cry. When John Gutknecht, in 1956, running for re-election as State's Attorney of Chicago's

FOREWORD

Cook County modestly advertised, "Gutknecht means Good Servant," one newspaper wondered why he neglected to mention also that John means "gracious gift of God." Then it observed, "But even if when you put them all together, they spelled 'mother,' we couldn't see that it proved very much, except the cogency of Shakespeare's query, 'What's in a name?'"

State Senator Nat Washington, in 1952, announced his candidacy for the Democratic nomination for Congressman-at-large for the State of Washington with the slogan, "Send Washington to Washington for Washington." When George H. Dern ran for Democratic governor in Utah in 1924, to replace the Republican incumbent named Mabey, his followers coined the slogan, "We want a Dern good governor and we don't mean Mabey." He was elected in a close contest although Coolidge carried the state. Bob Cherry running for the state senate in Illinois in 1958 started with the slogan "It's Cherry Picking Time." His opponent attacked with "Cherry Canning Time," but was quickly met with the counter attack "Cherry Preserving Time." Jim Muchmore, campaigning for Treasurer at Evanston Township High School, proclaimed, "If you want much more, vote for Muchmore." He won a hot election.

Perhaps we should cease our smug smiling at primitive man with his superstitious belief that to know the name of a person, or even a god, was to acquire power over him. If our use of names to influence the election of our top leaders succeeds, are we any better? Civilized man is really influenced by the sound of names.

Mrs. Peggy Ebeling was so enrolled on the voting lists in New Rochelle, New York, but felt that the pet form was not dignified enough when she desired to stand for election to the Republican County Committee in 1965. She found that she had to go to court to force the Board of Elections to list her on the ballot as Margaret Ebeling.

Judge Lewandowski sued in 1957 to force the election commissioners in Detroit to put his name on the ballot in the same size letters as those running against him. The director of elections said that the printer used his discretion when he found that Lewandowski would not fit in the space provided. Judge Toms (with four letters) dismissed the petition with the remark that this was an attempt to emphasize Mr. Lewandowski's candidacy. All politicians know of the influence of good names in winning elections.

In 1948, when Thomas E. Dewey, Harry S Truman, Henry A. Wallace, J. Strom Thurmond, and Norman Thomas were named on the presidential ballot, a newspaper reporter telephoned various persons with these surnames to find if the surname influenced the voters in any way, but could find no substantial correlation.

In the latter half of the sixteenth century in England the fashion of bestowing family names as given names arose. The custom became quite general among the upper classes who desired to perpetuate their names. Many of them have become recognized, popular Christian names such as Bradley, Clarence, Clayton, Clifford, Dean, Dudley, Gordon, Howard, Neville, Percy, Russell, Sidney, Stanley, and Wesley.

Only in America has the English use of surnames as Christian names been followed, and here it is a common practice. Names of well-known Americans have become common Christian names. Some of them are Calvin, Chauncy, Dwight, Franklin, Grant, Jefferson, Lee, Lincoln, and Washington. All the family names often used in England as given names are also found in America. Family names used as Christian names are almost always masculine. About the only ones commonly used by women are Beverly, Leslie, Lynn, and Shirley, and these have also been used by men.

Some of our given names which originated as surnames can be traced. Dwight became popular because many Yale students named their sons after Dr. Timothy Dwight, a popular former president of Yale University. Many friends of Harvard named their children Chauncy after Charles Chauncy, the controversial second president of that institution (1654–72). Sidney is due to the Whig party's regard for Algernon Sidney (1622–83) in England. The eponym of Clarence was the Duke of Clarence, the eldest son of Edward VII, although the first dukedom with this name was created for the third son of Edward III in 1362. Stanley is chiefly due to the popularity of the English explorer, Henry Stanley (d. 1904) whose name was originally Rowlands. Stanley was the family name of the earls of Derby and must also be reckoned with in connection with this Christian name. Names

FOREWORD

like Dudley, Percy, Howard, and Neville were influenced by the great English families bearing these names.

In our civilization the telephone directories of the larger cities are huge, bulky lists of names of the heads of households of most of the inhabitants. Compilers of these directories encounter some unusual problems. People want to be either first or last in the book. And many telephone companies accept almost any name the subscriber wishes to use, although when competition becomes too fierce, the companies do adopt some ground rules. In a Southern city one who demanded top billing with Aaaaaron was turned down when he could not produce proof that he was entitled to more than two of those five *a's*.

As each large telephone directory is issued, name collectors leaf through for oddities of nomenclature. Billy Rose called them Cognomen Collectors. Others work the names into a story. When the Manhattan Telephone Directory came out in 1957, a tour de force appeared in *The Herald Tribune Magazine* pointing out that "many subscribers are *Suffern,* a lot are *Blue* or *Down,* and then there are Elmer, who is *Sadd,* H.S., who is *Sader,* and Vincent, who is *Sorey.*" The writer found only one *Tears* but he did come across Frank and Patrick *Cryan.* Using misspellings almost anything can be found in the large city telephone books.

Many people make a game of searching out odd names. Mignon McLaughlin looked and found in the Manhattan book names like *Cash* and *Carry; Kiss* and *Tell; Win, Place,* and *Show.* She even found *Shirley Good, Shirley Better,* and *Shirley Best.* One can look for and find *Longs* and *Shorts; Diamonds, Hearts, Clubs,* and *Spades; Man* and *Boy.* Another, wrestling with the Chicago directory (the largest in one volume), came up with names pronounced approximately the same as each letter of the alphabet—from *Aye* to *Zeeh.* Well-known names in fiction, history, or science can be found. Ex-presidents can be located in profusion. With different subjects the game can be varied in a hundred ways. Truly surnames loom large in the minds of Americans. To understand them the background of customs existing at the time they arose, together with historical events which influenced them, must be taken into account. In this work, often through repetition, some of the more important aspects of American surname customs have been emphasized.

Throughout this book it will be observed that many names

originate in more than one way, and for any particular person's name it is impossible to be sure which one is the correct origin, although when the country and the part of a country where the person's ancestors lived is known, a more nearly accurate guess can be made. Since some surnames having several derivations are interpreted one way in one chapter and in another way elsewhere, one interested in a particular name and its different meanings should check it in the index. Not all interpretations, however, can be included in a work of this size. Genealogists are fond of asserting that the true meaning of a particular surname can be found only by tracing the family back to the time the surname was first used and ascertaining the circumstances under which it was bestowed. This is, of course, impossible. Not even one in a million families can be so traced, but from early records it is possible to ferret out the origin and meaning with tolerable accuracy in most cases.

In designating the meaning of names generally and comparing those from different countries with similar connotations in this work the common diminutive and patronymic terminations are ignored to avoid needless repetition. Attention is usually given only to the principal element of the name. Also the common and oftentimes meaningless terminal *s* is usually disregarded. Minor variations in spelling are usually not noted. At a time when spelling was in the discretion of the writer (happy time) vowel differences had little or no meaning. Use of *i* for *y* or vice versa did not have any reason except custom of the time and place. Doubling of consonants may be disregarded. Variants in spelling like Dixon for Dickson are easily recognized. Some variant forms are different merely because they accord with the custom or dialect in different parts of a country.

Practically every family name has various spellings and it is impossible due to lack of space to include all of them. Variant spellings are here noted only when they are exceptionally common or sometimes when their omission would mislead one searching in the index for his surname. It was Holyoak who in the preface to his *Latin Dictionary* (1612) wrote, "Also if you find not the word you seeke for presently after one sort of spelling, condemne me not forthwith, but consider how it is used to be spelled, whether with double or single letters, as Chappell, or Chapell."

Names are given with the spellings usually employed in America even though slightly different from the form found in the country of origin. Indeed, the spelling commonly employed in America may not be found at all in the country of origin. This book is about American names and not about names current in other countries. Many German, French, Spanish, and Italian names have been slightly altered in the United States to give them an English cast. Most of the German names terminating in -*mann*, for example, have had the final *n* dropped, but this has been ignored in classifying them as German in origin. In the same way the German *Sch-* is often condensed in America to *Sh-*. Names are spelled as they are commonly used in America influenced by the English language without those diacritical marks so sacred to many from other countries. With a knowledge of the various ways surnames were formed and classified, many unusual foreign names may be understood by simply translating them into English.

Today the dictionary meaning of names is disregarded by most people except when a pun can be used effectively. What little meaning most names have at the present day arises from their sound or evidence of nationality or association with outstanding men. Here, to save space, when one element of a name is obvious, often only the other is translated. Some names grouped together necessarily do not have the exact same shade of meaning due to differences in locality or circumstances.

Since surnames in America are derived from all languages, the forms they take are infinite. As an example, there are English surnames which may be from Anglo-Saxon, Old Norse, Norman French, French, Cornish, Manx, Celtic, Latin, and several other languages, or from the dialect of any county in the British Isles, also from slang and colloquial speech. For our purposes here it is enough to identify the language of origin as one from a presently existing European or Asiatic country. The language of every nation developed from several other languages and American surnames are the results. The different languages spoken at various times in the same area are responsible for many different names now ascribed to one nationality. And they are all swirling around together in that great melting pot we secretly think of as the heart of the universe—America.

It will be seen that a dozen or more English surnames may

have the same or similar meanings, some common, others rare. Norman French was spoken along with English in the British Isles during the time surnames became fixed and so the English have names with the same meanings from both languages. Every language, dialect, slang, and colloquial speech had to have words or terms for curly hair, baldness, size, shape, and every other common attribute that can be applied to Homo sapiens.

The surnames discussed are usually identified as to nationality, but this will frequently confuse the reader. Nationality is one thing and language of origin is another. Men known by French names may have resided in England since family names first became stabilized. Is such a name English or French? No ironclad rule can be followed consistently.

Not all names can be discussed in a book of this size but a special effort has been made to include all the common family names. Some uncommon names have been given attention where their interpretation illustrates some principle with respect to onomastics. Many names not listed here will be easily recognized as only variants of common names that are included. Often a perplexing name will become clear if it is looked up in a large telephone book where other forms or spellings are easily perceived. Names in other languages can be generally understood if they are first translated into English. In many cases the obvious meanings are given because in so many other cases the obvious explanation is the wrong one.

Many English, German, and Dutch names and many Italian, Spanish, and Portuguese are alike or with only very minor variations in spelling because they are derived from the same earlier language. Lowland Scottish names are like English names and it is difficult to separate them. Some names may be the same in more than one country (such as Borg in Sweden, Norway, and Germany), but for reasons of space they may be assigned only to the country where they are found most frequently.

More attention is given to conditions of life in England during the period when surnames were being adopted as permanent names because a larger percentage of our family names is English, but in general similar conditions and customs prevailed at the same time throughout Europe.

All names in capital letters are found today in the United States

FOREWORD

as modern surnames, most of them listed only in their most popular forms, although some other forms are sometimes included for one reason or another. Many readers will think of other foreign surnames with the same meanings which have not been included here. An important reason for their exclusion lies in the fact that they are not common names in America.

The journal *Names* is the official organ of the American Name Society, the first American periodical devoted to the study of names. The first issue was brought out in March, 1953, edited by Professor Erwin G. Gudde of the University of California, and it has appeared quarterly since that time. Each issue contains several articles relating to the subject of place, personal, or other names, by outstanding authorities, together with reviews of important works on the subject, brief comments, and notes. Bibliographies on the subject appear once a year.

Upon the resignation of Professor Gudde with the issue of December 1956, the editorship was taken over by Professor Madison Beeler of the same university who edited Volumes V, VI, and VII. Beginning with Volume VIII, March 1960, Professor Demetrius J. Georgacas of the University of North Dakota undertook the editorship for two years, being succeeded with the beginning of Volume X, March 1962, by Professor E. Wallace McMullen of Fairleigh Dickinson University. With the issue of March 1966, Volume XIV, Professor Kelsie B. Harder of the State University College at Potsdam, New York, became editor. In 1969, Professor Conrad M. Rothrauff took over the editorship.

The author has called upon many members of the American Name Society for aid in interpreting many puzzling names and is particularly obligated to Jack A. Dabbs, Geart B. Droege, Enrique Chelminsky L., Douglas P. Hinkle, Demetrius J. Georgacas, Gerald M. Moser, Jaroslav B. Rudnyćkyj, Yar Slavutych, and Wolodymyr T. Zyla.

The author's wife has spent long hours in counting names, typing various drafts, and aiding in numerous other ways.

None of these, however, can be blamed for errors and poor judgment, some of which are bound to creep, nay, even leap, into a work of this nature, and all errors must be credited to

Elsdon C. Smith

AMERICAN

SURNAMES

1

CLASSIFICATION OF SURNAMES

Rise of hereditary surnames—Names on the Mayflower—*Great American surnames—Names from* Who's Who—*Abbreviated names—Immigrant alterations—Four classes of surnames—Surnames from animals—Auxiliary words—Diverse origins of names—Attitude to foreign names—Change of names by immigrants—Jewish change of names—Summary of types of change—Common elements in American surnames indicating nationality—Surnames without vowels—*Idem *sonans—Spelling of names—Pronunciation—Names from words that have changed their meanings.*

AFTER THE ROMAN three-name system deteriorated into the single cognomen by the fourth century A.D., it was not until the tenth century that modern hereditary surnames first developed among the Venetian patricians. From there during the next six hundred years the custom of fixed hereditary family names spread, first to France and England, then to Germany and all of Europe. In these parts of Europe individual man was becoming more important, commerce was increasing, and the exact identification of each man was becoming a necessity. But even today the Church does not recognize surnames. Baptisms and marriages are performed through use of the Christian name alone.

1

AMERICAN SURNAMES

Thus hereditary family names as we know them today developed gradually during the eleventh to fifteenth centuries in the various European countries. In a few places the genesis and popular use was not completed until much later. Canon Bardsley explained it in his *English Surnames:*

By a silent and unpremeditated movement over the whole of the more populated and civilized European societies, nomenclature began to assume a solid lasting basis. It was the result, in fact, of an insensibly growing necessity. Population was on the increase, commerce was spreading, and society was fast becoming corporate. With all this arose difficulties of individualization. It was impossible, without some further distinction, to maintain a current identity. Hence what had been but an occasional and irregular custom, became a fixed and general practice—the distinguishing sobriquet, not, as I say, of premeditation, but by a silent compact, became part and parcel of a man's property, and passed on with his other possessions to his direct descendants.

In general, the development of surnames and their universal use throughout the world followed commerce. The countries and parts of countries where many were engaged in trade were the first to use surnames. Agricultural districts, where man was tied to the soil to make his living, had a smaller population where the need for more exact identification was not so pressing, and were, consequently, the last places to acquire universal family names.

When the first immigrants from Europe came to America, the only names current in the new land were Indian names which did not appeal to European throats, and the Indian names did not influence the surnames or Christian names already possessed by the immigrants. The Indians had no surnames. Hiawatha, Pocahontas, Massasoit, and Osceola were well-known Indian personal names, but they had no effect on the onomastic pattern in America.

Some have contended that there are no American surnames, but they are wrong. All family names are good American surnames. Since America first was colonized by adventurers from England, Holland, France, and Germany, they all came to this country with family names. The fifty English surnames of the men arriving on the *Mayflower* in 1620 were:

2

Classification of Surnames

ALDEN	CRACKSTON	LANGEMORE	STORY
ALLERTON (2)	DOTEY	LEISTER	THOMPSON
BILLINGTON	EATON	MARGESON	TILLEY (2)
BRADFORD	ELLIS	MARTIN	TINKER
BREWSTER	ENGLISH	MOORE	TREVORE
BRITTERIDGE	FLETCHER	MULLINS	TURNER
BROWNE	FULLER (2)	PRIEST	WARREN
CARTER	GARDINER	RIGDALE	WHITE
CARVER	GOODMAN	ROGERS	WILDER
CHILTON	HOLEBECK	SAMSON	WINSLOW (2)
CLARKE	HOPKINS	SOULE	
COOKE	HOWLAND	STANDISH	

Surely these are real American names, they being among the first American surnames known in America.

Some names that might be called particularly American surnames because their bearers made such significant contributions to American life and history are AUDUBON, BARNUM, BARUCH, CARNEGIE, EDISON, EISENHOWER, EMERSON, FRANKLIN, HANCOCK, HAWTHORNE, JEFFERSON, KNICKERBOCKER, LA FAYETTE, LINCOLN, LONGFELLOW, McCORMICK, PENN, PERSHING, PULLMAN, ROCKEFELLER, ROOSEVELT, THOREAU, WANAMAKER, and WASHINGTON. The mere mention of each of these surnames without first names brings a romantic story to the mind of every educated American. Who can doubt that these are truly American names?

Some native-born Americans picked almost at random out of the 1968–1969 edition of *Who's Who in America* are Berla, Crumpacker, Cubeta, Cudlip, Dingledy, Ducommun, Fangboner, Gazzolo, Huganir, Ihrke, Int-Hout, Kaloupek, Loosli, Ochiltree, Ockenga, Oladko, Owre, Pantaleoni, Plaxico, Polyzoides, Ponkey, Popma, Quencer, Rzasa, Schrunk, Skowbo, Stufflebean, Syphax, Tooill, Ughetta, Ylvisaker, Yutzy, and Zecca, all good American names, although not borne by many families. SMITH is no more of an American name than FERRER, GOW, KOVAC, LEFEBVRE, or SCHMITZ, all of which designate that worker in metal.

One explanation of the high proportion of unusual names found in *Who's Who in America* is the number of highly educated refugees who have fled to America in recent years, and have contributed their rare and exotic names to our national list. Some of the most active, adventurous, colorful, personalities from all over

3

the world have arrived on America's shores to pursue their goals in life free from arbitrary and unreasonable limitations. Unusual names are often more easily remembered and the names thus aided in their achievement of fame. Laura Fermi told the story of this "Big Brain Wave," the transplanting of thousands of European intellectuals to the United States during the 1930's to 1941, in her book *Illustrious Immigrants.*

The friends of Zbigniew Brzezinski, the brilliant young Washington political scientist, cherish the wisecrack about his success: "America is a place where a man called Zbigniew Brzezinski can make a name for himself without even changing it." Every name found in the United States is a good American name. It is in the American motion picture industry, which goes all over the world, where may be observed in the film credits some of the most extraordinary and unpronounceable American names.

A particular feature of "American" surnames is the many short or abbreviated names which have arisen through the bearer's shortening his awkward Old World name by summarily eliminating letters or dropping first or last syllables to create a pronounceable name with which he seems to be satisfied. After years have passed or a new generation has inherited the name without hearing an explanation of its origin, the name becomes impossible of any clearly correct interpretation. If it resembles a name or a word in another language, it is often saddled with an erroneous interpretation. A few of these names, some the meaning of which can only be guessed, are Adas, Arca, Dec, Gac, Hosna, Kaji, Marcu, Troc, and Peto. Such names as these originated as parts, first, last, or middle, of longer names from every country in the world. Without the distinctive prefixes, suffixes, or original spelling there is in many cases no way to ferret out the nationality of the original name unless it be by tracing the genealogy of the bearer in the paternal line. Family names in America present a complex, all inclusive pattern different from that found in any other country.

A Michigan college study showed that short, pleasant-sounding, common, easy-to-spell-and-pronounce surnames are the most favored and envied by Americans. Such names as LANE, MOORE, HOLMES, and BENNETT are smoothly handled in the United States. But such names as SMITH, BROWN, and JONES are considered to be too common.

Classification of Surnames

The only large groups of "foreigners" who arrived in America without family names are the Indians (from Asia) and the Negroes. As the Indians mingled with the European immigrants they tended to acquire their name patterns. After the Negro slaves obtained their freedom, one of the first things they did was to adopt a surname in imitation of their former masters. To them it meant status. Indian and Negro surnames are discussed in Chapter VI.

American surnames comprise the surnames found in every country throughout the world, many with differences in spelling not seen in the old country due to the inability of clerks and government officials to record correctly the names given them by unschooled immigrants not familiar with the English, French, German, or Spanish languages currently used in the port of entry or the part of the country where they settled. When an immigrant arriving in America with little knowledge of English gave his name verbally to the officials to whom it sounded odd or unusual, it was written down by them as they heard it, and being thereby "official," it was often accepted by the immigrant himself as a correct American rendering of his name. To say that there are no American names would be wrong; one might on the contrary affirm that there are no unAmerican surnames. All family names in the United States can be and should be classified as "American" names.

But it is not enough to declare that American surnames now embody all the surnames of all the world. Immigrants to America from European countries have also consciously altered their names to relate them partially to the English language, especially as to English pronunciation, so that many names have a form and spelling, as has been mentioned, which is different from that found anywhere else. Some familiar examples might be noted. Dutch VAN ROSEVELT "of the rose field" becomes ROOSEVELT, German BLUM "flower" becomes BLOOM, GELBFISCH "yellow fish" becomes GOLDWYN, HUBER "tenant of hide of land" becomes HOOVER, KUNTZ "Conrad" becomes COONS, ROGGENFELDER "rye field" becomes ROCKEFELLER, PFOERSCHING "peach tree" becomes PERSHING, SCHWAB "from Swabia (freeman)" becomes SWOPE, THALMANN "valley man" becomes TALLMAN, French GUIZOT "little Guy" becomes GOSSETT, Swedish SJÖSSTRAND "sea shore" becomes

5

SEASHORE, Irish QUIDDIHY "descendant of Cuidighthigh (helper)" becomes CUDAHY, Italian TAGLIAFERRO "iron worker" becomes TOLLIVER, and AMICI "friend" becomes AMECHE. General CUSTER of "Last Stand" fame had a Hessian soldier grandfather named KÜSTER, "minor church official in charge of the sacristy." Dutch VANDERPLOEG becomes VANDERPLOW, Finnish TERHUNEN becomes TERHUNE, and KIRKKOMÄKI becomes CHURCHILL. The list is endless.

The noble who held a manor or village or large estate acquired a surname from the name of the land; the newcomer became known by the name of the village from which he came; the country villager often was described by reference to the landscape feature near where he lived. Numerous men were called by reference to their occupation. Many were identified by some descriptive nickname. Some became known from the font name of the father who was well and favorably known.

William MADDOX refers to the son or descendant of Madog or Madoc "fortunate." William PACKER had a forebear who packed wool. William GOODALE descended from the brewer who made good ale. William BEVERIDGE now describes one whose early ancestor came from that village in Dorsetshire or who had a progenitor who lived at a farm or ridge frequented by beavers.

Thus almost all family names may be classified on the basis of their derivation in one or more of the four following groups:

1. From the Father's Name or other Relationships (Patronymics)
2. From Occupation or Office (Occupational Names)
3. From Description or Action (Nicknames)
4. From Village Names or Landscape Features (Place Names)

Some authorities have called these four classes:

Sire-names, Trade-names, Nick-names, and Place-names.

Virtually all surnames in the western world originated in one of these four ways, although the proportion in each class varied in different countries and districts. Even today, if one did not know the name of another, he would be referred to by the use of one of these four categories. Indeed, it would be difficult to describe or identify another in some way that could not be classified in one of these four divisions. In most countries, particularly

6

the western countries, the emphasis is on one or another of these classes. In Ireland, the Highlands of Scotland, Wales, and Spain, the majority of the names are patronymics. In England place names predominate, and they are common in Germany and France. In the Scandinavian countries there are very few occupational names. Italy and Portugal have many in the nickname class. More nicknames developed among the lower classes than among the nobility who were likely to become known by the name of their landed properties.

If all of our surnames were easily molded into this pattern of patronymical, occupational, nickname, and place name classification, they would be uniform and clear. But there are so many on the border line. A name like LONDON, for example, might originate because the man came from that place or because, being from the country, he aped what he thought to be big city ways. The exceptions and corruptions that have arisen make for anything but a consistent and logical outline. The neat pattern is marred by all the odd and unusual names that sometimes cannot be identified with certainty. GOLIGHTLY and LIGHTFOOT are nicknames for an efficient messenger, and although they became words for an occupation in the Middle Ages, they are noted in the chapter on nicknames rather than in the one on occupational names.

Some names may be derived from a personal name or from a village name. WINSTON may be derived from Wynston "friend, stone" or from Winston "Wine's or Wynsige's homestead," the names of several English villages. ALSTON may be from Elfstan "elf, stone" or from Alston, the name of several villages, such as the one in Lancashire meaning "Aelf's homestead." WILFORD may be derived from Wilfred or Wilfrith "resolution, peace" or from Wilford "willow ford" in Nottinghamshire. ALFORD may be from Alfred "elf, counsel" or from Alford "alder ford or ford of Ealdgyth," the names of villages in Lincolnshire and Somerset.

There are many surnames in various European languages which are derived from animals, birds, fish, and insects. Chaucer mentioned thirty-four birds in *The Parliament of Fowls* and the late Dr. P. H. Reaney found that all but four of them have survived in English surnames. Every familiar name of bird or beast became a European surname, some common, some quite rare. Outstanding exceptions are the dog and horse, although both were em-

7

ployed as nicknames in the Middle Ages. The three common explanations of these creature names are (1) from a house, shop, or inn sign (see page 219), (2) a nickname from some real or fancied resemblance to the animal (see page 176), and (3) from some incident in the family history, usually a nickname, the origin of which is lost in antiquity.

But there are many other explanations of these names. Several are from old given names. RAVEN and WOLF are old, amply attested personal names for men in surname times both in their simple form and as one element in dithematic, or two-theme names. They were held in especial esteem as beasts of good omen. Wolf, a personal name, both alone and as a short form of dithematic names containing this element, has produced many surnames. LAMB may be a shortened form of Lambert "land, bright," or a metonym for one who had charge of the lambs. LYON is often from Leo or Leon "lion." The lion was found in Palestine in Biblical times and was employed as a symbol of power and ferocity by Biblical writers, also as a symbol of the resurrection of Christ. Many other words for animals and birds were used as medieval font names. HAWK is a pet form of Harry and also derives from the old English personal name Hafoc "hawk."

Some of these animal names, such as LAMB mentioned above, are metonymic for occupation, having to do with the keeping or sale of the creatures. Names of domestic animals are short terms for the herder or caretaker of such beasts. Even names of wild animals may be indicative of occupation, such as BEAR for the bearward or keeper of performing bears. In the same way bird names sometimes designate the man who handled or raised them. HAWK sometimes designates the HAWKER, the keeper and trainer of hawks and falcons. Fish names, especially, often denote the man who fished for or dealt in that species. PIKE and HERRING in some cases were fishmongers dealing in such fish. Some occupations may have acquired their names by the words peddlers used in calling out their wares.

These animal and bird names are sometimes derived from localities so called because of the presence of such animals or birds (see page 228). A few animal names are derived from the device or crest of the owner. Frequently animal names are corruptions of other names. For example, GOSLING is a respelling of the Old

8

French personal name Goscelin "just"; OTTER is a corruption of Old English Otthar or Othere "terrible army"; PARROT is a diminutive from Perre (Peter). Any one animal or bird name can arise in many places from any or all of these origins. They run the full gamut of names.

Unusual names may often be placed in their proper classification by reference to the auxiliary words, articles, or prepositions used in the early rolls. Frequently patronymics are preceded by the Latin *filius* "son." Many occupational names and nicknames are preceded by the French definite article *le,* as *le spicer* and *le lang.* Place names follow the preposition *de* "of or from," while landscape terms may be preceded by the preposition *at* with or without the definite article, as *at shaw,* or *atten shaw.* The German *am, zu,* and *zum* have the same meaning and are found in such names as AMBACH "at the brook," ZUFELDE "at field," and ZUMWALD "at the wood." German place names used as surnames may be preceded by *von.* The Dutch use *van* and *vander.* Italians use *da, di, dal, del, della, la, lo,* and other similar prefixes. Modern family names have usually eliminated these descriptive elements, although many French and Italian names do retain them.

There is no clear distinction between status and occupation. FREEMAN, which designates the man free from bondage to the lord, a position every peasant yearned for, might be classed as an occupational name or as a status name and thus a nickname. KNIGHT is a similar name, higher in status than FREEMAN, but clearly one which pinpointed a man's chief occupation as a fighter. It is so easy to classify family names in these four main groups, but so difficult to assign certain names to the proper classification.

In a careful check of seven thousand of the most common surnames in the United States it was found that the proportions in each class are as follows:

	Percentage
Patronymics	32.23
Occupational Names	15.16
Nicknames	9.48
Place Names	43.13

Of the last class, the place names, 15.17% are landscape names, 3.32% are sign names, and 24.64% are village names. C. N. Mat-

9

thews in her *English Surnames,* London, 1966, analyzed the names of the members of the House of Commons to find that 33% were patronymics, 17.5% were occupational, 13% were nicknames, and 36.5% were place names. If Mrs. Matthews' calculations are based on a large enough sample to be accurate, it may be assumed that non-British names found in America tend to be more from places rather than from occupations or nicknames.

A separate chapter of this work is devoted to each of these classes but the names spill from one category to another dashing all efforts at a neat, systematic arrangement. Do shop or house signs belong to the nickname class, as Weekley suggests, or to address names? Many of them do clearly indicate occupations as well as locations.

When surnames are examined carefully it may be observed that many rest on the border line between two classes. Many occupational names have the patronymic element attached to them, as noted in the chapter on patronymics (page 45). Numerous names originate equally from two or more entirely different concepts. SEWELL is either a descendant of Sewal "victory, strength" or one whose ancestor came from Sewell "seven wells," the name of towns in Bedfordshire and Oxfordshire.

There is a group of surnames, much more common in French, German, and Italian than in English, which are really a compound of nickname and patronymic. They consist of an adjective indicating size or an attractive quality as a prefix attached to a given name. English names most frequently noted are GOOD WILLIE and LITTLEJOHN, the latter having another significance mentioned elsewhere. German names are GROSSHANS "big John," KLEINPETER "little Peter," and GROSSKLAS "large Nicholas." French examples are GRANDCLEMENT "big Clement," GRANDJEAN "big John," and PETITPERRIN "little Pierre." Similar Italian names such as BONGIOVANNI and BONZANI "good John" and BUONAGUIDI "good Guy" are numerous. Greece has produced such surnames as PAPANDREOU "Priest Andrew" (father and son, recent prominent Greek political figures) and PAPANICKOLAS "Priest Nicholas." Greek surnames of this type were adopted by a priest's relative as it was considered an honor to have a priest in the family because of the respect for their unselfish work during the Turkish occupation of Greece.

Classification of Surnames

When the immigrant to America could not read or write and had little or no knowledge as to the proper spelling, the obscurations suffered in this country by family names at the hands of government officials were long and extended. The spellings were further corrupted by the slurred, often uneven and halting, pronunciation employed by the man and his friends. PARSON "son of Par (pet form of Peter)" might become PASSEN; PARKHURST "dweller in an enclosure or on a wooded hill" became PARKIS; PRESCOTT "priest's cottage" slipped down to PRESCOD; and PICKERING from Pickering in Yorkshire "people at edge of hill" became PICKRAM, to mention just a few English names starting with P. Pick up any book on the genealogy of an immigrant family from Europe and observe the many variant spellings used in this country. To give more examples of alteration of surnames in America caused by the slurred, halting pronunciation of ignorant people would do little good here. The early town records are full of these misspelled names most of which gradually changed back to a more conventional spelling as education progressed. However, many incorrect spellings persisted to increase the number of family names not found anywhere else in the world.

Simple names like HEW, HOE, HOO, HOUGH, HOW, HOWE, HUFF, and HUGH are hopelessly mixed up. They can derive from Hugh "spirit," or from Middle English *hewe* "servant," or from Old English *hoh* "spur of land," or from Old Norse *haugr* "hill," or from Middle English *howe* "ridge," and some of them are also subject to other possible explanations.

Any particular surname may originate in more than one way—in several ways, in different places and countries, and at different times. Even the ubiquitous SMITH derives from words designating other than the worker in metals. SMITH sometimes comes from *smethe* "smooth" as in Smithfield "the smooth field" in London. Although no recorded proof has been found, it cannot be doubted that some with that name had an ancestor living by the Smite "dirty stream" from Old English *smitan* "to pollute." Several others will be here discussed, not to confuse the reader, but to emphasize the point that oftentimes a family name arose in different places with different antecedents all coalescing into the same form to make just one common family name. To add to these confusions, when such a name arrived in America, there was a powerful tend-

11

ency to equate an old, unfamiliar spelling of a word or place name
with a more familiar, easily spelled and pronounced word or name
not alien to American-English ears. Here it may be helpful to
direct attention to some common family names that have several
different derivations.

The original Gaelic man surnamed ADAIR may have been
descendant of Edzear or Edgar "rich, spear"; others with the name
had an ancestor who was a dweller near the river crossing by the
oak tree; in Ireland he was a grandson of Daire, an old Irish given
name. BALL dwelt at the sign of the ball; or was a descendant of
Baldwin "bold, friend" or of Balle, an Old Danish name; or had
a bald head; or resided on a knoll or rounded hill; or lived at
bald or bare place; or had a fat, rotund figure. Balls rolled all over
the landscape.

BARNES may designate one who came from Barnes "the barns,"
villages in Surrey and Aberdeenshire; or one who dwelt near
barn or grain storage building; the name may indicate the descendant of Barn, a pet form of Barnabas "son of prophecy or
consolation," or of Beorn "a nobleman"; or it may be a name derived from bairn or child, often a young person of a prominent
family. The common surname BELL may be a dweller at the sign
of the bell; a descendant of Bel, a pet form of Isabel; or a name
from the occupation of bellringer or bellmaker; or from the French
bel, "the handsome one."

BLANCHARD, both French and English, is a descendant of Blanchard "white, hard"; one who dwelt at the sign of the blanchard
"white horse"; or had a light complexion or white hair. BOLDT,
German, English, and Scottish family name, descended from
Baldo, a pet form of names beginning with Bald "bold," as Bald-
hart, Baldher, and Baldawin; or was acquired as a nickname for
a bold or fierce man; or dwelt at a hall or mansion; or was a short
heavy-set individual; or had an ancestor who originally came from
Bold "a dwelling" in Peeblesshire. BRADTKE is both Czechoslovakian and German, designating one who was a descendant of
the little brother, or of Brado; or dwelt at the sign of the little
bear.

The English, Dutch, and German BRILL came from Brill "a hill"
in Buckinghamshire; or from The Brill (Brielle or Bril) in The
Netherlands; one who made, or wore, spectacles; stranger who

12

came from Brill, the name of four villages in Germany; and as a Jewish name, an abbreviation of Ben Rabbi Judah Lowe. (On this Jewish name practice see page 266.) BROCK is a common English name, originally a dweller on the recently cleared and enclosed land; or dweller near the stream or swamp land; or dweller at the sign of the brocc "badger or young stag"; or resident near the Brock river in Lancashire; or, according to Professor Reaney, a stinking or dirty fellow, this latter derivation probably being the least likely interpretation.

BRODY is an Irish, Scottish, German, and Russian name, and refers to the son of Bruaideadh "a fragment"; or one who came from the barony of Brodie "muddy place" in Moray; or one with an outstanding or prominent beard; or dweller by the wide island; or one who came from Brody, "a ford or swamp" in Russia. This is a neat example of the trouble one may have in assaying nationality from the surname. BROEMEL is an English and German family name for the man who came from Bremhill "bramble hill" in Wiltshire; or who dwelt near a bramble or blackberry bush; as a German name it refers to a descendant of Broemel, a variant of Brumo, a pet form of names beginning with Brun "brown," as Brunfrid and Brunolf. In old Germanic names *m*'s and *n*'s easily interchange.

CAIN in Ireland descended from Cathan "warrior"; from Normandy he came from Caen, a city esteemed by William the Conqueror; in Anglo-Saxon England, he was a descendant of Cana "of mature judgment"; this name is also a nickname for a tall, slender individual. CLAIR, both English and French, descended from Clair "illustrious," a male name; it designates the light-complexioned man; one who came from Clare "clayey slope," the name of several places in England; one who came from St. Clare or St. Clair, the name of various villages in France. COLEMAN refers to a servant of Cole, a pet form of Nicholas "people's victory"; or is a corruption of Old English Coelmund "ship, protector"; or was a charcoal burner; or descendant of Coleman or Colman "little dove"; or an Anglicized form of German Kuhlman, that is, one who lived at, or near, a pool; or descendant of Old German Coleman "coal-black man." COLVIN is English and Gaelic, a descendant of Calvin "bald" or of Ceolwine "ship, friend"; one who came from Colleville "Col's farm" in Normandy.

13

CULLEN in its various spellings is Irish, English, and Scottish a grandson of Cuileann "holly"; an affectionate nickname for a cub or puppy; the handsome person; dweller in, or near, a small wood; dweller near a holly tree; one who came from Cullen "little nook" in Scotland. German DEGEN and DEGENER made rapiers descended from Thegan, a pet form of names commencing with Degen "young warrior," such as Theganbald and Deganhart; or designated a young warrior; or descended from Degenher "young warrior, army." FRANKEL is a German and French family name denominating a descendant of little Frank "free"; or one who came from France; or one who came from Franken, an old duchy in south central Germany. GABEL, from Germany, was one who made and sold agricultural implements such as pitchforks; or dwelt by a fork in the road; or came from Gabel "fork" in Germany; in England he descended from little Gabe, a pet form of Gabriel "God is my strength."

German GEISLER descended from Gisalhar "spear, army"; or was a vassal or feudal tenant; or was triumphant over another or who butchered goats and small animals; or who originally lived in Geislar or Geisler, the names of towns in Germany. German GELLER descended from Gelther "sacrifice, army"; it is a nickname for one in the habit of yelling or shrieking; one who moved from Geldern in Prussia. Goss, an English, German, French, and Hungarian surname, describes a resident in, or near, a moor or wood a descendant of Goss, a pet form of Gocelin "the just"; descendant of the Goth; dweller near a hedge of thorns; dweller at the sign of the goose; one who came from the former town of Goss, in Austria; a shortened form of names beginning with the Germanic element god "good."

GOODMAN is a common name in England, designating a descendant of Godmann "good man," or of Gudmund "war, protection" (-man is often substituted for -mund); the good servant the man or servant of Good, a common personal name; the good man or master of a household (once a title of dignity, and still so used in Scotland); also in Scotland, a landowner who held his land as a sub-tenant. HELM, an English, Dutch, German, and Swedish surname, means in England a dweller near the roofed shelter for cattle; or resident near an elm tree; in Holland and Germany it signifies a descendant of Helmo "helmet," a shortened form of names beginning with Helm, such as Helmhart and Helmold; or descendant of Helm, the Swedish name merely meaning "helmet." German HELWIG represents a descendant of Haluig "man, fight"; dweller at a military road; former resident of Hellweg "army road," a place in Germany; descendant of Hiltiwic, both elements of which mean "fight"; descendant of Hailwich "holy, fight."

HAROLD, HARROLD, HERALD, HEROD, and HARROD, to list only the most common forms, are names that cannot well be pinpointed and differentiated; the surname may be derived from Old Danish *Harald*, Old Norse *Haraldr*, Old Swedish *Harald*, Old German *Hairold* or *Herold*, or Old English *Hereweald* all possibly meaning "powerful warrior"; or from Middle English *heraud* "herald" or Old French *heraut* "herald"; or the name may be interpreted as a stage braggart; or one deriving from the Biblical family name, Herod.

HERRING, a German, English, and Scottish name, marks the descendant of Hering "son of Here (army)"; one who fished for and sold herring, a staple food in medieval England; dweller at the sign of the herring. Herrings were the principal fish used for food in western Europe. In medieval times the rent from sea fisheries along the English coast was normally expressed in herrings. English HOGG dwelt at the sign of the pig or young sheep; or descended from Hoga "careful or prudent" or from Hodge, a pet form of Roger; or was a self-indulgent, gluttonous, filthy person and thus qualified for the nickname.

HOLM, a Scandinavian and English name, specifies the householder living at, or near, a holly tree, or on, or near, a hill; the former resident of Holme "island," the name of numerous villages in England; dweller on the small island or on the raised dry land surrounded by marshy land. The most popular English form of the name is HOLMES. English HOOD made and sold head coverings; or came from Hood "shelter," places so called in Devonshire and Yorkshire; or was a descendant of Hood or Hud, hypocoristic forms of Richard "rule, hard" or of Hugh "spirit."

The aristocratic English family name of HOWARD has many possible derivations since the numerous families of that name arose in many different places; it marks the descendants of men with such names as Hugihard "heart, brave," Heward "spirit,

15

guard," Hereward "army, guard," and Howard "keeper of the swords"; it is the manorial official who guarded the hedges to protect the cultivated land from straying cattle; it is the eweherd in charge of the ewes; or is the high or chief warden. German HOYER was one who made hay; or one who came from Hannover a city and province in Germany; or the descendant of Hucge "spirit, spear." The English, Dutch, German family name, LEYDEN indicates a dweller at a meadow valley; or one who came from Lydden "pasture with a shelter" in Kent; or a former resident of Leiden "people" in Holland; or is a descendant of Liuto "people."

The English and German MADER had an ancestor who used or sold red dye; or came from Maden in Germany; or who cut and harvested grain; or who had a forebear named Matheri "court army." MARCH has five distinct origins; perhaps the most common is from residence near the *mearc* or boundary mark; others come from residence in or near a marsh; descendant of Mark "belonging to Mars, the god of war"; or of March, a name given to one born in that month; or from previous residence at March "boundary" in Cambridgeshire. MAZZONE was an Italian who resided or worked at the sign of the fish; or descended from big Mazzo, an aphetic form of Giacomazzo "the supplanter, or may God protect" or was a slow-moving individual; or who was housed in a field or meadow.

Two German names are MERTZ and METZ; the first one is a descendant of Mertz, a pet form of Mertens "belonging to Mars the god of war"; or of Maro, a pet form of names commencing with Mar "famous," such as Maruin and Maroald; or one who came from Metz in Germany; or one who dealt in small articles. Next, METZ came from Metz "middle" in Lorraine; or descended from Metz, a pet form of Matthias "gift of Yahveh"; or from Mar "belonging to Mars the god of war"; or from names beginning with Macht "might" such as Mahtulf and Mahtwald. PERRY, a Welsh or English surname, was ap Harry, the son of Harry, the English pet form of Henry "home, rule"; or one who lived near a pear tree; or one who descended from little Pier, a pet form of Peter "rock"; or descended from Perry, a pet form of Peregrin "the wanderer."

The simple name, PICK, is of either English, Czechoslovakian or German extraction, referring to a man who lived on or near pointed hill; or on a highway; or dweller at the sign of the pick or pickaxe; or one who lived or worked at the sign of the pic or woodpecker; or one who sold pike, the fish. The Dutch, English, Irish QUICK, with its Irish variant QUIGG, is the bright, lively person; or one who resided near an aspen tree; or grandson of Corc "heart"; or descendant of one who previously resided at Quickbury, formerly Cuwyk "cow farm" in Essex. RAINES is an English, sometimes Scottish, name, the descendant of Rain, a pet form of one of the old names beginning with Regen or Ragin "counsel," such as Raginhart and Reinold; or of Rayner "might, army"; or dweller at the boundary line; or at the sign of the frog from French *raine* "frog"; or a nickname for one supposed to have froglike traits; or from one who played the part of a queen in play or pageant; or one who came from Rayne "a division" in Aberdeenshire. RAY may be interpreted as a descendant of Ray, a pet form of Raymond "wise, protection"; or as a dweller at the sign of the roe deer; or one thought to possess some quality of the roe deer; or one who played the part of the king in play or pageant; or one who labored in the king's household.

RIDDLE has no connection with an enigma produced for solution by guessing, but usually refers to the man who came from Rydal or Ryedale "valley where rye was grown," towns in Westmorland and Yorkshire; or was the offspring of little Rada "counsel"; or from residence on or near a red hill. ROSNER is a German name meaning one who rode a horse; or a name designating the man from Rosna, Rossen, or Roessen, towns in Germany; or who was a descendant of Rozzo, a pet form of names beginning with the Germanic element, *hrod* "famous," found in such names as Hrodmund, Rothari, and Hrotfrid. SACCO, an Italian and German surname, is a descendant of Sacco, a pet form of Isacco or Isaac "he who laughs"; or is a descendant of Sacco, a pet form of names beginning with Sache "legal action," such as Saghart and Sacbert; or for one who dealt in sackcloth.

SAYERS in various spellings is the Englishman, progeny of Saer or Sayer "victory, people"; or one who had an ancestor who made or sold silk or serge; or one who assayed or tested metals; or one who cut timber into boards; or who sewed clothing, a tailor; or who appeared at fair and festival as a professional reciter or storyteller. SEYMOUR is an English surname referring to a descendant of Seamer "sea, famous"; or to the stranger who came from Seamer "lake, sea" in Yorkshire; or who came from St. Maur "black" in France. STELLA is both Italian and English, denoting one who descended from Stella "child of fate"; or from Stella, a pet form of Battisstella; or the name of the man who came from Stella "pasture with a cattle shed" in Durham; or who dwelt at the sign of the star. STENSON designates one from Stenson "Stein's village" in Derbyshire; or the son of Stean "stone" or the son of Sten, a pet contraction of Steven "crown or garland."

STRAUB is a German nickname for one with bushy or bristly hair; or for one who came from Straube in Germany; or descended from Strubo, a pet form of names commencing with Strud "destroy or rob," such as Strudolf and Strudmar; STROBEL has the same meanings as Straub, except that as a place name the town in Germany from where the bearers first came was probably Strobel. STUBBS is the English surname for one who lived near a prominent tree stump; or was a short, stumpy man; or who came from Stubbs "recently cleared land where the stumps were still evident" in Yorkshire. SWAN is English, Swedish, and Norwegian and designates the man who dwelt at the sign of the swan; or who was thought to possess the grace of that bird, and thus was so nicknamed; or in some cases the name points out the swain or servant; in others it is the descendant of Old Norse Sveinn or Swan "knight's attendant," a personal name; or it might be a metonym for the keeper of the swans; or in a few cases it may derive from Old English *swan* "herdsman."

TYSON, an English and Dutch family name, means the son of Ty, variant of Dye, a contracted form of Dionysius, "the Grecian god of wine"; or the son of Tys, a pet form of Matthias "gift of Yahveh"; or one who is known for stirring up strife and trouble. VESELY is both Slavic and English, a descendant of Vasily, a hypocoristic form of Basil "kingly"; or the man from Vesly "Virilius' estate," or Vezelay "Vitellius' estate" in France; or specifies the joyous or happy fellow. WAHL and WALL are German, Swedish, and English surnames for the resident at or near a wall, especially an old Roman wall; or one who lived at, or near, a stream or spring; or at, or near, a pool or bog; or in a field; or one who came from Wall "(Roman) wall," the name of several places in England.

Classification of Surnames

Wasson may be either English, Swedish, or German, the son of Waso or Wasso "sharp"; or of Wace "watchful"; or of little Waso or little Wace; or one who came from Wasa, a province in Finland; or was a descendant of Waso, a German pet form of names the first element of which was Was "sharp," such as Hwasmot or Wasmund. Weiner is a German family name, frequently used by Jews, which designates the man from Weine or Weiner, towns in Germany; or speaks of the man who made and sold wagons or carts; or manufactured and sold wine; or who descended from Winiheri "friend, army"; the name is sometimes confused with Wiener, the man from Wien (Vienna) in Austria.

German Weise refers to the offspring of Weise "wisdom"; or to the educated or learned man; or one who was an orphan; or one who descended from Wizo, a pet form of names commencing with Wid "forest," such as Widulf, Withar, and Widiman. Winter is English and German for the vintner or wine merchant; or refers to the progeny of Winter, a name bestowed on one born in the winter; or designates the dweller at the white water; or the man who descended from Winidhari "wind, army." Woodman may be the man who cut and sold timber in the wood; or one who hunted game in a wood; or who dyed cloth with woad; or who descended from the Old English given name, Wudumann "woodman." Word is an English and German family name for a resident near a thicket; or near a winding brook; or one who inhabited an open place in a village; or one who had an ancestor named Werdo, a pet form of names beginning with Wert "worthy," as Werdmann and Werdheri.

One cannot dismiss these various origins as merely a recital of disagreements among onomatological authorities; they are names that originated in different places at different times. What is today spelled in just one way had many origins among peoples the great majority of whom were illiterate. Even educated men spelled as fancy dictated at the moment. The common, easily spelled forms have swallowed up the other more unusual names. From these names the reader will note the powerful tendency of different names with different spellings to settle into common names spelled in an English way or what appears to be an English way. And no claim can here be made that all the interpretations of each of these names have been mentioned. In this book many

19

names are repeated in different chapters which have more than one origin, but for reasons of space not all contributory origins of every name can be noticed.

American people are no longer predominately of British stock. Yet British names are the popular pattern due chiefly to the fact that English-speaking people comprised by far the largest class among the earliest immigrants and later arrivals tended to "Americanize" their family names by "Englishing" them. The common American surnames, SMITH, JOHNSON, BROWN, and MILLER owe much of their popularity to the fact that they conceal large numbers of non-British family names that have been so translated in this country. Working with metal and the milling of grain were common occupations in every country which produced Smiths and Millers; due to the widespread familiarity with Bible names in Christian Europe, John in its various language forms was a very familiar name in all Christian countries; and as a nickname or forename the color brown and the given names Brun and Bruno were used everywhere.

America was colonized by peoples from all over the world in a very short period of time, a phenomenon that has not occurred in Africa, South America, or Australia, or anywhere else in the world. As settled, hereditary family names had developed long before this immigration started, all peoples brought their own diverse surnames to the new land bringing about an intermingling of every conceivable language background. A few groups of immigrants have stayed together such as the French in Louisiana, the Spanish in the Southwest, and the close-knit Pennsylvania Germans, but their numbers have not been sufficient to interfere with the stable English background. In late years many with common Spanish surnames have come into the country from Cuba and Puerto Rico. Earlier non-British immigrants were from Germany, Holland, France, and Sweden, and although some of their names were a bit discordant they were rather easily changed and absorbed by the English-speaking peoples. After about 1840 the Irish, German, and Scandinavian immigrations got under way. After 1880 great numbers of Slavic peoples came to the land of opportunity along with numerous East European Jews.

One could take any occupation common during the Middle Ages, a common sign name, a common descriptive term, or a oponymic term and translate the word into a dozen European anguages and have twelve different surnames, and find them all n America. Professor Weekley was fond of supporting his inter-retations of numerous surnames by inviting comparison with German and French names having the same derivations.

All the common surnames in England, Wales, Scotland, and reland are also popular in the United States. This is also true of panish, Italian, German, French, Scandinavian, and Slavic fam-ly names. In passing along the city streets in America, names rom these European countries are easily recognized. One might xpect the same world feeling in London or another of the Eng-ish cities since the same language is spoken in America as in the British Isles. But the English speaker has a feeling for names in England different from that in the United States. He may not now the meaning of most of the English names but they do, he eels, have an affinity with the language he speaks. This work eeks, in some measure, to reflect the overall pattern of Ameri-an surnames.

People in the land of the free distinguish between "ordinary" ames and those foreign "outlandish" names, generally meaning Polish, Russian, Hungarian, Czechoslovakian, South European ames borne by the laboring class—those Polacks, Ivanawful-ches, Hunkies, Bohunks—some of the more ignorant natives nunciate decisively, reflecting the prejudice and discrimination hat characterizes the hard, uncompromising attitude of many mericans. Names which require a bewildering array of conso-ants only lightly interspersed with vowels such as Czerny, Czyzewski, or Gzbelsuebzgy, or which involve unfamiliar twist-ng of the English tongue, such as Hlynka, Mkhalapov, or Antschichnij, appear to insult the culture of the lightly edu-ated WASP "White Anglo-Saxon Protestant," a phrase used de-ensively by those with the "unspeakable" names.

French, German, Italian, and Irish, particularly the latter, were a former years also deeply resented by Anglo-Americans, but he prejudice towards them was not nearly so virulent as that irected against the Slavs and South Europeans. Many unedu-ated Americans of British origin look down their noses upon oreigners in this country and are unduly proud of being Ameri-ans, forgetting that their own ancestors were "foreigners." They

21

remind one of the pompous Boston lady who, upon returning from a trip to Europe, was asked how she liked the people. "Not very well," she replied, "there was nothing but foreigners there."

This idea that foreigners are evil was recognized by William Henry Pratt to assure his stage success. Touring the country and playing minor roles, he was a mediocre success. He adopted Boris Karloff as his stage name about 1911 to make himself as much of a menace as possible. Thereafter, playing the part of monsters, maniacs, and other rough terrorists under the foreign-sounding name, he became one of the best-known thespians in the country. Yet KARLOFF is a simple name, "the son of Charles."

This discrimination against Slavic and South European peoples has, in the nineteenth and early twentieth centuries, made it diffi cult for them to obtain jobs. Even some not so narrowly biased who operated mercantile establishments insisted that prospective employees change their names. They were told that people needed to address the sales clerks and might hesitate to come into the store if they had difficulty in pronouncing the names Large American firms, understandably enough, do not want their outgoing letters to bear such foreign-looking signatures as would tend to repulse prospective customers. They require the name of employees who deal with the public to be easily remembered and used. They are afraid that when people are embarrassed to use an employee's name, they may possibly go elsewhere.

Although America is a nation of nations, still fast becoming one nation, one can be highly prejudicial against another particularly when it comes to a fight for jobs. Carl Sandburg, whose father shortly after his arrival from Sweden, changed his name from August Johnson to August Sandburg, aptly expressed his thought on the handicap of keeping an Old World name in the competi tion for jobs in this new country in the poem he entitled "Black listed."

The influence of the right name in obtaining jobs in Americ was used to their advantage by some industrial workers before the advent of Social Security laws which stabilized the names of the laboring class. Where personnel managers in the factorie were known to dislike all foreigners, a serviceable Anglo-Saxon name was often listed on the application blank. Where the fore men had Polish or Czech or German names the smart applican listed a corresponding cognomen and benefited from the prejudicial favoritism.

During war times employment managers in defense establishments eyed foreigners suspiciously and hired them only after others with more English-sounding names were employed. In the twentieth century many were required to exhibit birth certificates which disclosed their original names. References they were required to give were necessarily those of people who knew them well—people with the same kind of foreign names. Girls who desired to teach school were advised to change their names so the pupils could speak them properly, and of course the men on the school boards also needed to be able to pronounce them. Students with foreign names sometimes think that they receive lower grades because the teachers do not often call upon them to recite since they are uncertain as to the correct pronunciation. Others think that people hesitate to address them or write to them because they are embarrassed when they cannot pronounce or spell the name.

At the present time, after a half century of wars, this bias and dislike of "foreign" names has eased somewhat due in great part to the accomplishments of many second generation "foreigners." Some of foreign extraction resisted all importunities to change and by their work and character forcibly made their names American. Outstanding examples are the Dutch STUYVESANT, VAN RENSSELAER, VANDERBILT, and ROOSEVELT in New York, and the SCHUYLER family in Pennsylvania.

Perhaps the most prominent feature of onomastics in America, one emphasized by H. L. Mencken in his *The American Language*, is the tendency by ethnic groups to change the family name to adapt to American ears and tongues attuned to the English language. The stimulus is especially strong when surrounded by neighbors of English descent, weaker when they congregate in cities and districts with little contact with outsiders. Those from countries with alphabets other than the Latin had to transliterate them and different systems of transliteration produced many variant names. Foreign names are assimilated into words and names familiar to speakers of English. The most usual change of surname was by translation practiced in some degree by every foreign group.

People from every European country with names meaning smith, miller, woods, hill, stream, new town, descendant of John, brown, white, small, and the like have translated their names into the common English equivalents; their descendants after several generations will surely regard themselves as of English descent. Common German names were thus changed: Koch became Cook; Klein became Cline; Grün changed to Green; Pfeffer to Pepper; Schwartz and Weiss became Black and White respectively; König translated to King; Schumacher turned into Shoemaker; Zimmerman into Carpenter; and Sonntag into Sunday. Cognatic translation is seen in the change of Krankheit "sickness" to Crankright.

Because of the close relationship between the English and German languages, some Germans are able to transform their names to the English form just by dropping a single letter. Fleischer "butcher" drops the *i* to become Flescher and Fischer eliminates the *c* to become Fisher. Some change the German *k* to *c* as when Krebs "crab" becomes Crebs. Traut "faithful" changes a single letter to become Trout, Behn "bear" alters to Bean, and Behm "from Bohemia" does likewise to become Beam.

Many Germans have respelled their names in America, paying particular attention to the German pronunciation. Thus Koehler "charcoal burner" becomes Caylor; Kaufman "merchant" changes to Coffman; Kalb "calf" alters to Kolb and Culp; Tiefenbach "deep brook" becomes Diffenbaugh; Espenschied "aspen boundary" becomes Espenshade; Eberhard "boar, strong" becomes Everhart; Vetter "cousin" is spelled Fetter; Schnabele "beak" changes to Snavely; Theisen "son of Matthias" is written Tyson; Weik "from Wigo" is called Wike; and Jost "descendant of Jodocus or Justinius" was known as Yost even before the great Fielding H. Yost became so successful as football coach at the University of Michigan.

After the start of the first World War, Germans in great numbers quickly Anglicized their names in an effort to remove all doubt as to their patriotism. Afterwards some changed back, and then during World War II the problem became acute again, and the changing started all over again, although not with as much intensity as formerly. Families named Hitler "supervisor of salt-works," especially, hurried to change their names, and today very few Hitlers are left to endure senseless insults.

Slavic immigrants to America have made all sorts of more or less crude translations and transliterations of their family names, although many who have lived in America among their own kind have resolutely retained the old forms despite the fact that diacritical marks have been eliminated in most cases. Their apparently indiscreet grouping of consonants has made them unpronounceable by natives of Western European ancestry, although the spelling and correct pronunciation are usually closely related.

Those of foreign origin who do change their names, either because of insistence by the second generation or to obtain economic preferment in America, sometimes find that they suffer agonies and feel that they are lost with nothing to support them. They are not ready to sever all connection with the Old Country since they do not yet have confidence that they are fully accepted in the culture of the new. They are still deep in the process of adjusting to new ways, new things, new environment. There is even some feeling of inferiority enhanced by the attitude of Americans toward them and their names. To those with professional and white-collar status, change is a very personal and delicate matter.

Instances and discussion of change of names in America could fill several books and it does. The late Louis Adamic, the writer who emigrated from Slovenia, discussed the problem in America in his *What's in a Name?* published during the early stages of World War II. He attacked the matter from a psychological and emotional point of view. He advocated what he called organic change by Europeans, that is, change which comes about by itself or develops naturally without distortion under all the pertinent circumstances.

Adamic urged persons with difficult foreign names to change them—not to common British names, but by shortening and simplifying the spelling in such a way as not to lose the ethnic flavor of the name. He argued for change "which comes about mainly of itself with very little inner conflict; which grows or emerges naturally out of an undistorted interrelation among all the pertinent circumstances." His own name in his native Slovenia was ADAMIC, with the hook over the *c*, pronounced Ah-dah'-mitch meaning "little Adam, or son of Adam." He considered changing it to Adamage to fit in with the way most Americans pronounced it when they saw it written. ADAMICH and ADAMITCH were forms he occasionally used. He enlisted in the army as Adamič but the hook over the *c* was immediately dropped, and the name was pronounced Ad'amic and so remained, notwithstanding efforts by others familiar with the Slovenian language to give it a different pronunciation.

It is among the second generation, the children of foreigners with formidable, unpronounceable names, that the greatest anxiety arises over whether to change to a simple, pronounceable British name to acquire better jobs. In the army there is no official prejudice against foreigners; indeed, there is admiration for them, but there is teasing and more or less good-natured joking and application of undignified nicknames when the top sergeant has trouble in calling the roll. Some recent arrivals in this country think it best to change their names but cannot bring themselves to the point of actually doing so. Some who do, find that it affects their personality adversely—they cannot quite get away from the feeling that they have lost some indefinable part of themselves. Years after changing some revert to their former Old Country name. Persons who have never experienced any difficulty with their names cannot always comprehend the quandaries of others and in their lack of sympathy may offer only ridicule.

To discuss all the changes and alterations immigrants make in their family names when they settle in the United States would take unlimited space. Here only a few of the alterations characteristic of the principal national groups in the country can be mentioned. English names spelled the same as common English words in which the English spelling differs from the American practice have been altered to conform with usage in America. For example, NEIGHBOURS becomes NEIGHBORS in this country.

Some shortened their names by cutting off the first or last parts. Many Greeks with their long names dropped a part. PAPPAGEOR-GIOU "Priest George" became either PAPPAS or GEORGIOU. Others translated their names to English. French MEUNIER became MILLER. Some only partially translated their names: German ALTHAUS became ALTHOUSE, Swedish STENBERG became STONE-BERG, and NYQUIST became NEWQUIST.

Classification of Surnames

As French, or rather Norman French, was the language of the aristocracy and the upper class in England at the time fixed surnames were being developed, it is not surprising that many of our well-known English family names are French or derived from French words. There are, for example, ALGERNON, from *aux gernons* "bewhiskered," BEECHAM, from *beau champ* "beautiful field," BEWLEY, from *beau lieu* "beautiful place," and ALABASTER, from *arbalestier* "crossbowman," to mention only a few. The most important source of these French names is the place names of French villages from which the original bearers came.

Of the early immigrants to America the French have fared the worst in respect to their names chiefly because of the difficulties experienced by Americans in pronouncing them correctly. Many have been translated into English names, as LE BLANC into WHITE and DUBOIS into WOODS. Others had their spelling "simplified," as RULO from ROLEAU "shield, wolf, or fame, land," BUNKER from BON COEUR "good heart," and RENO from RENAUD "counsel, judgment." French names were not the only ones that Americans had trouble in pronouncing. Perhaps the most difficult English name to pronounce correctly is THISTLETHWAITE "field overgrown with thistles."

Italian names presented few difficulties and few were changed for that reason. The most common alteration is the dropping of the final vowel to fit in with the English language pattern of a consonantal ending. Sometimes the *i*-ending is changed to *y* as when BOVERI "oxen" becomes BOVERY, a more British-appearing form. Others change the *a*, *i*, or *o*, to *e* to give the name a slight American flavor. A few may drop the final part as when BONFIGLIO "good child" becomes BONFIG. In America the prepositions *da*, *de*, *di*, and the articles *la*, *li*, *lo* frequently merge with the name as in DAMATO "of the loved" and LAROCCA "the fortress." Few Italians seek to hide their national character by alterations in their family names.

Spanish names, especially the common patronymics such as GARCIA "spear, firm," FERNANDEZ "journey, venture," LOPEZ "wolf," GONZALEZ "battle, elf," and RODRIGUEZ "famous, rule," are familiar to Americans and few see the need to change them. The Spanish usually simplify their surnames by leaving out the awkward reference to the mother's maiden name. Those few who use

27

the family names of both parents, as is the Spanish custom, often drop the connecting *y*. Mexicans and Cubans who have come to the United States have usually settled in places where Spanish is generally understood so have made few changes. The Portuguese in this country settled more among English-speaking people and many of their names have undergone some changes in spelling and pronunciation. They use *de* instead of *y* as a connective between the parents' surnames and this, like the Spanish practice, is usually dropped. They have changed such names as Pereira "pear tree" to Perry and Rodriques "famous, rule" to Rogers.

The Swedes have made many changes in America. There are several sounds in their language which are particularly difficult for Anglo-Saxon throats, such as *ö*, *sj*, *bj*, *hj*, *lj*, and *lilj*, and many of these with difficult sounds are quickly altered upon arrival in America to aid in pronunciation. Sjögren, "sea, branch" is changed to Shogren; Ljung "heather" into Young; Hjelm "helmet" into Helm, although in Swedish it is the *h* which is silent; and Liljegren "lily, branch" into Lilygren. Many Swedes have been encouraged by their government to change to a so-called civil name, usually two plant or nature elements arbitrarily combined, as Sjoberg "sea, mountain" and Sjostrand "sea, shore," more fully discussed on page 269. When they are partially or fully translated in America to become Seaberg or Seashore, they produce names not found anywhere else in the world. A Swede by the name of Örnberg, "eagle, mountain," may alter it to Earnberg to keep the pronunciation of the first element or spell it Ornberg, dropping the diacritical marks in which event the usual English pronunciation of *o* would be adopted. In Swedish, the *g* in *berg* is pronounced like the English consonantal *y*, but Swedes usually accept the normal English pronunciation of the word.

Swedes and Norwegians with such names as Andersson, Karlsson, Nilsson, Ericksson, Larsson, and Olessen have eliminated one medial *s* in America to become Anderson, Karlson, Nilson, Erickson, Larson, and Olesen. Pettersson drops both a medial *t* and *s* to emerge as Peterson. The highly respected Swedish "priest" names terminate in *-ius* or *-ander* and are seldom changed. Many Swedes in America reverted to the names they received in military service, the soldier names. In earlier times the commanding officer assigned bynames to each recruit which served to identify them while in the army. These were usually short, warlike names such as Felt "battlefield," Granat "grenade," Hurtig "brisk," Pihl "arrow," and Strang "firm." Sometimes whimsy took over and names like Brud "bride," Drucken "drunk," Gris "pig," Kattunge "kitten," Trut "snout," and Vildgås "wild goose" resulted, more fully discussed in Chapter VI.

The Norwegians and Danes have brought their recently acquired patronymics to America, most of them terminating in -*son* or -*sen* (from Norway) and -*sen* (from Denmark). The -*sen* suffix has often been changed to English -*son*. At the time of the first emigration to America the patronymic was the name of the father to which the suffix was added and thus the surname changed with each generation. If a man were named Halvor Olsen, his children would not have Olsen as a surname, but would be surnamed Halvorsen. Each generation had a different surname.

In Norway custom decreed that men have two surnames, a patronymic and a farm name. Farm names are discussed in Chapter VI (page 267). Because of these double names family names of Norwegians in America were particularly unstable. In Norway neither the patronymic nor the farm name was hereditary. After they arrived in America they frequently wavered between the two if they did not change entirely to an "American" name. The Norwegian's problem was to confine himself to either the patronymic or the farm name. He tended to take the patronymic as his family name in America because it was more familiar and easier for Yankees to pronounce, but then many turned to the farm name because the patronymic was too common. Where the family had lived on more than one farm, although the family might not have owned all or any of them, several farm names were available. National groups favored the distinctive farm names for patriotic reasons; they were the only characteristic Norwegian names and they often awakened a fierce family pride. It has been estimated that farm names are now more commonly used among Norwegian-Americans than patronymics.

When sufficient pressure forced the Norwegian to settle on a single family name he had several choices. There would be several patronymics as in the past each generation had a different one, and any one could be chosen. The problem was usually settled on the basis of which was the most widely known. Due to the transitory nature of the use of patronymics and the casual use of either the farm name or a patronymic, the Norwegian in America did not feel a strong attachment to the surname and change to one permanent family name was not difficult. Brothers frequently adopted different surnames in America. Minor changes were sometimes made. For example, NELSON is not found in Norway, but many a NIELSEN, NILSON, or NILSSEN "son of Nils" has altered to Nelson.

The Finns have made fewer changes because many of their names could be easily pronounced by Americans. Some long names were cut up, as when HIETEMAKI "sand hill" became MAKI "hill," and KIVIJÄRVI "stone lake" became KIVI "stone." Others had one part translated. Finnish writers point with pride to the minority of Finns who have resisted all pressures to change their names and deplore the translation and transliteration of Finnish cognomens in the New World.

Ukrainians in the Americas insist on keeping themselves separate from the Russians. Their patronymic surnames may be easily recognized from use of the common suffix -enko, not found in any other Slavic language, originally a diminutive which later acquired the meaning of "son," as in IVANENKO "son of John." The origin of -enko goes back to the twelfth century, and this termination is found with many names not patronymics.

As many Ashkenazic Jews had surnames popularly recognized as "Jewish," men with substantial anti-Semitic bias paid particular attention to the names of those they met. This, of course, is an important reason why Jews have been so willing to change their family names. Many Slavic Jews adopted German-Jewish names because German Jews before them, by their work and industry in America, had won respected positions, and thus had added luster to such surnames. Educated Jews in America change their names more than the uneducated. Other educated newcomers are less likely to change their names generally because their names have become better known and they have become leaders in their group, so that a change would be detrimental. It has been estimated that at least half of the Jews in America do not now have "Jewish" names.

Yankee peddlers were for the most part replaced by German Jews in America beginning about the first third of the nineteenth century. Many entered the tailoring and clothing trades and developed dry goods, tobacco, the export and import trade, auctioneering, and general wholesale businesses, largely concentrated in New York City and the large metropolitan areas in the eastern half of the country. This was such a distinct group that American humor produced numerous stories about them in Yiddish dialect.

These Jewish immigrants, usually from south and western Germany, had characteristic surnames recently acquired, mostly of geographical origin and American folk humor concentrated on the *-heim(er)s* "home" and *-stein(er)s* "stone," since few Germans not of Jewish extraction had surnames with these endings. Many of these names were artificial, no place in Germany so named being in existence. Other Jews had surnames with other geographical name endings such as *-ach(er)* "abounding in," *-au(er)* "meadow," *-bach* "brook," *-baum* "tree," *-berg(er)* "mountain," *-burg(er)* "stronghold," *-dorf* "village," *-feld(er)* "field," *-hof* "court," *-thal* "valley," *-wald* "wood," and *-wasser* "water." (See pages 263 ff.) These terminations are not exclusively Jewish. The humorous stories in Jewish dialect produced such characteristic names as Grabbenstein, Burnstein for the insurance applicant, and Failinstein for the bankrupt, as well as Leviheimer and Cohnheim. DINKELSPIEL, "the man from Dinkelsbuhl" by its very sound stamps it as a humorous Jewish cognomen. Strong in commercial dealings, the Jews did not let their Jewish names interfere with progress.

The following is typical of Jewish persistence in mercantile affairs, its good humor enhanced by the names.

There was young Ikey Kabibble who applied to Steinheimer, a big cloak and suit man, for a job as salesman. "I have all the salesmen I can use," said Steinheimer, "but I have one suit that they can't seem to sell. It is there, the orange one with the bright purple and green polka dots. If you can sell it, you have a lifetime job." The boss then went to lunch.

Returning, he found Ikey smiling complacently with his clothing ripped and torn to shreds and his face and hands scratched and bleeding, but the suit was gone. "What's happened?" inquired Steinheimer.

"I sold the suit," exclaimed the new employee.

"Congratulations, but did you have to battle the customer?"

31

"Oh, no," replied Ikey, "the customer was perfectly delighted with the suit, but his Seeing Eye dog attacked, scratched and bit like the devil."

Even when Jewish names remain unchanged, they are often altered or modified in spelling or pronunciation. SCHLESINGER "from Silesia" becomes SLESSINGER, DALSHHEIMER alters to DALSEMER. MORDECAI "taught of God" collapses into MARCUS or MARKS, also spelled MARX. BURNSTEIN "amber" and similar names sometimes alter the spelling of the last element to -stine.

Before the first World War many Jews with names ending in -stein altered the pronunciation to make it rhyme with bean, although when standing alone it was kept to rhyme with brine. The pronunciation of the common LEHMAN "vassal" was changed from Layman to Leeman. Some STRAUSS "ostrich" families pronounce it Straws. KUHN "bold" is sometimes Coon, other times Keene. When the Jew changed his name it often involved some slight play or pun on the meaning because to a Jew the meaning has been the most important attribute since Biblical times. Illustrative of this tendency is the humorous story of the Jewish migratory businessman born in Lithuania with the surname Bevelterpisser. Moving to Germany he became known as Spritzwasser "squirt water." Residing in France he became La Fontaine, then in England the name became Fountain, and finally in America, Waters. Attaining success and moving to an ostentatious neighborhood, the family became Delawaters. To outsiders the newly chosen name often appears to have no reference to the former cognomen, but to the man himself it retains some secret connection. LEVINSKY changes to LEWIS or LEE; COHEN changes to CONN or CAINE; and WEINTRAUB "grape grower or merchant" changes to WINTHROP. Many of the changed names, it will be noted, have some faint allusion to occupation, Biblical phrase, or are even related in some way to the sound of the former name.

Although Jews throughout the world have hesitated little about changing their names to conform to the name-patterns of the locality in which they lived, it is in America where free change of names among Jews is legal and commonplace. In one act the Jew has tried to avoid the handicaps that go with both foreignness and Jewishness. H. L. Mencken estimated that, "Possibly half the Jews of New York now sport new names." BLUMENTHAL "flower valley" changed to BLOOMINGDALE and STOLAR, a Yiddish-Russian word, translated to CARPENTER, SHER "mole-catcher" is extended into SHERMAN. August Schonberg, the banker, translated to French, Belmont, but his enemies insisted on using his former name. GOLDWASSER translates to GOLDWATER. No law in America hinders them as it does in Germany, France, and elsewhere in Europe. Numerous Jews merely changed to Adams, Brown, Jones, Lowell, Smith, and all the other common "Anglo-Saxon" surnames. Today Jews in America cannot all be recognized by their surnames alone. The story is often told of the Jew who appeared in court to change his name to a typical Irish name. A month later he again appeared and asked to change to another common Irish surname. In answer to the judge's inquiry he said that people on hearing his name asked him what it was before and he wished to tell them his previous Irish name.

In America a good name is one whose bearer has contributed something of value to the growing country. Many German Jews are found in this classification. There are Berlin, Einstein, Frankfurter, Goldblatt, Rothschild, and Wise. Some of the famous German-Jewish financiers who operated out of New York are Bache, Goldman, Guggenheim, Hallgarten, Kuhn, Lehman, Lewisohn, Loeb, Seligman, and Wertheim. Baruch and Cardozo represent the Sephardim moiety. HALLMARK is "half a mark," a nickname from the coin worth six shillings, eight pence. Such names referring to money often arise from the bearer's paying that amount as rent each year for his land. The other names in this paragraph are interpreted elsewhere in this work.

The small Sephardic (Spanish-Portuguese) group of Jews were the first to come to America. They had surnames from ancient times and were fiercely proud of them. Few changed them as they experienced little difficulty with them. Some of these easily recognized Spanish and Portuguese names are: CARDOZO "from Cardoso," CARVALHO "dweller near the oak tree," CORDOVA "from ancient Cordoba," CASTRO "castle," COSTA "hillside," GOMEZ "son of Gomo," LOPEZ "son of Lope," MENDEZ "son of Mendel," PEREIRA "pear tree," SILVEIRA "brier tree," SOUZA "from Souza," SPINOZA "from Espino, thorny place," TOLEDANO "from Toledo."

MERCADO "market place" is found sometimes as a surname among Sephardic Jews, a name that arose from a superstition current in the Middle Ages. When a couple found that their babies were dying one after another, they assumed that there was a curse on them. To eliminate the curse they "sold" the next baby to a family with healthy children, and then took it back after a few days as caretakers of the "sold" child, giving it the name Mercado, "the bought baby." An analogous custom among Ashkenazim might account for some surnamed KAUFMAN. Further discussion of Jewish names is delayed to a later chapter (page 261).

Some people from many nationalities have shortened their names by retaining only the patronymical prefix or suffix, as Norman FITZ and FITTS, Gaelic MAC and MACK, German SOHN, sometimes spelled SONN or SONNE, and the Greek POULOS, or, infrequently, the English and Scandinavian SON. Old Norse Magnus "great" is occasionally a contributory source of MACK. Likewise a few of Dutch extraction have contracted their place names to the preposition or preposition plus article, VAN and VANDER.

Some with English names have contracted them, keeping only the topographical suffixes TON and LEY. Many merely slightly altered their names into familiar English words or compounds as will be seen by the numerous examples mentioned in the latter part of Chapter VI which discusses a sampling of these surnames that play havoc in orderly classification. This practice explains numerous odd and puzzling names. Others have merely arbitrarily corrupted or altered the spelling to conform to popular American pronunciation. LANGESTRAET, for example, becomes LONGSTREET and KUHLMAN becomes COLEMAN.

To summarize, the principal, albeit overlapping and vague, types of changes of name favored by immigrants in America, are eight in number. They are:

1. By respelling, as when English COCKBOURNE is spelled COBURN, French NOEL becomes NOWELL, and German ALBRECHT changes to ALBRIGHT.
2. By translation, as when Irish BREHONY becomes JUDGE, and German RUEBSAMEN translates to TURNIPSEED.
3. By transliteration, as when a Russian name spelled in the Cyrillic alphabet is changed to the Latin alphabet, or a Chinese name written in ideographs is expressed in the alphabet used in America.

4. By abbreviation, as when Welsh DAVIES contracts to DAVIS and German GOLDBERGER shortens to GOLDBERG.
5. By extension, as when JOHNSON increases to JOHNSTONE and RUSSEL becomes RUSSELL.
6. By conversion, as when the German MUELLER changes to MILLER and the Swedish JONSSON becomes JOHNSON.
7. By dropping diacritical marks, as when Czech RŮŽIČKA "little rose" strips naked to RUZICKA and Swedish SJÖGREN "sea, branch" unveils to SJOGREN.
8. By substitution, as when Smith becomes Jones and Black becomes Fields.

Before the system of war veterans' pensions and the adoption of Social Security laws, the change of names was smooth and easily done in the United States. Today the complexities of modern life make it almost imperative that legal action be involved by one desiring to change the family name, although in the United States court permission is not a legal necessity as it is in most other countries.

It may be helpful to note a few of the most common elements in American names which provide hints in recognizing the national antecedents of the bearer from inspection of his family name. Surnames terminating in *-ley, -ton, -ham, -ford, -field,* and *-brook* are usually from English village names. Some German locality endings are *-au, -bach, -baum, -berg, -bruck, -burg, -dorf, -heim, -hof, -horst, -reut, -stadt, -stein, -thal,* and *-wald.* The ending *-er* is found in English and German names and the ending *-mann* (often contracted to the English *-man*) connotes a German name; both indicate occupational names or denote that the original bearer came from the place or town indicated. *Von* may be observed in German names hinting at nobility while the *van, vander,* and *vanden* stamp the bearer as Dutch and merely mean "at" and "at the."

The patronymical terminations are very helpful in assessing the nationality of the bearer's paternal parent. The ending *-son* is found in English, Scottish, Swedish, and Norwegian names. When spelled *-sen,* it is Danish or Norwegian. The prefix *O'* indicates an Irish name while *Mac* or *Mc* is either Irish or Scottish. Most Armenian names terminate in *-ian,* sometimes changed to *-yan.* The ending *-nen* usually indicates Finnish ancestry. The Spanish patronymical form is *-ez* and *-es*, and the Portuguese form is *-es* and *-az*. Russian *-ovich*, Polish *-wicz*, Rumanian *-escu*, Ukrainian *-enko*, and Turkish *-oglu* are telltale patronymical elements. *Ibn* or *ben* is found in Arabian names. Common masculine names with the *-s* ending are often of Welsh derivation.

Most Russian surnames end in *-ov*, *-in*, or *-ev*. If the ending is *-sky*, the man is probably Russian; if it is *-ski*, he is likely to be of Polish descent. A common Portuguese suffix is *-eira*. The Frisian *-stra* indicates place or location while the ending *-sma* is used with occupational names. Common Swedish nature terminations are *-blad*, *-blom*, *-dahl*, *-ek*, *-gren*, *-holm*, *-lind*, *-lof*, *-lund*, *-kvist*, *-sjo*, *-strand*, and *-strom*. Many Belgian occupational names are preceded by the definite article *De*, but the same term in French names is the preposition "of" or "from." The French also use the article *Le* and the preposition or contraction *Du*. Arabs employ the definite article, *Al* or *El*. The simple endings *-is* and *-os* often indicate transliterated Greek names. The diminutives *-eau*, *-el*, *-iau*, *-on*, *-ot* and various combinations of these or double diminutives are frequently noted in French names. Common Italian diminutive endings are vowels enclosing double consonants, as *-ello*, *-etti*, *-illo*, *-ucco*, *-ucci*, and *-uzzo*.

Family names that do not contain vowels are most confusing to Americans when suddenly they are confronted with them and required to pronounce them. There are the following Czech and Slovak names: CHRT, DRS, KRC "cramps," KRCH, SMRT "death," SMRZ, SRB, SRCH, SRP "sickle," TRC, TRCH, TRFT, TRH, and VLK "wolf" found in American directories. These short names can be real stumbling blocks. Many Czechoslovakians with this type of name have been forced to insert a vowel for the convenience of Americans. A name like YFF, found in Chicago, can set an American back on his heels. NG is an Asiatic name not easy for Westerners to grasp. In 1958, there were 1647 entries on the Social Security list with this surname. The pronunciation is approximately *unn* with the lips pressed together.

To arrive at the exact derivation or meaning of a surname is not easy. Many are not what they appear to be. BARKER did not bay like a dog but devoted his working time to preparing leather from Old English *bark* "to tan." POINTER did not direct people where to go by the use of the extended forefinger, but was one who made laces and cords for fastening hose and doublet together. USHER did not show people to their theatre seats but was a doorkeeper, one who kept watch at the door to the king's apartment. SPITTLE does not mean that; it designates one who dwelt or worked at a hospital, a place of shelter or entertainment for travelers in the Middle Ages. But SPEAKER and SPEAKMAN did act as advocates or spokesmen for others. In contrast to European names, the correct interpretation of English surnames can be given with greater confidence because of the many early documents containing them still extant.

As we attempt to drag the meaning of our surnames from the dark, cloudy, murky past, it must be remembered that many names of diverse origins with only slightly varied spellings tended to freeze into the usual common, generally modern, English spellings familiar to most people. Any simple-looking name with an apparently obvious meaning can thus have become the end result of the cohesion of a half dozen or more completely different names several of which are from diverse languages. Ordinary vagaries of spelling and sound differences found even in adjacent communities are responsible in many instances.

Merely dropping the ubiquitous diacritical marks does not always solve the problem as it often changes the pronunciation for one's compatriots unless another letter is added. For example, eliminating the diacritical mark in VLČANSKY without inserting an *h* to make it VLCHANSKY, elicits the American pronunciation Vulkan'-skee. Adding the *h* would change the Slovak pronunciation.

The influx of names into the United States from non-British sources, an invasion unmatched in the history of the world, by peoples whose pronunciation of the vowels and consonants varied in every conceivable manner, forced the wide extension of the legal rule of *idem sonans,* which provides that a slight variation in the spelling of a name is immaterial if both modes of spelling have approximately the same sound. Names that sound alike are the same although spelled differently. The law regards the sound more than the spelling. Thus American courts have decided that the couplets such as Bulkley and Buckley, Burnon and Vernon, Chevrolet and Chevrole, Erwan and Irwin, Reinhardt and Reinhart, Vincent and Vinson, and Zulkowsky and Zulakoskie are the same name. Without the use of this rule the difficulties would be endless. However, as higher education has become more widespread, the courts are more reluctant to apply this rule.

Samuel Brown titled his work on family nomenclature, *Surnames Are the Fossils of Speech,* and they most assuredly are. Many surnames have retained the spelling of the Middle Ages, although the words from which they were derived have been modernized. There are TAYLOR from *taylor* modernized into *tailor,* LYONS from *lyons* now *lions,* and BRISTOW from Bristou, the English city, now spelled Bristol. When the words *reid, reed,* and *read* changed in spelling and pronunciation to *red,* the surnames REID, REED, and READ did not follow suit. On the other hand, some names have made the change along with the words from which they were derived. In the fourteenth to sixteenth centuries *smith* was always spelled with a *y,* but in the seventeenth century it changed to *i* and the surname, SMITH, changed accordingly. Middle English *brid* "bird" changed to *bird* and the surname BIRD followed. The early spelling *yonge* changed to *young* and the surname YOUNG in most cases changed in like manner. When one asserts that his name has always been spelled in just one way he is talking nonsense. Every name has been spelled in several different ways in the past.

While English pronunciation of names is not the purpose of this work, it may be helpful to allude to certain alterations in pronunciation, especially in regard to surnames derived from Christian names. In the Middle Ages until the sixteenth or seventeenth century, the *n* in Henry was silent, and the name was pronounced as Harry in England, as confirmed by the many families named HARRIS and HARRISON compared with the later form, Henry. Then Harry became considered to be the pet form of Henry. In Scotland they retained the *n* sound and even inserted a *d* to emphasize it, as in HENDRY and HENDERSON. Other names developed the intrusive *p* as in THOMPKINS, THOMPSON, and SIMPSON. The terminal *-d* or *-eds* is seen in SIMUND and SIMMONDS, HAMMOND and HAMMONDS. Walter, Gilbert, and Ralph were pronounced without the *l* sound which produced such surnames as WATTS and WATER, GIBBS and GIBBARD, and RAFE and RAFF.

Numerous names in America, among certain families, are pronounced locally one way and spelled another. CRENSHAW is pronounced *Granger;* CALLOWHILL is pronounced *Carroll* and BOUL-

WARD fades into *Boler;* and CAMPBELL is often *Camel.* This fuzzy slurring so common in early America tends to disappear except where it is stubbornly retained to keep a supposed patrician coloring. This is the same principle that is in effect in England where well-known CHOLMONDELEY is pronounced *Chumley* much to the humorous ridicule of people outside of the British Empire. In America the correct spelling and pronunciation of a name is the spelling and pronunciation accorded it by the bearer. He is the one most intimately concerned with its shape and form and is accorded the authoritative voice.

In the early European records the names were always written in their Latin forms by the clerks, although the names as used by the peasants in England were always in English. However, a few occupational names in their Latin form have come down to us, the most common of which is FABER "smith." Others are SUTOR "shoemaker" and TEXTOR "weaver."

One must keep in mind that the same word and thus the name derived from it had widely different meanings at different times and in different places. The duties of a particular servant or occupation varied a great deal even in the same country. Before the advent of the printed dictionary and universal education, the commonly accepted meaning of a word often varied in different sections of a country. Thus the meaning of a surname is the meaning given the word from which it is derived at the particular time and place when and where the name first arose.

Some examples may be noted. SADD does not mean mournful; when surnames were becoming fixed family names, the word meant "serious or grave"; and that is the explanation of the surname. MOODY is from Old English *mōdig* "bold, impetuous, brave"; it has no reference to fits of depression, the latter-day meaning. PRETTYMAN means the "crafty, cunning man"; his ancestor was not the elegant man his descendant has become. BLYTH is from Old English *blitha* "gentle, merry." QUICK refers to the living, the lively person, as in the phrase, "the quick and the dead." NICE before becoming "pleasant or agreeable" developed as follows: "foolish—simple—shy—modest—discriminating." As a surname it does not have its present day meaning, but it survived as a family name because the word changed into a pleasant one. SIMPLE, now usually spelled SEMPLE, originally meant "honest, free from guile or duplicity," not the meaning we usually ascribe to it today—"deficient in intelligence." SEMPLE, as noted elsewhere, however, also designates one who came from St. Paul, the name of several places in France.

More odd names exist in America than elsewhere because so many of them are ordinary foreign names which are also common English words with a different meaning. For example, KISS, the common Hungarian name for the small man, has a comic connotation for Americans. BOYS is from French BOIS, "a dweller in or near a wood." In others an ordinary English word or name has acquired a different conception. OUTHOUSE in rural America is too familiar to require further elucidation.

People generally are unaware of the origin and meaning of their family names, a subject not treated in most genealogies; struggling to keep apace of the rapid growth in America, people have lacked time for backward glances into the subject. Most of them have not given the matter any thought. Others, upon being asked the meaning of their names, will repeat something learned from family tradition, usually quite preposterous. Upon being asked by an inquiring reporter one man explained: "According to the story my grandfather tells, it was back in 1740 that the family was known as the Edward family. Then there was a son born, and as the family gathered around the newcomer the father said: 'This is the son of Edward; so we will call this new boy Edwardson.' Hence we became known as Edwardson." To the student of onomastics such an explanation is quite naive.

2

SURNAMES FROM FATHER'S NAME
Patronymics

*Patronymical elements: -ing, ap, O', Mc-, -son, -sen, De—Diminutive endings
—Other relatives—Plain forms—From Christian names: William, John, Richard, Robert, Roger, Walter, Allan, Henry, Ralph, Saints' names, Charles,
George, Gregor, Alexander, Anthony, Martin, Patrick, Lawrence, Christopher, Bennett—Old Testament names—New Testament names—More
Bible names—Anglo-Saxon names—Patronymics from occupations—Germanic
names—Pet forms—Lithuanian names—Dutch names—Slavic names—Scandinavian names—Irish names—Scottish names—Welsh names—Spanish names—
French names—Italian names—Metronymics—Miscellaneous patronymics.*

N OTHING COULD BE more natural than for children in the community to be known by their father's name. Boys and
young men would be referred to as the sons of their fathers, particularly when the parents were well known. Names identifying
the bearer as the son of the father may be classified as patronymics. These are not necessarily family names. In many countries
they are middle names with another name for the family. It has
been thought by some that these names arose through pride of
ancestry, but at times when family names were acquired from
reputation among one's neighbors and acquaintances, it is clear
that pride of descent had little or no part in the acquisition of the

name. However, almost all nations have adopted these patronymic surnames. The term *patronymic* is now often used as a synonym for a family name, the name acquired from the father.

Some names of this kind are so familiar to our ears that their root as a Christian name has now passed out of our knowledge, especially those from pet forms or nicknames now obsolete. For example, GOLD, GOULD, and the Scottish GUILD are sons of Gold or Golda, Old English masculine personal names derived from the precious metal; WHITE is sometimes from Hwita "white," BROWN is sometimes from Brun "brown," BURT is from Bert or Beorht "bright," all Old English font names. It might be noted here that Anglo-Saxon men's names often end in *-a,* a termination we now think of as feminine.

HARVARD, who left his library to the college in Cambridge, Massachusetts, had a name derived from Old English Hereward "army, guard." ALGER, the writer of all those American boy adventure, rags to riches books, owes his family name to a remote ancestor known as Aldgar "old, spear" or Aelfgar "elf, spear" or Athelgar "noble, spear"—at least the second element was undoubtedly "spear." Here it should be mentioned that most Old English and Old Germanic personal names usually consist of two words or elements with little or no relation between them. In the earliest names of this type there was some relation between the two elements, but as we shall observe, when two parts were taken from two different names, perhaps the names of the parents to form a new name for a child, relationship was lost and meaning of the separate parts only remained. When we dip into patronymic names we are likely to sink in over our heads and fail to come up the third time. But let's do it.

One of the most convenient ways of identifying a man is by reference to the father's name, particularly when combined with a patronymic suffix or affix. The most popular English and Lowland Scottish method was the addition of the word *son* to the father's given name, as MORRISON, the son of Morris "Moorish or dark," and GARRISON, the son of Garry, a pet form of Garrath "knightly." Others are STETSON, the son of Stedda or Stith, and LEVINSON, the son of Leofwin "dear friend." BRAMSON is from a shortened form of Abraham "father of multitudes." GOODSON does not usually mean "the good son" but refers to the son of Goda or

Gode, or of God, short forms of such names as Godric and God-wine. The element *God* in personal names is either from Old English *god* "God" or Old English *gōd* "good," and the two meanings cannot always be distinguished. In some cases the name GOODSON refers to the one who has been sponsored in baptism by another, the godson. Both the English and the Welsh were sometimes content to add just an *s* to the father's name, as in EDWARDS, EVANS, and EDMONDS, either to indicate filial relationship or the genitive case.

The Anglo-Saxon patronymic suffix is *-ing*, as in GUNNING, the son of Gunn "war," BROWNING, son of Brun "brown," WHITING, son of Hwita "white," CUTTING, son of Cutha "famous," and DENNING, son of Dene "the Dane." In many names the *-ing* is only a corruption of Early English *wine* "friend," as in GOODING from Godwin "God's friend," GOLDING from Goldwin "Gold's friend," and HARDING from Hardwin "firm, friend." SCHILLING is a German name from Scildwin "shield, friend." In other instances *-ing* is a corruption of a diminutive form as in GOSLING from Jocelyn or Goselin "just," and CUSHING "little Cuss," a pet form of Custance or Constance "firm of purpose."

The Welsh *ap* also means "son of," and in early times a long pedigree might be added to a man's name, as Lewis ap Rhys ap Rhydderch ap Howell ap Bleddyn ap Einion. The patronymic sometimes blended with the name to form surnames such as PRICE "son of Rhys," PROTHERO and PRATHER the "sons of Rhydderch or Rhudderch," and POWELL "son of Howell." Convenience in sound might change the *P* to *B* and we have BUNYAN or BEYNON "son of Einion," BRICE or BREESE "son of Rhys," BOWEN "son of Owen," and BEVAN or BEVANS "son of Evan." Just try to say "ap Owen" without getting the sound of Bowen.

For the Irish there is *Mac* meaning "son" and *O* from *ua* meaning "grandson or descendant." To illustrate, there is McBRIDE "son of the servant of St. Brigid," McCARTHY "son of Carthach," and McCALL "son of Cathal." *Mac* can come at the end as in CORMAC "Corb's son." Some names commencing with *O* (the apostrophe has no meaning unless it be a relic of the accent in Irish) are O'BRIEN "grandson of Bryan," O'ROURKE "grandson of Ruarc," and O'LEARY "grandson of Laoghaire." A very few names are commonly found in all three ways, as DONNELL, MACDONNELL,

and O'DONNELL and CONNOR, MACCONNOR, and O'CONNOR. Other
seldom or never lost the prefix, as O'HARE, O'TOOLE, McNAMARA
and McINERNEY.

The Norman patronymical element is *Fitz-*, from Latin *filius*
French *fils*, and many noble houses in England, Ireland, and Scot
land were so styled. *Fitz* names are an Anglo-Norman formation
which developed in the British Isles and are not found in France
There are FITZGERALD and FITZMAURICE who are usually Irish
Capitalizing the second part is merely a matter of personal style
Not all names with this element indicate illegitimacy, but a few
do, such as some originally named FITZROY, FITZCHARLES, FITZ
JAMES, and FITZCLARENCE, bastards of English kings, all of which
are quite rare as modern surnames. The royal house without a sur
name adopted this way of giving a surname to illegitimate son
who could not inherit the throne.

The Scots used the Gaelic *Mac* but not the *O*. Both the Irish
and the Scots contract the prefix into *Mc* and *M'*. Such contrac
tions are without special significance, notwithstanding some au
thorities who have affirmed that *Mac* is Irish and *Mc* is Scottish
and others who have declared just the opposite.

The Swedes use *-son*, as in SWANSON and FREDRICKSON. The
Norwegians use both *-son* and *-sen*, as in OLSON and THORSEN
and the Danes favor *-sen*, as in SORENSEN and JORGENSEN. The
Spanish patronymical element is *-ez*, as in MELENDEZ, from Her
menegildo "protection, strength," DOMINGUEZ "son of Domingo,
and ALVAREZ "son of Alva." The usual Portuguese element is *-e*
as in GOMES "son of Gomo." Some Slavic terminations with th
connotation "son of" are *-ov, -ek, -czyk, -wicz, -ovich, -ak,* an
-enko, as in UMNOV "wise man," KLIMEK "Klemens (merciful)
RYBARCZYK "fisherman," WOJTOWICZ "mayor (of a village)," Por
OVICH "priest," STASZAK "Stanislaw (camp, glorious)," and VASII
ENKO "Vasil (king)," the last being the typical Ukrainian form
There are many other patronymic terminations which arose i
different parts of the Slavic countries at different times so tha
every common given name can usually be found in various form

Italians employ *De*, as in DELEO "lion," DELEONARDIS "lion
bold," and DEVITO "life" and *Di* as in DIMAGGIO "May," DIORI
"honor," and DIVITO "life"; these patronymical words are some

44

times contracted to *D'* as in D'ANGELO "angel," D'ONOFRIO "giant, peace" and D'AGOSTINO "August." Modern Greeks use *-poulos*, and many of their names are quite long, as in THEODOROPOULOS, "the son of Theodore."

Patronymic suffixes and prefixes are sometimes applied to place names, occupational names, and nicknames in many countries thus alluding to the place of origin, occupation, or nickname of the father of the first so named. There is Polish SOBCZAK "son of the egotist"; Russian MALENKOV "son of the little man"; English MAN-NING "son of the servant"; Scottish McNAIR "son of the steward"; Slavic DUBOW "son of Dub (oak tree)"; Irish MOYER "son of the steward"; and McKNIGHT "son of the knight."

Another important element in many surnames derived from the name of the father is the diminutive ending. The chief English diminutives are *-cock, -et, -in, -ie, -kin, -on,* and *-y.* From Hamo "home," for example, there are the family names HAMMOCK, HAMMETT, HAMMAN, HAMON, and HAMMOND. The termination *kin* is said to have originated in Flanders, but the Flemish brought it to England during the early surname period. The principal French diminutives found in many English names are *-eau, -el, -elle, -et, -ette, -ot, -otte,* and *-on,* and with Hamo, there are HAMEL, HAMETTE, HAMILL, and HAMON. The French also are fond of the double diminutives, such as *-elin, -elet, -inet,* and *-elot,* as in HAMELIN and HAMELET, and these are sometimes contracted into *-lin, -let, -net,* and *-lot,* as in HAMLIN, HAMLING, or HAMLYN, HAMLET, HAMMETT, and HAMNETT. Many English names have double diminutives such as BARTLETT "very little Bart or Bartholomew," GIBLIN "very little Gib or Gilbert" and PARNELL and PERNELL "very little Peter." Numerous English diminutive forms are included elsewhere in this chapter so no further examples will be instanced here.

All the other European languages employ diminutive forms, especially the German, Irish, and Italian. Some German endings are the common *-ke,* as in DOMKE "judgment," GEHRKE "spear man," KIPKE "gift," LUEDTKE "people," REINECKE "counsel," STEIN-E "stone," WARNEKE "protection," and WILLEKE "resolution"; *-lein* and *-len,* as in EBERLEIN and EBERLEN "boar"; and *-el,* as in HER-CHELL "red deer." Names of this type are usually short forms with the diminutive suffix added. Dutch diminutives are *-je* and *-ke,* as in LUTJE "people" and HENKE "hedged place," and there are several other more rare ones.

Some Irish diminutive endings are -*an*, -*gan* (most popular), -*in*, -*on*, -*han*, and -*lan*, as in BRENNAN "raven," and NOLAN "noble, famous"; FLANAGAN "ruddy man" and BRANNIGAN "raven"; CRONIN "brown" and FLAVIN "lord"; BRANNON "raven" and DILLON "spoiler"; HOULIHAN "proud" and LENIHAN "clocked"; DONNELLAN "world mighty" and PHELAN "wolf." Some common Italian diminutive suffixes are -*elli*, -*ino*, -*ello*, -*etti*, -*illo*, -*occo*, -*ucci*, and -*uzzo*, as in PACELLI "good peace," LUPICINO "wolf," MORELLO "love," MORETTI "love," LEONCILLO "lion," BERTOCCO "bright," SANTUCCI "saint," and MATTIUZZO "gift of Yahveh." Double diminutives are often used, as ALBERTINELLO "noble, bright" (-*ino* + -*ello*) and PETRUZELLO "rock" (-*uzzo* + -*ello*).

Since each European language influenced the others, the diminutives are similar and in some cases the same in different languages. In all of them there are different spellings by reason of differences in the vowel used. All the different forms of surnames from the popular Christian names cannot be listed, but many will be recognized easily by remembering the abbreviated, pet, and diminutive forms found in every European country. In this study where meanings are given the diminutive element is often ignored in the interest of avoiding repetitious phrases.

The Norman Conquest in 1066 brought about a revolutionary crisis in the personal names used by the people in England, the effect of which is still clearly discernible in the United States today. Some names popular before the Normans came did manage to hold on long enough to influence surnames. For instance, Ketil "a pot or sacrificial cauldron" is an Old Norse name found in England and Ireland and occurring frequently in the Saga literature and in Domesday records, from which such surnames as KETTLE, KETTEL, and KITTEL are derived. KEATS, familiar to everyone because of the poet, probably derives from Ket, a pet form of these Ketill names. SWEET is sometimes from Old English Sweta "sweet." DARWIN is from Deorwine "dear, friend." LOVEDAY refers to a descendant of Loveday, a name given to a child born on a loveday, i.e., a day appointed for the settlement of local controversies. PACE and PEASE are from Pace or Pash, a name given to a child born during the Easter season.

Surnames from Father's Name

Introduced into England by the Normans was GUY from Old German *wido* "wood." Diminutive forms are WYATT and WYOTT in England and GUYON, GUYOT, WYNOT, and WHYNOT in France. Geoffrey from Old French Geoffroi "God's peace" is the etymon of the names JEFFERIES, JEFFERS, JEFFERSON, JEFFERY, JEFFREY, and JEFFRIES, proof of its popularity at the font in the Middle Ages. Geoffrey of Monmouth, the twelfth-century English ecclesiastic and chronicler, and the two sons of Henry II of England both named Geoffrey, one having been illegitimate but acknowledged, made the name well known in England just at the time given names were frozen into permanent family names. GIFFEY, GIFFIN, and GIFF are from the pet or diminutive forms. HUMPHREY with the Welsh HUMPHREYS and HUMPHRIES became popular from the French Onfroi "giant, peace," although there was an Old English form Hunfrith "young bear, peace" from which some with this name are derived. Hubert Humphrey, vice-president of the United States under Lyndon Baines Johnson, who uses the most popular form of the surname, is the best-known American with the name. He was nominated for the presidency by the Democrats in 1968, but the pleasant meaning of his name did not help him. Augustine "majestic," not found before the Conquest, produced AUGUSTIN, AUGUSTINE, and the vernacular form AUSTIN from Old French Aoustin. AUGUSTYN and AUGUSTYNIAK are Slavic forms.

A very few surnames are derived from relatives other than the parents, but most of these have died out. In the early English records many long, awkward names of this kind may be observed, but they have been discarded long ago. Some of them are Manningestepsune "Manning's stepson," Hughesneve "Hugh's nephew," Geppedoghtersone "Gilbert's daughter's son," Edesdohter "Ede's daughter," Raweswyf "Ralph's wife," Vikercister "the vicar's sister," Prestcosyn "the priest's cousin," Huwechild "Hugh's child," and Nicbrothere "Nicholas' brother." Simple names such as BROTHERS, COUSINS, and EAMES "uncle" are sometimes shortened forms of the above names. As they are more properly classed as nicknames they are included in that chapter (page 180).

Many Christian names are used as family names without change or addition of any patronymic element. In America the most common are THOMAS "a twin," LEWIS "hear, fight," JAMES "the supplanter, or may God protect," JORDAN "flowing down," HENRY

47

"home, rule," and LAWRENCE "laurel, symbol of victory" in descending order. However, the three most common are Welsh surnames which already end in a genitive or patronymical *s* so their patronymic meaning is clearly implied.

In fact, almost all given names common in the Middle Ages have come down without alteration as familiar surnames. To list more of this type, also widely spread today, there are: AMBROSE "immortal," AMOS "burden-bearer," ARTHUR "Thor's eagle," BALDWIN "bold, friend," COLBERT "cool, bright," EMERY "industrious," GODFREY "God's peace," GODWIN "God's friend," HARVEY "bitter or carnage-worthy," HERMAN "army, man," also spelled HARMAN and HARMON, LAMBERT "land, bright," LEONARD "lion, bold," MAYNARD "strength, hardy," REDMOND and RAYMOND "counsel, protection," ROLAND "fame, land," and SYLVESTER "forest dweller." MILES "soldier" is a Welsh name, probably from Latin *miles* or in some cases from Old German Milo, a name of doubtful etymology. Spanish ROSADO descends from Rosado "rose." MILOS is a Czechoslovakian and Yugoslavian form from Milos "pleasant." Hungarian BORIS is from Boris "stranger." Many German given names have in the same way become surnames such as ERNST "earnestness," CONRAD "bold, counsel," FRIEDRICH "peace, rule," LUDWIG "fame, warrior," and ULRICH "wolf, rule." As mentioned before, it must be noted that most Germanic names are composed of two themes or elements with little or no relationship between them. Consequently, in giving their meanings, a comma is put between them to indicate that one word does not necessarily modify the other. Almost all of the popular font names produced surnames without change in most countries, but they are noted here only if frequently observed in America.

Our common patronymic surnames are derived mostly from the popular Teutonic given names like Robert, Richard, William and Henry (the four sons of the Conqueror) or from the well-known Biblical names, the latter being popular in their various national forms all over Europe and even in many parts of Asia.

After the conquest of England William the Conqueror was on the throne, followed by his son William Rufus, and although William I was feared and William II was hated, William soon became the most common font name in England just before the period when surnames became fixed family names. Consequently the name became the etymon of the second name of many persons. In its simple form, WILLIAM "resolution, helmet" is not particularly common, but the Welsh and English WILLIAMS is the third most popular surname in the United States while the longer WILLIAMSON is only two hundred forty-eighth in popularity. The common pet form WILL became a surname along with WILLS and WILLIS, and with the English and Scottish termination *-son* became WILSON, the eighth most common surname. To Will was added various diminutive endings to produce such family names as WICKS, WILCOX, WILKE, WILKES, WILKIES, WILKS, WILKINS, WILLETT, WILLEY, WILLIE, WILLING, and WILMOT. WICKS and others of these names which include the sound of *k* sometimes derive from residence on or near the dairy farm, from Old English *wic,* which had that connotation at the time surnames were becoming universal. The patronymic element can be added to many of these forms, as in WILCOXSON, WILKINSON, and WILKERSON. The Scots and Irish use McWILLIAMS. The Irish fashion is Mc-ELLIGOTT from Ulick, a pet form of William. The Manx condensed MacWilliam into QUILLIAM. The German form WILHELM is frequently found in America. Influenced by the French, there is GILLIAM. Teutonic *w* and the Celtic and Romance *g* are convertible letters. GUILLEMET and GUILLET are French diminutive forms of the name. GUILLEMIN, another French form sometimes corrupts into GILMAN, which also has meaning of "Gilbert's servant." GUILLOTIN, the French form with the double diminutive, has probably been driven out of America by its relation to the well-known French instrument of death, the guillotine. The Welsh ap William produced PULLIAM.

William continued as the most common forename until the seventeenth century when it gradually gave way to the ubiquitous John "gracious gift of Yahveh." Some authorities just define it as "gift of God or Jehovah." This connotation "gift of God" is a concept that has been used by almost all nations in naming their young. With this meaning there are Theodore and Dorothy from the Greek, Bohdan among the Slavic peoples, Nathaniel among the Hebrews, Devadatta among the Hindus, Ataallah among the Arabs, Godgifu among Germanic peoples (seen as Godiva in England), and Deodatus among the Latins (found as Dieudonné and Déodat in France). Specific gods are mentioned in

49

many such names, as the African (Ibo) Aniveta "gift of Ani," the Egyptian-Greek Isidore "gift of Isis," and the English Matthew and Matthias "gift of Yahveh."

In its various national forms John has been exceedingly frequent in use throughout all of Europe. Its popularity is due chiefly to the two outstanding Biblical characters, John the Baptist and John the apostle, beloved disciple of Jesus. In England the name, not being common in the early 1200's, was not hurt by the hated King John. In Wales its acceptance was aided by several prominent Johns. Various sovereigns of Bohemia, the Roman empire, several French and Germanic states, Portugal, and Spain, as well as numerous popes and saints living during the surname period, all contributed to the prevalence of the name throughout the world.

Thus JOHNSON from England and the Scandinavian countries became the second most popular surname in America, and the Welsh JONES the fifth in frequency. John Paul Jones, the Scottish-born American naval officer, was the most famous American Jones. He was born John Paul and added Jones shortly before coming to these shores, possibly to escape detection since he had been involved in the killing of a crewman aboard a vessel of which he was master. Johnson was sometimes hardened by the intrusive *t* to make JOHNSTON which is then confused with the Scottish place names, Johnston and Johnstone "John's manor." From the nickname Jack comes JACKSON, the seventeenth in popularity. Jon is an early English form. Other English surnames are JANES, JAYNES, JAXON, JENNINGS, and JENNISON. From the short form Hans are derived HANCOCK, HANCOX, and HANKINS.

John Hancock is a name that has come to be a jocular term for one's signature, from the first signer of the Declaration of Independence. It also, in some cases, has acquired the connotation of "name." When presented with the Declaration of Independence, Hancock is reputed to have exclaimed, "I will write it so large that the King will be able to read it without spectacles," and his signature stands out boldly. John Hancock of Columbus, Ohio, complains that he has had a lot of trouble with his name. As a boy he once went to a store where his father, William, had a charge account and made some purchases, whereupon the clerk asked him to put his "John Hancock" on the sales slip. When he did, the clerk became most indignant and abusive. His biggest frustration came after marriage when he took over insurance payments on his wife's policy with the John Hancock Life Insurance Company. Every time he called the office and identified himself by name, the operator would hang up.

The Welsh also produce UPJOHN (from ap John), JENKINS, JOHNS, and JONAS. JACK together with all the popular English forms is found in Scotland. In Ireland SHANE, McSHANE, McCAIN, and McCLAIN proliferate.

German family names developed from John, or its short form, are HANS, HENSEL, HENSCHEL, HENZEL, JAHNKE, JANISCH, JANKE, JESKE, JESCHKE, JOHANNES, JOHANN, YOHANAN, and YONAN. Dutch forms are JANS, JANSEN, JANTZEN, and YANKE. From Sweden, Norway, and Denmark will be found EVENSEN, HANSEN, HANSON, HENSON, JAHN, JENSEN, JENZEN, JESSEN, JOHANSON, and JONSSON. Italy has GIANNINI and DI GIOVANNI and, after dropping the first part, the various diminutive terminations produce the unrecognizable NITTI, NOTO, NUCCIO, and NUZZO, among others. A Spanish surname is IBAÑEZ, the "son of Iban" (a Basque form of John). Greece gives us GIANOPOULOS.

Surnames derived from John are very popular in the Slavic countries. Polish JANICKI, JANICKE, JANIK, JANKOWSKI, JANOWICZ, and JASINSKI are easily located in America. IVANOV is the common Russian form, and it is the most popular surname in Russia. Other Russian family names from forms of John are EVANOFF and EVANOW from different systems of transliteration, and the aphetic VANA. From Czechoslovakia come JANA, JANAS, JANDA, and VANEK. Hungary produces JANOSFI and Lithuania has JANIS and JONIKAS. Numerous other family names derived from John could be cited, but the above forms are the most common.

The love and admiration of the people of England for the adventurous Richard the Lion-Hearted in the latter part of the twelfth century caused many to bestow his name on their sons. The best-known surname form is RICHARDSON followed closely by the Welsh RICHARDS and RICHARD. Other forms are RICKARD and RICKERT. Shortened diminutive forms are RICH, RICHEY, and RICHIE. The three popular nicknames for Richard "rule, hard" in the Middle Ages were Rick, Hick, and Dick. From Rick come RICKS, RIX, and RICKETTS. Hick produces HICKS, HICKOX, HICKEY,

51

HICKMAN, HITCHCOCK, HIXSON, and ICKES, and the softened forms HIGGS, HIGGINS, HIGGINSON and HISCOCK. Forms from Dick are DICKENS, DICKEY, DICKINSON, DICKSON, DIGGINS, DIGGS, DIX, DIXIE, and DIXON. RITCHIE is popular in Scotland. From the Welsh ap Richard come PRITCHARD and PRICHARD. The German surnames are REICHERT and REICHARDT. RICARDO is the form in Spain and Portugal. The Italians sometimes start the name with S and have SCARDINA, a descendant of Cardo, the aphaeretic form of Riccardo.

The Normans brought the French Robert "fame, bright," from the Old German Hrodebert, to England at the time of the Conquest. Robert, Earl of Gloucester and illegitimate son of Henry I of England, who fought with his cousin, King Stephen, undoubtedly prompted many to adopt Robert as a given name. There were two Roberts, kings of France, in addition to two Dukes of Normandy named Robert, three Counts of Flanders, and three Roberts, kings of Scotland, which influenced given names during the surname period. In the thirteenth century the diminutive form, Robin, inspired by the ballads of that popular hero, Robin Hood, was more widespread than Robert. Today ROBINSON is the twenty-second most common surname and ROBERTS, the Welsh form, is thirty-fourth, followed much later by ROBERTSON and ROBERSON. The most popular medieval pet names for Robert are Rob, Hob, and Dob. From Rob we get the surnames ROBB, ROBBIE, ROBIE, ROBIN, ROBBINS, ROBESON, ROBISON, and ROBSON. Hob produces HOBBS, and HOBSON, together with the sharper HOPKINS, HOPKINSON, HOPPE, and HOPSON. In the same way Dob gives us DOBBS, DABBS, DOBSON, DOBBINS and DOBLE. Welsh ap Robert coalesces into PROBERT. Bob was never a pet form for Robert in the surname period, so no family names are derived from it. The rare name BOBB is from Bobba, an Old English lall name.

Roger of Montgomery distinguished himself at the Battle of Hastings, and was granted vast estates throughout the south of England, together with most of Shropshire, and he, along with other Norman nobles of this name, stimulated the English and Norman adventurers after the Conquest to choose Roger "fame, spear" as a given name at the time surnames were becoming hereditary. From this name the surnames ROGERS and ROGERSON have developed, as well as the Welsh PROSSER and ROSSER, and the Scottish RODGERS. Two common nicknames for Roger appeared in the Middle Ages, HODGE and DODGE, both of which are also surnames. From Hodge come HODGES, HODGKINS, HODGKINSON, HOSKINS, HOTCHKISS, and HOTCHKINS. And from Dodge there are DODD, DODDS, DODGSON, and DODSON. Names commencing with Dod are also from the personal names, Dudda or Dod "rounded summit," and sometimes designate the lumpish or fat man. Dutch cognates are RUTGERS and RUTSEN, while Italians recognize RUGGIERO.

Walter "rule, army" was introduced by the Normans into England at the time of the Conquest. Walter was a cousin of the Conqueror and was given a great deal of land. In the next two centuries there developed such surnames as WALTERS, WOLTER, WELTER, and WELTHER. The early pronunciation was without the *l* which brought about the surnames, WATERS, WATTERS, and WATTERSON. From the pet form Wat come WATTS, WATT, WATSON, and WATKINS. WATMOUGH refers to the brother-in-law of Walter. A Manx name from Gaelic MACWALTERS is QUALTERS. GAUTHIER is a common French form, and WALTHER the common German name.

Count Alan of Brittany brought a large contingent to fight at Hastings and was rewarded by the Conqueror with great estates throughout England. He married one of the king's daughters. Upon his death his nephew, Alan the Black, succeeded him. From this popular font name are derived the popular family name of ALLEN, also ALAN, ALLAN, and ALLEYNE. ALCOCK is a diminutive form. Alan is an old Celtic name of obscure etymology, thought by some authorities to have a connotation of "comely or harmony."

During the twelfth and thirteenth centuries three strong kings named Henry "home, rule" were on the English throne and various other Henrys ruled in continental European countries. Consequently, the name was popular everywhere with the common people at the time family names were becoming stabilized. The standard English form of the French Henri was HARRY and that became a surname. The omission of the *n* and the broadening of the vowel created Harry, a name more suited to the English tongue. Some surnames from Harry are HARRIS and HARRISON.

Harrison has absorbed the uncommon animal nickname, herisson "hedge-hog." Haw, Har, and Hal were pet forms of Harry and produce HAWK, HAWKES, HAWKINS, HAWKINSON, HARKINS, and HALLETT. From Henry the English have HENDRY, HENDRIES, HENRY, and FITZHENRY. The English and Scots share HENDERSON and HENRYSON. From ap Harry the Welsh produce PARRY. The Irish use McHENRY.

From the German Heinrich the following surnames arise: HEINRICH, HENDRICKS, HENDRIX, and from pet forms, HANKE, HANKES, HEINZ, HEINTZ, and HEINS. The Dutch surname is HENDRIKS. Scandinavian countries use HENRIKSEN and HENDRICKSON. French names are HENRI and HERRIOT. Italians are familiar with the diminutive forms HENRICI and the aphaeretic RICCI. JINDRA comes from Czechoslovakia and ENRIQUEZ from Spain.

Ralf de Tankerville was William the Conqueror's chamberlain. There were several other followers of William with that given name who received lands and earldoms. The name was also used in England before the Norman Conquest, in the form Raedwulf "shield wolf," which became Radulf and then Ralf from which the surnames RAFF, RALPH, RAND, RANDALL, RANDOLPH, RANKIN, RANSOM, RANSON, RAWLINGS, and RAWSON developed. RAND is also one who came from Rand "marshy edge," the name of places in Lincolnshire and Yorkshire. RANK is a German form. There are various French forms none common in the United States. If Ralf, like other Norman names beginning with R, had rhymed forms with H (such as Hick for Richard, Hob for Robert, and Hodge for Roger), perhaps such names as HANKIN, HANSON, HANCOCK, HAND, and even HANDY can be derived from Ralf. Several authorities suggest this theory, but the evidence is not strong as in the other Norman names mentioned.

Although some monks and other religious adopted the names of saints and the more important New Testament characters, ordinary people thought them to be too sacred for mundane use. Of the first fifty-one popes before St. John I in the first five centuries only one had the name Stephen and one Mark. After the Normans came into England and the returning pilgrims and Crusaders felt a more familiar acquaintance with the men revered by the Church, ideas changed and the names of the apostles and

54

disciples of Christ were widely employed in England and on the continent.

The French have many names from saints. From Severian "severe," the name of several saints, are derived SEVERIN and SEVERANCE. SAINT-GAUDENS, the surname of the great Irish-American sculptor, commemorates Gaudentius "rejoicing," the name of five different saints. TOUSSAINT is a French surname meaning "all saints." Some people just do not want to put all their eggs with one saint. DAL SANTO is Italian "from the saint." GERMAIN is a descendant of Germain "spear, people," the name of two French saints.

Probably popularized by St. Bernard of Clairvaux and Bernard of Cluny in the twelfth century, the name Bernard "bear, firm" was popular in France from where it became widely used in England. The original name of the divine Sarah (Bernhardt), so well-known in America, was Rosine Bernard. The name produced the family names of BERNARD in both France and England. BARNARD and BARNETT are English variants. BERNARDI is the common Italian name. BARNAS is known in Poland and BARNET in Scotland.

Many surnames are derived from the Christian name Hugh "spirit," the Latin and German form of which is Hugo. In the north of England the popularity of the name owes much to St. Hugh, Bishop of Lincoln (1186–1200), and it was intensified by the death of the nine-year-old boy martyr, Hugh of Lincoln, according to legend crucified by the Jews in 1255, just at the right time for its effect on surnames. Several French saints living during the surname epoch also added to the luster of the name. The common Welsh and English surname is HUGHES. Variations in spelling and patronymic and diminutive suffixes produce the English HEWES, HEWSON, HEWITT, HEWLETT, HUGHEY, and HUEY. Middle English *hewe* "servant" is a contributory source of many of the above names. HOWE, HOWES, HOWELL, and HOWIE are sometimes from Hugh. Pet names Hug and Hutch give us HUGGINS, HUTCHINS, HUTCHINGS, and HUTCHINSON. In Scotland McCUTCHEON refers to the "son of Hutcheon," a diminutive pet form of Hugh. In France and Germany the surname HUGO is found. The French also use HUCK (from the pet form Huc), HUGUELET, and HULETT. HAUCK and HAUKE are from Germany. Italian DUGO and Welsh PUGH mean "son of Hugh," as does the Irish McHUGH. Like Hugh, Nicholas "people's victory" was a very popular saint's name known throughout the Western World. St. Nicholas, Bishop of Myra in the fourth century, was the popular patron saint of children. From Nicholas many different surnames are derived, particularly because of the many variant spellings of the name. The usual Old English form of the name was Nicol; the common intrusive *h* and *k* came in later. Most popular in America are NICHOLS and NICHOLSON, but NICHOLAS, NICHOLL, NICKEL, NICKELS, NICKERSON, and NICKLES surname many families. The first part of the name produces NIX, NIXON, and NICKSON in England. Nis, a pet form, brings forth NISSEN in Denmark. NICKELSON is popular in Sweden and Norway. From the Slavic countries there come MIKRUT and MIKULA, the initial letter there changing from *N* to *M*. The Irish use McNICHOLAS.

In many places surnames have been derived from the middle or last part of Nicholas. Some of the English names, COLE, COLES, COLSON, COLLETT, COLLINS, COLIN, and CLASS are so formed, as is the Welsh COLLEY and the Scottish CLASON and CLAYSON. Likewise, there are the German names, KLAUS, KLOSS, and LASSEN, and the Dutch KLASS. The Italian form is COLONNA. In Sweden and Norway CLAESSON, CLASSEN, and CLAUSEN, with various other spellings, are prominent.

Admiration for St. Francis of Assisi, the Italian founder of the Franciscan order, produced widespread use of the name on the continent. The prevailing Welsh and English name is FRANCIS "the free," spelled FRANÇOIS in France, but few Americans stoop down to include the cedilla. The German forms are FRANZ and FRANCKE and the Swedish is FRANZEN. Polish forms are FRANCZYK and FRANCZAK. In Spain the name is FRANCO, made familiar to us by the Spanish dictator. All of these names cross in meaning with FRANCE and FRANK and other names designating one who came from France. The Italians extended the name to FRANCISCO, and then used CICCO as a pet form from which is derived CICCOLO. CICCONE is the augmentative "big Cicco."

Clement "merciful" was the name of four popes before the end of the thirteenth century, one a saint of the first century, and two of them during the surname period, and the name became well established throughout Europe. Clement was a fellow worker with Paul in Philippi. His name is written in "the book of life" (Phil. 4:3), a feature that made the name a great favorite in all Christian countries. English and Scottish forms of the resulting family name are CLEMENS, CLEMENT, CLEMENTS, CLEMONS, and the pet form CLEM. The French also favored CLEMENT and the diminutive form CLEMENCEAU. Scandinavians used CLEMENSON and CLEMENSEN. A German form is KLEMM. The Italian names are CLEMENTE and CLEMENTI. The popular Slavic form is KLIMA, while the Lithuanians preferred KLIMAS. A Czechoslovakian form is KLIMEK and the Polish surnames are KLIMCZAK and KLIMKIEWICZ.

During the Middle Ages GILBERT "pledge, bright" was a favorite name, and with its nicknames of Gip and Gib formed many last names. Gilbert of Sempringham founded the Gilbertine order in the twelfth century and was canonized in 1202. GILBERTS and GILBERTSON are found in England. MACCUBBAN is a Manx mutation. The pet forms produced the following names: GIBBONS, GIBBS, GIBLIN, GIBSON, GIPSON, GIVENS, and FITZGIBBONS. Gib became a common designation for a male cat.

CHARLES was introduced into England by the Normans, but was never a popular font name in the surname epoch, so not many with this name are of English extraction. Its preponderance in France and other European countries was due to the reputation in song and story of Charles the Great or Charlemagne, king of the Franks and emperor of the West (768–814). The name is from Germanic *karl* meaning "man, husbandman, or rustic," and KARL is the principal German form. From this stem is derived the word *churl*, originally the simple freeman, but now a word of moral reprobation, a coarse, rude, surly ill-tempered person. In Holland KAREL is used. The French like the diminutive forms CARLIN and CHARLET. In the Scandinavian countries the names KARLSON, CARLSON, CARLSEN, and KARSON are quite prevalent. The Russians look with favor on the names KARLOV, KARLIN, and KARLINSKY. In Czechoslovakia a form is KADLEC. From Italy DECARLO is quite common.

The Greek name GEORGE "farmer" is common in Wales and in France, where in the latter country the surname is also styled GEORGES. The nominative case in Old French is indicated by the suffix -s. The common form of the surname in America is the plain

GEORGE. Although the name was brought to England by the returning Crusaders, St. George did not become the patron saint of England until 1349, and the given name had little effect on English surnames, although there are some GEORGESONS, especially in Scotland. George was used only by the upper classes in England and therefore did not develop into pet forms. In Italy there are DE GEORGE and DE GIORGIO; in Romania the form is GEORGESCU; in Czechoslovakia, JIRIK; in Poland, JUREK, JURICO, JURKIEWICZ, and JERZY are popular; in Germany, YERKES; in Greece there are GEORGACAS and GEORGACOPOULOS; and in Holland the name is JURGENS. A Danish cognate is JURGENSEN, and the Swedish form is GORANSON.

Gregory, the name of ten early popes, is derived from Gregor "watchman." Both GREGORY and GREGOR are found as surnames in England and the pet forms GREIG, GREGG, and GRIGGS have produced family names with these spellings. The Scottish form is MACGREGOR, the name of one of the greatest of Highland clans. In Scotland the surname is sometimes contracted into GREER. GREGOIRE is the French family name. GRZEGORSKI, GRZEGORZEW-SKI, and GRZEGORCZYK are Polish forms with the simple intrusive z giving the names a foreboding cast.

From ancient times Alexander "helper of mankind" has been a popular name with kings, saints, and popes throughout all Europe. The epic of Alexander the Great has been called the most widespread story in the world, so well-known, remarked Chaucer's Monk, that every man who was not a simpleton had heard much or all of it. Numerous surnames are derived from the name. The family name ALEXANDER is very common in Scotland due in part to the three Scottish kings with that name in the twelfth and thirteenth centuries. The name is also well-known in England owing to the immense popularity of the Romance of Alexander in the Middle Ages, where the terse form ALEX is also used. The Scots also favored MCALLISTER in the Highlands, and, elsewhere, the aphaeretic forms, SANDERS, SAUNDERS, and SANDERSON. The German abbreviated forms are ZANDER and SENDER. D'ALESSANDRO is from Italy. ALEXOPOULOS is the Greek patronymic form. OLEKSY is a Ukrainian form.

St. Anthony, the fourth century Egyptian ascetic, about whom many legends recording his temptations were current in the Middle Ages, caused his name to become a popular font name which produced surnames in various spellings throughout Europe. AN-THONY "inestimable" is a common surname. Its short form TONEY is also common. ANTON is the German surname. ANTONELLI is the Italian form along with TONELLI; ANTANAITIS is Lithuanian; AN-TONESCU is Romanian; ANTONOPOULOS is Greek; and ANTOINE is French.

The popularity of St. Martin of Tours, the patron saint of France, made the name MARTIN "diminutive of Martius (from Mars, the god of war)" the most common family name in France, and also very common in England. The story of his dividing his cloak with a beggar, followed by a vision of Christ recognizing the charitable act, was a favorite subject of medieval art. St. Martin's festival in the Roman and Anglican churches is November 11, in England called Martinmas, celebrated over most of Christendom, a time when cattle are killed for winter use and the new wine is drawn and tasted, a somewhat jovial occasion.

MARTINET and MARTINEAU are diminutive forms of the surname in France. Martinet is an odious surname because of the auto-cratic, strict, and tedious military drill bearing this name, devised by Jean Martinet, Inspector General of Infantry, in the reign of Louis XIV of France. MARTINSON is occasionally observed as an English surname. In Ireland GILMARTIN is "the son of the servant of St. Martin." The Danish name is MARTENSEN; in Spain it is MARTINEZ; in Czechoslovakia, MARTINEK; in the Ukraine, MAR-TIKKE; in Italy, MARTINELLI, MARTINI, and MARTINO; and in Switz-erland, MARTI. The many countries where the people revered the saint give the United States so many common variants of this surname, where the first six letters are alike, that it has been used as an illustration in Chapter VI, irrefutable evidence that the esti-mate of 1,500,000 different surnames in the United States is not too far out of line when the machine count of different names with differences only in the first six letters in the Social Security Account Number File located only 1,091,522 surnames.

PATRICK, and many other surnames, are derived from the Chris-tian name Patrick "patrician." This Christian name was a great favorite in medieval times because of the popularity of St. Patrick, especially in Ireland, Scotland, and the north of England. Other Irish forms are PADDEN, FITZPATRICK, and KILPATRICK, the last

AMERICAN SURNAMES

name meaning "the son of the servant or disciple of St. Patrick." In Scotland PATTERSON and the short forms, PATE, PATT, and PAIT, are also found. Scottish McFADDEN refers to the "son of Pad," a pet form of Patrick. The Scottish people also used Peter as a pet form of Patrick, and so some of the surnames derived from that name may be closely related to Patrick. PATTON is not uncommon as a family name in England. A related Italian form is PATTI. PADEREWSKI, the name of the great pianist and statesman, derives from the Polish form of Patrick.

Because of the affection of the people in the Middle Ages for St. Lawrence "laurel, symbol of victory," deacon of Pope Sixtus II, who was martyred in the third century, the English surname of LAWRENCE and the Welsh surname of LAURENCE arose. The spelling of Laurence for the given name is slightly more popular in England, while Americans prefer the name spelled with a *w*. The saint's name is spelled both ways. LAWSON, LAWS, LARK, and LARKIN are also English forms while LARSON and LARSEN are popular in the Scandinavian countries. The pet forms LAURIE, LAWRIE, LOWRY, and LOWRIE are common in Scotland. McLAREN in the Scottish Highlands refers to the son of Lawrence. German variants are LEVERENZ, LORENZ, and the short forms, RENTZ, and RENTSCH. The French form is LAURENT, but a contributory source is one who came from Lorraine, the medieval duchy adjoining France. The Polish cognate form is the formidable WAWRZYNIAK.

Both CHRISTOPHER and CHRISTOPHERSON from the third-century Christian martyr, meaning "Christ bearer" (one who carried Christ in his heart), and CHRISTIAN, meaning "follower of Christ," arose as surnames in England from the font names, although the latter may have been applied as a nickname to one who was especially religious. An early legend recites that Christopher would not pray or fast, but offered to carry all Christian pilgrims who came that way across a certain raging torrent. One day a child he carried revealed himself as Christ, who then said, "Marvel not, for with me thou hast borne the sins of all the world." The pet forms CHRIST, CHREST, CRIST, and CRISS, used as family names, can be derived from either Christopher or Christian. In Scotland and in the north of England the surnames CHRISTIE and CHRISTY are derived from both font names. In Scotland CHRYSTAL and CRYSTAL, both with other spellings, are diminutives of Christo-

60

pher. In Norway and Denmark CHRISTOPHERSEN, CHRISTIANSEN, and CHRISTENSEN are forms used. CHRISTMAN and KERSTEN, the latter clearly from Christian, are from Germany; CHRISTIANO and CHRISTIANI are found in Italy, Spain, and Portugal, while CHRIS-TOPOULOS is the Grecian form.

Bennet, "blessed," a popular font name during the Middle Ages, and its less common form, Benedict, were the stems for several surnames, such as BENNETT, BENEDICT, and BENDIX. Benedict was the name of fifteen popes. In the early part of the sixth century, St. Benedict of Nursia, not a pope, founded the Benedictine order, considered by many historians to have been the chief civilizing agency in Western Europe during the following three or four centuries. Bennett comes directly from Benet, the colloquial French form. BENSON refers to the son of Ben, usually the pet form of Bennet rather than of Benjamin, a name little used at the font during the Middle Ages. From the nickname also come BEAN, BEEN, and BEANE. BENDA is a German name. In Italy Di BENE-DETTO and BENEDETTO are used, while the French name is BENOIT. BENES is the cognate Czechoslovakian name.

The greatest influence on Christian names in the Western World at the time surnames were becoming hereditary was the Bible, both the Old Testament and the New. Since the ordinary person had no access to the Bible or Biblical literature, and couldn't read if he did, he had an acquaintance with only the most prominent Biblical characters through the mystery and miracle plays and pageants and the images of saints displayed in the churches. There was only a mere superficial knowledge of the very outlines of the sacred narrative. This is understandable since the Bible was not translated into English until the work initiated by Wyc-liffe in the fourteenth century. Even the village priest was likely to be quite illiterate with a most imperfect understanding of the Bible. The first printed Bible was made in 1456, in Germany. Manuscript Bibles in Latin were owned only by the wealthier religious houses and the great rulers and nobles.

In the British Isles Adam "red earth or man," the name of the first man, became a favorite thirteenth century font name, and produced the surnames of ADAMS and ADAMSON. From the abbreviated form used by the English in everyday medieval life the surnames ACHESON, ADCOCK, ADDIS, ADDISON, ADKINS, AIKEN, AIT-

KEN, AITKINS, AKINS, and ATKINS were formed. Both the Scots and the Irish are familiar with McADAMS. Unusual Scottish names are EASON from Aye or Aythe, pet forms, and KEDDY from the effect of the *Mac* upon Adie. Polish forms of the name are ADAMCZYK, ADAMOWICZ, ADAMOWSKI, and ADAMSKI. ADAMEK is a Czechoslovakian form. ODOM is sometimes seen, the Hebrew pronunciation of the name of the first man.

Although often regarded as very Jewish names, Abram "high father" and Abraham "father of multitudes" were in general use from the thirteenth century in England and throughout Europe. ABRAHAM, ABRAHAMS, ABRAM, ABRAMS, ABRAHAMSON and ABRAMSON are English surnames. ABRAHAMOWICZ and ABRAMOWITZ are Polish forms.

As the patron saint of Wales and the name of several Scottish kings, David "beloved" naturally influenced British nomenclature. More English-speaking people have family names derived from David than any other Old Testament name. The most common patronymic is DAVIS with DAVIES the Welsh form. In the British Isles Davies is the prevalent form, but in America there are twenty-six men surnamed Davis for every one named Davies. This is a peculiar difference in temperament between British people and Americans, possibly due to the latter's impatient shortening of the vowel. DAVID, DAVIDSON, and DAVISON also are frequently noted. From pet forms of David in the British Isles are formed the following family names: DAVY, DAVEY, DAWES, DAWSON, DAYS, DEAKINS, DEVITT, DEWEY, and TAFF. In medieval script the letters *v*, *u*, and *w* were easily and frequently interchanged. McTAVISH is a Gaelic form.

DANIELS, DANIEL, and DANIELSON, from the Old Testament name of the Hebrew prophet, Daniel "judged of God," are popular in Wales and England. Daniel also comes from France where the regard for the name was undoubtedly influenced by the French troubadour, Daniel, who flourished in the twelfth century, called *gran maestro d'amore* "grand master of love." DANILEVICIUS is from Lithuania and DANIELEWICZ is the Polish form. Job "persecuted or enemy" was a favorite subject in medieval plays and gave rise to such surnames as JOB, JOBE, JOBBE, JOBIN, JOBSON, JUPP, and CHUB, none particularly common. Some of these latter names may also be occupation names for a maker of jubbes, a vessel holding about four gallons of liquor, or of jupes, a long woollen garment for men.

Salamon, the usual medieval form of Solomon "peaceful," the colorful King of Israel in the ninth century B.C., produced such surnames as SALMON, SOLOMON, and SAMMONS. Samuel "God hath heard, or name of God, or Shem is God" was not common in the Middle Ages, but the use by Jews made SAMUEL, SAMUELS, and SAMUELSON common surnames. SAMPSON and SAMSON with the contraction SAMP derive from Samson "sun's child," the Biblical Hebrew famous for his superhuman strength and unshorn hair, although these names are also related to Samuel. SAMP plus a diminutive termination is also a contributory source of SAMPLE. The Italian form is SANSONE.

Michael "who is like God," the archangel and leader of the heavenly host, is mentioned three times in the Old Testament and twice in the New Testament. As the patron of the Christian warrior during the Crusades, his name was a favorite one from the twelfth century onwards. Both in the plain form and with the genitive *s*, MICHAEL, MICHAELS, and MICHELS served to surname many families. The most popular form in England, however, is MITCHELL, a pronunciation influenced by the French Michel. This name is also derived from Middle English *muchel* or *michel* "big," and thus sometimes designates the big or fat man. MICHAELSON is also easily found in English name lists. The abbreviated form produces MIX "the son of Mick," together with MIXON and MIXSON. In Germany the name is MICHAELIS, and in Greece it is MIKOS from the pet form Michos. French forms are MICHAUD and MICHEL, both very common in America, while the Italian name is MICELI. Danish and Norwegian forms are MICHAELSEN, MIKKELSEN, and MICHELSON. The usual Finnish surname is spelled MIKKONEN. Popular Polish names are MICHAL, MICHALAK, and MICHALSKI.

Two Bible names that have produced many surnames but have slightly different forms in the two testaments are: Jacob in the Old Testament and James in the New Testament; Simeon in the Old Testament and Simon in the New Testament. Authorities are not in agreement as to the meaning of Jacob-James. Some define it as "the supplanter"; others contend it means "may God protect." British James is from Old French Jacomus-Gemmes-James. English and Welsh surname forms are JAMES and JACOBS; the English also use JACOBSON and sometimes COBB from the pet form. From Scotland come JAMISON, JAMESON, and JEMISON. Scandinavian forms are JACOBSEN, JAKOBSEN, and JEPSEN. The Old Testament name is popular in Germany as JACOB, JACOBI, JAKOB, JAKOBI, KOPP, and KOEPP. The French forms are JACOBI, JAQUES, and JACQUES. The Italian names are GIACOMINI and GIACOMO, and from pet forms, CHIAPPETTA, COMO, MAZZUCA, MELONE, and PUCCI—what a list of variants! The Spanish favorite is DIAZ, a corruption of Diego from Iago. A Dutch name is KOBUS. Many Poles are surnamed JAKUBOWSKI, KUBICKI, KUBIK, and KUBIAK. Czechoslovakian forms are KOUBA and KUBA. The accent on the second syllable of JACOB has produced, it may be noted, many surnames in Europe derived from that syllable.

The popularity of Simon "gracious hearing" in the Middle Ages was due to affection for Simon Bar-Jonah surnamed Peter, rather than to Simeon the second son of Jacob by Leah. The name gave rise to many family names, especially in England where SIMMONS and SIMPSON became the most popular forms. Both the latter form and SIMPKINS were sharpened in pronunciation by the intrusive *p*. Other popular English names are FITZSIMMONS (also popular in Ireland), SIMCOCK, SIMCOX, SIMS, SIMONDS, SIMON, SYMONS, and SYMMES. In the Scandinavian countries SIMONSEN and SIMONSON are popular. An Italian form is DE SIMONE, while JIMENEZ is from Spanish-speaking countries, and SHIMKUS is Lithuanian. Polish names are SIMEK, SZYMCZAK, and SZYMANSKI. From the pet form Sienko, comes the Polish and Russian SIENKIEWICZ.

Some Bible names, especially some from the Old Testament, are really nicknames arising from playing the part in the early miracle plays. Names of outstanding characters particularly subject to this interpretation of their origin are ADAM, NOAH, JACOB, SAUL, and SOLOMON. They would naturally take the same forms as the patronymical surnames derived from these font names.

As previously noted, the names of the principal New Testament characters were rarely used in England before the Norman Conquest. After that, through the Norman-French influence, the New Testament names became popular in England and served as the etymon of numerous family names. The prominence of St. Luke, the Evangelist beloved by Paul, caused many to use the name.

The surnames LUKES, LUKE "light," and LUCAS are common in England. From the sobriquet, Luck, come LUCK, LUCKETT, LUCKEY, and LUCKY. In the Isle of Man they have CLUCAS, condensed from McLUCAS. LUCE is a French surname. LUKAS, LUKASIK, LUKASZEWSKI, and LUCZAK are popular Slavic forms. LUX is a short German form and DE LUCA is a form favored by Italians. A Spanish form is LUCERO, a word which also means "a star or the morning star."

After the Norman Conquest the name of Peter, the most vivid and vigorous of the twelve apostles and founder of the Church in Rome, was introduced into England. It is a translation of Cephas "stone." The story of Peter appealed to the imagination of the Church in the Middle Ages. Many ecclesiastical dignitaries bore the name, and people were quick to adopt it for their sons throughout Christian Europe. However, in English towns the name was often rejected because of the odious Peter's Pence, an annual tribute of a penny exacted from each householder for use by the papal see at Rome. The most common early form in England was the French Piers from which such surnames as PIERCE, PEARCE, PIERS, PEARSON, PIERSON, and PEARY are derived. French forms are PERRIN and PIERROT. PETERSON owes its outstanding popularity to England and the Scandinavian countries. English forms of the surname from the pet form, Par, are PARKINSON, PARNELL, PARLIN, and PARROTT (when this latter name is not a nickname for one with the characteristics of a parrot). Norway and Denmark favor PEDERSEN while Sweden and Norway have PERSON and PETTERSON. The Welsh have made PETERS and PERKINS well-known and also have PARSONS (from the nickname Par when not referring to the parson) and BEARSE from the coalition of ap Pearse.

Just plain PETER is both an English and a German surname. PETRIE and PIRIE are Scottish diminutive forms. PEET comes from Holland. FERRICK is an Irish form. The name in its various national forms is common throughout all of Europe. Italian forms of the family name are PERRI, PETRI, PETRILLO, and PETRONE, while the Spanish name is PEREZ, and the Portuguese form is PIRES. PETROV and PETROFF are from Russia and Bulgaria. PETRENKO is the Ukrainian name. Polish forms are PETROSKI, PIOTROWSKI, PIETRZAK, and BIESCHKE. From Lithuania come PETKUS, PETRAITIS, PETRAUS-

AMERICAN SURNAMES

KAS, and PETRONIS. PETRAKOS and PETROPOULOS are from Greece. The Hungarian name is PETOFI, and in Romania it is PETRESCU. The widespread popularity of family names derived from Peter, the fisherman who received the name from Jesus, is rivaled only by the names which owe their universality to John.

Although the name of Paul has always been frequently coupled with Peter, the name was not an object of particular devotion in the surname period. In the United States the most common cognomen derived from the apostle Paul, whose original name before his conversion to Christianity on the Damascus road was Saul, is just the simple PAUL sometimes spelled PAULL, PAULE, PAWL, or PAULY, and the early form POWEL, all from the Latin *paulus* "small." Men in the United States who bear these surnames descended from ancestors originally from England, Scotland, and France. Scottish MACPHAIL means "son of Paul," and the Manx have condensed this name into QUAIL. German spellings are PAULI, PAULUS, and PASCHKE. A French diminutive form is POLLEY. In the Scandinavian countries, as well as in England, PAULSON, PAULSEN, and POULSON are used. In Italy the name is PAOLI. The Polish forms are PAWLAK and PAWLICKI, while the Ukrainian names are PAVLIK and PAVLENKO and the Czechoslovakian forms are PAVLOV and PAFKO. Surnames derived from Paul fade into other names with other explanations, such as the Welsh POWELL "son of Howell (eminent)" and POOLE "deep water or pool."

Andrew "man," the first of the disciples called by Jesus, had a name much revered by the Church in medieval times. St. Andrew is the patron saint of both Scotland and Russia. ANDERSON is the ninth most common surname in America. It owes its position to the regard for Andrew in England, Scotland, and the Scandinavian countries. ANDRES is also frequently observed, especially as a Spanish form. Norway and Denmark often spelled the ending *-sen*, but many changed to *-son* in the United States. ANDREWS is from Scotland and MCANDREW is from both Scotland and Ireland. The pet form is the aphaeretic DREW, which as a surname is also from Old German *drogo* "carrier." Forms of the surname from Norway are ANDRESEN, ANDERS, and ENDERS. The Swedes eliminate the extra *s* in America to become Anderson. The French form is ANDRE, which often appears as André; the accent outside of France is sometimes an affectation. The Italian form is D'AN-

66

DREA, the Polish is ANDRZEJEWSKI, the Czechoslovakian, ONDRUS, and the Ukrainian, ANDRIJENKO.

Bartholomew, one of the twelve apostles, had a name which was already a surname in form. With the Hebrew *bar*, it means "son of Talmai" and Talmai translates to "furrow." If, as some authorities contend, this was a surname, and Nathanael was his given name, we have an instance of a surname becoming a font name in medieval times and then again becoming a surname as family names became universal. BARTHOLOMEW with its variant terminations, -*may* and -*mae*, became well known in England. Such a long name was very quickly reduced to short, pet forms, the most popular one being BATES, together with BATESON, BATTY, BATTS, BARTLETT, BARTELS, BARD, BART, and BATTLE, although this last name also designates one who came from Battle, the site named after the Battle of Hastings, where the Conqueror was victorious in 1066. From the medial syllable there are TOLL, TOLSON, and TOWLE. Scottish names are BEATTY and BEATON; also these names derive from Bate or Beat, pet forms of Beatrice "she who blesses." Scottish McFARLAND refers to the son of Parlan, Latin Partholomaeus, and so Bartholomew. Czechoslovakian names are BARTA and BARTOS. Hungarian forms are BARTO and BARTOK. An Italian surname is DE BARTOLO.

There is Matthew the tax collector who was called by Jesus to be one of the twelve and Matthias the apostle selected to fill the place among the twelve left by Judas Iscariot. Both mean "gift of Yahveh." Both were common names at the font in England and Europe during the surnaming period. Many surnames were derived from one or the other of these forms, but in most cases it is impossible to segregate them. Common British names are MATTHEWS (a favorite with the Welsh), MAYS, MAY, MAYO, MAYHEW, MATSON, MATTESON, MADDEN, MADISON, and MATHESON. Danish names are MADSEN, MATHISEN, and MATHIESEN. German family names are MATTHIS and the aphaeretic THEIS. MATTHIES and MATTHIAS are both German and English. The French form is MATHIEU and the Finnish name is MATTINEN. Both Czechoslovaks and Poles use MATUS, MATOUSEK, and MATUSZAK, while the Polish peoples also recognize MACIEJEWSKI, and even MATUSZKIEWICZ.

Although not quite so popular in England, Mark "from the god Mars," the companion of early Christian missionaries and author of the second gospel, was revered in European countries. Surnames derived from the name are: in England, MARCUS, the Latin form of the name, MARKUS, MARX, and KUSS; in Germany, MARX and MARKOWITZ; in Czechoslovakia and Yugoslavia, MAREK and MARCINIAK; in Poland and Russia, MARKIEWICZ; and MARCO, DEMARCO, and MARCHETTI in Italy. As an English family name MARK is usually the dweller at the boundary mark. MARQUIS is also derived from Mark when not connected in some way with a marquis' household. MARKS is the most common form of the name in the United States, an instance of the American penchant for the terminal -s as an aid in enunciation.

The popularity of Philip "lover of horses" in medieval times was due not only to the reverence paid to Philip, one of the twelve apostles, but to four French kings on the throne in the eleventh, twelfth, and thirteenth centuries. From France the name came into England at the time of the Conquest. The uncertain use of one or two l's and one or two p's provided various spellings of the name. The very common Welsh and English surname is PHILLIPS. Other English names are the shortened PHIPPS, PHELPS, and PHILBIN. Adding the French diminutive -ot there is PHILLIPOT which shortens into PHILPOT and PHILPOTT. Dropping the first syllable leaves POTT which, with the addition of s, settles into POTTS, apparently a far cry from a descendant of Phillip. Again, adding a diminutive ending, there is POTTLE. How names do originate! The passage in a seventeenth century letter to Philpot from John Careless has been often quoted: "Oh good Master Philpot, which art a principal *pot* indeed, *filled* with much precious liquor —oh, pot most happy! of the High Potter ordained to honour." Germans have used the second syllable to form the equally anomalous LIPP and LIPSON. Poles use the patronymics FILIPIAK and FILIPOWICZ, and San FILIPPO is a form found among Italians.

Stephen "crown," the first Christian martyr, was recommended to many through the description in Acts as a man "full of faith and power" doing "great wonders and miracles among the people." Stephen was also the name of ten popes before the twelfth century, one English king, and several European rulers during the Middle Ages, all of which commended the name to ordinary people, and it became the etymon of various surnames, the most common of which are STEVENS and STEVENSON, STEPHENS and

STEPHENSON in Wales and England. Other English forms are STEFFENS, STEEVES, STINSON, STIMSON, and STIMPSON. A German name is STEPHAN. The name was quite popular in Poland and STEFAN, STEPANEK, SZCZEPANIAK, SZCZEPANIK, and SZCZEPANSKI are the results. From the Ukraine come STEPAN and STEC. The Italians use DESTEFANO. An Icelandic form sometimes seen in America is STEFANSSON.

Henry II of England appointed his friend, Thomas à Becket, Archbishop of Canterbury. Bitter conflict between the two developed quickly. In 1170, in a furious outburst of passion, Henry complained that his subjects allowed Thomas to make him a laughing stock. Four knights who overheard the king hastened to Canterbury and murdered the Archbishop in the Cathedral. This became the most publicized event of the twelfth century. Thomas à Becket was almost immediately idealized as a martyr. He was quickly canonized and remained a popular saint all through the Middle Ages. Henry did penance before the Pope, but the deed was done. In addition, the story of Thomas, the doubting apostle, was well known and this also influenced many parents in the Middle Ages to name their sons Thomas "twin." The font name THOMAS without change or addition is a very common Welsh family name. English surnames are THOMPSON (also Scottish), THOMPKINS, TOMPKINS, TOMLINSON, THOME, THOMA, and TOOMBS. Also popular in Scotland are MACTAVISH and McCOMB, the latter sometimes being extended into MACOMBER. In a name like Mc-Comb the *c* sound overwhelms and eliminates the *t*. Polish forms are TOMCZAK and TOMASZEWSKI (when the latter is not from a place name). The Danish family name is THOMSEN, the Lithuanian is TUMAS, and the Czechoslovakian is TOMAN. The Germans have dropped the first syllable to leave MASS, and the Italians did the same leaving MASSA, while the French added the diminutive to make it MASSON. MASSEY and MASSIE, influenced by the French and Scots, are similarly diminutive forms found in both France and Great Britain. Massey and Massie also derive from Massy or Macy "Mathieu's estate" in Normandy.

Other surnames derived from popular Biblical names are TIMM, TIMSON, TIMMONS, and TEMPLIN from Timothy "honoring God," the youthful and faithful associate of Paul in the propagation of the gospel. English Moss and MOSES and Slavic MOSKOWITZ are derived from Moses "child," the leader of the Hebrew tribes in their exodus from Egypt. Not all of the people in the Middle Ages with this name were Jews. Many named Joseph "He shall add" in medieval times were Jews because of the story of Joseph, the favored eleventh son of Jacob who was imprisoned and sold by his older brothers only to rise to great power in Egypt through his ability to interpret dreams. Also devotion to St. Joseph, husband of the Blessed Virgin, especially among Roman Catholics, made the name a familiar one to Christians at the time family names were becoming hereditary. From Joseph are derived the surnames JOSEPH, JOSEPHSON, and JESSUP, the latter from a medieval pronunciation of the name. German SEPP is an aphaeretic pet form. JOZWIAK is a Polish version of the name.

From Noah "rest" come NOY, NOYS, and NOYES, none particularly common. Abel "breath" produced ABEL, ABELL, ABELSON, ABELMAN, and the Italian ABELLA and ABELLO. GABOR is the Hungarian form of Gabriel "God is my strength." In its simple form GABRIEL is an English surname. The Czechoslovakian and Ukrainian HAVLIK descended from Havlik, a pet form of Gabriel. RUBIN and the pet form RUBY are from Reubin "behold, a son." TOBIN is a diminutive of Tob, a pet form of Hebrew Tobias "Yahveh is good," and JEWELL often comes from Hebrew Joel "Yahveh is God." KISSACK is a Manx condensation of the surname, MAC-ISAAC "he who laughs."

From Elijah (or the New Testament form Elias) "My God is Yahveh," a name very popular in the Middle Ages, are derived the English surnames ELLIS, ELLISON, ELIAS, ELLIOTT, and ELKINS, and the Welsh BELLIS. ELY is usually from the early English form Elie, when not from the Isle of Ely "eel district" in Cambridgeshire. Elliott can have several different spellings dependent upon one's predilection for l's and t's. LAZAR usually derives from Lazarus "whom God helps," the brother of Martha and Mary, raised from the dead by Jesus. Also possibly influencing the name was Lazar, a character in the York plays, from Middle English *lazare* "leper." German LASSER also descended from Lazarus. Jordan "flowing down" became a popular given name because so many pilgrims returned to England with holy water from the river Jordan which was used to baptize infants who then received the name, and in its plain form it became the popular surname JORDAN.

70

A regular part of the pilgrim's costume was the leathern bottle carried for this purpose. From the nickname Jud come JUDD, JUDKINS, and JUDSON. GIORDANO is an Italian form.

Gaspar or Caspar "master of the treasure," the traditional name of one of the Three Kings, the three wise men of the East who came to Bethlehem to worship the infant Jesus, has been the eponym of several surnames in England and Germany, such as CASPER, GASPER, JASPER, and KASPER, all of which sometimes have the variant termination, -*ar*. The French form is GASPARD. Italian forms are CASPARI and GASPARO. A Polish form is KASPERSKI. Other Slavic names are GASPEREC and KASPRZYK. The other two wise men, Melchior and Balthasar, did not capture the imagination of the people to the same extent, although the surname MELCHER in some cases may be interpreted as a descendant of Melchior "king of the light," and German BALTAZAR and BALTHASER derive from Balthasar "Bel has made a king."

Dionysus, the Grecian god of wine, made the name Dionysius quite popular during the early centuries of the Christian era. Dionysius the Areopagite was converted by St. Paul. St. Dionysius became pope in 259 A.D. A name of so many syllables was naturally abbreviated and from Denis and Dion, the popular pet forms, we have the surnames DENIS, DENNIS, DENNISON, TENNY, and TENNY-SON, the last made familiar by the poet. DWIGHT, now more familiar as a given name because of Dwight David Eisenhower, derives from Dwight or Diot, other pet forms of Dionysius. DYE is another English surname from a pet form of Dionysius, and it produces DYSON. DION and DIONNE are the French surnames from the pet form, Dion, the latter made famous through birth of the Dionne quintuplets in Canada. St. Denis is the patron saint of France.

There are some Anglo-Saxon names and name elements common before the Conquest which lasted long enough afterwards to become the etymon of family names. From Brun "brown" come BRUNS, BRONSON, BROWN, and BROWNELL. The German BRUNO and BRUNKE are cognate forms. From the very common Godwin "God's friend" is derived GOODWIN. KENRICK and KENDRICK are derived from Cenric or Kenric "bold, rule" or from Cynric "royal, rule." From Serlo "armor" come SEARLES and SERLIN. From Hard or Hardwin "firm, friend" comes HARDIN. From Folki "people" come Folk, Folkes, Foulkes, Ffoulkes (for ff see page 295), Fewkes, Fulk, Fawke, Voke, and Volk. Fulk de Neuilly was a famous French fanatical preacher who aroused the people to undertake the Fourth Crusade in 1198. From Gegn "straight" come Gaines and Gaynes.

Other English surnames frequently observed derived from short Anglo-Saxon personal names are Baggett and Baggs from Baga or Bacga "fat one," Bott from Botta "help," Budd and Budde from Budda "beetle," Calloway and Callaway from the font name Calewa "bald," Cates from Cate, a pet form of Cato "cautious," Chada from Ceadda "battle," Darling from Deorling "beloved," Dare and Darrell from Deor "brave or bold," and Dill from Dill or Dila "spoiler." Edgett is derived from little Ecga "sword," Giles from Giles "shield bearer," Hackett from little Hack or Hache "hook," Haskins from little Aesc "ash or spear," Mann and Man sometimes derive from Mann "man," an old name not particularly common in the surname period. Neal and Neil from Neil "champion," Sommer from Sumer or Somer "summer," Twigg from Twicga "twig," and Wiggins from little Wicga "warrior," although in some cases this last surname denotes one who came from Wigan "Wigan's homestead" in Lancashire. Many of these names are also descriptive nicknames rather than names from old Anglo-Saxon font names. Snow had a remote ancestor with that name which was sometimes given to one born during a snow storm, although this name again alludes in some cases to the man with a snow-white head.

Various family names were developed in England derived from given names not only from the Teutonic languages but from the classical tongues as well. English Basil, as well as the Italian form, Basile, are descendants of Greek Basil or Basilio "king." Both Constantine and Considine derive from Constantine "constant" as do Costin and Costain from early English forms. Cornell is from Latin Cornelius "hornlike." Fithian is a variant of Vivian "animated." Julian is from Latin Julius "downy-bearded or youthful." Kay descended from Latin Gaius "rejoice." Titus is from Latin Titus "safe," the name of a companion to St. Paul. Two other Latin names have produced English family names: Valentine "vigorous or healthy" and Vincent "conquering."

Other English family patronymic names which should be

noticed because of their frequent occurrence in America are: ALDRICH from Alderich "noble, rule" (when not from Aldridge "village among alders" in Staffordshire); ARNOLD "eagle, rule," and its diminutive form ARNETT; BERTRAM "bright, raven"; CULBERTSON from Culbert "cool, bright"; GODDARD "God, hard"; HILDEBRAND "battle, sword"; and INGRAM "Ing's raven." Ing was a popular Scandinavian hero of remote antiquity. JARVIS is from Gervais "spear, servant." JARRETT and GARRETT descended from little Gerard "spear, firm." KINSEY is from Cynesige "royal victory" when it is not merely a slurred form of Kingsley "the king's wood," the name of several English towns. LUTHER is both English and German, from Lothair "famous, warrior." MERRILL derives from Muriel or Merel "sea, bright." MURDOCK is the descendant of Murdoch "seaman," an old Irish name introduced into England before the Conquest. OLIVER is both English and French from Oliver "elf, host," although the French form is usually OLIVIER.

Names beginning with *Os*, the name of an Old Norse god, often translated as "god or divine," about whom little seems to be known, are OSBORNE "god, bear"; OSMAN from Osmund "god, protector"; OSGOOD "god, goodness"; and OSWALD "god, power." This last name has been temporarily besmirched by the man generally believed to have murdered President Kennedy. RICHER is a descendant of Richere "mighty, army." SEARS, an American name made famous for successful retail merchandising by mail, derives from Segar "sea, warrior" or from Sigehere "victorious, army." TALBOT and TOLBERT descend from a French name, the correct etymology of which authorities cannot agree to, but possibly means "to cut fagots" or "bandit." English TALBOT also denominates a dweller at the sign of the talbot, a white sporting dog. TERRELL comes from Turold or Thorold "Thor, strong," while TERRY derives from a pet form of Latin Terence "smooth or tender" or Old German Theudoric "people, rule." Other English family names are THAYER from Thaider "people, army"; THURMAN from Thormund "Thor's protection"; WILBUR from Wilburh "beloved, stronghold," originally a woman's name; WILLARD from Wilhead "resolute, brave"; and WINCHELL, the family name of the controversial American journalist, from Wincel "child."

There are several surnames terminating in *-mann* or *-man* which are from popular Old English given names, and as such do not indicate servants, although all of them do have other origins with the connotation of servant or an occupation. WHATMAN and WATMAN are from Hwaetman "bold man"; WHITEMAN and WHITMAN are from Hwitman "white man"; BLACKMAN descends from Blaecman "dark man." SEAMAN is sometimes from Saemann "victory, man," and SWEETMAN is sometimes from Swetmann "sweet man." All of these names together with COLEMAN, GOOD-MAN, and WOODMAN, mentioned in the previous chapter, may be found in Domesday Book, the results of a census completed in 1086.

A small class of patronymics is formed from occupations. The principal English names that have survived are CLERKSON, COOKSON, GRAYSON "grieve's son," SMITHSON, and WRIGHTSON HINSON is the "son of the hind or servant." MASTERSON designates the "son of the leader or teacher." Some Irish names are Mc CAHEY "son of the horseman," McCORD and McCURDY "son of the navigator," McINERNEY "son of the steward of church lands," and MAGOUN "son of the smith." Greek PAPADOPOULOS, in various spellings, is "son of the priest," and MARANGOPOULOS is "son of the carpenter." The Scots prefixed *Mac* to words indicating occupation, description or status. There are McINTYRE "son of the carpenter," MACPHERSON "son of the parson," MACGOWAN "son of the smith," and McWARD "son of the bard." MACMILLAN i the "son of the bald or tonsured one"; McINTOSH is the "son of the chief or leader"; McLAUGHLIN is the "son of the man from Norway." Polish OLEJNICZAK is the "son of the maker of oil from seeds for food purposes." Dutch CONKLIN or CONKLING probably designated the "descendant of the petty chieftain."

A Scottish family named Lockhart contended that the name arose from the fact that a member had conveyed the heart of James Lord Douglas back to Scotland after his death in the Holy Land, in a locked casket, and the family bears as its arms a heart clasped by a padlock. This, unlike most romantic tales recited to explain the origin of a surname, could be true because it was not unusual for the hearts of knights and nobles dying abroad to be returned to the homeland during the Crusades. The heart of Richard Cœur de Lion, who died from an arrow wound near Limoges, France, is preserved at the museum in Rouen. Never

heless the most likely explanation of the origin of LOCKHART is
hat it is derived from the personal name Locard "enclosure,
mall." Another Scottish name from a given name is BLAINE re-
erring to the son of the disciple of Blaan or Blane "the lean," an
early Scottish saint. CADY is from little Cadda "battle." CALL is
a descendant of Cathal "battle, mighty." KITTRIDGE is derived
rom Sitreac or Sitrig "true victory." FARQUHAR is from Gaelic
earchar "very dear one."

Rather easily recognized are many German family names, that
ndicate descent from men with old Germanic given names, com-
osed of various name elements, mostly relating to armed conflict,
uch as war, bold, castle, hard, battle, sword, protection, spear,
ictory, peace, counsel, noble, bright, people, fame, servant, and
ule. For example, GUENTHER, GUNTHER, and GUNTER derive from
Gunter or Guntard "war, bold"; BORCHARDT from Burghard
castle, hard"; ENGELHARDT from Engelhard "angel, hard"; HILDE-
BRAND and HILLEBRAND from Hildebrand "battle, sword"; GUTT-
MAN from Gudmund "war, protection"; GERHARDT from Gerhard
spear, hard"; SEIFERT from Sigifrith "victory, peace"; REINHARDT
and RINEHARD from Raginhart "counsel, hard"; ALBRECHT and
ALBERS from Albrecht "noble, bright"; VOLKMAN from Folcman
people, servant"; DIETRICH from Theodore "people, rule"; and
RUDOLPH which is both German and English, from Hrodulf
fame, wolf."

Other German surnames from old Germanic first names are:
BERNHARDT from Berinhard "bear, firm"; DITTMANN descended
rom Teutman "people, man"; EWALD comes from Ewald "eter-
nity, power"; HEIMAN had an ancestor, Hagiman "enclosed place,
man," although in some instances he came from Hagen "enclo-
ure" in Germany; HOWALT comes from Hugold "spirit, rule";
KIMMERLE comes from Khunemar "race, famous." There are
URATH from Chuonrad "bold, counsel," LEPPERT and LIPPERT
rom Liutperaht "people, pride," MEYNER from Maganhar
strength, army," PILLER from Bilihar "sword, army," and REICH-
MAN from Ricman "powerful, man." RADER is from Radheri "counsel, army." REIMER derives from Raginmar "counsel, famous,"
while REINER probably comes from Raginhari "counsel, army,"
and REINERT and RINEHART descend from Raginhart "counsel,
ard." RIEGER is the descendant of Hrodgaer "fame, spear."

75

SIEBERT derives from Sigibert "victory, bright," while SIEVERS and SIEVERT are from Sigiwart "victory, worthy." TROST is from Trad stilo "helper." WACKER derives from Wacar "vigilant." WENDEL is a descendant of little Wendimar "wander, famous." ZIEMAN is from Sigiman "victory, man," while ZIEMER is from Sigima "victory, famous."

AMORY, EMERY, EMMETT, EMERSON, and EMMONS descend from Emery or Emory "industrious," or from Old German Emmerich "work, rule." Emerson, whether the spelling is with one or two, means "the son of Emery." ERVIN and ERWIN, sometime spelled IRVIN and IRWIN, descend from Eorwine "sea, friend These names also derive from Irvine or Irving "green river places in Scotland. Eberhard "boar, strong" is the etymon o EBERHARD and EBERHARDT. The element *hard* in various spelling terminates many German family names. ECKERT is an instanc the first element meaning "sword edge"; HARTMAN "strong ma or servant" is an example where it is the first element; MOZAR is a variant of Muothart, the first element translating to "spir or courage"; FREDERICK "peace, rule" in several forms is both German and an English name; FRIEDMAN has the same initia element. GOEBEL and GOBLE descend from an early ancesto called Godbeald "God, brave." German YODER comes from Theo doric "people, rule" or from Jodocus "fighter." DIAMOND is fro Daymond "day, protection," although in some cases it may be metonym to designate the dealer in those precious stones whic in America are said to be girls' best friends.

Similar English names from Old English may be observed, suc as GUNNELL from Gundwulf "war, wolf"; GOODRICH from Godri "God's rule"; ALBERTS, ALBERTSON, and ALBRIGHT from Ethel beorht "noble, bright"; WOOLSEY from Wulfsige "wolf, victory (the *g* oftentimes softens into a *y*). BRANSON descends fro Brand "sword"; BARRETT descends from Barret "bear, rule BURKETT derives from Burgheard or Bouchart "fortress, hard The etymon of GERLAND and GARLAND is Gaerland the first el ment of which means "spear." In some cases Garland denote the dweller in the triangular field or at the sign of the garlan HUBBARD had an early ancestor named Hubert, the first eleme of which is the same as the given name, Hugh "spirit." REYNOL comes from Regenweald "counsel, force." All these family nam

re reminders to us of the types of names borne in medieval times
y our ancestors.

There are other English patronymics from Old English or
:ermanic personal names and these have found their way to the
Inited States where many such are noted in goodly number.
.SHER, when not a respelling of German Ascher, descends from
sher "spear, army." ATLAS descends from Edel or Eidel "noble,"
name corrupted through Edlin and Eidles to settle into the
ame of the god who supported the world on his shoulders.
·RAINERD is from Brandhard "sword, hard." BRITTERIDGE comes
:om Brictric "bright rule." BURRAGE looks to Burgric "castle, rule"
s an early ancestor. ELMER, a surname often used as a Christian
ame in America, descends from Old English Aethelmaer "noble,
imous." EVERETT, also often used as a font name in this country,
omes from Everard "boar, strong." FILLMORE, the family name
f the thirteenth president of the United States, is derived from
'ilimar or Filomor "very famous." GILLARD descends from Gail-
ird "gay." Then there are GLADWIN and GLIDDEN from Gladwin
kind, friend."

There is a small group of names starting with *H* with the sound
f *b* in the middle that are sometimes confused, such as HEBERT
:om Hebert "combat, bright," HEBBARD from Hibbert "high,
right," HIBBARD from Herbert "army, bright," HOBART and
IUBERT from Hubert "mind, bright," and HUBBELL from Hubbald
mind, bold." INGALLS identifies a descendant of Ingeld "Ing's
:ibute" when not the man from Ingol "Inga's valley" in Lanca-
hire. JARRELL comes from Jarrold, a spelling variant of Gerald
spear, firm." JERNIGAN is a descendant of French Gernigon "iron,
imous" or Old Teutonic Gerwig "eager, warrior." JOSLYN, spelled
1 various ways, derives from Jocelyn "the just." KENNARD is
ither from Cenhard "bold, strong" or from Cyneweard "royal
uardian." LIPSEY is a corruption of Old English Leofsige "dear,
ictory." MENARD is a shortened respelling of Maynard "strength,
ard" found also as a French form. MERRICK, when not the man
:om Merrick "pronged place" in Scotland, derives from Merick
ir Almeric "work, rule." OATES is a descendant of Odo "prosper-
·y." ORDWAY is a modern spelling of Ordwig "spear, warrior."
'URNELL comes from Pernel, a contraction of Petronella "little
ock." RAYNER comes from Rayner "counsel, army," and RUPPERT

77

is from Rupert "fame, bright." SEAVEY looks to Saewig "sea, war as an ancestor. SEAWARD is from Sigeweard "victory, protection" or Saeweard "sea, protection." SHERROD, when not a corruption of Sherwood "wood belonging to the shire," is a descendant of Scirheard "bright, hard," while SHERWIN is derived from Scirwine "bright, friend." SIZEMORE is a softened corruption of Sigmar "victory, great." STANNARD is extended from Stanard "stone, firm." THEOBALD means "people, bold." THEODORE is usually from Germanic Theodoric "people, rule," seldom from Greek Theodore "gift of God," not common in England during the surname epoch. THURBER comes from Thurgar "Thor's spear." WARING is derived from Old German Warin or Old French Guarin "protection." WYAND is a descendant of Weigand or Wygan "warrior."

Some other German names that might be noted are EBER from Ebilo or Eble "boar," FAUST from Faustus "fortunate," GARBER from Garibert "spear, bright," HEDRICK from Haidrich "heath, rule," HUMBOLDT from Hunbeald "bear cub, bold," LIEBER from Liubheri "dear, army" (when not from the town of Liebau in Germany), and MANDEL from little Manto "pleasure or joy." BRUNER and BRUNNER descended from Brunheri "brown, army." OTT and OTTO are from Otta or Odo "prosperity," the former being sometimes an English surname. REICHEL descends from little Rico, a pet form of Riculf "powerful, wolf." RUCKER is from Hrodgaer "fame, spear." SEIBERT derives from Sigiperaht "victory, bright." WERNER descends from Warinhari "protection, army." YOST comes from Jodocus "fighter."

Many short German names are derived from the kurzform, the short form or nickname of the font name. For example, KUNTZ, KUNZ, and KURTH derive from Conrad "bold, counsel"; REINKE is from Raginulf "counsel, wolf"; GATZ and GATSCH are from Gato, a pet form of Gadafrid "comrade, peace"; MANN is often from Manno, the short form of names beginning with Man, "servant," such as Manifred and Manowald. WITZ and WEITZ are from Wizo, a pet form of names beginning with Wid "forest," such as Witbald and Wittimar, or from Wig "fight," a pet form of names such as Wigibald and Wigbrand. STARCK and STARK are from Starco, a pet form of Starculf "strong, wolf." ZACH is a pet form of Zacharias "whom Yahveh remembers." RADKE and RASCHKE are from Rado, a pet form of Conrad "bold, counsel."

RATH is from Rado, a pet form of names beginning with Rat counsel," as Radulf, Ratward, and Radoald, when not one who came from Rath "advice" in the Rheinland. LOTZ is from Lotze, a pet form of Hludizo "clear, plain." FRITZ and FRITSCH are from Fritz, a pet form of Friedrich "peace, rule." GOETZ and GETZ are pet forms of Godizo "God." SHOOK is from Cak "expectation" a Kurzform of Zschacke. KERN is from a pet form of Gernwin "spear, friend," when not a former resident of Kern "kernel" in Germany.

The Germans have always been partial to family names from short or pet forms. Additional names of this type that should be mentioned are: BECHTEL is a descendant of Betto, a pet form of many names beginning with Bercht "bright or famous," as Berhari and Berhtolf; BRETZ derives from Briddo "bridle"; LANTZ, LENTZ, LENZ, and LENTSCH from Lanzo or Lando "land"; LIETZ comes from Liuzo, a pet form of names commencing with Liuto people," as Liutbald, Liutgard, and Liutwin. MATZ has two derivations: it is from Mazo a pet form of Math "assembly place," or from Matz, a pet form of Matthaus "gift of Yahveh." MAX is well-known as the short form of Maximilian "the greatest." MERKEL with its variant spellings of MERKLE, MERKELL, and MERKL descends from little Merk or Mark "from Mars, the god of war." REIF and REIFF come from Rifo, a pet form of Ricfrid "rule, peace." RIECK is from Rieckert "rule, hard." WOLFSON is the son of Wolf, often a short form of the numerous German given names beginning with this element.

Some nickname or short forms stand for several different given names. BILL comes from Bil "sword," a nickname for names beginning with that element, as Bilihar and Biligarda. As a nickname for William it came into use too late to become the etymon of an English family name related to William. BUTTS and BUTZ descend from Bucco, a pet form of names beginning with Burg "castle or fortification," as Burghard and Burcward. DIETZ and Doss come from names beginning with *diet* "people," as Theubald and Theodulf. EPPS is from a pet form of names beginning with *eber* "boar," as Eburhard and Eburwin. GERTZ derives from *ger* "spear" beginning such names as Geremar, Geribald, and Germund. HEITZ is a pet form of such names as Heinrich, Haidrich, and Haidulf. HINTZ and HINZ are pet forms of names beginning with *hag* "hedged place," as Haginold and Haginher.

79

LUEBKE is a descendant of a pet form of names beginning with *leute* "people," as Liudberct and Liutbrand. WERNICK is a descendant of little Waro "protection."

LEMKE is a descendant of little Lem or Lampo, pet forms of names beginning with Land, as Lambico, Landbald, and Landebert (when not from Lemke, a town in Germany). LUTZ is a pet form of such names as Liutbald and Liutgard (when not from Lutz "small place" the name of a village in Germany). MIELK derives from little Miel, a pet form of Aemilius, Milan, and Miloslaw and other names with the element *mil* "beloved." MINT is a short form of names beginning with Magin "strength," such as Maginbald and Maginhard (when not from Mainz "great water" in Germany). MUNDT derives as a short form from Mundhart, Munderich, and such names beginning with *munt* "protection." MUTH descends from Muth "courage," a short form of names containing that theme such as Helmuth, Muotfrid, and Mothar.

RAPP derives from names beginning with *rabe* "counsel," as Hrabanolt and Rappmund. RUTH is from Ruodo, a pet form of names beginning with *hrod* "fame," as Hrodmar and Rothhari. SEITZ, SEIDEL, and ZICK as surnames derive from names beginning with *sieg* "victory," as Sigibald, Sigismund, and Sigiswart. Seidel is also from a town of that name in Germany. SIEGEL is a descendant of little Sigo, another pet form of names beginning with *sie* "victory." WALDO as a surname derives from Waldo a pet form of names commencing with *wald* "forest," as Waldomar and Waltheof. There are many other German surnames derived from the pet forms of the old Germanic personal names, but lack of space prevents the presentation of all but the most familiar ones found in the United States.

English nicknames that have become surnames standing for several different Christian names are also frequently encountered. EDDY is the familiar pet form, together with EDISON, of names beginning with Ead "richness" as Edward, Edmund, Edwin, and Edgar. GOOD, when not referring to the good man, is a short form of such names as Godmund, Godric, and Godwine. NILES is a hypocoristic form of Nicholas "people's victory" and also of Cornelius "hornlike." STARKEY is a familiar form of names commencing with *starc* "strong" as Starcbeorht, Starcfrith, and Starcwulf. SILLS and SILL are pet forms of such divergent names as ilvester "forest dweller" and Cecil "blind." TRUMP is from Trum "strong," a pet form of names having that as the first syllable, uch as Trumbald, Trumbeorht, and Trumwine. GRIMES and GRIMM derive from *grim* "mask," the first element of names such s Grimbald, Grimulf, and Grimkell. This method of forming urnames from diminutive or pet forms of given names is espe-ially prevalent among peoples speaking the Germanic languages.

BODKIN derives from little Baud, a pet form of Baldwin "bold, riend." BURCHETT descends from little Burchard "castle, firm," lthough in some cases the name designates the dweller at the ead or edge of the grove of birch trees. BURDETT descends from 3ordet "little shield," although in some instances his ancestor was dweller near the border or on a rented farm. BURDICK descends rom little Borda "shield," but can also be the newcomer from 3ourdic, the name of two towns in France. DUCKETT is from little Juke, a pet form of Marmaduke "sea leader." LAMKIN and JUMPKIN are descendants of little Lamb or little Lump, pet forms f Lambert "land, bright," which also produces the patronymic JAMSON. PICKENS and PICKETT are descendants of little Pic "pike." RUSKIN is the diminutive of Rous "red."

Often the present day meaning of words has nothing to do vith the medieval heritage of surnames. BASSETT is a descendant f little Bass or Bassa "short." Dog lovers with bassets will find hat their animals are well-described. DAGGETT is a descendant f little Dagr or Daegga both meaning "day." DERRICK is a cor-uption of the pet form of Theodoric "people, rule." FOGG comes rom a pet form of Fulcher "people, army." GARNETT descends rom little Guarin "protection, friend." JEWETT is a descendant f "the little Jew," also it may be a pet form of Julian "downy-»earded or youthful." LANCE is from Lance "land," the double liminutive of which is Lancelot from which, in turn, again comes Jance as a short form. LIGGINS is a descendant of little Lig, a hort form of Ligulf "spear-shaft, wolf." LUFKIN is a descendant f little Luf, short for Lufa "love or wolf." PENNELL is derived rom a diminutive of Pinn "peg" or Pain or Pagan "rustic or :ountryman." PUCKETT is a descendant of little Puca "goblin." 3ACKETT comes from little Sacq "adversary." TEBBETTS and TIB-»ETTS descend from little Tebb, a pet form of Theobald "people, »old."

Hann is a nickname for John, from the medial syllable of the full form, Johannes; also for Ralf or Randolph, as previously suggested (page 54); and also for Henry. Adding the diminutives -kin, -cock, and the patronymical termination -son, we have the surnames of HANKIN, HANCOCK, and HANSON where the parent of the original bearer may have been named either John, Randulf or Henry. Hudd is a nickname form for both Hugh and Richard. HUDSON is a popular family name in the north of England, but there is no evidence as to whether the remote ancestor was named Hugh or Richard. A phonetically sharper form is HUTSON.

There are many other English family names, not too uncommon, that have developed from hypocoristic forms. EBY derives from a pet form of Ebbe or Ebba "boar." TIPPETT is a descendant of little Tibb, a pet form of Theobald "people, bold." ROLLINS and ROWELL are diminutive forms from Roland "fame, land"; and RUDY naturally comes from Rudolf "fame, wolf." RAINEY is a Scottish surname from little Ren, a pet form of Reginald "counsel judgment"; GUNN, also Scottish, is from Gunn "war" an abridged form of longer names such as Gunnar, Gunulf, and Gunnhildr.

All the Western countries delighted in forming hereditary family names from pet forms. In Greece PANOS is from a pet form of Panayotis "pertaining to Our Lady"; MANOS is from a shortened form of Manolis, "God is with us"; and DEMOS refers to both Demosthenes "strong with people" and Demetrius "of Demeter, goddess of fertility and harvests." Italian CORSO is a pet form of Bonaccorso "good help," and ZONA of Franzona "little Frenchman"; COZZI, GUZZO, and NERI are pet forms of various names with these terminations. Spanish RUIZ is the son of Ruy a pet form of Rodrigo "famous, rule"; GOMEZ refers to the son of Gomo, a pet form of Gomesano "man, path."

Many surnames are easily recognized when it is remembered that in many places the second element of a Christian name was the pet form which became a family name. STACY is the descendant of Stace, a pet form of Eustace "steadfast"; and NUTT is from Canute "hill or white-haired." Today Nutt as a surname is not regarded with favor because of the slang meaning accorded it. DUKE and DUKES are sometimes from Marmaduke "sea leader," but in other cases they merely have the connotation of "leader." French names, especially, favor aphaeresis, the retention of only the last element. CHARDIN and CHARD are from Richard "rule, hard," JAMEN is from Benjamin "son of my right hand," and COTIN, COTON, and COTOT are from Jacquot "the supplanter, or may God protect" and Nicot "people's victory."

Lithuanian surnames occasionally noticed in America are from pet forms of names favored in that country. BUTKUS descends from a short form of Butkintas, a name Alfred Senn, the authority on Lithuanian names, says is not translatable. There are MINKUS, a descendant of Minkus, a pet form of Minkantas "remember, suffer," NORKUS from Norkus, a pet form of Norkantas "wish, suffer," and RIMKUS from Rimkus, a pet form of Rimkantas "peaceful, suffer." Were the Lithuanians more fond of suffering than other peoples? TANIS is from a pet form of Athanasius "immortal." TUBELIS denotes descent from Tobiosius or Tobijas "goodness of Yahveh."

There are some Dutch patronymics that should be noticed because they have become familiar names in the United States. One might start with AARSEN, the son of Arthur "Thor's eagle" simply because it would head most alphabetical lists. BASTIAN descends from Bastian, the aphaeretic form of Sebastian "venerable." LEFFERTS is the son of Leffert "dear, hard." JOOST derives from Joost "the just," the Dutch form of Justus. ROELANDTS is the son of Roeland "fame, land." RYERSON is the son of Reyer or Reijer "rider."

Various Slavic surnames are patronymics. Yugoslavian RADDATZ is a descendant of Radac, a pet form of Rad "happy." Czechoslovakian MRAZEK had little Mraz "frost" as an ancestor. Russian RIFKIN is the son of Rifka "a snare." Polish WALCZAK is the son of Walek, a pet form of Walenty "valorous," while his countryman BERCOVITZ is the son of Berko, a pet form of Baruch "blessed." Polish KOSCIUSZKO is a descendant of Koscia, a pet form of Konstanty "constant."

Magnus I was king of Norway and Denmark in the eleventh century. He was born when his father Olaf II was not available and the priest in an emergency baptism gave him the name of Magnus "great," a name which he thought would be pleasing to the king. The name became popular among Scandinavian monarchs and was consequently favored by the people, giving rise to the surnames MAGNUS and MAGNUSON. From the pet form Man

AMERICAN SURNAMES

come the Scandinavian MANSON and MANS, although this latter name is usually spelled MANNS. Irish McMANUS derives from Maghnus "great," a form of the Scandinavian given name.

Various names stemming from the father's name are common in this land from the several Scandinavian countries, some in slightly different spellings. Sweden, Norway, and Denmark all favor such names as MORTENSON "from Mars, the god of war," MUNSON and MUNSEN from Mans, a pet form of Magnus "great," IVERSON "archer," ERICSON and ERICKSON "ever king," and NEILSON "champion." As an English family name, a contributory source of MUNSON is from Mun, a pet form for Edmund. All these names and many other similar ones are found with both the -son and -sen suffixes. Whether Lief Ericsson, born in Iceland of Norwegian parents, was the first to set foot in the new world or not, his name is forever linked to America, and we may well regard him as "ever king." ARENSON "eagle, rule," AMUNDSEN "protector, forever," and BJORNSON "bear" are well-known in Norway and America. RAS-MUSSEN "amiable" is both Danish and Norwegian. ARENDT is Norwegian while ARENZ and ARNDT are Danish. They all mean "eagle, rule." GUSTAFSON "Goth's staff" comes from Sweden. GUNDERSON "war, bold," hails from Norway. KNUTSON, the son of Knut or Canute "hill or white-haired," in several spellings, comes from either Sweden or Norway. KNUDSEN is very popular in Denmark. SWENSON is Swedish, SWENSEN is Danish, both referring to Swen "young boy or servant." Scandinavian BARNEY is a pet form of Bjorn "bear," but Irish BARNEY is a pet form of Barnabas "son of prophecy."

An Irish sept or clan is simply a group of persons living in the same locality who bear the same surname. As most of the Irish names originally included Mac or O or the Norman Fitz, most were patronymics even though altered in spelling by elimination of the prefix. Irish surnames are now generally Anglicized and spelled approximately as they are pronounced without regard to the earlier Irish spelling. The Fitz was dropped quite early as the Norman practice was to use the plain given name as a surname. Many Fitz prefixes were replaced by Mac. This accounts for such Irish and Scottish names as MACDAVID and MACWILLIAM.

DUGGAN and DUGAN are Anglicized names meaning the "grandson of Dubhagan or little black one." The O has been dropped

84

n the same way BOYLE, no matter how spelled, is the grandson
f Baoigheall "vain pledge," and SHEA is grandson of Seagh-
lha "learned." CONNORS derives from Concobair "meddlesome"
r Conchor "desire"; DOHERTY, from Dochartach "unfortunate";
MALONEY, from Maoldomhnaigh "devoted to the church"; KEEFE,
rom Caomh "beautiful or noble"; DONNELLY, from Donnghal
brown, valor"; FOLEY, from Foghlaidh "plunderer"; CASEY, from
Cathasach "vigilant"; DONOVAN, from Donndubhan "brown Dub-
an"; DUFFY, from Dubhthach "black"; QUINN and COYNE, from
Conn "freeman" (CONN is also from Conn, a pet form of Constan-
ine "constant"). RILEY in all its spellings is from Raghallach
"sportive"; SULLIVAN is from Suileabhan "black-eyed"; KELLY and
CALLAHAN, the latter being the diminutive form, are from Ceal-
ach "contention"; and HOGAN is from Og "young"; all grandsons.
HALPIN, HALFPENNY, and HALPENNY are the grandsons of Ailpin
little stout man." HOYT, when not a descendant of Dutch Hoyte,
s a grandson of Ud. REAGAN, the governor of California, derives
is name from an ancestor who was a grandson of Riagan "little
king." A shorter spelling is REGAN.

There are other Irish patronymics, most of which originally
ad the prefix O referring to grandson or descendant. Some of
hem most often seen are: BREEN from Braon "sorrow" (some-
imes a variant of O'Brien or of Bryan); CARNEY from Cearnach
'victorious"; COCHRAN from little Cogar "a confidant"; CONDON
rom Cudubhan; CONLEY from Conghalach "valorous"; CORCORAN
rom Corcran, a diminutive of Corcair "purple"; and COUGHLIN
rom Cochlan, which is little Cochal "hooded cloak," a forename
hat originally developed from a nickname. DORSEY is both Irish
nd French; it refers in Ireland to the descendant of Dorchaide
'dark man" and in France to one who came from Arcy "strong-
old." DOWLING is the grandson of Dubhfhlann "black Flann."
FERRELL derives from Fearghal "super valor." FLAHERTY was a
lescendant of Flaithbheartach "bright ruler." These personal
ames transliterated from the Irish alphabet present some fearful
ppearing names to the eyes of those accustomed only to the
Latin alphabet.

GAFFNEY descended from Gawain "calf," GRADY comes from
Grada "noble," HENNESSY and McGINNIS are from Aonghus "one-
choice," while FARRIS is from Fearghur "better choice." KINNEY

85

comes from Cionaodh "fire sprung." MEEHAN is from Miadhachan, a diminutive of Miadhach "honorable." MONAHAN is a descendant of the little monk from Manachan, a diminutive of *manach* "a monk."

Some frequently encountered Mac names are McCAFFREY who is the son of Godfrey "God's peace" or of Eachmharcach "horse rider"; McCANN, the son of Annadh "storm"; McCLENDON, the son of little Leannach "cloaked"; McCONNELL, son of Domhnall "world mighty"; McCRACKEN, the son of Neachtan "pure one"; McGOVERN, the son of little Samhradh "summer"; McKINNEY, the son of Cionaodh "fire sprung"; McGONAGLE, the son of Congal "high valor"; and McGERRIGAN, the son of Geargan "the little fierce one," those musical old Irish names.

It is especially difficult to distinguish Irish names denoting descent from an ancestor through use of his name and one referring to a descriptive characteristic, since the words from which the name is derived may be either just a description or a personal name with that meaning. Some such names are LAUGHLIN, grandson of Lachtna "gray," COYLE, the son of Dubhghall "black stranger," CROWLEY, grandson of Cruadhlaoch "tough hero," COSTELLO, the son of Oisdealbh "fawn-like," SHANNON, grandson of Seanach "old or wise," SHERIDAN, grandson of Siridean "peaceful," TALLEY, the descendant of Taithleach "quiet, peaceful," TIERNEY, grandson of Tighearnach "lordly," O'MALLEY, grandson of Maille "noble or chief," O'HARA, grandson of Eaghra "bitter or sharp," O'KEEFE, grandson of Caomh "beautiful or noble," O'CONNELL, grandson of Conall "world mighty," and NEELY, son of Conghal "high valor."

A very good estimate of the character of the early Irish or Celts in their occupation of much of Europe may be made from an inspection of the meaning of their present day family names from Ireland. Their warlike attitude is made evident by the many names originally meaning soldier, warrior, or champion, such as CLANCY "ruddy warrior," DOOLEY "dark warrior," DUNCAN "brown warrior," DUNPHY "brown warrior," FINNY "soldier," GLANCY "ruddy warrior," HANLON "great hero," HANRAHAN "champion," HORAN "champion," KANE "warrior," KEANE "warrior," McDONOUGH "brown warrior," McMORROW "sea warrior," MURPHY "sea warrior," PHINNEY "soldier," and SLOAN "soldier." The distinction between a soldier, warrior, and champion at the time when surnames were being adopted is quite nebulous. The joy of fight or battle is clearly reflected in such Irish family names as CAHILL "battle powerful," CALHOUN "battle hero," CALLAN "battle mighty," DONAHUE "brown battler," HARTNET "battle bear," KEARNEY "victorious in battle," and MULCAHY "warlike chief." In each name the exact shade of meaning cannot always be brought to light, but the general implication is clear. ROONEY and SHANLEY refer to "hero." CURRAN is from Corran, a diminutive of Corradh "spear."

The early Irish love of hunting is brought to light by the many family names that include a reference to dog or hound, especially a hunting dog. Some of them are CONANT "little hound," CONBOY "yellow hound," CONCANNON "fair-headed hound," CONROY "hound of the plain," CONWAY "yellow hunting dog," CARMODY "black hunting dog," CUNNIFF "black hound," GARY "hunting dog," GEARY "hunting dog," McADOO "black hound," McNAMEE "hound of Meath," McNIFF "black hound," and MADIGAN "dog." CONNERY is the "grandson of the dog keeper." Because of the affection for the hunting dog some of these names may refer to a house or inn sign, although few Irish names derive from house or inn signs. Hound was also used figuratively for a warrior or chieftain.

Irish saints enter into many Irish family names. KAVANAUGH and CAVANAUGH are descendants of Caomh or Caomhan "beautiful or noble," the names of fifteen Irish saints. CONNELLY refers to Conghalach "valorous," the name of seven saints revered by the Irish. HEANEY is the grandson of Eanna, an early saint. Corb or Cormac "the son of Corb" the name of eight saints produced the surnames, CORB, CORMAC, and McCORMICK.

Names beginning with mul, maol, kil or gil meaning "follower, servant, or devotee" are common. There are MULVIHILL "servant of St. Michael" and MULLANEY "devotee of St. Senan." MALONE and McLAIN were "servants of St. John," and MALLOY "servant of St. Aedh." There are KILKELLY "follower of St. Ceallach," the name of three Irish saints, and KILGALLEN "servant of St. Caillin." GILMORE is descended from the servant of Mary. COOLEY is from St. Mochuille. McGILL is an abbreviated form of surnames commencing with MacGiolla "son of the servant of . . . ." GILLEN and

GILLIGAN descend from the little servant. Other Irish names tha
begin with the words *giolla* or *maol* meaning "disciple or servant"
are GILCHRIST "servant of Christ," GILFOYLE "follower of St. Paul,"
and MacGILLICUDDY "son of the servant of Mochuda," an early
Irish saint of Lismore. Some of these Irish saints are local, no
recognized as such by the Roman Catholic hierarchy or are more
commonly known under different names. MALONEY was a grand
son of Maoldombnaigh "devoted to Sunday or to the Church."

Aodh "fire," the name of a pagan Irish deity, a common per
sonal name, is the etymon of several common Irish family names
such as EGAN, KEEGAN, KENNEY, MAGEE, McCOY, McCUE
McKENNA, MacGEE, MacKEY, McKEE, and MacKAY, the las
being a popular clan name in Scotland, also called Clann Aoidh
Some names from Aodh have been twisted into such spellings a
HAYES or HUGHES. How English can one get?

Even many names that started out as nicknames or occupa
tional names are really patronymics as indicated by early in
stances with the prefix *O* or *Mac*. The Irish were liberal in ap
plying descriptive nicknames to their neighbors and with the
addition of *Mac* or *O*, later dropped, they became patronymics
Some nicknames became personal names before becoming family
names. SHEEHAN is the grandson of little Siodhach "peaceful."
GALLAGHER descended from Gallchobhar "foreign helper." MAHEI
is the grandson of Meachar "hospitable." McELROY is the son of
the red youth. MULLIGAN, McMULLEN, and MULLEN descended
from Maolan, also spelled Maolagan, "little bald one." MILLIGAI
also refers to the grandson of "the little bald one." DAUGHERTY
descended from Dochartach "unfortunate." Other similar Irish
names are included in the chapter on nicknames.

A few Irish surnames have been changed little or not at all
from the personal names from which they are derived. MORAN,
having dropped the *O*, is the grandson of Moran "little great
man." CONNELL is the grandson of Conall "high powerful." RYAN
is the grandson of Rian "little king." FARRELL is the grandson
of Fearghal "super valor." An unusual name is McGRATH, also
spelled McGRAW, McCRAY, and McRAY, "the son of MacRaith,"
MacRaith meaning "son of grace or prosperity," the full form
including the *Mac* being the personal name.

Some Irish personal names derive from the animal kingdom.

88

Mathghamhain "bear" produced the family names MAHAN, MA-HONEY, and McMAHON. Faolan "little wolf" is the etymon of WHALEN and WHELAN. Drean "wren" brought forth DRAIN. Colum "dove" produced McCULLUM and McCALLUM. Art "bear or stone" produced the popular McCARTNEY.

Many present day Irish are descendants of English settlers and traders with English names, as a result of the Anglo-Norman invasion starting in 1172. Throughout the troubled years the Irish have translated or Englished their names, or have altered them in some way to give them an English appearance. The chief concession was the dropping of the *O* and *Mac*, although certain names, such as McADOO "son of Cudabh" and McNAMEE "son of Cumidhe," seldom lost the prefix. A name like McDANIEL refers to the son of Domhnall, not the son of the Old Testament character. Indeed, it will be seen from an inspection of the Irish names and the given names from which they were derived that almost everyone bears some alteration in capitulation to the overbearing influence of the English tongue. McDERMOTT is the son of Diarmaid "freeman" or of Dermot "free from envy." Some names do not look too Gaelic, as CARROLL, the grandson of Cearbhall "stag," BRADY, the grandson of Bradach "spirited," BYRNE, the grandson of Bran "raven," and DWYER, the grandson of Dubhodhar "black Odhar." However, the common names have a distinct Irish flavor that is unmistakable. In more modern times when they began to re-Gaelicize the names, they added *O* and *Mac*, sometimes to names that never had the prefix in early times.

Because of the complex nature of Irish surnames, their development from ancient Gaelic given names often of obscure origin, the Irish fondness for descriptive nicknames and diminutive pet forms, together with the changes and alterations due to transliteration and the oppression by the English, it is most difficult to set them out in any proper, classified outline. Emphasis has been placed on including the Irish surnames one encounters most frequently in America.

Closely allied to patronymical surnames are the Scottish clan names and names of septs and tribes. In the Highlands of Scotland, where family names became fixed much later than in the Lowlands and in England, it was the custom to take the name of the leader or head of the clan as the surname without reference to blood relationship. Taking the clan name was joining the clan, affirming allegiance with the clan chief. Septs and tribes allied themselves with the more powerful clans for protection. It has been estimated that about half of the clan names begin with *Mac*. Highlanders mixing with people in the Lowlands who were antagonistic changed or translated their names to acquire some protective coloring. Highlander McDONALD, for instance, translated his name to English DONALDSON. Others merely dropped the *Mac*.

Some Scottish surnames as in the similar Irish practice embody the term *gille*, an ancient Gaelic expression meaning "disciple, follower, or servant." Thus, GILLESPIE is *Gille* plus *easpuig* "bishop" meaning "servant of the bishop." McCLURE is "son of the servant of Odhar." Names of saints are coupled with *gille*. McCLINTOCK is the "son of the follower or servant of St. Findan"; both MacCLELLAN and GILLILAND mean the "son of the servant of St. Faolan (little wolf)." MacLEAN is the "son of the servant of St. John." MacLEISH designates the "son of the follower of Jesus."

Other common Scottish patronymics refer to the ancient Gaelic name of an early tribal leader. FINLAY derives from Fionnla "fair hero." MacDOUGALL derives from Dougal "black stranger"; MacKENZIE, from Coinneach "fair, bright"; McKINLEY, from Finlay "fair hero"; McKINNON, from Findgaine "fair-born"; McQUEEN, from Suibhne "good going" or from "son of the peaceful or quiet man"; and FERGUSON, from Fergus "manly strength or super choice." McRAE derives from Macrath "son of grace or prosperity," the full form including the *Mac* being the original given name. McMURRAY and McCAULEY are both Scottish and Irish, the first being the son of Muireadhach "belonging to the sea" and the latter being the son of Amlaib, a Scottish form of Olaf "ancestor's relic" or of Amhalghaidh, an ancient Irish name. Some of these ancient Gaelic names are most difficult to translate. The meanings were understood in ancient times, but have been obscured through the passage of time and the change in customs and use of language. McLEOD is the son of Leod "ugly." English and Scottish ARCHIBALD and the Scottish diminutive ARCHIE are from Old German Ercanbald "simple, bold."

Between 1272 and 1377 England had three kings named Edward "rich guardian" but this hundred years came too late to exert a great influence on surnames. EDWARDS is a Welsh surname, which became common by reason of the stabilization of family names in the seventeenth and eighteenth centuries in the principality. Ned and Ted are well-known as pet forms for Edward but the complete absence of Neds and Teds, Nedsons and Tedsons as surnames today reveals that these pet forms were not popular in the Middle Ages. DUARTE is the Portuguese and Spanish form of the name.

There are many Welsh family names that are quite common because at the time they were becoming hereditary they were mostly derived from only a few given names in common use. Welsh surnames did not become fixed until after 1542, the date when Parliament passed the Act which united England and Wales. The great majority of the Welsh people formed their surnames from the names of their fathers or grandfathers. LEWIS "hear, fight," VAUGHN "little," GRIFFITH "fierce lord," and MORGAN "great, bright" descended from forebears with those names. Griffith and Morgan were the names of Welsh princes during the Middle Ages. MADDOX and MADDOCKS derive from Madoc "fortunate." When the young pedant asked the country acquaintance, "Do you know mathematics?" the reply was, "No, I know Tom Maddicks and Will Maddicks, but I never heard tell of Mathy." Madoc was the name of a legendary Welsh prince credited by his countrymen with the discovery of America before Columbus— about 1170. However, the only evidence is the supposed discovery of a tribe of American Indians speaking Welsh.

MEREDITH, another Welsh prince, derives from Maredudd "sea lord." MORRIS is from Maurice, the Moorish or dark-skinned man. Morris was an early spelling of the given name now usually spelled Maurice. St. Maurice was martyred by the Romans in Switzerland in 287. BLEVINS comes from Bleddyn "little wolf," a popular early Welsh forename. ROWLAND descends from Roland "fame, land." OWENS and OWEN are the sons of Owen, a Welsh form of Eugene "well-born." FLOYD is a variant of Lloyd "gray." RHYS descended from Rhys "ardor, a rush," a name made famous by a great South Wales family. Rhys ap Tudor checked the Norman advance into South Wales. His grandson, Rhys ap Gruffydd, became so powerful that Henry II of England appointed him

King's Justiciar for Wales. From Rhys are derived the surnames of REECE, REESE, and RICE.

Many Spanish names are patronymics with the familiar -*ez* termination. A few of the more popular surnames are FERNANDEZ and HERNANDEZ from Fernando and Hernando both translating as "journey, venture"; GONZALEZ derives from Gundisalv "battle, elf"; LOPEZ, from Lope "wolf"; MARQUEZ, from Marcus "belonging to Mars"; MENDEZ, from Mendel "wisdom"; MUNOZ and NUNEZ, from Muno "hill" and Nuno "nine," respectively; ORTIZ, from Ordono "the fortunate"; RAMIREZ, from Ramon "wise protector"; and RODRIGUEZ, from Rodrigo "famous, rule." Rodrigo Diaz de Bivar, called El Cid Campeador, "The Lord Champion," famous for his exploits in the wars against the Moors in the eleventh century, is the great national hero of Spain, and the adventure tales about him influenced many parents to use his name. SANCHEZ is from Sancho "sanctified"; and SUAREZ is from Suero "family." GARCIA, the most common Spanish family name, is from Garcia, a Spanish form of Gerald "spear, firm." Some authorities translate it as "youth or prince." Garcia was King of Navarre (998–1001). CHAVEZ descends from a corruption of Spanish Jaime, Iago, Diego, or Jacobus "the supplanter, or may God protect." SANTANA commemorates Saint Anna. VIGIL is from Vigil, that is, one born on the feast of the nativity. MALDONADO designates the "son of Donald." MORALEZ derives from Moral "right and proper." VELAZQUEZ and VELASQUEZ and the shortened form VELEZ are all descendants of Bela "raven or crow."

There are numerous French surnames derived from the given name of some early ancestor. BOUDREAU is a diminutive form of Boudon "armed courier." BERTRAND "bright, raven" and DURAND "lasting" are descendants of forebears with these names. GAUTHIER derives from Gautier "rule, army." GILLETTE is not only a razor all over the world but is the name of an American who descended from little Giles, a variant of the Latin Aegidius "shield or protection." The meaning is appropriate because King Camp Gillette's razors are of the safety variety—with a shield for protection. GIRARD "spear, firm" comes from a given name with the same spelling, as does GIROUX "old man," although this latter name also derives from Girulf "spear, wolf." HARDY is a popular French, Scottish, and English surname, derived from Hardi, a pet form of Hardouin "bold, friend," found in various spellings in the different countries. It may be observed that many of these French surnames are derived from font names which are composed of Norman-French variants of the Old Germanic elements.

French MELIN is an aphetic form of Amelin "labor, bright." PACKARD, before becoming the name of a fine car, now extinct, was a family name from Bacard "combat, strong." REGNIER and REGNER are descendants of Raginhari "counsel, army," while RENAUD and RENAULT "counsel, judgment" come from the given name, Renaud, although some bearing these names had an ancestor who formerly lived in Renaix in Belgium. RODIN is a descendant of little Rod, a pet form of Girard "spear, firm," in the same way as ROSIN is a pet form of little Rose. However, ROSIN is also a German family name designating one who previously lived in Rosien, in Germany. SECORD comes from French Sicard "victory, hard" and THIBAULT is derived from Theudbald "people, bold." Although the French people speak a Romance language, many of their early personal names are Germanic due to the Norman influence.

Many Italian patronymics are formed from the second or final syllable of a given name plus a pet or diminutive ending. For example, BERTUCCI descends from little Berto "bright" which is a pet form of several names with that ending, such as Alberto and Gilberto. NARDI is the pet form of Leonardi "lion-like" and of Bernardi "bear, firm." PARRILLI, which often appears with other vowels at the end, is a descendant of little Parro, an abbreviation of Gasparro "treasure." POLITO is short for Ippolito "one who frees horses." RINELLA is derived from little Rina, a familiar form of Catrina or Caterina "pure." Some names can be formed by taking the diminutive ending and adding another diminutive ending. For example, MUSSOLINI may not be related to a gnat, but could be the "rear end of something" (Giacomusso perhaps?) plus a diminutive ending.

Some surnames are metronymics, referring to the son of the mother. This is a difficult subject. Several authorities have contended that such names indicate illegitimacy. While this is true in some cases, it falls far short of explaining numerous others. Sons of widows or children of parents where the dominant one is the mother are likely to become so known, as well as a child

93

adopted by a single woman or one who has been widowed. All the common female Christian names popular in the Middle Ages with their nickname forms can be found as actual or apparent etymons for surnames now in use in America. Many women's names are merely feminine forms of men's names, so some surnames derived from women's names are concealed by that fact since, in most cases, names that can be ascribed to either a feminine name or a masculine name have been interpreted as masculine.

From the beginning of the twelfth century Mary came into use in England and Europe as a popular girls' name. The true interpretation of Mary is a subject of controversy among the authorities. The three most probable theories are that it means "bitterness, wished-for child, or rebellion." From it in England comes the surname MARISON. From various diminutive forms there are derived the French and English MARION and the English MARRIOTT, MALLIN, MALKIN, and MALLETT, the latter name being also French. MARION may also be a diminutive of Latin Mario "belonging to the god Mars." MALLETT also derives from diminutive forms of names such as Malcolm, Malculf, and Maldred, as well as Maclou, a seventh century saint.

ALLISON "little Alice" is from the old forms of the name Alis, Alys, and Aliz "noble, kind"; and from that source it employs the French diminutive ending -on. But ALLISON may also be derived from Ellis "God is salvation" or from the Scottish "son of Allis," from Alexander or Alex "helper of mankind," in which cases the English -son would be the suffix. In some instances it is a slurring of Allanson. Even the surnames most certainly derived from a woman's name often have other origins from men's names. Some authorities have estimated that as many as ten percent of the "patronymic" names are derived from the names of women. Any reasonable proof, however, is impossible to obtain.

Matilda was the name of three queens of England during the Middle Ages, including the wife of the Conqueror. The Empress Matilda was the wife of Henry V, Holy Roman Emperor who died 1125. Stirred by these active women, Matilda "might, battle" became a very popular font name during the time surnames were becoming fixed family names. From the middle syllable came the pet form, Till, which produced such surnames as TILL, TILSON, and TILLOTSON. MADISON and MAUDE (from the pet form Maud) sometimes derive from Matilda.

Margaret, a venerated third-century saint, made the name a common one in medieval times. Miss Withycombe in her *The Oxford Dictionary of English Christian Names* ascribes Margaret's popularity to her last prayer, reported to be: "Hearken to my prayer, O God, and grant to every man who shall write my life or relate my works, or shall hear or read them, that his name be written in the book of eternal life, and whosoever shall build a church in my name, do not bring him to thy remembrance to punish him for his wrong-doing." Not all saints put away pride in their accomplishments. Several Margarets were queens in European countries during the Middle Ages. MARGESON designates the son of Margery, a pet form. From Magg, a nickname for Margaret, come the English surnames MAGGS and MOGGE. MARGOLIS is a Ukrainian and Russian Jewish family name derived from the Hebrew *margalit* "pearl." Margaret means "a pearl" and PEARL and PERLE are German and English surnames so derived. These last two names may be metonymic for a seller of pearls or designate one who came from Perl in Germany.

MAPP and MAPES in some cases derive from Mab, a pet form of Mabel or Amabel "lovable," girls' names in vogue in medieval times. In other cases they are variants of Welsh *map* "son." LIBBY is a Scottish, English, and German surname designating a descendant of Ibb, a pet form of Isabel "oath to Baal or oath to God." Florence "flourishing" was a common name for both men and women in the Middle Ages, and the surname, FLORENCE, when it does not designate one who came from Florence, Italy, refers to a descendant of a person so named. Joyce "joyful" was also used for both men and women in early times and the surname JOYCE is derived from it. Russian SORKIN refers to a descendant of Sorkeh, a pet form of Sarah "princess." SIBLEY is a descendant of Sibley, an English pet form of Sibyl "prophetess." French CATLIN and CATRON are from pet forms of Catherine "pure." TRUDEAU, the family name of the Prime Minister of Canada, denotes descent from little Troude, a pet form of Gertrude "spear, strength," although in some cases it derives from a pet form of Thorvald "Thor's power."

During the surname period Agnes "pure" was one of the most

95

popular girls' names. St. Agnes was a revered fourth-century saint, the patron saint of young maidens who might through certain rituals on St. Agnes Eve (Jan. 20) see the visage of their future husbands. The name was usually pronounced and spelled without the g and ANNES and ANNIS are the chief surnames derived from it. Ann was the pet form of Agnes during the surname epoch, and produced such forms as ANNOT and ANSON. Anne, the western form of the Hebrew Hannah, was quite rare as a girl's name during the period. Edith "richness, gift" survived the Norman Conquest due possibly to the popularity of St. Eadgyth (d. 984), daughter of King Edgar. The full name does not seem to be the basis of any surnames, but the pet forms Ede and Eda may have influenced such surnames as EADIE, EADS, EADY, and EDDY, although most of these names undoubtedly owe their origin to men's names commencing with Ead "richness," as explained earlier in this chapter.

Certain unusual surnames commemorate the fact that some people gave their children names with reference to some festival, holy day, event, or period of time usually commemorating the day of birth. Children born on a holy day might be called HOLIDAY, HALIDAY, HOLLIDAY, HALLIDAY, or HOLEDAY which developed into hereditary family names. One born on Sunday would give rise to the Italian surnames DI DOMENICO, DOMINICK, and DOMENICO. RAMOS is a descendant of Ramos "palms," a name given during the religious fiesta of Palm Sunday. However, RAMOS sometimes is from Ramos "branch," a small town in Spain. Children arriving on December 25th would bring about such names as NOEL, CHRISTMAS, YULE, and even MIDWINTER, a term sometimes applied to the Christmas season, all of which became fixed surnames.

In December, newspapers are wont to exhibit pictures of girls bearing the name Merry Christmas. They are eligible even if they spell their name Merrie, or even Mary. Some even quote the girl as liking her unusual name saying that it is a wonderful conversation piece. Don't they ever get tired of the conversation? As long as the girl is single, she can count on attention once a year during the happy Yuletide season, to coin a hackneyed phrase. Some boys are even named Merry Christmas. Christmas is not a particularly uncommon surname. It may be found in any large city directory.

Birth on PENTECOST (seventh Sunday after Easter) would produce that name, and birth on Epiphany (January 6th) would in some cases eventually bring about TIFFANY, as a family name, although Tiffany is also a pet form of Theophania "manifestation of God." Birth at Easter would cause babies to be so named, such as ASTOR, EASTER, PACE, PACK, PASCAL, PASCO, PASKE, PASS, and PATCH, and these names became family names. Children born in the month of MARCH would sometimes be so named and eventually produce the surname MARZULLO in Italy or MARZEC in Poland. Similar birth in May would produce MAJEWSKI in Poland and MAGGIO in Italy. English children born on Monday might be so christened and produce the surnames MONDAY and MUNDY. Names like MIDNIGHT and MIDDAY call attention to the hour of birth. All of these names thus eventually became family names without change.

There are many popular American surnames that while they do not defy classification do require a tedious outline to include all of them. Some of them will therefore be briefly mentioned here. ADRIAN "of the Adriatic" became a popular name because it was adopted by Nicholas Breakspear in 1154, the only Englishman ever to become pope. BALDWIN "bold, friend," a Flemish name, was common both before and after the Conquest. BARRETT denotes the descendant of Barret from Germanic Beroald, "bear, rule" or from Old French *barat* "commerce or trouble." The name was introduced into England by the Normans. BRANSON is the son of Brand "sword," sometimes a pet form of Hildebrand "battle, sword." BRIGHT is both English and German from Old German *beorht* "bright." GARNER is a descendant of Garner or Warner "protection, warrior," although sometimes it is a softening of GARDNER, the occupational name. VARNER is a French form. REYNOLDS is a variant of Reginald or Regenweald "counsel, force." SERLIN is a diminutive form of Serle "armor." WOOLRIDGE is not a place name but denotes a descendant of Ulrich "wolf, rule."

EWING and EWEN are descendants of Ewen, a corruption of Eugene "well-born." OTIS comes from Old English Odo "prosperity." AMES is the son of Ame or Amis "friend," but in some cases it is from Old English *eam* "uncle," thus meaning "son of the

uncle" or cousin. ESTES is the son of East "easterly" or Est "gracious." BUGG and BUGGS are not completely obsolete being descendants of Old English Buga or Bugga "to stoop" although some
with these names have changed them in recent times. RUFFIN is a
descendant of Rufinus "red," the name of several saints and
martyrs.

French COLOMB, Italian COLOMBO, and Spanish COLON are all
descendants of Columba "dove." St. Columba in the sixth century
was the apostle of the Picts. The name is related to Columbus
regarded by most Americans as the discoverer of their homeland.
Sometimes these surnames derive from one who raised and sold
doves.

Some other German names prevalent in America must be mentioned here. ARENDS is a descendant of Arend "eagle, rule."
BARUCH comes directly from Baruch "blessed"; BERKSON from the
pet form Berk is both German and English; and BERKOWITZ from
the pet form Berko is the Polish form. CAPEHART is an American
variant of the German personal name Gebhardt "gift, brave."
ELLMAN descended from Hellmann when the name does not
refer to the stranger who came from Germany. FAUBUS is from
Phoebus "bright." ROSEN, from German "roses" refers to a descendant of Rose "horse or rose." WIMMER is a descendant of
Winimar "friend, famous." VOLKMAN is from Folcman "people,
servant."

Stanislaw "camp, glorious" is a very popular Polish given name.
Stanislaw, Bishop of Krakow in the eleventh century, is the patron
saint of Poland. Pet forms of this name are STACHNIK, STANEK,
STANKO, and STANKUS, and all of them have become popular family names. STANKIEWICZ is the son of Stanko. STACH is an augmentative and may be interpreted as a descendant of big Stanislaw.
Russian SLAVIN is the son of Slav "glory," a pet form of names
terminating with this word. WIENCEK is a diminutive form of
WIENCYSLAW "more glorious than his parents," another given
name well liked in Poland. WOJCIECH is a Polish form of Voitech
"noble, bright," a Czech missionary who converted Poland to
Christianity. The Polish form became a family name without
change. From a diminutive of the name comes WOJCIK and from
an augmentative comes WOJTAS. MIKA descended from Mika, a
Polish pet form for Marika (Mary).

Surnames from Father's Name

Since the following names derived from given names or pet forms are interesting and possibly give some insight to Slavic thought, they are here included even though some are not frequently encountered in this country. There are BLAZEK, a pet form of Blasius "babbler," LEBOVITZ from Leyba "life," MRAZ from Mraz "frost," and PROKOP from Prokop "progressive." The given name Sawa "desire" has produced such Slavic surnames as SAWA, SAWICKI, SAWIN, and SAWINSKI. Bogdan "gift of God," a popular given name, has given rise to BOGDAN, BOGDANOWICZ, and BOGDANOVICH. Ukrainian SYDORUK is the son of Sydor "gift of Isis." Urban "city" is a given name that has produced the Polish family names URBANSKI and URBANEK. English URBAN also descended from Urban or Latin Urbanus.

3

SURNAMES FROM OCCUPATION
OR OFFICE

*Overseers—Manor officials—Smith—Miller—Forester—Manor servants—Carter
—Messenger—Shepard—City occupations—Names from land tilled—Taylor—
Shoemaker—Occupations in the woolen industry—In food industry—Hunting
—Fishing—Leather—Stone—Merchants—Music and carnival—Coining money—
Watchmen—Metal industry—Roofing—Rope—Books—Ecclesiastical offices—
Fighting—Miscellaneous occupations.*

MAN WORKS eight hours a day in order to make his living, sleeps and rests eight hours, and devotes the remaining eight hours to eating, minor chores, and recreation, although part of this latter period may be expended in traveling to and from work. Since man's work involves such a large portion of his life, it must be taken into account in any adequate system of identification. In many directories men are more definitely identified by listing their occupation. The ordinary pursuits during the Middle Ages have become some of the most common surnames in the United States. In order of frequency they are, in America, SMITH, MILLER, TAYLOR, CLARK, WALKER, WRIGHT, BAKER, CARTER, STEW-

100

ART, TURNER, PARKER, COOK, and COOPER. These are the ordinary occupations in which men engaged during medieval times. When translated into other European languages they make other popular American family names.

Many English and German occupational surnames end with the agential suffix -*er* normally used to make agent-nouns from verbs; many others terminate in -*man* or -*mann*. These endings do not necessarily point to occupational names alone as they are also frequently found in toponymical surnames and nicknames. It must be remembered that the man who crafted an object commonly also sold it at retail. There were few middlemen.

In many cases it is not easy to distinguish between occupation and office. For example, the SMITH might be either the king's smith, an important official, or merely one who plied the trade from a shop in his home for the benefit of the peasants. The STEWART might be the king's seneschal, the keeper of the royal household, an important public official. Other stewards might be merely servants in charge of a manor on behalf of an absent lord. Ecclesiastical officers are discussed at page 130.

In earlier times most men lived in small villages or country manors where they made their living from the soil. The larger villages were just starting to develop into towns and cities in England as men returned from the Crusades, yet there were several large cities on the continent of Europe. In England, in the eleventh century, with a total population of less than two million, it is estimated that London had only about 40,000 with York and Bristol next with about 12,000 each. Consequently the occupations of men in the country manors who worked the land for the lords tended to be somewhat different from city crafts and trades.

A manor, during the centuries surnames became stable, might have had about two or three hundred persons living on it, most of whom worked strips in the two or three large fields of the manor to produce their food. The manor would be owned by the king, an important noble who held it of the king, or by a religious house, or even by a freeman who held it, perhaps, of a mesne tenant who in turn held it of a noble or churchman or who even attorned only to the king. The tenants would be of three kinds, (1) the freeholders who worked substantial land for which they paid a money rent which freed them of most, but not all, services to the lord, (2) the villeins or serfs who cultivated about thirty acres for which they worked for the lord two or three days a week, and (3) the cotters who held smaller plots and worked shorter periods for the lord. Villeins and cotters were often manor servants.

In the center of the manor would be found the church and the hall. The latter building was the principal residence, which would be occupied by the lord of the manor or, in his absence, by his principal overseer. Around these two buildings would be grouped the rude houses or cots of the inhabitants. As overseers usually enjoyed a higher rank, their occupations first appeared as recorded descriptions in manor accounts and church rolls, and then tended to become hereditary family names which they were content to retain.

For example, the STEWARD or BAILIFF was the steward of the manor or of several manors or manager of an estate, whose duty it was to protect the lord's interests and preside at the hallmote or manor court in the absence of the lord, dispensing justice among the serfs. In many cases these stewards were important officers of royal and noble households. The New English Dictionary says that the word "steward" from Old English *stigweard* refers to a house or some part of a house and that there is no ground for the assumption, as some have thought, that it meant "keeper of pig sties." The Lord High Steward of Scotland was the chief officer of the Scottish king in early times. STUART is the French form of the name. John Stewart, Lord of Kyle, became Robert III, King of Scotland in 1306. But the name is no proof of royal descent as evidenced by the remark of James VI when he exclaimed, "All Stewarts are not sib to the king."

The principal officers in charge of the large and important households in Germany were the MAIER, MEYER, MEIER, or MYER, common spellings often found with the -s termination, especially as MEYERS and MYERS. These were head servants. Later, the term also designated a substantial farmer. MAYER, occasionally spelled MAYOR, MEYER, and MEIER, was also an English name, the mayor of a borough or town who often held the office for life. Henry Fitz Ailwin became the first mayor of London about 1193. VOGT was a German overseer or manager of a household. SCHAFFNER was also an important official, the manager or steward of a German estate. HOFFMAN worked a large farm either as owner or manager; HOFMEISTER was a steward or chief servant. OBERMAN, WERCKMEISTER, and KAMMERER were supervisors or foremen. SCHULTZ and SCHOLZ with their various spellings were German magistrates or sheriffs, also overseers. FACTOR managed the business or estate of another. GRAFF, sometimes shortened to GRAF, was an overseer in the lord's establishment, also in some cases having the connotation of a mayor of a village, a judge, or even a noble.

In Poland, MARSZALEK was the officer in charge of military affairs in the household of a medieval king, prince, or noble. SENN was the headman of a Swiss Alpine dairy farm. In Greece, ECONOMOS managed a large household. LEMAITRE was a French overseer or head servant. Russian KORELEV was an important functionary in a king's household. Many highly skilled and specialized craftsmen were employed by the kings and great nobles.

It is not to be wondered at that an undue number of surnames are derived from positions as overseers of the work of the serfs. When these underlings received little or no pay for their toil on the lord's demesne, they were not likely to do their work quickly and efficiently, and constant supervision was necessary. The principal officers who performed this supervisory duty for the lords were naturally better paid than the serfs and occupied positions of respect in the community. Various lesser positions involving some supervision or responsibility also created surnames.

The serfs in the English manors usually elected one of their number annually to oversee their work for the lord (and you can be sure that he had also to satisfy the lord), and from this official the surnames REEVE and REAVES are derived. In the north of England he was called a GRAVE, a name related to the German Graff, but which did not attain the higher status that it did in Germany. Sometimes an *s* is added for phonetic reasons to make GRAVES, and the bearer has nothing to do with places of burial. Other titles for the same office are PROVOST and PRATER. Sometimes the servant in charge of the fields and intrusted with the responsibility of overseeing the reapers and mowers was called a MESSER. The GRANGER, in Scotland, had charge of the manor house with its outbuildings; in England he had charge of a barn

103

or farm. The shire-reeve was the chief civil officer of the Crown in the county, the SHREVE or SHERIFF.

To understand better the country surnames that arose on the English manors it might be well to look at the usual occupations. Perhaps the two most important men who served both the lord and the peasants were the smith and the miller, which produced the ubiquitous SMITH and MILLER. It was Verstegan, writing in 1605, who quoted,

> From whence came Smith, all be he knight or squyre,
> But from the Smith, that forgeth at the fyre.

On the manor the smith's duty was to shoe the lord's horses, mend and sharpen his plows, and make all the small and large metal objects required. For this he received certain perquisites from the lord such as charcoal and wood from the lord's forest and the right to have his land plowed by the lord's plows. He also did work for the serfs in the manor from whom he received payment in produce or in money. Henry II, of England in 1181, ordered every holder of a knight's fee (land worth £10 a year) to provide himself with a coat of mail, a helmet, a shield, and a lance. Many smiths were required to make these articles besides the plows and other articles the peasants needed. The earliest spelling of the word was smith or smithe, then in the fourteenth to seventeenth centuries the universal spellings were smyth and smythe. In the eighteenth century the common spelling reverted to smith, and that is the usual spelling of the family name today.

The smith as a worker in metals was important in every country. In the Bible, God says, "Behold, I have created the smith that bloweth the coals in the fire, and that bringeth forth an instrument for his work" (Isaiah 54:16). Many surnames in America have been translated to SMITH from many different languages. The common German forms of the surname are SCHMIDT, SCHMITZ, and SCHMITT. SCHMITH is the Smith undecided whether he wants to be German or English. Low German and Dutch forms are SMIT, DESMET, and SMIDT. Gaelic names are GOW, GOWAN, and GOFF. Various French names, mostly influenced by the Latin *Faber*, are FAURE, FERNALD, FERRIS, Le FEVRE, and Le FEBVRE. TAILLANDIER made and sold iron objects in France, also acted as a cutter or tailor of clothing; the name is fairly common in France but rare in the United States—it is just not right for Americans. From Italy the name for the smith is FERRARO; from Spain, FERRER and HERRERA; from Syria, HADDAD; from Finland, SEPPANEN; and from Hungary, KOVACS. In the Slavic countries many names beginning with *K* designate the worker in metals, chiefly iron. The common Russian names are KOWALSKY and KUZNETSOV. The Polish names are KOVALIK, KOWALCZYK, and KOWALSKI. Czechoslovakia uses KOVAR and KOVARIK, and Lithuania has the form KALVAITIS. Several countries recognize the smith as KOVAC.

Some occupational names one might expect to exist can yet be observed in our directories; others cannot be found now. Before the author's marriage he noted that the KISER, KISS, KISSMAN, and CUSSER, from Old French *cuisse* "thigh," made cushes or armor for the thighs. There should, he reasoned, be a Kissmith since so many similar names terminated in -*smith*, and he persuaded his affianced to make a search in various telephone directories. The name was not found, and if it ever existed, it apparently became obsolete. However, in many cases thigh armor was made of heavy leather in which the smith, who worked in metals, would not be employed.

MARSHALL originally cared for the lord's horses, treated their diseases, and shod them, a shoeing smith or farrier. Later the word developed into a name for an official in a king's or great noble's household having charge of military affairs and the title frequently became hereditary. The marshall is the highest ranking officer in the French army, and under the form Field Marshall is the top officer in the British army. MARTELL, when not a hypocoristic form of Martin, used a hammer in the smithy, although the name is sometimes a nickname for a warrior, one who wielded the mace or spiked hammer of medieval warfare. BLOWERS helped the smith at the forge with the bellows. STAHL, in Germany, worked with steel.

Smiths needed good fuel. MINOR and MINER dug coal and also excavated other minerals. COLLIER mined and dealt in coal, or made charcoal, as did BERNER and BRENNER. In Germany, KOEHLER and KOHLER burned charcoal. WEGLARZ in Poland and CARBONE in Italy were coal miners. ARQUILLA operated a kiln in Spain. RUDNICK in Poland and HORNIK in Czechoslovakia worked in the mines. French MÉNIER was a miner. English GROVER was

a lead miner. Mining for lead was carried on long before co;
mining became important.

Most manors were situated on or near a stream where wa
located a mill operated on behalf of the lord by the MILLER c
MILNER, sometimes called the MILLWARD which was usually co1
rupted to MILLARD. The serfs in both England and France wer
required to have their grain ground at the lord's mill. Each se1
had to pay the miller for his services by leaving a portion of th
grain. Medieval records disclose a tendency on the part of mille1
to substitute grain of poor quality for the good grain they wer
given to grind. Millers thus as a group were not popular, althoug
many were among the most considerable men of the villag
Every cluster of settlements throughout Europe needed a mille
In Germany the form was MOLLER, MUELLER, MOELLER, or MU1
LER; in France it was MOULIN, MOULINIER, MEUNIER, or MOL1
NEAUX. The Czechoslovakian forms of the name are MLYNA1
MLYNEK, and MELNICK, while in Hungary it is MOLNAR. MELNIKO
is the Russian name with the same connotation. Italians nam
them FARINA and MOLINARI, and the Dutch use MULDER. MIL1
MAN was the English miller's servant helping with the operatio
of the mill.

There were various minor servants who served both the lo1
of the manor and his serfs. These men usually did not fan
enough land to support themselves and their families and wer
thus forced to work for others. Some did so little work for th
lord that he was glad to release them upon payment of a sma
money rent and they expended all their time in work for other
PLOWMAN and AKERMAN or ACKERMAN plowed the lands of th
lord as well as that of the peasants. The acre really denoted th
ager or land open to tillage—not a definite measure. PFLUEGE
plowed the lord's lands in Germany, and, in Poland, SKIBA desi
nated a plowman, by referring to the strip of soil thrown up b
the plow. The Slavic term for the man who used the old woode
plow was SOCHA. The Dutch VANDERPLOEG followed the plov
The German who worked by the day was HEISLER; HERBS
worked for the lord in harvesting the crops. MANNERS was
servant or domestic in a manor. Sometimes, though, MANNEF
refers merely to the man who came from the nearby manor.

Forests or woods were always within the immediate confines of the manor or nearby. They belonged to the lord who received fees from the serfs for allowing them to gather firewood or use timber in building or repairing their houses. As the inhabitants of the village had few compunctions against trespassing on the lord's preserves, forest wardens or gamekeepers were required. In many manors the serf could take all dry wood lying on the ground as well as any he could knock down with poles or hooks; this gave us the phrase "by hook or by crook." In England the forest wardens might be called FORSTER, FORESTER, FOSTER, FROST, WOODWARD, WOODRUFF, or WOODMAN. A mounted guardian of the forest would be RIDER or RYDER. If he had charge of the lord's park, an enclosed forest or woods, the name might become PARKER or PARKMAN; WARREN and WARNER were employed to watch over the game in a park. WARNER also designates the descendant of Warner "protecting warrior," an Old English personal name. The Irish gamekeeper might be named FORRISTALL, and the French counterpart would be VERDIER. There were many woods in Germany belonging to the estates of the nobility and the guardians would be called FOERSTER, HEINTZLEMAN, or HEINEMANN. If they just took care of the shrubs or bushes, the name might be STOUDEMIRE or STAUDENMAIER. LESNIK in Czechoslovakia was a forest keeper.

Some servants who worked for the serfs as well as the lord were, in some manors, elected by them. There was the HAYWARD or HAYMAN who had nothing to do with hay but who had charge of the hedges or fences, protected the cultivated land, and impounded straying cattle found damaging the lord's fields. He also often supervised the plows and harrows and assisted the reeve. In France, he was DELAGE, and in Germany, HECKMANN. MOORMAN had charge of the cattle on the moors or waste ground, except in those cases where he acquired the name simply by residence on the moor. The DAY, DEY, DEGMAN, or WICKMAN was the servant who worked in the dairy, caretaker of the cows and a maker of cheese and butter. The word also meant a kneader of bread, a bread-baker. The dey in early times was a female servant but the term was applied later to men. As surnames could be acquired from the given name of the mother, they could also be acquired from the occupation of the mother, and some with the name of Day undoubtedly descended from a mother who made her living from working in a dairy.

As many manors were often owned by one lord, it was necessary to have a CARTER, PORTER, or LEADER to transport produce from one place to another by awkward carts which were usually two-wheeled affairs with high sides, drawn by two animals not necessarily horses. No matter how badly wounded or sick he was, no baron or knight, conscious of his station in life, would consent to ride in a cart; if not able to ride horseback, he might be conveyed on a litter between two horses. SANDLER carted sand or gravel, except in some instances where he was a cobbler, one who repaired shoes. The DRIVER in England and HOTCHNER in England and Scotland drove cattle to distant markets. BOYER was a drover of cattle in France. German SCHROEDER drove a dray, a drayman. The WAGNER or WAINER drove a wagon or cart, or made these conveyances. KERNER and KARNER are the German forms; the French name is CHARTIER; and the Hungarian form is KOZSIS. In Italy, FARINELLA conveyed flour from the mill to the home.

When telephones and postal services were non-existent the king, nobles, and others required messengers to carry their letters. In England they were called MESSENGER or TROTTER, the latter from Old French *trotier* "runner," both names being also Scottish. HEROLD or HERALD delivered formal proclamations for the sovereign or military commander. LIGHTFOOT, another name for the swift courier, was a messenger. ANGEL was a religious messenger, an emissary from God. This name, however, can also signify a descendant of one named Angel, or one thought to have an angelic disposition, or a dweller at an angle or corner, thus being capable of correct listing in all four categories of family names. The runner who carried messages on foot or horseback in England and Holland was RENNER. In the Ukraine HAJDUK was the footman or messenger in Cossack uniform. HICKENLOOPER was the Dutch battle runner. When Bourke Blakemore Hickenlooper, former Governor of Iowa and Senator, was running for office he found his name to be a political asset, and employed it in his campaign. "See here," a gaunt, elderly countryman approached him after a rural crossroads speech, "I'd like to know just what your name is. I heard you tell it three times. My wife says that

I'm a mite hard of hearing and maybe I am. But every time I heard you, it sounded just like Hickenlooper."

Between the times a civilization eliminates slaves and turns to labor-saving machinery a host of paid servants is necessary to cater to the needs and desires of the upper classes. People who owe their surnames to an ancestor who was a servant are found everywhere and several have already been mentioned. There are many names designating a servant without in any way indicating his duties. Irish CODY is the helper or assistant. The English LADD, LACKEY, MANN, and SWAIN were general servants. German servants were DIENER, FOLGER, KNECHT, ROBACK, SCHALL, and SCHALK. HINES and HYNES were English domestic servants. Young male servants in English noble houses were PAGE or PAIGE and PADGETT. They stood behind the lord holding his cup, a position sought after by sons of the lower nobility. The number with these names reflect the honorable position of the page. PRENTICE is the young man bound through indenture to a master craftsman to learn a trade, an apprentice; in Germany the term is GESELL.

As *mann,* or *man,* is the general Germanic term for a vassal or human being, the word is frequently found as a termination in surnames with the connotation of servant, vassal, or follower in England and Germany. Many names ending in *-man,* the first element of which is a forename, originally designated the servant or assistant of that person. For example, there is ADELMAN, the servant of Adal or Edel; BATEMAN and BATMAN, the servant of Bartholomew; GILMAN, the servant of Gill or Gilbert; GOLDMAN, the servant of Gold or Golda; HARDIMAN, Hardy's man; HARRIMAN, Harry's servant; HITCHMAN and RICHMAN, the servant of Hitch or Hick or Rich, pet forms of Richard; JACKMAN, the servant of Jack; LIPMAN, the servant of Lipp, a pet form of Phillip; and WATERMAN, the servant of Walter. In Holland, FEIKEMA was the servant of Feike.

In other combinations the termination designates just a general servant. TALLMAN was not particularly tall, but was the able, obedient servant, from Middle English *tal* "obedient." BURMAN was the servant of the peasant. LANDSMAN tended the open wood. ERDMANN was a land worker or farmer. FELDMAN worked in a German field or open country. HALLMAN was a general servant in the hall or manor house. In Germany, JUNGMANN or YOUNGMAN was the young servant; ALTMAN was the old servant. CARL has the meaning of man, particularly a countryman or husbandman, a fellow of low birth.

Where the herdsman kept the animals was important. In some places the lord had the unrestricted right to the manure of his own herds and sometimes had the right to fold all the animals of the peasants. To accomplish the best results the shepherd had the duty of moving the flocks around from place to place on the lord's demesne. Names derived from the general occupation of a herdsman in England are HEARD, HURD, and HERDMAN. In Holland the name is HERTER; OVCIK in Czechoslovakia; PASTEUR in France; PASTORE in Italy; VERGARA in Spain; SENER in Switzerland; HARDER in both England and Germany; and VLAHOS in Greece. POUNDS and POUND had charge of the animals in an enclosure, except in some instances where these names denominate the men living near the pound or enclosure for animals.

Those who tended the sheep of the villagers as well as those of the lord in England might be SHEPHERD or SHIPMAN, a functionary generally chosen by the villagers. They might also be called WEATHERS. BARKER, when not a tanner, is from Old French barker "shepherd." German shepherds might give rise to the surnames SCHAEFER, SHAFER, SHAFFER, and SHAVER. This name can be spelled in many ways but the most common one in the United States is Schaefer followed closely by Shaffer. In France, BERGER means a shepherd, while PECORA is the Italian name. In Spain, VAZQUEZ, VASQUEZ, and VELEZ designate those who herded ewes or sheep, although some with the first two forms of the name came from the Basque country. COULTER tended colts, and STEDMAN and STODDARD had the care of horses or oxen in England. FOREMAN or FORMAN was often the swineherd who tended the pigs, from Old English for "pig," although in some places he was an overseer of the serfs. BACON was also a swineherd at the time the word meant a live pig; in other cases he was a bacon or lard dealer. BOUVIER took care of cattle in France. In England the COWHERD, or COWARD as the name might be pronounced, tended the cows. In Ireland, the name LEARY designates the descendant of one who herded calves. CALVERT tended calves in England where BULLARD kept the bulls. Polish BYCZEK took care of young bulls. Cows were tended by KROWA in Poland, SCHWEIGER in Germany, and VACCARO in Italy. Goats were handled by SHIVERS, from French *chevrier* "goatherd"; by KOZA, KOZAK, and KOZEL in Czechoslovakia and Poland; and by KOZLOWSKY in Russia.

On the estates of the king or wealthy nobles many servants were required whose specific duties were means of identification which developed into hereditary family names. The officer in charge of the private household was the CHAMBERLAIN, who, like the steward, developed into an important public official. CHALMERS was a Scottish, and CHAMBERS an English, overseer in such a household although this official sometimes served only as a chamber attendant or valet. The BUTLER was often a head servant, the bottler in charge of the butts or casks of wine, sometimes an officer of high rank. PAINTER or PANTER was the title of the official in charge of bread, a pantry-keeper. In a monastery he had charge of the distribution of bread to the poor. SPENCER, SPENCE, LARDNER, PURVIS, and STORER were the ones who dispensed the provisions generally. KELLER and KELLNER did this work in Germany. NAPIER had charge of the napery or table linen. EWERS supplied guests at the table with water to wash their hands—before table forks were invented they merely used their hands. In the *Boke of Kervynge* is the injunction, "Set never on fyshe, beest, ne fowle, more than two fyngers and a thumbe." The USHER was the doorkeeper, the one who had charge of the door of the king's apartment. The flower and vegetable gardens were cultivated by the GARDNER, GARDINER, or GARTNER in England, by the RACINE in France, and by the ZAHRADNIK in Czechoslovakia.

The lord's oven, or the communal oven, in charge of the BAKER, was the place where the villagers cooked their food. The bakers, like the millers, were full of crafty tricks for swindling their neighbors. In many places in both England and France the peasants were fined for not baking at the lord's oven. When the great oven was hot, a bell was rung to inform the villagers to bring their bread to be baked. The public baker was well known in the towns. The feminine form of baker is sometimes spelled BAXTER, although most bakesters were men. The French names for the men who operated the public ovens are BOULANGER, BULLINGER, DUFOUR and FOURNIER. PFISTER and BECKER are the German breadmakers. PIEKARZ is the Polish baker, while PEKAR does the same for the Czechs and Slovaks. KUCHENBECKER baked cakes in Germany.

Men who cut and sold meat were prominent everywhere and there are many family names which reveal the ancestor who was a village BUTCHER, the common English surname. In England KELLOGG slaughtered hogs and KNATCHBULL cut up and sold meat. Perhaps this latter name arose as a nickname for the man who slaughtered the bull by knocking it on the head to kill it, from Middle English *knatch* "to knock." FLESHER, the dealer in flesh, has been absorbed by FLETCHER, the arrow maker. German surnames for one who cut meat are FLEISCHER, FLEISCHHAUER, FLEISCHMAN, METZGER, SCHECHTER, and SLAGER. RAUCH smoked meats. In France where the Gauls were great eaters of meat, especially pork, butchers were respected and became prominent tradesmen whose wealth often enabled them to hire servants to cut up and sell the meat, and there the surname is BOUCHER. Czechoslovakian butchers are MASEK, MASARYK, and REZNICK. RESNICK is a common Slavic form, especially for one who slaughtered animals for meat in compliance with Jewish ritual. SCHACHTER is the Hebraic, ritualistic slaughterer of meat animals.

It is, of course, impossible to separate the country occupations entirely from those more prevalent in the cities or larger towns. Most of those discussed previously in this chapter can be described as country or manorial pursuits. The majority of the occupations described in the balance of this chapter might be termed city occupations, but may also be found here and there in a small village or in the outlying estates of rich nobles. In the larger towns the occupations were more specialized. The smith was a GOLDSMITH, NAYSMITH or NAYLOR "nail maker," or WHITESMITH "tinsmith," often not just a smith. Occupants of a town were usually free men engaged in a trade or industry. Towns had markets; villages did not. One who lived in a town as compared to one in an outlying village might be designated BURGER in England, or BOURGEOIS in France; they were townsmen. BURGER and BOURGEOIS might be better labeled as nicknames rather than occupational names.

In the manors and small villages the cottages of the serfs were simple in construction and as their erection did not usually require the services of a skilled CARPENTER, the peasant himself ordinarily built them. Some had the aid of the local carpenter if there were one in the neighborhood. But it was in the cities and wealthy estates where the buildings were more substantial that skilled woodworkers were required. The French CARPENTIER or CHARPENTIER often went to the forest to cut and gather his own wood. Another important surname arising from the early English worker in wood is the Anglo-Saxon WRIGHT. (CARPENTER is an English name from the French language.) Other names are JOINER and JOYNER, more particularly for those expert craftsmen who did woodwork for the interiors of houses, ships, etc., by joining pieces of timber by mortise and tenon and by panels fitted in grooves, all without nails. BOARDMAN and SAWYER cut timber into boards. CARVER was usually a wood carver or cutter, although some carved in stone. The German woodworkers are SCHREINER, SHRINER, TIMMERMAN, and ZIMMERMAN. The Dutch worker who cut timber into boards is ZAGAR. The Czechoslovakian forms for carpenter are KOLAR, TESAR, and TRUHLAR. In Poland the name is CIESLAK, in Lithuania DAILIDE, in Hungary ASZTALOS, and in the Ukraine TESLENKO. Italian MARTELLO designates the carpenter, that is, one who worked with a hammer.

Closely allied to the carpenter's work are the men who made wheels and wheeled vehicles. The WHEELER and WHEELWRIGHT may have specialized in making the wheels. The WAINWRIGHT made wagons and the CARTWRIGHT made carts, both active in English communities long before wheeled vehicles consisted of autos and trucks. RADERMACHER and WEGNER did the same for Germans, and KOLODZIEJ made wheeled vehicles for Poles.

The universal use of ale, beer, and wines in the Middle Ages by people of all classes made a considerable need for the maker of casks, tubs, and barrels in which to store the liquid refreshments. The usual English surname with this meaning is COOPER sometimes spelled COWPER. Others are TUBBS, TUPPER, HOOPER, HOOPS, COOPERMAN, and COOPERSMITH. Cooper and its compounds cross with COPPER, the maker of copper utensils, and its similar compounds. German makers of casks and barrels produced the following surnames: BENDER, BITTNER, BOETTCHER, BUETTNER, KIEFER, and SCHEFFLER. KIEFER in some places was the servant who had charge of the wine cellar. Franch COVIER was a cooper. From the Slavic countries have come the following names for a cooper: BECVAR, BEDNARCZYK, BEDNAREK, BEDNARZ, and KADOW. KUBILIUS and KUBILUNAS "son of the tubmaker" made tubs in Lithuania, while the Dutch worker was called KUYPER, and the Frenchman, TONNELLIER.

To make round objects either of wood or of clay a lathe or potter's wheel was necessary, and they have been in existence in one form or another from remote antiquity. There were many who fashioned objects on a lathe in England and the very common name TURNER amply evidences the fact. TURNER derives from Old French *tornour* but the surname, unlike Barbour, does not have the ending *-our*. Many in Germany worked industriously at the lathe and the following surnames have this connotation: DREXEL, DREYER, KREISLER, SPIES, and TRAXLER. Some named SPIES came originally from Spies in Germany. The Polish turner was called TOKARZ. Similar to the turner in his work was the POTTER or CROCKER who made utensils of earthenware or metal. Other English names for one who made concave vessels or bowls were BOWLES, BOWLER, and BOLLER. The German form for the artisan who fashioned pottery was HAFNER or HEFFNER. The similar Czechoslovakian name is HRNCIR. German KRIEGER made and sold jugs or drinking vessels; in some cases he was an innkeeper.

The manufacture of alcoholic beer and ale and the fermenting of wines was necessary in every small village. Ale was "the people's food in liquid form," and was consumed by everybody at all times. The extreme poverty of the Franciscans when they first settled in London was exemplified by the writer who related, "I have seen the brothers drink ale so sour that some would have preferred to drink water," yet in our times even very wealthy people are not ashamed to drink water, our national drink. In early times each villager usually brewed his own drink although he often had to pay the lord for the privilege. The BREWER in the manor was often a woman, and BREWSTER, the feminine form, since it was often inconsistently used for a man, is also a common surname. Brewers often charged more than the price fixed by law, and the records are replete with instances of fines assessed for that reason.

GOODALE and GOODALL were men who brewed and sold goodale, a kind of beer. German names for the brewer are BRAUER,

BREYER, and MELTZER, while the Dutch forms are BROWER, BROUWER, and TAPPAN. Germans who dealt in wine acquired the surnames WEIN, WEINMAN, and WEINTRAUB. WEINMAN also made and sold wagons and carts. WYNKOOP and SCHENK sold wine in Holland. SCHENK was also a cupbearer or butler in Germany. In later times the manufacture of ales and wines became an important monastic industry. By the close of the Middle Ages beer had supplanted ale as the universal drink.

Many serfs on the manor owed their names to the amount of land they tilled or the social position they occupied, such as the COTE, COTTER, COTTLE, COATES (also shortened to COATS), COTTRELL, or BURMAN—men who planted only five or ten acres in England and occupied small cottages. YARD was one who tilled a yard or yardland, about thirty acres. BORDERS held a cottage at his lord's pleasure, for which he rendered menial service. The English serf who worked so many days a week for the lord in return for the land he held was designated a WORKMAN or WERKMAN, or if he worked or was paid by the task or piece, a TASKER. A freeholder, that is, one owning a small landed property, would be called YEOMANS or YOUMANS; they also acted as retainers or gentlemen attendants in a noble household. BOND and BUNDY were householders or peasant proprietors. All of these names could be classified properly as nicknames rather than occupational names but they do seem to belong in this chapter as they really tell us the man's occupation.

Villeins who tilled the land or were farmers would not acquire such names on the manor but might if they removed to a large town or city. Then where everyone else was engaged in other pursuits, the fact that they had been farmers might produce the term as a surname. One who tilled the soil in England might be TILLMAN or TILLER. The surname FARMER meant a tenant who cultivated the demesne of the lord paying for it a "farm," that is, a settled, established rent. In other cases FARMER designated a tax collector. That there are few families with this name is due to the fact that the custom of working land for which a money rent was paid did not arise until the latter part of the fourteenth century, long after surnames became fixed family names. In Scotland the name designated one who farmed the revenue, a tax collector. In Germany the name acquired by one who tilled the

115

land might be BAUER, BAUGHMAN, BAUMAN, BURMEISTER, HOF-BAUER, or HOFER, or if he were tall, LANGBAUER. WIDMEYER worked a farm the produce of which went to the support of a church. SEDLACEK operated a farm in Czechoslovakia. The peasant in Holland who tilled the land would have a surname in the form of BOER, or DE BOER. In France the name is GAGNON, and in Poland it is KMIEC together with the diminutive form KMIECIK. REUTER cleared land for farming in Germany.

In the parts of Europe where the winter weather was severe everyone needed the "great cloak" required by nobles, or other warm clothing which was made by the TAYLOR whose talent commanded respect. In medieval times clothes made the man—the difference between the lord and the villein—showing everyone the class in which one belonged and the deference due him. Laws restricted the lower classes from wearing the clothes of their "betters." Others who made and sold outer garments were MANTELL and PARMENTER. COPE made the long cloak or cape. In almost all European countries the family name derived from the occupation as a tailor became a popular one. The Italian SARTORI is common but not so popular as the English and German names—in the south of Europe heavy, warm garments were not so important. The German variants were SCHNEIDER, SCHNEIDERMAN, SCHRADER, SCHROEDER and SHRADER. SNYDER and SNIDER are the Dutch forms. FELLER, PELZ, and PILCH dealt in fur garments. In Poland KABAT, KRAWCZYK, and SZEWCZYK made overcoats. PORTNOY is the Russian tailor, along with KREJCI in Czechoslovakia, and TAILLEUR in France. SZABO or SABO made outer garments in Hungary. Other Slavic tailors are KRAVITZ and KUSHNER, the latter a furrier. CHAIT is a Hebrew name for the tailor.

Also important everywhere in the economic life of all European peoples was the BOOT, SHOEMAKER, or SUTTER. SUGAR and SUGARMAN shoed horses—not a sweet occupation. English SHOESMITH and German HUFSCHMIDT made horseshoes. The practice of nailing iron plates or rim shoes to the hoofs of horses was in regular usage during the Middle Ages.

Common German variant forms for the medieval cobbler are REUSS, SCHUBERT, SCHUMACHER, SCHUMAN, SCHUSTER, SHUBERT, and SHUMAN. SHOEMAKER in America is mostly the Anglicized form of the German name. In France the name is LESUEUR;

CHAPIN dealt in low shoes. The Italian shoemaker is SCARPELLI; the Polish one is SZEWC; the Czechoslovakian term is SVEC; and the Ukrainian word is SEVENKO. In Hungary, VARGA made shoes for men and BALOGH did the same for horses. CHAUCER in England made and sold pantaloons or tight coverings for the legs and feet. The maker of caps, hats, or hoods was CAPPS, HATT, or HATTER in England, MICEK in Poland, and HUTMACHER in Germany. POINTER made laces for fastening hose and doublet together in England, and HOUSER made and sold stockings or socks. HOUSER also names one employed at a house, probably a religious house.

In the cities the craftsmen were severely restricted by guild laws. Shoemakers could only make shoes; they were forbidden to mend them. Bowyers made only bows, and fletchers made only arrows. Weavers were prohibited from dyeing their yarns and cloth and the dyers were prevented from weaving. This deliberate policy of protection for the guild members made for the proliferation of many different trades and crafts and consequently the multiplication of surnames disclosing the livelihood of the first bearers.

The chief industry in England during the centuries when surnames became hereditary was the weaving of coarse woolen cloth. Sheep were the mainstay of the British farmer. Most of the early skillful weavers were Flemings. They were attracted to the country famed for its wool, and with dexterity settled into the woolen industry. The CARD or CARDER smoothed the fibers, and the SPINNER spun the wool or yarn to be woven into cloth. Since almost every woman in the Middle Ages was a spinner (whence comes the term *spinster*), the surname did not become particularly common. SPINDLER made the spindles, and WHEELER the spinning wheels. The names WEAVER, WEBB, WEBBER, and WEBSTER were forms current in different parts of England and became extremely common family names. TAKACS is the Hungarian form. WEBER is the German name.

As early as the middle of the twelfth century the weavers of London, Winchester, Lincoln, Oxford, Huntington, and Nottingham and the fullers of Winchester had organized themselves into guilds. The laws of the weavers and fullers of Winchester, Marlborough, Oxford, and Beverly, based upon those of London, provided that no weaver or fuller could sell except to merchants of the town. The laws also required that if any became prosperous and desired to become a freeman of the town, he must first abandon his trade and get rid of all the tools and implements connected with it and satisfy the town officials of his ability to keep up his new position without working at his old trade. How snobbish social rank developed in Great Britain! Perhaps the evolvement and attainment of a "pecking order" with the discipline imposed to uphold it made for a national stability in the precarious medieval society.

After the raw cloth left the loom, it had to be cleansed, scoured, and thickened, and this was done by the WALKER trampling upon it in a trough. Other common names for this work were FULLER, TUCKER, and TUCKERMAN. DRESSER or DRESSLER worked to give the cloth a nap or smooth finish. PACKER packed the wool in bales for transportation or storage in England. In Germany, WOOLNER prepared the wool for manufacture.

CUTTER, SHARMAN, SHEARER, and SHERMAN cut the cloth. DEXTER, DYER, and LISTER, also spelled LESTER, put color into the material. WADMAN or WOODMAN, when not cutting timber, used woad, a blue-green dyestuff in great demand in the Middle Ages. CORK and CORKER used Middle English *cork*, a purple or red dye. DRAPER made and sold woolen cloth. PLUNKETT made and sold *plunket*, a coarse, white or pale blue woolen cloth. BURRELL made and sold *burel*, a coarse-grained woolen cloth much used in the peasants' clothing. In the thirteenth century the Sheriff of London ordered a thousand ells of burel for use by the poor in that city. MOTLEY made and sold a mixed colored cloth. MERCER dealt in silks, velvets, and the more expensive materials; the name also had the connotation of merchant, a dealer in all commodities. Linen cloth also provided occupations for many Englishmen. FLAXMAN and SWINDLER beat and dressed flax. LANDERS, LAVENDER, and WASHER washed and bleached flax and wool. TELLER made and sold the linen cloth. The occupation of alnager, the officer whose duty it was to inspect all cloths for proper quality and length and attach his leaden seal of approval, apparently did not come into existence early enough to produce a surname. By the very nature of his duties the alnager was an unpopular official which fact would militate against the use of the term as a permanent name. The alnager who presided at the Philips Norton Fair so enraged the populace that they mobbed and mortally wounded him.

Many other English occupations having to do with woolen and other cloth could be mentioned but are uncommon as names in America and must be omitted to save space. Gustav Fransson, in his *Middle English Surnames of Occupation 1100–1350,* collected 165 surnames relating to the manufacture and sale of cloth or clothing. Capitalism first made its appearance in England through the cloth industry, operating through the guilds. So many and diverse crafts were required from the first shearing of the sheep to the finished cloth that some agency needed to be organized to deal with the various crafts to see that the material proceeded smoothly from craftsman to craftsman, and such a venture required management and some capital. However, during the time that family names were becoming fixed capitalists played such a minor role that they influenced names not at all.

Other than English names the number of surnames found in America derived from the clothing trades are not particularly important. In Germany, WESLAGER prepared wool for manufacture into cloth and FARBER dyed the cloth. In Holland, BLEECKER bleached the cloth and KLOPPMAN was the inspector who was required to stamp his approval on the cloth. LANIER was the weaver in France who manufactured and sold woolen cloth, and TKACENKO did the same in the Ukraine.

The most common surname for one who cooked or prepared food was COOK. Sometimes COOK was one who sold cooked meats. In Germany the form is KOCH, and in Poland KUCHARSKI. One who operated a granary or dealt in grain would be CORMAN, KASTNER, KOERNER, or KORMAN if he came from Germany, or GRENIER if a Frenchman. HABER grew oats in Germany. MOSER operated a vegetable garden in France while CONDIT was a merchant of pickled foods. SELZER sold salted or pickled foods in Germany. Most of the names in America dealing with food are not too common but do often reveal where a certain crop is popular. KIRSCH grew and sold cherries in Germany; POIRIER cultivated and sold pears in France; OLIVA grew and sold olives in Spain and Italy. CITRON raised and sold lemons in France; KOHL and ZIELKE raised and sold cabbages in Germany, while ZIEBELL and ZIBELL raised and sold onions, except in those instances where the name is derived from Zibelle "place where onions grew" in Germany. RZEPKA and PASTERNAK raised and sold turnips and parsnips respectively in Poland; REPA did the same for beets in Czechoslovakia; BENNER produced crops of beans in England. CIMINO and KIMMEL produced caraway seeds in Italy and Germany respectively. ZUKOR dealt in sugar in Hungary while ZUKERMAN and ZUCKER did the same in Germany.

As salt was a necessary condiment, it is not surprising to meet SALTER from England, SAULNIER from France, and SALZMAN from Germany. Some ancestor of unlovable Adolf Hitler, if his relative acquired the surname in the customary manner, supervised the salt works. PEPPER was the pepperer who dealt in that and other condiments in England. Names ending in double -er would naturally lose one syllable. SPICER was a dealer in various spices, sometimes an apothecary or druggist. The nobles and wealthy churchmen spent considerable money on aniseed, cinnamon, caraway, coriander, cummin, ginger, licorice, pepper (the most common of spices), and saffron to enable the cooks to spice meat which tended to spoil quickly in the absence of modern refrigeration.

Polish ZIOLKO and ZUELKE grew and sold herbs, while CHMIEL was a hop grower, and ZUREK made sour meal pap. NUTTER collected and sold nuts in England. KAWA is a Slavic name for a dealer in coffee. SCHMALTZ, in Germany, dealt in fats, lard, and butter. GRZYB may not sound to us like a mushroom, but that is the surname of the Pole whose ancestor picked and sold them (if he did not get the name by dwelling among them).

When meat animals could not be kept well throughout the winter months, an important source of meat came through the game killed by the HUNT or HUNTER whose work was both a necessity and a pastime for the ruling classes. HUNT is the early form from Old English *hunta*. Hunta "huntsman" was also a pre-Conquest personal name, so some with the name HUNT are descendants of Hunta. The British were famed for their hunting dogs. Gaston de Foix, in France, was said to have had sixteen hundred hounds in his kennels and six hundred horses in his stables. Favorite quarries of the nobility were the stag and the wild boar. The chief or royal huntsman in England was the GROSVENOR.

TODHUNTER was the man who specialized in hunting the tod or fox, not so much for sport but to exterminate them as vermin. The sport was developed much later. The large retinue of the visiting prelate often included a huntsman to provide fresh meat. The MARKER marked the spot to where the game had retreated, although some with that name dwelt at the boundary mark. The peasants and minor clergy, in imitation of the nobility, had a passion for the chase. Since they were prohibited from hunting in the lord's forests, they could only supplement their larders by poaching, which they did most cheerfully. Civil disobedience which we decry so much today is not new. From Germany there are many family names which denominate the huntsman. The more important are JAEGER, SCHUETZ, WEIDMAN, WEIDNER, YAEGER, and YEAGER, all with about the same meaning.

Hawking was a favorite recreation with the nobility and both sexes enjoyed it. The rough medieval knight bestowed almost as much care and affection on his falcon as he was claimed to have done upon damsels in distress, and often carried the falcon with him even when he attended church. Men were needed to keep and train falcons and other hawks to hunt game. In England the surnames arising from that occupation were FALCONER, FAULKNER, HARKER, and KIDDER. FALCONER was a term also used for one who worked a crane or windlass in a fortified castle. In Germany and Norway the names for the falconer were FALK and FALKE.

The birds selected for the sport were based strictly on the rank of the sportsman. According to the *Book of St. Albans,* a fourteenth-century treatise on falconry, the prince and important noble hunted with the peregrine, the yeoman was allowed a goshawk, while the sporting priest and lower classes were only entitled to use a sparrow hawk. (Today, status depends rather upon the kind and model of car or boat owned.) Status and rank were most important among all classes. It was Lady Bemers, the Prioress of Sopewell, who was able to discover and with much pride announce that, "Christ was a gentylman on his moder's side." GENTLE in medieval times meant one of noble birth, one well-born, and with that meaning the word became a surname. The more complete word GENTLEMAN also served to name many families. Gentle and gentleman have now narrowed in meaning

121

to one aspect of noble behavior, another illustration of the fact that the meaning of a name is only the meaning of the word at the time surnames became common, and not necessarily the present day connotation.

FOWLER in England, and FINKLER and VOGLER in Germany, trapped small birds by means of nets. They could be caught in great numbers and sold in the market or used as welcome additions to the housewife's pot. After the birds were caught, they were kept alive in cages until wanted for cooking. These names are not too common because each peasant and peasant's wife snared birds for their own table. BIRD and FINCH were sometimes metonymic for a bird-catcher.

From time immemorial fish has been an important food in all countries. FISH, FISHER, and FISHMAN got them out of the water and sold them in England. If there is a distinction between FISHER and FISHMAN, it is the FISHER who caught the fish while the FISHMAN was engaged in selling it. FISCHER is the form of the name in German-speaking countries. POISSON sold fish in France while VISSER and VISCHER were the workers with the fish nets in Holland; PISCIOLO so labored on the water in Italy, and FISK in Sweden. For the finny tribe Polish people relied on RYBAK; the Czechoslovakians spelled it RYBAR. Crabs were caught and sold by RAK in Slavic countries. BODFISH in England caught and sold flat fish such as the sole, plaice, and turbot, and may have had a painting of a flat fish outside of his shop to advertise his calling if he didn't think the odor would be notice enough.

One who fished for and sold herring, the fish in greatest demand, would acquire the name HERRING in England, sometimes spelled HERING. Yarmouth was an important center for the herring industry. Herrings were salted and packed in barrels which were slung over packhorses and taken away to the market. When there was no cold storage it was necessary to salt the fish for keeping and transportation. Herrings were so important an article of commerce that rents along the seacoast were often stated in herrings rather than in money.

Early man used the skins of animals for protection against the elements, and soon learned to manufacture them into leather, a most useful material, known since ancient Egyptian times. SKINNER prepared the skins for the TANNER to manufacture into leather. BARKER tanned leather with bark. All three of these craftsmen merely made leather an important occupation which produced three popular surnames in England. The first name is sometimes found as SHINNER from Old English *scinn* "skin," a skinner. HYDER and LEDERER are less common names for a tanner of hides. CURRIER and TOWER dressed leather. WHITTIER tawed or dressed skins into white leather. BOLGER or BULGER made leather wallets or bags. The German GERBER, KIRSCHNER, and LEDERMAN tanned leather, as did LAUER, although this last name is often confused with Laue "lion," and sometimes designated the man who formerly lived in Lau or Laue in Germany. In France PELLETIER prepared skins, and SKORA did the same in Poland. In Germany, KOLLER and RIEMER made leather harness and LOESCHHORN made leather horns used as drinking utensils. KUZNIAR and KOZELUH in Czechoslovakia prepared skins and furs. Closely allied with the leather workers are the saddle-makers. SADLER and SADDLER are the English forms while SATTLER and SATTELMACHER are the German counterparts.

About the middle of the twelfth century the castles of the king and important nobles and the great cathedrals of mother church commenced to be built of stone. Previously they had all been built of wood with the castles surrounded by a ridge or mound of earth and a wooden stockade for protection. When the Roman occupation of Britain ended, the manufacture of bricks ceased and was not revived in England until the Flemish came over in the fourteenth century. Formidable castles were first constructed in stone by the Normans after the Conquest in England, not for protection of the town but to overawe the townsfolk. Thus the work of the mason, the builder with stone, came to be important, and MASON became an esteemed family name. He became one of the most skillful of craftsmen, and up until the end of the twelfth century the elaborate carving was a significant part of his work. Many were employed in the cities in the construction of the magnificent cathedrals and important castles. The masons congregated in the places where the great cathedrals or castles were being built. STONER is another name for the rockhewer or mason. The French form of the name is MAÇON. French CARRIER prepared the stone in a quarry. Germany in the fourteenth century had more than ten thousand castles and strongholds throughout the country, many built of stone, and the masons who constructed them acquired such names as MAURER, STEINMAN, and STEINMETZ. STEIN is occasionally a metonym for the stone worker.

The earliest merchants were the itinerant peddlers, always on the move, who carried their small stock of goods strapped to their backs between castle, manor house, and cottage. Not having the benefit of advertising they often congregated at the church door on Sundays to exhibit their wares and attract buyers. They were usually enthusiastically greeted, especially by the feminine half of the country. The king exercised the sole power of licensing the right to hold a fair or market which was profitable to lord and trader alike. Some fairs were annual events or held only a few times a year; others were open one day a week, resorted to by those who had produce to sell and by those desiring to buy. PEDDLE was a peddler; BADGER, BAGGER, CODMAN, and HARKER carried their wares and produce from place to place in a bag or pouch.

The CHAPMAN or CHATMAN and the MERCHANT, MUNGER, and SELLERS were the more solidly established traders often attaining the more enhanced status through the buying and selling of woolen cloth. They were attracted to the larger cities where the fairs were held most frequently and, in a city like London, they grew wealthy and became respected citizens of consequence. BIGGERS was a purchaser, probably selling elsewhere. There were not so many traders and merchants during medieval times in proportion to the population as there are today because usually the man who made an article or raised a crop was the dealer. The middleman was not so important as he is today. EASTERLING was the eastern merchant from the shores of the Baltic, a member of the Hanseatic League, with a reputation for fair and honest dealings. The name became the etymon for our word "sterling."

The French traders were MARCHAND and MERCIER while MINOT acquired the surname from measuring goods for sale. Various rules and regulations restricted the merchants. For example, in Paris no sales could be made from the shop on Saturdays. On that day sales could be made only at the *campelli*, a market attended by traders from nearby towns. Saturday is still a market day for the farmers in the small towns of America, although fast becoming only a holiday. The German KRAEMER, found also as

KRAMER, KREMER, and CRAMER, was the tradesman who traveled throughout the countryside buying butter, chickens, and eggs which he carried to the market in a cram or pack on his back. SCHOTT was also a peddler. The more important German shopkeeper brought about such surnames as COFFMAN, HANDELMAN, HANDLER, KAUFMAN, and WINKLER. KOOPMAN was the tradesman in Holland while POLZIN was the merchant who engaged in transactions for profit in Russia.

The merchant who extended his activities into other countries needed to depend upon boats and crewmen to transport his goods. In and out of England BARGER worked on a small sailing vessel, along with SEAMAN, SHIPP, and SHIPMAN, although the latter name often referred to the shepherd or caretaker of sheep. KEELER operated a keel or long boat; PITCHER caulked ships with pitch; and SAYWARD was a sea warden or coast guard. French GALLUP used a flat-bottomed boat to load and unload ships. German WASSERMAN, SCHIFF, SHIFFMAN, and SEEMAN were sailors. The Dutch sailor was STURMAN. In Czechoslovakia KORANDA operated a flat boat or raft. Most of these occupations did not serve to name as many families as their numbers would suggest because they would be found only in small groups located on the waterfront, where the term would not properly differentiate the man from his neighbors. FURMAN was a ferryman in Germany.

Fairs and festivals attracted entertainers, jugglers, and carnival men of all kinds to cater to the pleasure-seekers. They created a picturesque, animated scene. Perhaps the most important of those who played a musical instrument was the HARPER who played the harp or other stringed instrument in places where people gathered. Some harpers, men of family, were so substantial that they were able to employ a servant to carry their instrument. (Reminds one of the golfer out for exercise who employs a caddy to carry his clubs.) Other harpers were retained in the castle by wealthy nobles and the harper sometimes became a sort of hereditary official. The wide distribution of the name attests to the popularity and standing of the harp player.

Many others owe their names to the instruments they played. CORNETT played the cornet; CROWDER played a crowd, an ancient Celtic instrument similar to a viol; FIDLER played the violin; FLAUTER used the flute; PIPER was a strolling musician, or in some cases the name just designated a shepherd, who played the pipe or the rustic English bagpipe while attending to his duties; ROTTER performed on the rote, a stringed instrument of the violin class; SALTER played the psaltery, a stringed instrument like a harp; TABOR beat the tabor, a small drum; WHISTLER merely whistled or, in some cases, blew a pipe. From such a man was descended James Abbott McNeill Whistler, the great American painter. The HORNBLOWER or HORNER was the trumpeter who was sometimes used to call the peasants to their work. DUDZIK, in Poland, played the bagpipe.

Most of these were jongleurs or strolling musicians who, although paid little respect, were gladly received to break the monotony of medieval life. They were a source of news and idle gossip of neighboring castles and the lord usually took the time to speak with them. Before they left they were often given a good meal and a few coins to encourage them to speak well of the lord at the next place they visited. Some not musically inclined entertained by performing tricks, clowning, or juggling. These might be named PLAYER, or, if they entertained by stories and song, the name might become SPELLMAN or SPILLER. SINGER, SANGER, or CANTOR performed in church or synagogue. HAZEN was the Spaniard who served as a cantor in the synagogue. SAYLOR, SAILOR, DANCER, HOPPER, and TRIPP all danced at fair and festival. The first two names do sometimes designate a seaman, but the more usual derivation is from Old French *sailleur* "dancer." Not the least of the wandering entertainers was the BERMAN in England and Germany who owned a bear and paraded it about for the public to be amused by its tricks. And of course we know from the man met by Simple Simon that the pieman was handy to feed the hungry. His descendants might be surnamed with the shortened form PYE.

Ireland paid homage to her poets. The word for poet was *tadhg* and Tadhg became a personal name which originated the family names TIGHE, TAGUE, and McTIGUE. Descent from the royal poet, Rioghbhardan, produced the family names REARDON and RIORDAN. BEGLEY as an Irish name refers to the grandson of the little poet, but as an English name it designates the man from Beckley "Beocca's meadow." BAIRD was the Scottish bard who recited poetry. George Fraser Black in his *The Surnames of Scotland,* however, contends that Baird is a name of territorial origin, from the lands of Bard.

Strolling minstrels were popular everywhere throughout Europe. German PIEPER and PFEIFFER played a fife or pipe or just whistled, and GEIGER played the violin. STELZER amused the populace by walking and performing tricks on stilts. The German who sang liturgical music in the synagogue was known by the name, KANTOR. Poland's singer would be named SPIEWAK while the entertainer on some musical instrument would be GRACZYK. In the Ukraine SPIVAK was the singer where DUDA played a bagpipe. DUDEK played the bagpipe in Czechoslovakia.

With many complicated international borders and especially when many important nobles and even churchmen were permitted to mint their own coins, the money-changer was a necessity and a man of importance. In Germany the money-changer was GELMAN, WEXLER, or WECHSLER. They sometimes developed into bankers. The Hebraic-Germanic forms are HALPER or HALPERIN. The trades that developed into the lending of money and banking became Jewish names since Christians were forbidden by the church to lend money at interest, and the Jews had this lucrative occupation to themselves, although wealthy churchmen sometimes competed with them. The money-changer was chiefly interested in the amount of silver in the coins. Silver was harder than the counterfeit metals used, and when the merchant was doubtful he satisfied himself by biting the coin with his teeth.

In England, MINTER and MONEYSMITH coined money. The occupation was hazardous. Henry I of England subjected those suspected of coining false money to loss of eyes and genitals. In the absence of bankers people often kept their coins in the homely stocking-foot or in a chest or cask. COFFER made coffers, boxes, and chests in which treasure was kept; and WHITCHER made whitches, that is, chests and coffers. When the lord or high churchman traveled, it was necessary to take along the cofferer or treasurer who had charge of the coffer containing the valuable articles, jewelry, and money. HOARD and HORDER were treasurers, keepers of the savings. SCHATZMANN did the same in Germany.

Guards and watchmen were necessary for the protection of chattel property during the Middle Ages when unbridled passion and violence were a way of life, more so even than at the present time. Violence in the streets was commonplace. There was law in abundance but little means of enforcing it as far as the common man was concerned. Policemen as such were unknown. WARD was the common guard or watchman in England. Watchmen usually carried a trumpet or horn to sound the alarm, and upon hearing it every peasant was supposed to give chase. MARCKWARDT was the warden of the border or marches, the guard, in Germany. In England SPEER, SPEAR, and SPEARS were watchmen or lookout men; WAITE and WAKEMAN were the watchmen for a village, castle, or fortified place, usually manning a watch tower. The German watchmen produced the surnames WACHTER, SPIELMAN, and SCHUETZ. In Lithuania the guard or watchman acquired the name SARGIS. The Italian sentinel was FAZIO. These men, it must be noted, were watchmen in a castle or manor, often without particular authority, who endeavored to prevent theft and burglary; they did not have the powers or support that policemen have today. SCHLEGEL and SCHLUETER were guards or turnkeys in a German prison. GALER did similar duty in England.

It was in the cities and large towns that the various workers in metal of one kind or another developed. Protected and matured by the craft guilds they formed in the Middle Ages, they rose in rank above the peasants in the country districts. In England the worker in brass became BRAZIER or COPPERSMITH. LEDBETTER and PLUMMER worked in lead in England while SPANGLER did the same in Germany where BLECHMAN worked with tin. One who cut iron and was a worker in that metal was EISENHAUER in Germany, now spelled EISENHOWER by the late president. Also working with iron in Germany were EISEN, EISNER, and EISEMAN. In England the ironcutter was TELFER from Old French *taille fer* "ironcutter"; and in Italy it became TAGLIA and TAGLIAFERRO and developed into English TOLIVER and TOLLIVER. KNIFESMITH and CUTLER made and sold knives in England. NAYLOR, NESMITH, and SPIKES made nails. Nails were made in Germany by NAGEL, and by CLOUTIER in France. NADLER made and sold needles in England and NUDELMAN did the same in Germany.

GOLDSMITH, a highly skilled craftsman, made and sold gold articles and repaired crown jewelry, coined money as well as lending it, and became the first of the bankers. His counterpart in France was ORFEVRE. SILBERMAN made and sold silver articles

Germany; SILVERMAN is the Anglicized form. LOCKYER in England, SCHLOSSER in Germany, and SERRURIER in France all made locks. The elaborate iron locks of the Middle Ages seen in our museums are evidence of the skill of those early locksmiths. KEY sometimes a metonym for the KEYER, the maker of keys. KLEINSCHMIDT in Germany made small metal objects such as locks and nails and KLINGELSCHMIDT made bells. LORIMER made bridle bits and spurs in England. MARRERO made hoes in Italy. HACKER made hoes or hacks, although the occupation of some of them was in cultivating the soil with such tools, or even in hacking or cutting wood.

Men did not hesitate to engage in fierce combat in the Middle Ages but they desired as much armor and strong weapons as possible. ARMOUR made defensive armor for the body. CUSHMAN, as mentioned on page 105, made protective covering for the thighs. Blades and swords were made by KLINGER in Germany. LEEPER made scabbards for swords and polished and sharpened blades in England where BILLER made bills, those long staffs terminating in a hook-shaped blade. BOLSTER and ARROWSMITH manufactured bolts or arrows.

The houses of the people were crude affairs made of wood, mostly roofed with thatch in very early times. In England the skilled craftsman who covered the roofs with straw, thatch, rushes, reeds, or the like was variously referred to as the RADER, READER, REDER, REEDER, REDMAN, or THATCHER, all well-known surnames. REDMAN, though, was perhaps more often a descendant of Redmund "counsel, protection," or a man with red hair. Some early churches were even thatched with reeds or straw. A good thatched roof will last for forty or more years but skill is required in the installation. Because a thatched roof was so vulnerable to fire, other materials tended to replace thatch, especially in the towns where by-laws forbade the use of thatch. TYLER and TILLER made and sold tiles or covered buildings with them, while SLATER roofed buildings with flat rock or slate. HELLYER was a general roofer using reeds, thatch, tile, or slate as the customer demanded. Hellyer's German and Dutch counterpart was DECKER. German ZIEGLER or ZEIGLER made bricks or roof tiles, while SCHINDLER made shingles. LEDBETTER beat and flattened lead for roofs.

The English CORDER and ROPER made and sold cords and rope.

RAPER was not one who committed sexual crimes; the word is an early form of roper. The same craft names from France were CORDES and CORDELL and from Germany, SEILER. Baskets and boxes all required cords and rope to secure them. TIBON is the Spanish straw merchant.

Printed books and their manufacture did not give rise to surnames because printing did not develop until after the end of the surname period in England, but the copying of manuscripts and the binding of them into books produced several surnames in use in this country today. The German noun *Drucker* refers to the printer, but the surname DRUCKER is explained as "one who pressed cloth." It is derived from the noun *Druck* "pressure" from which comes the common noun Drucker "printer," that is, one who makes marks by pressure. High churchmen owned bound books, and many important religious houses owned good-sized libraries. ROLLER made and sold parchment rolls for manuscripts. SCRIBNER, BOOKER, and BOWKER copied books and manuscripts in England while BUCHER did the same in Germany. BINDER in England and BUCHBINDER in Germany were bookbinders. The official or public writer in Germany was SCHREIBER or SHRIVER. LATIMER in England was the latiner, or translater of Latin, the universal language of Medieval Europe. DRISCOLL in Ireland was also an interpreter.

There are many surnames which seem to indicate that a remote ancestor was an official of the Church who performed sacerdotal functions, and this may appear puzzling in view of the rule of celibacy enjoined on its ministers by the Catholic Church. Notwithstanding the inflexible rule of the Church against marriage by its clergy, many were married in medieval times. There were instances where the last representative of an ancient family obtained from the Pope a dispensation to marry upon the death of an older brother or other relative whereby his family was in danger of becoming extinct. It was not an uncommon thing in the Middle Ages for widowers to go into the Church, a significant act which might affect the names of their children at the times surnames were becoming hereditary.

Particularly before the Norman Conquest, clerical marriages were quite common. Efforts to abolish them were only partially successful especially in the north of England. Anselm, Archbishop

f Canterbury, forbade clerical marriages in 1102, and Henry I
eceived substantial funds from priests for license "to live as be-
ore." The story is told of a certain vicar in Scotland who, keep-
ng a mistress, was overcome when informed that his bishop was
o visit him to order that he put the woman away. The good lady
vas indomitable. She cannily packed her basket with pudding,
:hickens, and eggs and set out. Meeting her the bishop asked
vhere she was going. "I am taking this basket to the bishop's
weetheart who has been brought to bed," she replied. The pious
nan made no reply but quietly visited the vicar without saying
mything about the subject on which he had come. Several of the
)ishops of Durham and at least one archbishop of York had chil-
lren. Besides the clergy who were formally married there were
nany who had consorts or hearth-mates. Children of such unions
vould not be scorned and would be known in the community by
ι sobriquet referring to their clerical father.

The number of these surnames is not surprising when one con-
;iders the large, practically overwhelming part played by the
Church in the daily life of the people of the Middle Ages. People,
:specially in towns, were churchgoers. One man in every fifty in
England in the thirteenth century was a clergyman. The Church
)rovided the one opportunity for advancement by the poor peas-
ints as well as by the younger sons of influential people. One in-
:lined toward scholarship found the Church a haven as well as
m inspiration. An old proverb truly says, "The Church, the sea,
)r the royal household for those who would thrive." Some went
nto the Church for security, others for prestige, and others be-
:ause it was an easy way to make a living, although most did
1ave a strong sense of vocation.

The gulf between the clergy and important men of the time
vas not great. This is illustrated by the ease with which Thomas
ι Becket, trained in the law, who became chancellor under
Henry II, quickly abandoned the courtly ways appropriate to the
high government office to become the reverend Archbishop of
Canterbury. The association between princes of the Church and
royalty was a close one.

There are other clear explanations of the origins of many of
these ecclesiastical names separate from their apparent meanings.
POPE, sometimes spelled PAPE, is not an uncommon name and it

131

is obvious that no person with that name could claim the Arch
bishop of Rome as a direct ancestor. Most of the people with
this name undoubtedly had an early forebear who played the im
portant part of the pope in the numerous mystery plays and
pageants. In some cases POPE and other ecclesiastical names may
be nicknames for men of a solemn, austere, ascetic appearance
POPE is also a dialectal term for the puffin and some other birds
The Italian form of the ecclesiastical surname is PAPA.

Many of the other common ecclesiastical names are nickname
from participation in the miracle plays, morality plays, pageants
and the various holiday revels. There was the Abbot of Unreason
the Pope of Fools, the Boy Bishop, and the Lord of Misrule to
list only a few of best known. A boy chosen as the Boy Bishop
led around the streets gorgeously dressed in the garb of a bishop
during the feast of St. Nicholas, would remember the honor to
his dying day and would often acquire BISHOP as a nickname
which might well cling to him for life, and descend to his progeny

The BISHOP (BISCHOFF in Germany) usually indicated one who
was a member of the bishop's entourage or who played the part
of the bishop in play or pageant. Some, however, arose from pre
vious residence in Bischof in Germany or in one of the towns in
cluding the word in its name in England. Biscop was also an Old
English personal name which would be the basis of some family
names by an alteration in spelling to the more familiar BISHOP
ABBOTT was the abbot, the official in charge of the monastery
In some cases there were lay abbots who inherited their office
not bound by the rules of celibacy. Scottish McNABB is the "son
of the abbot." The name can also derive from the "son of little
Abb," a pet form of Abraham or from Abet or Abot, pet forms for
Abel. The German form is ABT, the Italian is ABBATE, and ABBEY
is the Scottish surname. Most of the names evidently arose from
the fact that the bearer was the abbot's servant, probably one who
accompanied him on his travels. PRIOR or PRYOR was a monastic
official next in rank below that of an abbot, and that surname
arose from service in a prior's entourage or from acting the part
in play or pageant. Bishops, abbots, and priors were constantly
on the move from manor to manor looking after the property of
the Church or monastery and supervising the work of the priests.
The RECTOR was the official in charge of a church or parish.

Many lords or other nobles had the advowson, that is, the right
to appoint the parish priest, and they often named a younger son
or other relative, paying little attention to his learning, his capability to serve a church, or even whether he were old enough.
Many of these totally unfit to perform their duties used a small
part of their income from the church to employ a vicar, a priest
who had the cure of souls and who was more or less suitable for
the position, to discharge their responsibilities in the parish. From
the position of vicar come the English surnames of VICKERY and
VICKERS, and the Italian name, VICARI.

CANNON was a canon or clergyman on the staff of a cathedral
or important church. Sometimes the name is derived from the
fact that the original bearer was the canon's servant. The CHAPLIN
was a chaplain in a monastery or in charge of a chapel either in
a church or cathedral or at a distance from it and subordinate to
the main building. Some lords, with the consent of the bishop,
erected their own private chapels where they employed their
own personal chaplain.

The surnames, PRIEST, PREST, or PROST designated one who performed sacerdotal duties. Scottish TAGGART was the son of the
priest. Of course, in some cases the name arose as a nickname
for one whose behavior, spirit, or appearance resembled that of
a priest. The German forms are PFAFF and PABST; POPOV is Russian; PAPP is Hungarian; the Greek name is PAPPAS; the Italian,
PRETE and QUILICI; the Slavic form is KOGAN; and in the Ukraine
the cognate POPENKO is found. In Germany and Poland the chaplain or high priest is KAPLAN or CAPLAN. The rabbi in Russia and
Poland is KAGAN or KAGANOVICH. DEACON is an order of ministers,
lower in rank than the priest, who assisted in divine service, read
the Scriptures in the church, instructed the youth in the catechism, and relieved the poor.

By no means the least important official in the parish was the
parish clerk, pronounced CLARK in England as the surname is
spelled, who kept the records. The Irish form is CLEARY. The
clerk was licensed by the bishop, paid very little, but had a measure of security, holding the office as a freehold. Sometimes clerks
renounced their benefices on condition that they be conferred on
their sons. Perhaps the most important attribute of a clerk was his
ability to read and write. The name was sometimes bestowed as

133

a nickname for one who could read and write. Officials of th church in English law had "benefit of clergy," the right to b tried when accused of serious crime by the ecclesiastical court which were notoriously easy on the offender. Proof of the righ to the privilege was made by reading the first verse from th fifty-first Psalm in the Bible, popularly known as the neck-verse Men who were employed to draw up deeds and other paper were also called clerks, and the term was also used for people o learning and even for merchants and tradesmen who could rea and write.

The male member of a religious order or monastery is th familiar MONK, MUNK, or MUNN in England. NUNN is a femal member of a religious order, although the name was sometime applied in derision to a timid or demure man. The German forn for the male is MUENCH with MUNCH in Norway. FREYER, FRYER or FRIAR as a surname designated the members of the four impor tant mendicant orders, which became prominent in the thirteentl century, the Dominicans, Franciscans, Carmelites, and Augustin ians. They lived among their fellowmen, engaged in endless wan derings, preaching throughout the world. The villagers wer quick to appreciate their courage, enthusiasm, and service anc welcomed them, but the established monastic orders recognizec them as formidable rivals and resolutely opposed them. Probabl some named FRIAR acquired their surname from playing the par of Friar Tuck in the popular Robin Hood plays and pageants.

Not all of the population of a monastery consisted of monks Halfway between the monks and their servants were the la brothers or *conversi* who lived according to a rule but one not s strict as that required of the monks or canons. They were illiter ate, engaged largely in manual work and had their own livin quarters; some were adults who had retired to religious houses Because of their frequent unruly and sometimes violent behavior they were gradually replaced by paid servants who proved more manageable. The surnames BROTHERS and CONVERSE designatec them, although the latter name sometimes denominated one, par ticularly a Jew, who had been converted to the Christian religion In 1154 there was a school for converts in Bristol. During the thirteenth century King Henry III founded the House of Con verts on the site of the present Public Record Office in Chancery

,ane, London, as a home for Jews who had abandoned their faith nd embraced Christianity, but it had to be closed for want of ımates about a hundred years later. Chancery Lane was earlier alled Convers Lane because of the presence of the home for con-erted Jews.

A servant in the monastery or religious house was the KITCHEN r KITCHENER in charge of the room or building appropriated to ookery. The kitchen of wealthy lords was generally a building eparate from the manor house and the name sometimes merely esignated the peasant who lived near the kitchen. The DURWARD r DORWARD held the office of doorkeeper at monastery or abbey ı both England and Scotland. The religious houses also em-loyed almost all of the domestic servants found in a king's or nportant noble's household, most of them listed elsewhere in his chapter. The parlor was the room set aside in a monastery or conversation either between the monks, who often observed he strict rule of silence elsewhere, or with outsiders who came or an interview or request. The servant in charge of such a room vas the PARLER.

Surnames with the genitive ending -s, as in PARSONS, VICKERS, nd MONKS, clearly refer to the parson's man or servant, the icar's man, the monk's man. In some cases they point to the one iving or working at the parson's house, the vicar's house, the nonk's place. That these names usually point to the servant or ne associated in some way with the person in holy orders rather han the occupation itself is emphasized by the greater numbers f names with the s than without it. The name of PRIEST is not ound with the s because of the sibilancy it produces.

The minor officials connected in one way or another with the eligious life of the Middle Ages gave rise to many surnames. For xample, the official in charge of the sacristy and its contents in ingland was the SEXTON. The similar German under-officer was ᴍᴏᴍᴏᴍᴏᴍᴏᴍᴏᴍᴏᴍᴏᴍᴏ ᴋᴏᴍᴍ, KOESTNER, KOSTER, or KUESTER, and WIDEMAN took ;eneral care of church property. Dutch forms are KOSTER and ᴏᴏᴍᴏ. In the Ukraine the name is KOSTELNY. PATNODE, from the irst words of the Lord's Prayer in Latin, is the man who sang or :hanted in the French church. PRIMMER in England was the ›fficial who read at prime, the first canonical hour, and CROZIER ›ore the bishop's crook or pastoral staff or cross in the proces-

sions. PROCTOR was an attorney in an ecclesiastical court. CHAN
DLER made and sold candles and other small wax images used in
ecclesiastical offerings. ROSARIO made and sold rosaries in Italy
while SANTORO manufactured saintly images.

SCHULER, SCHULMAN, SHULMAN, and LERMAN taught school in
Germany. LERNER, however, was one who came from Lern "to
learn" in Germany. In Holland the name for the teacher appeared
as SCHUYLER, and in France it was CYR. This last name also de
nominated one who came from St. Cyr in France. The Slavic
SKOLNIK was an important functionary or student of a school or
synagogue. While it is unlikely that a schoolboy would acquire
the word as a surname, ZAK means just that in Czechoslovakia
but the name probably arose as a nickname for someone who
resembled a student. A name once applied, especially if it was
originally an apt nickname, can continue long after it ceases to be
descriptive. The learned person or teacher was MASTERS and
MARSTERS in England, MEISTER in Germany.

KNIGHT in England acted as a military servant to the king or
great baron while CHEVALIER did the same in France, and RITTER
the same in Germany. They were mounted soldiers owing loyalty
to their liege lord bound to fight in his quarrels. SQUIRES is the
surname which originally designated the squire, a young man of
gentle birth, attendant on a knight before becoming old enough
and skillful enough to acquire knighthood himself. CHILDS also
refers to a young noble awaiting knighthood. SARGENT was a
tenant of the king by military service ranking under a knight
although his duties were often similar to those of the steward or
bailiff. A young knight who served under the banner of another
either because he was not old enough or because he had too few
vassals to display his own banner, might be called a BACHELOR
in England or BATCHELOR in Scotland. Bachelor as a word later
acquired the signification of an unmarried man or one who had
had the first or lowest academic degree conferred upon him by a
college or a university, but the surnames did not have these
meanings. DVORAK was a courtier or attendant at the court of a
prince in Czechoslovakia.

Many names have arisen from the fact that the original bearer
was a fighting or military man. If he fought with the bow and
arrow, he became ARCHER, BOWMAN, or SCUDDER. BANNISTER

136

andled the once deadly crossbow and FLIGHT the longbow.
BANNISTER also was the name of the man who made and sold
baskets. The ordinary warriors or soldiers acquired such names
s KAMP, KEMP, or KEMPER, and WYMAN, the latter name having
Vigmund "war, protection" as a contributory source. SPEARMAN
vas the soldier armed with a spear. French LA POINTE was a
ighting man, a soldier armed with a point such as a lance. In
arly courts, guilt was sometimes assessed through the outcome
f combat between the litigants. One who could not do his own
ighting might engage a CHAMPION or HELD to fight for him,
specially in disputes about the ownership of land. A CHAMPION
vas a regular member of the household of some bishops. The
German form of the name is HELDT.

The German warriors acquired names such as HERRMANN,
KRIEGER, or REISMAN. If one fought with the crossbow, the name
might be ARMBRUSTER. In Italy, the German mercenary soldier
vas called LANZA, while others engaged in combat were BAT-
TAGLIA and GUERRERO, the latter name also being a Spanish form.
A guard of the Doge of Venice armed with a broadsword was
SCHIAVONE, although this name also designates one from a Slavic
country. The Polish fighter with a bow and arrow would be
LUCZAK, while if he fought with the sword, it would be ZAREMBA;
f he attacked by laying in ambush, the name would be DYBAS.
The French archer is FLECHE, the Dutch crossbowman, CUYLER,
and the Irish soldier, FEENEY. AMIRAULT was the highest ranking
naval officer in France, although the surname was more often a
nickname applied in derision. The GFROERER was the man in
Germany to whom the warriors resorted for superstitious protec-
ion while engaged in combat.

Warriors needed weapons, and since the bow and arrow were
supreme during the surname period, many were engaged in pro-
ducing them. BOWYER and BOYER made and sold bows in Eng-
and, and ARCARO did the same in Italy. STRINGER from Old
English *streng* "string or cord," a common Yorkshire name, specialized in making strings for the bows. Arrows were made in
England by FLETCHER, and TEPPER furnished them with metal
ips. ARSENAULT in France had charge of the arsenal where
weapons were stored. JENNER is the Scottish engineer, that is, the
operator of an engine of war, a device capable of hurling heavy

137

stones against a fortress. The word was also sometimes used o
the men who combined the work of the mason and architect i
the construction of important buildings.

The officials who manned the law courts contributed their titl
as surnames. CONSTABLE was originally the count of a stable, the
became the chief officer of a household court, an attendant on
bailiff or sheriff. CRYER, BEADELL, BEDELL, and BIDDLE were th
surnames attached to the town crier, the man appointed to mak
public announcements. Some of the Biddles of Philadelphia a
tribute the origin of their name to original residence in Biddulp
"place by the mine" in Staffordshire, or from the personal nam
Beaduwulf "battle, wolf." BELLMAN went around the streets o
a town with a bell to attract attention and broadcast decrees. Th
similar official in Holland and Germany was BODE. BODE is als
from Bod "messenger," a pet form of names beginning with thi
element as Bodewig and Butulf.

LAWYER and LAYMAN declared the law and gave legal opinion
in England, and LAMONT did the same in Scotland. A LAWMAN
holding his office by hereditary right in the north of England
functioned much like a city alderman. LAYMAN and LAWMAN ar
also derived from the Old English personal name, Lagema
"lawyer." SOMMERS and SUMNER were the petty officers, the sum
moners, who warned the peasants to appear in court. The Polis
name for this official was WOZNY. WEDGE acted as a pledge o
security for an accused. A magistrate would be PROVOST in Eng
land and France, and PROBST in Germany. JUDGE occupied tha
office in England, although JUDGE is sometimes derived fror
Judith "praise." RICHTER in Germany and TSCHUDI in Switzer
land were judges. ZENNER in Germany was an officer of a hun
dred, a district in medieval times chiefly important for its la\
court.

ALDERMAN in England and RATHMANN in Germany were cit
officers or magistrates. Most aldermen in England were the im
portant governing officers of the many craft guilds. As the guild
endeavored to regulate most minutely the quality of work, hours
and charges of their members, many aldermen were require
for inspections, and enforcement of the regulations. In Polan
SOLTIS performed the duties of a magistrate or was mayor of
village.

Surnames from Occupation or Office

On roads where tolls were charged it was necessary to station a toll collector who would be called GABLER, TOLL, TOLER, or TOLMAN. ZOLL and ZOLLER are cognate German forms. French SHOCKETT collected taxes on wine. These toll and tax collectors usually purchased the concession and then greedily garnered all they could. Some monasteries levied a toll on traffic past their property. Tolls were exacted on all merchandise brought in or taken out of a town or into a fair. In 1281 tolls were inaugurated on London Bridge, a penny for a horseman, a farthing for a pedestrian, or if he carried a pack of goods, a halfpenny. A collector of rents in Germany would be ZENDER, and one who collected a farm rent equal to a tenth of the income would be the TEGTMEYER.

In England and Scotland CHANCELLOR is the official who kept the registers of an order of knighthood. In some places he was more of an ecclesiastical judge. LEGGETT was the ambassador, a minister of state. BAILEY, BAYLIS or BAYLIE, in England and Scotland, and BAILLY in France, were the chief magistrates of a barony or part of a county, sometimes the chief officers of a hundred or wapentake, a part of a shire sometimes consisting of a hundred heads of families.

During the Middle Ages the innkeepers or tavernkeepers were prominent men. Apart from the monasteries and other religious houses, inns and taverns were the only places of refuge for the weary traveler. Quite naturally, the owner or operator of the inn acquired the word as a surname. The English surnames were HOST or HOSTLER, INMAN, and TAVENNER. SELLARS worked in the cellar where the wine was stored. The German publican became KRUEGER, KRUG, or WIRTZ. The Dutch form was KROEGER, and the Italian, PUSATERI. TAPPER in England and KRETSCHMER in Germany tapped casks and sold ale and wine and also were tavernkeepers.

In Scotland there were physicians called DOCTOR who enjoyed lands by virtue of their office which was hereditary. The name is also German, indicating a highly educated man or teacher. BARBER or BARBOUR in England, HOLIC in Czechoslovakia, and BADER and SCHERER in Germany were barber surgeons as well as hairdressers. SCHERER was also a mole catcher. Barbering of both beards and hair was a grave social matter in medieval times. Ecclesiastics inveighed against men with curls and fancy facial

139

hair calling them effeminate and debased, but that did not stop them, as in the present day, from following the current fashion. The Council of Westminster decreed in 1102 that men's hair must be cut short enough to show their eyes and at least part of their ears. That surgery was relegated to the haircutter in the Middle Ages is not surprising when it is remembered that all educated men were clerics and the study of medicine was discouraged by the Church. Men who had taken religious vows "should not touch those things which cannot honorably be mentioned in speech." In 1163, the Council of Tours forbade the practice of surgery by the clerics on the principle that "the Church abhorreth blood shed."

Some people have not been able to believe that their name derived from honest craftsmen and workers but have insisted that their ancestors were noble Normans who must have come over with the Conqueror to England. Dr. Ebenezer Cobham Brewer, for example, the compiler of the famous *Dictionary of Phrase and Fable* (1870), explains his own name: BREWER "which exists in France as Bruhière and Brugière, is not derived from the Saxon *briwan* (to brew), but the French *bruyère* (heath), and is about tantamount to the German 'Plantagenet' (broom-plant). No statement is too ridiculous to use if it will enhance the status of the man aspiring to some empty title.

Even writers and authorities on surnames cannot become reconciled to the fact that their own family name might have a plebian origin. Dr. Henry Barber, in his *British Family Names* published in London, 1894, carefully asserts that BARBER is "from St. Barbe sur Gaillon; a local name in Normandy, where was the celebrated abbey of St. Barbara; or French Barbe, Barbiaux, Barbry; Dutch Barbe; German Barber; place name." Although suggesting several other places that might have originated the surname he makes no mention of the honest hairdresser or barber surgeon who was undoubtedly his eponymous ancestor. Leslie Gilbert Pine, the genealogist and author of *The Story of Surnames* (1965), after stating that numerous names come from trees and giving examples, ends up by saying, "but not Pine, which is admittedly a place name but has little to do with the tree which forms the heraldic pun on the name in most of the Pine (or Pyne) coats of arms. There is little doubt that the name is mostly derived from the ree, although in some cases it is a nickname for a tall, thin man.

There are countless miscellaneous occupations that have provided surnames. BELLER made and sold bells; CUSTER made eather beds and cushions; COMER made and sold combs; COKER ut up hay in cocks, a hayworker; GRAVER was an engraver or culptor; LICHTERMAN was a lamplighter in Holland and Germany; 3OGARD in Holland tended an orchard and BAUMGARTNER, sometimes shortened to BUMGARDNER, did the same in Germany. GREEN-PAN made and sold verdigris, a substance much employed in the early chemical arts. Glass was well-known but window glass was not too common during the period in which surnames became table. GLASS and GLASSER made and sold glassware in England; GLASSMAN did the same in Germany; and GLASER, GLAZER, and GLAZIER are similar names in France. German ASCHENBRENNER was an ashburner, making potash used in the manufacture of soap and glass. LEEPER made and sold baskets in England, while VANAMAKER did likewise in Holland. LEEPER also exhibited as a eaper or dancer at fairs, or in some cases acted as a runner or courier.

CALDERON in Spain and CALDERONE in Italy, together with KESSEL in Germany and England, made and sold kettles, while TINKER in England and CAIRD in Scotland repaired pots and kettles. Gloves were made and sold by GLOVER in England, GANT in France, and WANTENAER in Holland. KUKLA in Russia and the Ukraine operated a puppet show for the amusement of both adults and children. English SPONNER and SPOONER made spoons in England and LOEFFLER did the same in Germany. They all came to America, the land of freedom.

Sometimes names seem to dispute ability. A Memphis, Tennessee, plastering company's truck carried the sign: "Expert Plastering, Will Crumble & Son." John Dye was an undertaker in Deadwood, New Jersey, in 1956. Dr. J. C. Toothaker, in 1956, practiced dentistry in South Bend, Indiana, while Dr. H. A. Toothacre was the school dentist in Burlington, Iowa. Doctor Lawyer is a dentist in Philadelphia. C. W. Buggs was professor of bacteriology at Wayne University in Detroit, Michigan. Rodney Prior Lien became a vice-president of the Cleveland Trust Co. Forest Burns was hired in Marquette, Michigan, in 1967, to man a forest fire lookout tower. With a little assiduous reading of newspapers one can collect a hatful of such names. These examples all prove that the present-day meanings of words sometimes have little to do with medieval names and occupations.

Just as the surnames men bear today tell us the common occupations during the Middle Ages the lack of names pointing to certain crafts tells us that they were unimportant or non-existent. For instance, our lack of names referring to the manufacture of furniture strikingly confirms the fact that the houses of both nobles and peasants were sparsely furnished. Even a wealthy man's hall might have only one chair. Tables were set up by boards placed across trestles. There were no bedmakers. The word "bedstead" merely meant a place for a bed. Beds of straw stuffed into sacks would be spread on tables, benches, or chests. The lower orders merely slept on the earth floor. The expression "making a bed" originated in medieval times when one was given a sack and some straw and did that very thing.

There seem to be fewer English names for the shoemaker and the maker of coverings for the head than one would expect from the importance of these two articles of clothing. Hood is not uncommon but it is also from Hood, the name of small places in Devonshire and Yorkshire and also a corruption of Hud, a pet form of Richard. Hatter is not a common name. Capps and Capper, the makers of caps, are occasionally seen. The surname Sutor and Sutter, the maker of shoes, are not particularly common. All in all this is a remainder that in medieval England most of the peasants made their own coverings for the extreme upper and lower parts of the human body.

The absence of names meaning a maker of, or builder with bricks tells us that brick buildings were not constructed in Europe during the Middle Ages. All buildings were either of wood with layers of mud or constructed with stone. In very ancient times bricks were used extensively in building as may be observed in Egypt and India and in places occupied by the Romans but with the fall of the Roman empire brickmaking ceased, not to be revived in Europe until just after the surname period. The common names Bricker and Brickman refer not to brickmaking but to the dweller near, or keeper of, a bridge. Cihlar from Czechoslovakia does refer to a brickmaker, but the name arose later than in other parts of Europe. Playing cards did not become

142

known in Europe until after the fourteenth century. CARD or CARDE had nothing to do with games, but their early bearers were engaged in carding or combing wool, as mentioned earlier in this chapter.

Although some surnames derived from the trade or craft in which an individual worked are among the earliest family names, many others are from a later period. It is known when certain trades or crafts arose. Such names cannot antedate the vocation or industry. SMITH and MILLER are among the most ancient names. But such names as HOST, INMAN, and TAVENNER came later since no taverns offering regular shelter for the night are known before the fourteenth century. MERCHANT as a name is thus much later in origin than the BADGER, the peddler who carried his pack on his back to display his wares to the prospective customer. The comparative absence of such occupational names as GROCER and GROSER, aphetic for engrosser or wholesale dealer, is to be expected; the wholesaler is an occupation of comparatively late occurrence.

For most of the occupations mentioned in this chapter there are surnames designating them from almost every language current in Europe during the surname period. They have been explained here usually only when they are found to surname a substantial number of persons in America. There are numerous other occupational names attached to men with unusual or rare pursuits, but there is not space to mention all of them. Both Gustav Fransson and Bertil Thuresson, as noticed in the Bibliography, have written on the subject of Middle English occupations and have explained many rare ones.

If occupational surnames were being adopted at the present time, there would be many strange, if not glamorous ones. The United States Department of Labor issued the third edition of its two-volume *Dictionary of Occupation Titles* in 1965 listing some 36,000 different job titles. For example, one might be a "mud man" or a "kiss setter." The mud man reclaims rubber particles from sludge in the rubber industry, while the kiss setter is engaged in shaping chocolate candy called "kisses." Today with the existence of complicated machines that do man's work and possibly even his thinking, the different occupations have been increased enormously.

4

SURNAMES FROM DESCRIPT·ION
OR ACTION

Nicknames

*Nicknames from complexion—Hair color—Facial hair—Size—Body build—
Mental or moral characteristics—Action—Strength and courage—Speech—
Dress—Stranger—Economic condition—Status—Comparative age—Animal re
semblance—Play or pageant—Relationship—Verb plus noun—Miscellaneous*

T HE WORD NICKNAME is derived from "an eke-name" or adde
name, and since surnames originated as added names fo
help in identification, all surnames are, in a sense, nicknames
There has been some controversy among authorities as to th
tendency of nicknames to settle into stable, fixed family names
Ewen would derive few family names from nicknames; Reane
and Matthews probably swing too far in the opposite direction
Part of the dispute, as in many controversies among authoritie
rests on semantics, the exact definition of terms. In this wor
trouble has been experienced in deciding in which category
given name belongs, particularly as between nicknames and occu

national names, and not all authorities will agree with the author.

Love of the use of nicknames for others is a universal trait, found in most all countries, civilized and uncivilized, to some extent among all classes, but some peoples and groups have accepted them more docilely than others. Crude, even vulgar, nicknames are employed more among the lower classes than among the propertied set. An outstanding exception is Claudia Alta Johnson, the wife of Lyndon Baines Johnson, who acquired the nickname *Lady Bird* at the age of two, by which she was thereafter known, even as First Lady, and is so listed in *Who's Who in America*. The higher civilization a nation possesses, the less a need for nicknames is felt, and the ones coined are more on the polite, or at least the neutral, side. Civilization provides a better use of language and communication so that awkward nicknames are not required so much for identification of the individual. In the United States today nicknames are heard chiefly among participants in team sports, in the school yard, and among the criminal element.

It is often difficult, as has been stated, to decide in just which class of surnames a particular name falls. Nicknames are especially intricate because any name in any classification could have been acquired as a nickname from some habit, external aspect or casual act. For example, a man might be nicknamed *Shoemaker* because he once made a particularly good pair of shoes for his wife, or *Bishop* because he looked like an ecclesiastic, or *Newcastle* because he was always talking about the place, or *St. Paul* because he was continually quoting the saint. Or each of these nicknames could come about for any of a dozen reasons. Nicknames not infrequently have an ironical cast. Pet forms are classed by some authorities as nicknames, but they are mostly a shortened form of font names and have been discussed in Chapter II. Sign names are by some contended to be nicknames; these are examined in Chapter V.

The circumstances attending the bestowal of most nicknames which became fixed family names have been lost in antiquity. But one can be sure that they were originally applied in exactly the same manner as nicknames are given today. Particularly apt nicknames spring forth suddenly in ridicule, rage, or satire when circumstances warrant. Many start in childhood where they are conferred in the family or on the playground. Everyone knows of the bestowal of nicknames among friends and acquaintances which have clung fast throughout life. Medieval nicknames in all countries at all times came about in exactly the same manner. Few general statements can be made about the meaning of family names that have come down to us from nicknames. One important principle might be noted: the majority of nicknames when first applied carried a derogatory connotation, a definite sense of contempt.

Bardsley cites various disagreeable nicknames found in early English records such as Thomas *Colfox* "deceitful fox," Roger *Piggesflesh*, John *Pourfishe*, Thomas *Catsnose*, William *Cocksbrain*, Matthew *Goosebeak*, and John *Bullhead*. Of course, these names have become obsolete. Descendants quickly discarded them or concealed the obvious meaning by changes in spelling. Even the simple change from Colfox to COLFAX "black hair" produced an acceptable appellation and the name is now found in our directories, although most of them do derive from the dark hair of the first bearer. The early rolls contain many frank nicknames that have failed to stand the test of time and have been shuffled off.

Most of the unusual and often colorful epithets of the Middle Ages have not survived and therefore have never entered America for which we must be most thankful. Terms referring even to the *membrum virile* are found as surnames in very early times. Instances of the free use of synonyms for both the male and female organs may be observed both in Chaucer and in Shakespeare. Opprobrious or indecent nicknames are discarded as soon as the opportunity presents itself.

Many of the kings of France are known to us by nicknames that do not describe them. Louis VIII was called *the Lion*, but was feeble in mind and body. Philip II, a selfish king, was nicknamed *the Magnanimous*. The next Philip was *the Daring*, but was far from fearless or adventurous. Philip VI, a most unfortunate monarch, was called *the Lucky*. Jean, a bad king, was known as *the Good*. Charles VI, who was an idiot, and Louis XV, a depraved libertine, were dubbed *the Well-Beloved*. Henry II, a man of safe pleasure, was known as *the Warlike*. Louis XIII, who was any

hing but moral and upright, was *the Just.* Louis XVIII, who was
ot desired by the people, was called *the Desired.*

All the French kings bearing the name of Charles (from 714
o 1483) acquired unusual nicknames. In chronological order they
vere *the Hammer, the Great, the Bald, the Fat, the Simple, the
3ad, the Sage, the Idiot, the Dauphin, the Bold,* and *the Foolish.*
Che father of William I of England was Robert *the Devil,* Duke
of Normandy.

Raymond of Barcelona was called *Stuffing-Head.* Foulques
l'Anjou was known as *Gray-Beard.* In Scotland there were Alex-
ınder I, *the Fierce,* Malcolm IV, *the Maiden,* and William, *the
_ion.* More than forty kings, rulers, and popes have been sur-
ıamed "the Great." Many others have been given such sobriquets
ıs *the Lion, the Pious, the Red, the Saint,* and *the Wise.*

Early English kings were Edward *the Elder,* Edward *the
Martyr,* Ethelred *the Unready,* Edmund *Ironside,* Harold *Hare-
oot,* and Edward *the Confessor.* There were William *the Con-
jueror* also called *the Bastard,* William *Rufus,* Henry *Beauclerk*
good clerk," Henry *Curtmantle* "short robe," Richard *Crookback,*
Richard *Cœur de Lion* "Lion-Hearted," John *Lackland,* Edward
_ongshanks,* and Edward *the Peacemaker.* Henry VIII was given
easier treatment as *Hal,* and the first Elizabeth was called *Bess.*
Nicknames of rulers are almost never hereditary. *Plantagenet,* the
exception, is a nickname first applied to Geoffrey, count of Anjou,
lerived from his wearing in his cap a sprig of the broom plant,
vhich descended as a dynasty name.

Since there are so many surnames derived from nicknames,
orimary attention has to be given only to the more common ones
n the United States. Names in other languages will occur to many
eaders with the same meanings as for names listed here. While
t is not possible to list all the surnames found in the land of the
ree, income-taxpaying people, practically all the meanings or
lerivations are found here. This is especially true of nicknames.

Surnames connected with the church, ABBOTT, BISHOP, CLERK,
MONK, PRIEST, and VICAR, sometimes arise from nicknames ap-
olied to men who exhibited some ecclesiastical accomplishment,
moral trait, or mannerism. People are quick to deprecate another
when they think he is exhibiting a "holier than thou" attitude
oward them, and a contemptuous nickname is an easy way to

accomplish one's purpose. The more important origins of these official nicknames are discussed in the chapter on occupational names.

By far the most common nickname is BROWN, an appellation applied to one brown, or dark red, of hair or complexion, principally the latter. A few Browns refer to the ancestor named Brun "brown," but this was not a common forename in England after the Conquest in 1066. As BRUN and BRUNS it is found in Germany, BRUNO in Italy, and the French say LE BRUN. Other English spellings are BROWNE, BROUN, BROUNE, BRON, and BURNETT, the diminutive form; this latter name also designating the man who lived in or near the place cleared of trees and bushes by burning. The explanation for several different spellings or even several different nicknames with the same or similar meaning ascribed to one country is that they arose independently in different parts of the nation due to differences in regional dialect.

The English not being predominantly light of skin had many with extremes of dark coloring and some of them became Brown. Basically an unexciting name and in this country not very descriptive, Brown arose to the notice of all when John Brown, the American abolitionist fanatic, seized Harpers Ferry, Virginia, thereby becoming one of the first civil rights leaders who resorted to violence; he was convicted of treason and hanged in 1859.

Other Englishmen became BLAKE or BLACK from their swarthy complexion. Some named BLACKMAN had a swarthy complexion but generally that name derives from the Old English personal name Blæcman. Some BLAKES derive from Old English *blac* meaning white or pale. Thus BLAKE or BLACK, curiously, may have originally designated either a light or a dark person—black or white. BLACKIE and BROWNIE, rather rare names, refer to the color of the eyes, except in Scotland where they may be diminutive forms.

Some family names that designate an ancestor who had skin darker than his companions are MURRELL and MORRILL. SORRELL, like the horse, indicates a reddish, yellow-brown skin. In northern England and in Scotland BISSETT might become the name for the brown or dark-complexioned man. Similar German names are BRAUN, BRAUNEIS, and BRUHN. The Russians would call their dark people CHERNOFF while in Czechoslovakia they would be satisfied with CHERNEY. CAREY, DORGAN, DUFF, DUNN, DUNNE, and KERWIN or KIRWAN are all names for the dark Irishman. The French names are BURNELL and MORIN, the latter in Spain and Italy becoming MORENO. CARDENAS, the bluish person in Spain, also had skin darker than most. Italy also described some with dark complexions as FOSCO. Greek MAVROS was darker than his neighbors. In Finland, MUSTANEN designated one with a remote ancestor who was dark of skin. PINCUS is a Hebrew surname for one darker than average. They all came to America and live in peace here now.

If the ancestor had a very dark complexion, the name was likely to become MOHR, SWARTZ, SWART, SCHWARTZ or SCHWARZ in Germany. NEGRON is the Spanish masculine augmentative of *negro* "black," signifying the very dark or black man. ZWARTZ is found in the Netherlands. The Irish were quick to call their swarthy neighbors who were dark or black by such names as DOLAN, DOODY, DOW, DOWD, DOUD, DRUMMEY, DUFFIN, and KEARNS or KERNS. Greek names with this connotation are KARAS and MELAS. From Hungary comes FEKETE. In Czechoslovakia they have CERNY sometimes spelled CZERNY. In the riots of 1212, in what is now that country, Chancellor Scornir was driven out and his castle of Chudenitz burned and all but one of his sons massacred. The nurse concealed the little boy in the chimney of the castle. When the mob departed, the boy was found to be so covered with soot that he was passed off as Czerny "black." It being unsafe to resume his former name he and his descendants elected to call themselves CZERNY. In the Ukraine the form is CORNEY. Similar Polish names are CZARNIK, CZERNIAK, and CZARNECKI. In France, MOREAU was a dark-skinned man, perhaps a Moor. Other countries have names for their dark or swarthy people, but in America they are not so common as most of the names mentioned.

Those with unusually light complexions are BLANK, from Old French *blanc* "white," and BLOUNT or BLUNT from Old French *blund* "blond or yellow-haired" in England; BAINES or BAYNES in Scotland; and BANNON, GAYNOR, GAINER, GALVIN, and GALLIGAN among the Irish. Wales and Ireland both have TEAGUE and TEGGE, and GWYNN and GWIN are Welsh forms. For those unduly light the Germans and Dutch use LICHTER, LICHT, and WITT or

WITTY. Also some Dutch include the definite article to make i
DeWITT or DEWIT. Those from Greece are named ARGOS and
from Italy BIANCO or BIANCHI, or with the article, LoBIANCO. The
French prefer BLANC or LeBLANC, BLANCHARD, and BLANCHET
Polish light-skinned people are BIALEK, BIALAS, BIALY, and LABNO
BILEK, BILKO, and BILY have this same meaning in Czechoslo
vakia. A gray youth in Ireland might be dubbed KILLELEA. In
Finland the name is VALKOINEN. It must not be forgotten tha
many of these names that seem to refer to the color of the ski
also designate the color of the hair.

This nicknaming by reference to color is found everywhere
Our forefathers used color in referring to the familiar animals
Their hides furnished their current designations. As Bardsley illus
trates in his *English Surnames,*

Thus we find the horse familiarly known by such titles as 'Morell
from its moorish or swarthy tan, or 'Lyard,' that is, dapple-grey, or
'Bayard,' bay, or 'Favell,' dun, or 'Blank,' white. The dark hide of the
ass got for it the sobriquet of 'Dun,' a term still preserved in the old
proverb, 'As dull as Dun in the mire,' while again as 'Burnell' it
browner aspect will be familiar to all readers of Chaucer. Thus also
the fox was known as 'Russell,' the bear as 'Bruin,' and the young hind
from its early indefinite red, 'Sorrell.'

Today young women are popularly differentiated as "brunettes,
"blondes," or "redheads."

Most of the color names, or names indicating light or dark
refer to the color of the hair or complexion. As to any particula
person's name it is impossible to say whether it originally referred
to hair or complexion. The Venerable Bede, writing of two mis
sionaries in the early part of the eighth century both of whom
bore the name Hewald, observed that one was called Hewald
Black and the other Hewald White being distinguished by the
color of their hair. With most of the color names it can be said
that they definitely designated hair or complexion. Some, how
ever, are patronymics showing descent as when WHITE derive
from the Old English given name, Hwita "white," and Irish
DINEEN, DONEGAN, and DOONAN are descended from little Don
"brown."

The names meaning "red" definitely refer to the red-haired
person, although it must be admitted that a few denote the man

with a ruddy complexion. Back in the family drug store in Huron, South Dakota, Hubert H. Humphrey, the Democratic party's choice for the presidency in 1968, was known as *Pinkie* because of his complexion. In most European nations the genial, red-topped man stood out from the crowd and received a nickname which called attention to his head color. The stranger with red hair can often be so addressed and he will answer without irritation. The strength of nicknames for the red-haired person is illustrated by the many slang terms which are easily understood such as brick top, carrot head, hot top, hot head, ginger top, red thatched roof, rusty, sandy, and kewpie; a girl might be called a strawberry blonde. Red for a redhead is such a solid term that it has not been as yet tarnished by the use of the word for a Communist.

In English the word *red*, during the origin of surnames, was pronounced with the long vowel and spelled READ, REDE, and REED and these were the forms that became surnames for those with redheaded ancestors. REID is the Scottish spelling. Not until after the time surnames became fixed was the vowel shortened to make the pronunciation and spelling our familiar "red." As a surname the spelling RED is almost non-existent. REDMAN is sometimes observed, but usually this name is a variant spelling of Redmond "counsel, protection." HUDAK is the Slovakian name for the man with red hair. Italian PINTOZZI "the painted or colored one" includes the connotation of red.

Other English names designating the reddish-brown head are BAY, GOUGH, RUDD, RUDDY, RUFF, RUSS, RUSSELL, RUST, and RUUD. The French called them LAROUSSE, ROUSE, ROUSSEAU, and ROUX, while in Germany the name was ROTH. Italian PURPURA, ROSSINI, ROSSETTI, with other variants, were quite popular. VOROS in Hungary, CERVENY and CERVENKA in Czechoslovakia, and COKINOS and PYRRHOS in Greece served well. The Irish FLYNN and GOOCH had red hair, as did the well-traveled KILROY.

James I. Kilroy, for those who have grown up since World War II, was a shipyard inspector when the war came in 1941. To remind his superiors that he was on the job, he began chalking "Kilroy was here" on the metal plates of tanks and ships which came under his critical eye. The war material went all over the world and so did his slogan. Then the soldiers took it up. Everywhere was found the assertion of Kilroy's former presence, and legend put him everywhere—when our soldiers broke through or captured a place they were sure to find the confession already written, "Kilroy was here." The name is consequently regarded as a definitely American name all over the world. James I. Kilroy died in Boston in 1962.

There are some names strictly denoting the man with light hair or dark hair, such as FAIRFAX "fair hair" from Old English *fæger* "fair" and *feax* "hair" and Irish GANNON with the same meaning. German GELB, Greek XANTHOS, Irish McEVOY, BOWIE, and BOYD and Czechoslovakian ZLATY named the person who had golden or yellow hair. Not many surnames can be clearly said to connote dark or black hair probably because the dark-haired people outnumbered others and it was not a truly significant distinction. The German SCHWARTZKOPF translates to black head as does the English BLACKETT and BLACKLOCK, and the Irish DEEGAN and DIGNAN. BLAYLOCK or BLALOCK had dark or lead-colored hair. The white head in German is named WEISKOPF or WEISHAUPT. Then there are WHITEHEAD, WHITELOCK, and SHERLOCK in English. SHERLOCK also named the dweller at the bright or clear stream or pool. BELOHLAV in Czechoslovakia is the man with the white head. SNOWMAN generally means the white head. WEISSMAN, WEISS, WHITMAN, WHITE, and WHYTE are the white-haired gentry in Germany and England. NIEVES meaning "snow" describes the white-haired man in Spain.

The names that connote gray refer generally to hair and because gray-haired people are usually old people it can be said that they also often merely designate "the old man." Such names found in America are GRAY, GREY, and HOAR (English), GROH, GRAU, and GRAUER (German), STARZYK and SEDIVY (Slavic) while the Spanish and Italians use PARDO and PARDOE. A contributory source of these last two names is Pardo, a pet form of Leopardo "lion, hard." LLOYD and LOYD from Welsh *llwyd* "gray or brown" are color names that carry the significations of both brown and gray.

Besides color of the hair there are various family names that call attention to some peculiarity of the hair in a remote ancestor. With curly or wavy hair Germans are surnamed KRAUSE, KRUSE and KRULL, also KRUMHAAR. Hungarians with curly hair are

Surnames from Description or Action

FODOR, Italians are RICCIO or RIZZO, Slavs are KUCERA, KENDZIOR, or KENDZIERSKI, and Irish are CASHIN and CASSIDY. Irish QUIRK had bushy hair, although in some cases this name designated the grandson of Corc "heart." Bristly haired Germans may be BORST or STRUBE. The Frenchman with shaggy, unkempt hair would likely be surnamed BROUSSARD, literally "brushwood." The German with unusual body hair would be called RAUCH, RAUEN, and RAUHE; the Hungarian so decorated might be KOSSUTH; the Italian would be CESARIO; and a Ukrainian with a prominent hair tuft would become CHUBATY. With shorn or close cut hair the Englishman would be POLLARD and the Italian would be CARUSO. Robinson Crusoe did not necessarily have any mythical ancestor so shorn, because, the reader will remember, Daniel Defoe, in the very first paragraph, had Robinson say that his surname was corrupted from Kreutznaer. Kreutznaer designates the German who dwelt at the cross or boundary mark.

The bald man even today often hears himself so called. Hairless heads were ancestors of family heads today with such names as BALCH, BALD, and BALLARD, in England. BALD is sometimes a short form of such names as Baldwic and Baldwin; at other times it fades into BALL. CALLAWAY and CALLOWAY are derived from Old English *calewa* "bald." COFFIN is sometimes from French *chauvin* "bald" to refer to the little bald man, and the French surname is CHAVIN. Gösta Tengvik in his *Old English Bynames* maintains that KNOTT (sometimes simplified to NOTT) usually designates the bald or close-cropped head. GLATZ in Germany and MULLINS in Ireland were known for their bald heads. LUNA "moon-headed" refers to the absence of head hair in Italy. The prophet Elisha had a bald head as we learn in the Bible, from II Kings 2:23, when the small boys mocked him with "Go up, thou bald head! Go up, thou bald head!" Probably only the reverence paid Elisha by reason of his position as the beloved leader of the prophetic guilds and the high esteem in which he was held by King Joash prevented him from going down in history by this generally repugnant nickname.

Facial hair sets a man apart. Since the outline of the face is the part we look to in order to recognize and like the person, any unusual facial hair or other feature is certain to provoke a descriptive sobriquet. BEARD and SKAGGS, together with Spanish

153

BARBERA, are men with large or unusual beards. The Slavic nations call such men BROD and BRODSKY, or if with a small mustache, WASIK. The "man with the beard" in Germany becomes BARTH, or without a beard, GOLZ and GOLTZ. Greek SPANOS had an ancestor noted for being beardless. USENKO has a long beard while BILOUSCENKO has a white one in the Ukraine. Italian LOMBARDO sometimes denotes the man with the long beard, and even if it suggests only a man from Lombardy, the ancestor probably had a long beard, as some contend that the Italian province was the land of the men with the long beards.

The man with the black beard would receive the words as a nickname, but the surname is now obsolete, possibly due to the reputation of the English pirate, Blackbeard (Edward Teach), who harassed the Spanish Main until he was killed in the attack on his ship, *Queen Anne's Revenge,* by two naval sloops sent by the governor of Virginia. The uncommon name BLACKBIRD is a corruption of Blackbeard. ROTHBART, the German with the red beard, is found in our American directories. GRAUBART is the old man with a gray beard. Every line and conspicuous feature about the face and hair have been used in verbal and written identification.

Size always attracted attention and the names for the tall, big, lanky man are many and varied. Common ones are: BIGGS, HAGER, LONG, and LONGFELLOW (English); LAING (Scottish); LANGAN (Irish); FELTZ, HOCH, HOMAN, LANG, and LANGER (German); LONG, LELONG, and LEGRAND (French); DE GROOTE and GROOT (Dutch); LONGO (Italian); STATURA (Spanish); WYSOCKI (Polish); and MAKRIS (Greek). The names LONG and LANG have more the connotation of large or big rather than great linear extent or length, except where they have the meaning of tallness. When a Mr. Longworth was presented to Henry Wadsworth Longfellow, Longworth remarked upon the similarity of their names. "Yes," said Longfellow, "but I believe that you have the advantage. Didn't Pope say 'Worth makes the man, and want of it the fellow'?"

Closely allied and often indistinguishable from this group recognized by reference to size are those numerous names meaning large, fat, plump, stocky, husky, such as CHOATE, GRACE, GRASS, GREET, MAJOR, ROUNDS, STUCKEY or STOCKEY, and TRAPP in England; HALPIN and HALFPENNY in Ireland (Halfpenny is not always an ironic term and may at times as a patronymic refer to the grandson of Ailpin "the little stout person"); DICK and DICKMAN, GROSS and GROSSMAN, GROTH, MOCK and MOCKLER, RIES, RUND, SCHMALZ, and STUMPF (the big man stands out) in Germany; GRAND, GRAS, GROS, and ROUNDLETT in France; BUICK in Holland (not always one who would "really rather have a Buick"); WASKEY in the Ukraine; NAGY in Hungary; WIELGUS in Poland; also GRANT and GRAND in Scotland, France, and England; and among the Hebrews, LEVITON or LEVITAN. Truly the big man had to be respected everywhere.

During and after the Civil War, Grant was not only a big man but a big American name, the eighteenth president of the United States. The future general was baptized Hiram Ulysses Grant. The story goes that in registering at West Point he reversed the order of his given names to avoid the kidding he knew was sure to come over his initials H.U.G. But his congressman in appointing him had mistakenly reported his given names as Ulysses Simpson, giving him the maiden name of his mother. Grant tried but was not successful in an attempt to correct his name in the record and accepted it.

The Early English words for large, fat, bulky were *michel* and *muchel*. From these words are derived the modern surnames MICKLE, MICKEL, MUCH, and MUTCH. However, as the old words became obsolete the surnames tended to become lost in the common MITCHELL and even in the Christian name MICHAEL. Gluttons or gourmands are observed in all nations and the general overweight of the American people is evidence of this universal characteristic. French BOUFFARD is a nickname acquired from an ancestor's habit of overeating observed by others. Irish GLAVIN was a grandson of Glaimhim "glutton." The fat person not so named trying to slim down may take what solace he can knowing that the problem has attracted attention at all times everywhere.

As the old poem says, names often go by contraries, and this is especially true of nicknames relating to size or bulk. Almost everyone knows of a fat man or boy who acquired Tiny as a nickname. Thus many of the names with the connotation of small or little mentioned in the next paragraph may have been originally applied to the large man in derision. Much less frequently does one

155

observe the opposite—a small man is seldom denominated by a term meaning large or fat.

In contrast to the large or fat man is the small, little, thin, or dwarfish man, and he is nicknamed BASS, BLOCK, GRUBB, LITT, LITTELL, LYTE, LYTLE, MURCH, PRIME, SHORT, SMALL, SCRUGGS, and SPRIGGS in England; KLEIN and KLINE (often Englished into CLINE), KURTZ, KUS, RAHN, STUTZ, and WENIG in Germany; MALECKI, MALEC, MALY, and NIZIOLEK in Poland; MALEK and MALYSHEV in Russia; LACOUR and PETIT in France; BASSO and CURCIO in Italy; MAGER in Holland; BEGGS, SMAIL, and PETTY in Scotland; MALY in Czechoslovakia; MAZEIKA in Lithuania; NESTOR in Ireland; KOROTCENKO in the Ukraine; and the popular KISS and TOTH in Hungary. BASSETT is the English spelling and BASSET the French for the short man, from Old French *basset* "of low stature." Ralph Basset is listed in Domesday Book (1086). At a time when both English and Norman-French were spoken in England such names would often need to be listed in both English and French.

The thin, slender man of Spanish extraction would acquire the surname DELGADO. The Poles may call a small man GUZIK "little button." Also, sometimes with affection, the Dutch denominate a man as BOYKIN "little boy." An English endearment name is CHICK, while the affectionate Italian name for the small child or man is PICCOLO.

Body peculiarities are an important source of nicknames which developed into family names. Among our rude ancestors there was little hesitancy in referring bluntly to the crippled or lame man and he became CROCKETT, CROOKS or CROOK, CRUM or CRUMP, and GEE in England (GEE also derives from an ancestor who formerly lived in Gee in Cheshire); KROM, SCHEEL, or SCHRAM among the Germans; while Czechoslovakians made it PALKA; the Ukrainians called them KRYVENKO; and the Dutch named them MANKE. The crippled or deformed man in Scotland might be called SPIVEY. SCHEEL is also Dutch for a cross-eyed or squinting man. German KRUMBEIN designates the man with a crooked leg. Irish CROTTY and CURTIN had an ancestor with a hunchback.

The simple name of a part of the body is frequently used as a nickname to call attention to a physical part or characteristic of the person. For example, when a person acquires such a byname as HEAD, those who originated the name did not intend to emphasize the fact that the man possessed a head. They merely wished to point out that his head was large, misshapen, or had some peculiar quality easily and quickly perceived upon inspection. In our own day Marie MacDonald, the actress, was known as "The Body." Of course, she had a body; the viewer observed its perfection. Students who earn good grades are sometimes nicknamed "The Brain." Thus such anatomical surnames as FOOT, LEGG, CHEEK, HAND, FINGER, and BACK are sometimes nicknames calling attention to such a peculiar or unusual member, although these names have other and more usual derivations. A name such as BEARD could call attention to the fact that the man had a beard especially in a neighborhood where most men were without facial adornments, but probably the name usually indicated a beard with some peculiar quality.

If the head were large, ugly, or misshapen, that fact would likely figure in the nickname by which the man was known and could easily descend to his posterity. In England the ancestor would become BROADHEAD, BULLITT, HEAD, or TATE, or in Germany HAUPT, KOPF, or GROSSKOPF. This last name has been corrupted into the more genteel GROSSCUP by some families in America. The Germans had many nicknames terminating in -*kopf* "head," such as HIRSCHKOPF "hart's head" and RINDSKOPF "ox head," although undoubtedly many names of this type came from house signs.

Italian names for the large head are CAPUTO, CAPONE, and TESTA, although this last name is sometimes a condensed form of the given name, Battista "Baptist." In Italy CAPUTO and CAPONE were also applied to one who was stubborn or dull-witted. "Scarface" Al Capone, the notorious American gangster, made the name almost an "American" name throughout the world through the murderous activities of the "Capone mob." MALATESTA had an ancestor with a bad or deformed head in Italy. Polish GLOWACKI, Ukrainian HOLOVATENKO, and French TESTER (this last name from Old French *testard*) also surnamed the family having an early forebear with a large or peculiar head.

KENNEDY is the Gaelic name for one with an ugly or misshapen head. But the great Kennedy families of Ireland, Scotland, and

America did not allow public attention to the big, ugly, mis-shapen head of their ancestor to keep them down. One member became president of the United States; his brother's bid for the presidency was curtailed by an assassin, and another brother is now in the wings. Some of the clan do contend that the name is derived from a word meaning "head armor," and they could be right. Robert Grosseteste "big head," nicknamed *Greathead*, the famous thirteenth-century English theologian and scholar, did not let his name interfere with defense of his rights and privileges against the pope and King Henry III. The name has, however, become obsolete. SMOLLETT is the man with a small head; the termination *-head* sometimes shrinks to *-ett* or *-itt*, as in BULLETT "bull head." In France, CABOT had a small head. The ugly man in Holland would acquire HESSLICH as a name, but this surname, understandably, is quite rare.

French NASON had a small nose while German ZINK or ZINKE had a large or prominent one. ZINKE is also metonymic for one who played the medieval cornet, the zinke. The great Highland CAMERON clan in Scotland descended from one with a crooked or wry nose. It has been stated that a hooked nose was a characteristic of the old Clan Cameron families. The Lowland Camerons, however, came from Cameron "crooked hill," a parish in Fife. The CAMPBELL clan originated from a crooked or wry mouth of the early ancestor, although the name may have really indicated arched lips. Opposing clans have contended that the Campbell name came about because of moral rather than physical defects. Scottish GIFFORD had an ancestor with fat or chubby cheeks. The Italian ugly mouth is BOCCACCIO. In Germany and England the name MAUL or MAULE called attention to one with a large mouth. FIGURA in Spain and Italy names one with an unusual face or figure. CHEEK is the man with a jutting jaw in England, although in some cases it is a name of endearment meaning "chick or little chicken." Spanish CARRILLO probably had an ancestor with a small but prominent jaw.

One with bow or peculiar legs, especially Scots, would become SHANK or SHANKS and perhaps CRUIKSHANK, although this name also depicts the dweller near the crooked, projecting point of a hill. The usual term in medieval times for legs was shanks. LEGG as a surname usually refers to the dweller in or near a meadow,

158

from Old English *leage* "meadow," although it does in a few cases denominate the person with a crippled or deformed leg. The Russian LAPIN originally had big feet. German KUHFUSS "cow foot" probably denominated the man with a club foot, as did KAULFUSS. These names have crossed the Atlantic unchanged and are found in some American directories. Kuhfuss has come into prominence with William J. Kuhfuss as president of the Illinois Agricultural Association.

The German FINGER may have had an unusual digit or the name may have arisen from a landscape feature using the word in some transferred sense. Polish PALUCH also means finger. DAUM in Germany may have had a large or unusual, possibly deformed, thumb.

Russian Premier, Aleksei KOSYGIN, has a family name that suggests a squint-eyed ancestor, as does Ukrainian KOSJACENKO. A disfiguring spot or mark originated the name FLECK or FLICK. PINTO was the Spaniard with a scar or blemish. Spanish CAMACHO had a hunchback or was otherwise crippled, although some of that name merely came from Camacho in Granada. Any part of the body that was unduly large or particularly small or was too prominent or deformed would tend to give rise to a nickname that became a surname for succeeding generations. Medieval people were cruel in openly noticing bodily defects.

There are probably more different nicknames suggesting mental or moral qualities than any other condition. Some are, of course, applied in an ironic manner. The cheerful, merry, gay, agreeable, pleasant man or companion evoked a nickname which, being a commendable characteristic, was not likely to be exchanged or altered. Some of these are BLISS, BLYTH, CORLISS, GAY, GAYLORD, JOY, MERRIAM, MERRIMAN, MERRIWEATHER (Merry formerly meant "pleasant and agreeable" as in the term, Merry England), PLEASANT, and ROOT. A contributory source of MURRAY is Middle English *murie* "merry." The Germans with this quality are named FROEHLICH, FUNK, and LUSTIG. The Slavs appreciate BLAHA, MELE, and ZMICH. French names are DOUCETTE and JOLY. Mr. ALLEGRETTI comes from Italy and Mr. FELICITAS from Spain.

The friendly, dear, beloved person is responsible for such family names as DARLING, FEARS (from Middle English *fere* "comrade"), FRIEND, GOODFRIEND, LEAF, SWEET, SWEETMAN, SWETT, and TREAT, all having been bestowed because of the endearing nature of the original bearers. Scottish FARRAR is a corruption of Farquhar "friendly." DORMAN and DEARMAN also have this connotation of neighborliness when not derived from the man who had to do with deer or wild animals. Old English *deore* "beloved" is related through sound with Old English *deor* "wild animal," and the resulting surnames are inextricably interwoven. BLOOD is a child or dear person when not metonymic for a bloodletter or not a contraction of the Welsh ap Lloyd. BUNTING, as in "Bye, baby bunting," also developed as a term for a good little child. In some cases this name may be a sign name from the bunting "finch." Germans use such similar names as FREUND, LIEB, SCHATZ, and SUSSMAN. With the Slavs it is LUBY or LOOBY. The Italians use AMATO, familiar to all with a smattering of Latin, and the French name is PAQUETTE. English DRURY from Old French *druirie* "love or friendship," nicknames the sweetheart or lover. Such a man would be notorious in a small village where idle gossip was the favorite recreation.

The lucky or fortunate men in Germany are Messrs. GLICK, GLICKMAN, and GLUCK; in England and Scotland there is FORTUNE, with FORTUNATO from Italy, and FELICIANO from Spain. One may wonder what particular good fortune fell to the lot of the first ancestor so named. MALLORY designated the unfortunate or unhappy man. SEELEY and SILLIMAN from Old English *selig*, now our word *silly*, meant "the happy or prosperous man" at the time of the origin of surnames, later "the good, simple man." Sely with the medieval meaning is also found as a woman's font name. This word "silly" as we use it today illustrates the shift of meaning over the years of words and names. Starting as "blessed, happy, or prosperous" the meaning degenerated thusly: "innocent—simple—simple-minded—foolish." The English still use the phrase "Silly Suffolk" with the connotation of "happy or blessed." In Germany the name is SELIGMAN.

The beautiful or handsome person would be so labeled, and his descendants might be surnamed FAIR or FAIRCHILD or even BELCHER (not now a very genteel or polite term, but originally influenced by the French to carry the connotation of beauty and love). The early meaning of fair was "beautiful." FAIR is derived sometimes, though, from Middle English *fere* "comrade." Ger-

man names for handsome men are HUBSCH, SCHOEN, SCHON, and
SHAIN. French names are BELLAMY "beautiful friend," sometimes
in an ironic vein, BEAUREGARD, LE BEAU, DUBEAU, and LE BELLE.
A Hebrew name with a similar meaning is JOFFE sometimes
spelled JAFFE.

Other nicknames, now family names, are those with the connotations of "good" or of "friend," most of the English ones having been influenced by the French. There are BONE, BONNER,
BONNEY, GOOD, GOODBODY (sometimes just an epithet of courteous address), and GOODFELLOW. BUNKER is a similar name from
the French, voicing the English tongue stumbling over *bon cœur*
"good heart." Italian names are BONELLI, BONFIGLIO, BONO,
BONOMO, and BUONO. The Polish people use the name DOBRY.
GUZMAN refers to the good man in Spain; however, this name has
other interpretations such as the good, competent noble who in
medieval times aided in the enlistment of soldiers, and "descendant of Guzman," or one who came from the village of that name.

Although our early forebears are sometimes regarded as crude
and ill-bred, at least during the time surnames were becoming
fixed, they appreciated the courteous, polite man with elegant
manners. In merry old England he acquired such names as
CURTIS, FINE, GALLANT, GENTRY, and HANDY. In feudal society
CURTIS also denoted a man with a good education. GALE is the
gay or lively person, except in some instances where it refers to
the man who lived near the jail, from Old Norman French *gaiole*.
The Italians use GENTILE and GRAZIANO, the French, GALLAS and
the Germans, FEIN. PANEK and ZEMAN are Slavic names with a
similar meaning. KLOTZ designates the German without a grace-
ful manner, and HARNACK for the hard-necked or obstinate man.

As admiration and respect for the wise or learned man is found
everywhere in the civilized world, so there are noted men with
that quality expressed in their family names. There are SAGE,
SENNOTT, WISE, and WISEMAN from England; KLUG and WEISMAN
from Germany; VROOMAN from Holland; MADURA from Poland;
and PREUCIL from Czechoslovakia. LEARNED might have been an
educated man, but the name is more correctly derived from
Leonard "lion, bold." The stupid, dull, or foolish individual acquired the name of LAPP in Germany, FOLLETTE in France, and
DURKEE and KAPUSTKA among the Slavs.

The fair-dealing or honest man is Mr. JUST from England and Herr EHRLICH from Germany. Perhaps this characteristic was not rare enough to set men apart and originate many surnames. The particularly loyal or faithful servant was denominated GOODHUE or GOODHUGH, and TRUEBLOOD. TRUMAN, the family name of a former president of the United States, denotes the true, faithful, or trusty man or servant, and much has been made of this name by the news media. The Germans used BIEDERMANN, GUTKNECHT, LIEBMAN, and TRAUTMAN. In Gutknecht the German *gut* can blend with Goth and Gott to produce the meaning "God's servant," as in GOTTSCHALK. GOODENOUGH was a nickname applied to one who was just sufficient or satisfactory in some sense; the name is often contracted to GOODENOW and GOODNOW. MAXIM specifies "the greatest."

The bold, brave, audacious man or soldier was esteemed, and today his descendant is known as CREWS, CROUSE, FRICK, MOODY (from Old English *modig* "bold, impetuous, brave," another word the meaning of which has changed since surname times), and the diminutive PRUITT. LEON and LEONE "lion" are sometimes nicknames for a brave man. From Germany, such men were nicknamed BOHL, BRAVERMAN, COON, FRECH, GUTH, KECK, KUHN, and PAHL. The opposite, the humble and submissive, were MEEKS or MEEK in England, KALBISCH in Germany, and POKORNY among the Slavs. Merely quiet men were STILL in England, FROMM in Germany, and CICHON in Poland. STILL may also designate the Englishman who lived near the fishing place or trap, from Old English *still*. SWEENEY was the peaceful, quiet man in Ireland, a country where peace and quiet were not always the natural order of things.

KEEN, LIGHTBODY, SMART, SNELL, SHARPE, SPRAGUE, and SPRY were the alert, lively, quick men in England with RASCH, SCHNELL, and SCHARF in Germany. SMART also had a meaning of fierce, one who inflicted pain, from Old English *smeortan* "causing pain." ZIV and ZIVIN are the vigorous, alert Slavs. SLEIGH and SLYE were dexterous or skilled in England. Germans who were excitable and hurried were RAUSH, STURM, and HUMMEL. PODRAZA was a Pole who stimulated others to action. England produced many grave, austere men who were labeled SEAVER, STARK, STARNES, STEARNS, and STERN. Different names or differences in

162

pelling and pronunciation for all these common mental or moral
ualities are due to the different languages and dialects current
1 England and other countries during medieval times. The seri-
us or solemn man in Italy was SERIO. The sour, morose, moody
1en in Germany were SAUER and WUNDERLICH, while SMUTNY
vas their counterpart in Czechoslovakia and DURKIN in Ireland.
VUNDERLICH also designated the curious German, the one who
oked his nose into everything.

Although nicknames calling attention to admirable qualities
vere more likely to persist down to modern times, many connot-
1g crude gaucheries or unattractive characteristics were con-
inued. COUTTS and COOTE are English nicknames from the coot,
pplied to a stupid man. RUNYON and SQUIBB were mean, mangy,
r scurvy men, and LORDAN was lazy, a vagabond; in Holland,
3ROFF was a coarse or boorish man while BOOZ was the angry
r cross man; in Poland, BURDA was a brawling fighter while
:WIK was cunning and ZMUDA was sluggish and lazy; English
'ETTIFORD, denoting an iron-footed person, probably indicated
he slow-moving man, or possibly a tireless walker. In England
{OYSTER was a blustering bully, PROUT was the proud, arrogant
ype, as was Irish DEMPSEY. English and Welsh GERRISH was the
howy or resplendent person.

SAVAGE and SALVAGE were   wild and fierce. RAMAGE, not a
ommon name, is from Old French *ramage* "wild." The name
lso designates the wild man who lived in the forest in Scotland;
ie must have found a wife in order to have his name live at all
n succeeding generations. In France, BOBBITT was the haughty,
ompous individual. Italian CONFORTI craved comfort. Scottish
ind Irish HASTIE was the impatient, violent man.

Our early ancestors had no qualms against labeling a man as
ι bastard, and in England Bastard as a surname was not unknown
ιs late as the seventeenth century. But since then most English-
nen so cognominated have been able to discard or alter the name
ieyond recognition. In France, Bastard can still be found, un-
:hanged, in the present-day directories. Americans by exercising
heir tendency to ridicule have completely eliminated the name
n the United States. German KEGEL, sometimes KAGEL, has this
lefinite connotation of illegitimacy, although in America some
iave changed the appearance to CAGLE, an innocuous English-

like name. FRUEHAUF in Germany designates the man born a bastard, although the German onomastic authorities soften the meaning somewhat to give the connotation of a child born before marriage. In many places marriage legitimizes children born previously.

The Italians were very free in labeling love children, and many with such names as INNOCENTI, TROVATO, RITROVATO, and DA MORE, also spelled D'Amore, are found in our directories. Whether these Italian names are meant merely to specify found lings or the more crude term "bastard" is often not clear. See on foundlings, page 277. Disclosure of such a disagreeable origin to an innocent-appearing name is no reason to cause distress to bearers of the name. Every family has this stain on its escutcheon whether it is visible or not. We are not answerable for the actions of our forebears, only for our own. Most surnames that had any connotation of contempt are likely to have been dropped before modern times. But there are a few left. The Russians designate a man from the Ukraine as KHOKHLOV, a name which expresses disdain. The Polish term of contempt for a little Jew is ZIDEK.

Everyone remembers boyhood friends who acquired nicknames through some stupid or ingenuous act or event which stuck to them for life. In many cases the action or event that called forth the sobriquet was forgotten but the nickname stuck like glue. When the nickname was acquired by a progenitor during the time family names were becoming fixed, the descendants who failed to change them were condemned to bear the name forever, or at least until the time of the generation that moved to America where change of name could be easily accomplished. There are numerous names of this nature although few of them became common. PUDDISTER is a curious name; it may have designated one, especially a woman, who was very busy in doing what was of little or no practical value. PINGREE was the Frenchman who was fond of playing the old game of cockles. One who walked with a haughty step or arrogant gait would become PROUDFOOT sometimes altered into PROUDFIT. Nikolai BULGANIN, the former Soviet premier, must have had in his family tree an early branch whose actions gave rise to scandal for that is the meaning of the name.

BAREFOOT is a nickname sometimes observed, although it is

Surnames from Description or Action

ltered to BARFOOT by simply dropping the offending *e*. What scapade did the original bearer indulge in to acquire the name? urely he did not acquire it from Whittier's "Barefoot boy, with heek of tan"! Some friars frequently traveled around the coun- ry barefoot, and that could give rise to such a nickname. Another ossible explanation for BAREFOOT is that it is a corruption of arford "barley ford" since the English tongue is apt to slip cross word endings. John Roy Barefoot, Jr., is president of IcKay Machine Co. of Youngstown, Ohio. Italian SCALZITTI de- cended from one who undoubtedly acquired the nickname hrough a habit of going about barefoot, a reminder that our odd Inglish nicknames are also found in other countries with exactly he same connotations.

There are several English nicknames for the swift courier, the nessenger, some of which describe the expeditious performance f the occupation in colorful language. GOLIGHTLY describes the unner who was fleet of foot, the Scottish corrupted form being GELLATLY. However, George F. Black in his work, *The Surnames f Scotland,* questions this explanation, and thinks that the termi- ation discloses it to be from some local name. Another nickname or the swift courier or messenger was LIGHTFOOT. SWIFT would asily nickname the runner who moved with great speed. Ralph wift was a courier to Edward III of England. The messenger vho was forced to travel by foot could be called PROCHASKA, "a valker" in Czechoslovakia. STURTEVANT, literally meaning "start orward" could be used to describe the messenger quick to re- pond. GOFORTH is undoubtedly another nickname for the mes- enger ordered to start out for his destination. With all the irritat- ng "messages" one is forced to listen to over the radio and tele- ision such communications are not the most soothing and trust- vorthy facts of life.

Habits which were open and obvious brought forth many nick- iames. A beggar might become LAZZARA in Italy or THIGPEN in Germany. English THIGPEN denotes a dweller at or near Thyga's nclosure or hill. If one were in the habit of belching or vomiting n public, the name RIHA would fit in Czechoslovakia. Among Czechs a man who tended goats might be PRK or PRCH because of he goatish odor he emitted. The slow or sluggish person in Spain ind Portugal was PACHECO. One who worked only in the winter

165

might be ZIMA among the Slavic peoples. In England STARK WEATHER was one who labored in severe weather; the man who would work only when the weather was good might find the name FAIRWEATHER bestowed upon him, although this name more often originated from residence at Faweather "many-colored heather" in Yorkshire. Irish DALY or DAILEY undoubtedly had an ancestor who was fond of attending meetings of various kinds, a gregarious sort of individual. Dutch CONKLIN designates one who plots or conspires; did he enter into intrigue with others? These names relating to action have been popular among all people from antiquity to the present day.

Habits in respect to the Demon Rum could give rise to permanent nicknames. The eastern European who frequently drank tall glasses of vodka might be known as STOPKA. One who drank unwisely in merry old England might be ironically named CAUDILL or CAUDLE from *caudel*, a mild, thin gruel mixed with ale, except in those cases where the man came from Caldwell or Caudle "cold spring," now Caudle Green in Gloucestershire. Nicknames for a teetotaller are DRINKWATER in England, BEVILACQUA in Italy, the rare TRINKWASSER in Germany, and BOILEAU in France, the names being sometimes applied in derision to an over-enthusiastic toper. Or these names might indicate one so poor that he could drink only water at a time when ale, the universal drink, was so cheap that it cost only a farthing a gallon. DRINKWINE is also occasionally found in America; the trait that gave rise to the nickname can be guessed even if the exact circumstances cannot be narrated.

Most of the men named LITTLEJOHN undoubtedly owe their appellation to playing the part in the Robin Hood plays. MERRIMAN, sometimes contracted to MERIAM or MERRIAM, arose in some cases from acting the part of one of Robin's men, an outlaw, as illustrated in the phrase, "Robin Hood and his Merry Men." It has been noted that GREENLEAF was also a character in the same pageants.

One who liked to sing, either in France or England, might be called CANTRELL, a diminutive form of cantor. In Poland, one who unduly enjoyed women's company could become BABIARZ. Slavic peoples appreciated freedom as much as others and their nickname, SVOBODA, has that meaning. It is curious to note that

Ludvik Svoboda was president of Czechoslovakia when the country was invaded by the Russians and their satellites in 1968 in order to crush the people's yearning for more freedom. A nationalist broadcast sheet entitled *Svoboda* emphasizes their hunger for liberty. The restless man of Russian ancestry would be called VOROSHILOV.

Visits to the Holy Land or to some sacred shrine could call for the application of an appropriate sobriquet. Some sent as a penance were often ordered to go barefoot; others did so to heighten the merit and efficacy of their good deed. This is the most probable origin of the surname BAREFOOT, mentioned a few pages back. One who had been to Jerusalem, in fulfillment of a vow or in repentance for sin, would bring back a palm branch to be deposited on the altar of the parish church. To advertise his piety he might carry a palm branch or a cross made of two short slips of a leaflet from the palm tree. Such a man would surely become known as PALMER. As it was easy to acquire the name and reputation by carrying a palm branch, some pious frauds undoubtedly became so named without having made the arduous trip. Others who had returned from Jerusalem might be called ZION "monument raised up," a hill in Jerusalem, also a religious name for the Holy Land of Palestine. A Frenchman returned from the Holy Land would be RAMEY.

Jerome's observation that the way to heaven is as short from Britain as from Jerusalem did not quench the zeal of those who yearned to see with their own eyes the places hallowed by the presence and deeds of their Lord. A traveler who had made a trip to a distant shrine would be glad to be known as PILGRIM in England, PULGRAM in Germany, and PELLEGRINI in Italy. If the destination had been Rome, the hallmark would be ROME or ROMAN in England, ROMANO in Italy, or ROMERO in Spain. TURCOTTE "the little Turk" was a French medieval nickname applied to a crusader. In early London the Pilgrim's Guild was founded to aid its members to go on pilgrimages to distant shrines. MEDINA is a Spanish surname for one who had returned from Medina "market," the holy city of Islam in Arabia.

One who visited another country could easily acquire its name as a nickname especially if he insisted on repeating continuously his adventures to his bored companions. Or a merchant might

167

have been quite successful in his commercial transactions with
foreign country and thus receive a nickname in accordance wit'
that fact. A surname embodying a reference to another place o
nation would not in all cases mean that an early ancestor ha‹
resided there. Names first applied as nicknames can be mos
elusive.

In a primitive community where machinery was scarce and a]
except the privileged classes worked with their hands, one wh‹
was stronger than others was admired and aptly named. The mos
common such name is ARMSTRONG which merely refers to th
strong-armed man. The great Scottish family of that name like
to explain the origin of the name from the act of their ancestor
the king's armor-bearer, who, it is claimed, helped an ancien
king of Scotland to remount when his horse was killed under hin
by bodily lifting the king onto another horse. The grateful mon
arch, to perpetuate the memory of such an important service
gave him the appellation of Armstrong and assigned to him for ‹
crest "an armed hand and arm; in the left hand a leg and foot i›
armor, couped at the thigh all proper." The strength of the earli
est Armstrongs was probably prominently displayed as partici
pants in the frequent wrestling matches on the village green.

The more awkward name Strongi'th'arm persisted down t‹
modern times; it is still part of a business corporation name i›
London but has not been found in American directories. Othe
English surnames calling attention to the fact that the origina
bearer was uncommonly muscular or powerful are DOTEY, DOTY
DOUGHTY, FORT, STITT, STRANG, STRENG, STRINGFELLOW, STRONG
and WIGHTMAN. A name with this connotation that looks like ‹
place name is STALLWORTH from Old English *staelwierthe* "sturdy
robust, brave."

KRAFT was the powerful man in Germany, and the strong
robust man in Holland was known as HARTIG. The French POIN
CARE meant "square fist," designating the virile man. In the Slavi‹
countries DUBIEL was "strong as an oak." MUSKIE, in Czechoslo
vakia, was strong, a tower of strength. Edmund Sixtus Muskie
United States senator from Maine, selected by Hubert Humphrey
to be his vice president, was chosen to give strength to the Demo‹
cratic ticket in 1968. Senator Muskie, nevertheless, is the son o
a Polish tailor surnamed MARCISZEWSKI "descendant of Marcin"

from Mars, the god of war) who shortened his name to Muskie .fter arrival in this country in 1903. The little, strong, fierce man n Ireland bequeathed the name LONERGAN to his descendants. Closely akin to the neighborhood man of great strength was the bold, brave, valiant leader: STOUT lived in England, VAILLANT in France, VALENTE in Italy, and WYETH, sometimes spelled WYTHE, mong the Welsh and Scots. WYETH in some cases refers to the dweller near a ford or wood.

A defective or unusual voice is the basis of some family names. LAWLER was the Irishman who mumbled or was unable to enunciate his words clearly. HRUBY in Czechoslovakia talked in a low r gruff voice. SPROUL in England spoke in a slow, drawling manner, while his neighbor SPRAGGINS was the little, lively, garrulous man, and JAY, from Old French *jay* "chatterer," was the person who talked and chattered incessantly. In Germany, SCHALLER was the one who was over-talkative.

An overworked word or phrase can easily initiate a nickname. Those who were addicted to the excessive use of the oath "by God" became BIGOTT, PARDEW, PERDUE, PURDUE, and PURDY in England and PARDIEU in France. PERDUE in France with the meaning of "lost" was a name given to foundlings. Most of the surviving oath names are of French or Norman-French origin. Roger Bigod was one of William the Conqueror's chief advisors. BLOOD in some instances is probably derived from excessive use of the phrase "God's Blood," timorously abbreviated to s'Blood. The plain and fancy use of profanity has been regarded with more or less approval in different places and at different times. The habits that affected people during surname times put their stamp on the names borne by families forever after.

The Italians called the man BONGIORNO or BONDI who habitually saluted others with "good day." GODDAG is a Swedish soldier name meaning "good day." An unusual English name is GOODAY; the speaker may have meant the English salutation of good day to be a short or slurred form of "God give you a good day." GOODNIGHT is not a parting expression but is a perversion of the German GUTKNECHT "good servant or God's servant." Charles Goodnight in the latter half of the nineteenth century laid out several Goodnight cattle trails and, along with John Adair, developed a cattle ranch in the Texas Panhandle covering more

than a million acres. The Americanized GOOTNICK is a respellin
of the German name keeping closer to the correct pronunciatio
The Englishman who frequently wished others a successful jou
ney with the phrase "God speed you" acquired the name shor
ened into GOODSPEED. One whose repetitious expression wa
"bless (you)" would certainly be nicknamed BENEDICT, fro
Latin *benedicite* "bless (you)." DABNEY is the Frenchman wh
habitually exclaimed, "God bless," except in those cases whe
the name is derived from Aubigny or some other village in Franc
with a similar name.

DRINKALE or DRINKALL was sometimes in the habit of replyin
to the drinking pledge with the words *drinc heil,* a wish of goo
health or good luck. Wace, the twelfth-century poet, in h
Romance of Rollo tells how the English spent the night befor
losing the battle of Hastings in revelry with cries of *drinc hei*
The Slavic goodfellow who continually exclaimed "gajda" (sim
lar to our "hi" or "hey") might be named GAJDA. English GOO
YEAR, a name along with Goodrich familiar because of the Ame
ican automobile tire industry, originated because of the excessiv
use of the new year's greeting, wishing one to have a good yea
or good harvest. Reaney suggests that the name came from th
expletive used in the question "What the good year?" Sometime
it is a translation of the German GUTJAHR which grew out c
similar good wishes, although the German name also has a mear
ing of "new year's present."

Some with the name CUMMINGS or CUMMINS affirm that a
early member of the family living in Scotland who spoke onl
Norman French was keeper of the King's bedchamber. H
learned only two English words, "Come in," which he spoke whe
anyone applied for admission. He thus became known as Williar
Come-in or Comyn. A good, interesting family tradition, but ab
solutely incapable of any kind of proof!

Normally dress does not give rise to a permanent nicknam
because any particular article of dress may soon be worn out. An
yet some named BLUE in England, BLAU in Germany and Ho
land, and GORMAN in Ireland undoubtedly did derive the nam
from some article of dress so colored. The green ones, ZELEN
and ZELENKA in Czechoslovakia, were so named from the colo
of their garments. Possibly a few in England named GREEN o

GREENMAN acquired the name from the color of their clothes. Mr. GREENLEAF, dressed in green leaves, represented the wild man in public pageants. The Russian KRASNOSHTANOV was known for wearing red trousers. CAPABLANCA, the great Cuban chess player, must have had an ancestor conspicuous for wearing a white cloak. In Italy, the dandy who was most particular about his dress became known as ZIZZO. A smart, stylish, well-dressed man in Germany caused his descendants to be surnamed SCHICK.

Most names referring to an article of dress derive from the occupation of making or selling the article. However, a few of them may have originated from the bearer's habit of wearing that particular article. For example, some surnamed HOOD do point out the man so attired; some called MANTEL do nickname the one wearing an unusual mantle; some with the name CAPE or COPE usually wore such a garment; some with the name COAT wore a conspicuous coat. Remember Joseph, Jacob's son in the Bible, with the "coat of many colors"? Some with the cognomen FURR proudly wore a prominent garment made of, or trimmed with, fur. But the overwhelming number of persons with these names acquired them because of other reasons—usually because they made or sold them. GILDERSLEEVE probably wore a rich garment with sleeves braided with gold, or made and sold them.

In small provincial communities in Europe where most men never ventured more than a few miles from the place where they were born, a stranger attracted attention, and was considered foreign for many years. Outsiders were distrusted. The recent arrival would be referred to as STRANGE, NEWMAN, NEWCOMER, or NEWCOMB. GUEST does not have the meaning known today for how could one stay long enough to be so known? The term meant the accepted stranger, the newcomer. A wanderer arriving in the village could engender the name PEREGRINE. In Wales, SAYCE or SEYS was the Saxon, that is, the foreigner or Englishman. The stranger in Scotland was termed GALBRAITH, that is, "the stranger-Briton." GALL, GAUL, and GAULT are Gaelic terms for the stranger. GILL and DORAN have the same meaning in Ireland. DOYLE is the swarthy stranger in Ireland.

All nations have these surnames, originally applied as nicknames, to designate the foreigner or newcomer. The most common ones in each country, of course, denominate the man from

an adjoining country. A curious one is Spanish MALDONADO,
corruption of the Scottish McDonald. Undoubtedly the name fir:
arose to designate a Scotsman because of some prominent Sc(
named McDonald or from the fact that several Scots living i
Spain were so named, that surname being the most common i
Scotland except for Smith. The Greeks and Romans could n(
understand the language of foreigners. To them it was just "b;
bar" from which comes the word *barbarian* or foreigner, whic
may be traced to the Sanskrit *varvara* "foreigner." Strangers i
Italy thus became surnamed LA BARBERA and SBARBARO.

German natives were quick to name newcomers with su(
names as NEIMAN, NEUMAN, NEUBAUER, NIEMAN, and NIEBUHI
In Czechoslovakia, the stranger who did not understand tl
Slavic tongue was called NEMEC or NEMECEK meaning "dumb
because he could not converse with them. As most of them we1
Germans, this came to be the term for them. The Polish surnam
for the man from Germany is NIEMIEC. The stranger in Swede
would become FREMLING, and in Greece, XENOS. The Dutchma
who moved from a big city to a small village might acquire tl
name GROOTSTADT. Foreigners in Czechoslovakia would becom
NOVAK, NOVICK, or NOVOTNY. In Poland they would be calle
NOWICKI, PRZYBYLSKI, or BLOCH, the latter name scornfully sign
fying "stupidity," used because of the foreigner's trouble with tl
language or lack of acquaintance with the locality, a name som
times Englished to BLOCK. As a German name BLOCH includ(
the signification of a wandering or foreign Jew—one from Polan(
or in later times, from France or Italy.

"Rich man, poor man, beggarman, thief," the children's fortun(
telling rhyme runs, and the man who stood out in the village k
reason of his wealth might acquire the name. The first ones :
England called RICH and RICHMAN had names referring to wealt
although in later times these names blended with the familiar p(
forms of Richard. Czechoslovakians applied the name BOHAC
a wealthy man, and the Irish bestowed the name MOONEY. MAN
PENNY and MONEYPENNY designated the man with many penni(
the rich man, but sometimes these names were ironic for a po(
man. As there were more poor men than rich men, the nam
designating a pauper were more numerous—POWERS and POOR
England, McNALLY in Ireland, and CHUDAK in Czechoslovaki

CHOLL, in Germany, meant one who was indebted to others, a
ebtor, perhaps one who had extended his credit unwisely. In
ontrast Polish DZIEDZIC rented land to another, a "rich" land-
ord, undoubtedly the wealthiest man in the village.

John, youngest son of Henry II, who became king of England
1199, was nicknamed Lackland because he had received no
rant from his father, who had assigned territories to the older
ons. At a time when land was the only important source of
ealth and distinction, a noble without it was poor indeed. LACK-
AND, with the connotation of no landed estates, has survived as
modern surname in Scotland and has crossed the Atlantic to the
nited States where real estate is no longer the most important
ource of wealth.

There are many family names originally applied because they
gnified status in some manner. SCHILLING is a German who has
aid money to his lord for his freedom. The villein who tilled
nly a half acre could acquire HALFACRE as the name to be passed
n to succeeding generations. Mr. HALFKNIGHT held his land of
e lord of the manor at half a knight's fee, that is, two hides of
nd—about 240 acres. HALFYARD tilled half a yardland—about
fteen acres. One who farmed a full yardland might become
ERGE or NEAT. A NEAT is also one who herded cows. HUSBAND
ultivated a husbandland—about twenty-six acres. HYDE con-
olled a hide, which is as much land as could be tilled with one
low during the season—about 120 acres. Mr. MOLL held his land
y paying a money rent to the lord and working for him only
n special occasions, except in those cases where the name is
erived from Moll, the pet name for Mary. HOLDER was a tenant
r occupier of land. Spanish QUINONES farmed land on shares.
rench QUINTRIE held land a fifth of the produce of which went
the lord. LOTT merely worked his allotted portion. DOLLARHIDE
wned and tilled a hide of land.

AYERS, AYRES, and EYRE were descendants of the heir, i.e., the
erson in whom the fee of land vested at the owner's death. Some
ave suggested that the name is derived from the personal name
ier or Aer, short forms of the Old English name Ealhhere "noble,
ear." To explain the origin of this family name the absurd
gend is told concerning William at the battle of Hastings being
nhorsed and his helmet beaten into his face. The early ancestor

of the family, observing the incident, quickly pulled the helm off and horsed him again. The grateful Duke then said to h rescuer, "Thou shalt hereafter be called Eyre (or Air) for tho hast given me the air I breathe." All such stories end with re erence to the King after the battle granting extensive lands the man as reward for his services. The fact that William cou speak no English seems to be a minor technicality.

The hide or hube in Germany—also about 120 acres—was common measure and the farmer who worked it would be know as HUFF, HUEBNER, HUBER, or HOOVER as it might be, and h been, Americanized. Not the only prominent American so name but the best known, was the thirty-first president of the Unit States, Herbert Clark Hoover, who descended from good Germa farm folk. The worker on such a farm of 120 acres might becon HUFFMAN. A vassal who held land on feudal tenure in Germar would be surnamed LEHMANN. HEUER would be the German wl paid rent for the land he tilled, and the French equivalent wou be MERRITT. English TENNANT rented his land of another. LEHN worked for a German lord in a feudal estate.

The FRANKLIN, FREEMAN, and BURGESS were men of free birt but not of noble birth, who held substantial land for which th paid only a small rent and were obliged to render little or service to the lord or king. FRANKLIN was slightly higher in ra than FREEMAN but below the rank of KNIGHT. Knight is a wo that has gone up in the world; the name is derived from O English *cniht* "a boy or youthful servant," and the knight w originally just a boy, a young servant. GENTRY was a man gentle birth just below the nobility. BARON was an importa landowner who held of the king. FREELAND and FRY worked plot without obligation of rent or service. The Finnish counte part is VAPAA, and the German ULLMAN. The lord of the man or one who aped the lord, might be LORD in England, LAIRD Scotland, HERR in Germany, and GUZMAN in Spain. KERNAN w the Irish son of the lord or owner of the village. The lord or he of the household in Hungary might be referred to as BANAS.

Nicknames which call attention to noble birth or exalted ra are common and become permanent family names in vario countries. A few of them are BARON, DUKE, EARL, NOBLE, a PRINCE from England; CHEVALIER "knight," GRAFF "count," L

ᴏᴍᴛᴇ "the count," and Lᴇ Dᴜᴄ "the duke" from France; Fᴜʀsᴛ
prince," Gʀᴀғ "count," Hᴇʀᴢᴏɢ "duke," Jᴜɴᴋᴇʀ "squire," Pʀɪɴᴢ
prince," and Rɪᴛᴛᴇʀ "knight" from Germany; Dᴇ Gʀᴀғғ "the
ount" from Holland; Cᴏɴᴛɪ "count" and Mᴀʀᴄʜᴇsᴇ "marquis"
om Italy; and Lᴇᴄʜ "noble" and Hʀᴀʙᴇ "count" from Czecho-
ovakia. Sᴀʀᴏʏᴀɴ, the American writer, has a name corrupted
om the Armenian *Saro Khan* "mountain prince." Yᴏɴᴋᴇʀ or
ᴜɴᴋᴇʀ in Holland was the young nobleman or squire. The Ger-
an and Dutch Eᴅᴇʟᴍᴀɴ and the Polish Pᴏᴄɪᴜs were noblemen.
lso men who exuded inordinate pride, boldness, or aped the
obility were sometimes nicknamed with these nobility names.

On the other hand the rustic or countryman in England was
ᴀɢᴀɴ, Pᴀɪɴᴇ, or Pᴀʏɴᴇ. Some have explained these names as
iven to children whose baptism has been postponed or to men
hose religious zeal is not what others think it should be. In
ermany such names as Hᴇɪᴅᴇʀ and Hᴇɪᴅᴇᴍᴀɴɴ have this mean-
g of rustic or countryman. The Irish form is Fᴀɢᴀɴ and the
alian name is Pᴀɢᴀɴᴏ. The gospel of Jesus Christ made its early
dvance in the larger towns especially those in which there was
monastery or important cathedral. Those in the country without
ch advantages came to be known as pagans, so that the word
mbraced both declared non-Christians and country peasants.
he French Dᴜʜᴀᴍᴇʟ designates the man from the hamlet, prob-
bly the neighboring place, but also carries the connotation of a
ountryman and thus is similar in meaning to the English Pagan.

Naturally, comparative age is a conspicuous imprint which
asily distinguishes one man from another in a small community.
ᴏᴜɴɢ is a very common name, sometimes found with the old
pelling of Yᴏɴɢ. Jᴜɴɢ is the German form and Jᴀʀᴏs is the same
Poland. Yᴏᴜɴɢᴇʀ and Yᴏᴜɴɢʜᴜsʙᴀɴᴅ distinguished between
vo men or two farmers bearing the same Christian name. The
erman Jᴜɴɢᴍᴀɴ and Jᴜɴɢʙʟᴜᴛ are Englished into Yᴏᴜɴɢᴍᴀɴ
nd Yᴏᴜɴɢʙʟᴏᴏᴅ. The latter name is also a Swedish-American
orruption meaning "heather, leaf." The Dutch Dᴇ Jᴏɴɢ "the
oung" becomes Dᴇ Yᴏᴜɴɢ in America. The boyish or young
erson in Poland becomes Pᴀᴄʜᴏʟsᴋɪ; in French the name is
ᴇᴊᴇᴜɴᴇ. The young, immature person was sometimes termed
ʀᴇᴇɴ in the same way we use the word *green* today for the in-
xperienced boy.

175

AMERICAN SURNAMES

When it is necessary to distinguish between two men on th basis of age, the younger is usually the one designated becau there is a tendency to distinguish the younger man from his fath who may already have acquired a descriptive surname not y hereditary. But occasionally, it is the older, and ELDER is four in England, AULD in Scotland, and ALT and ALTER in German although all three of these names have other and more commc derivations. OLDER is usually a corruption of Alder "dweller the alder tree." A very old man in Germany might even be irre erently alluded to as ALTERGOTT "the old god." WNEK meanir "grandson" is a Czechoslovakian name for a young man ass ciated with his grandfather.

As the peasant of the Middle Ages lived surrounded by woo where every species of animal and bird made dens or nests, I naturally attributed to each certain definite characteristics ar nicknamed his neighbors when he observed the same quality them. Animals and birds with some striking color, size, or oth characteristic are very likely to be used as nicknames. Articles c numerous real and mythical animals to which were ascribe moral and other qualities are found in the enormously popul bestiaries in medieval times. *Aesop's Fables* and *Reynard the F* are but two of the best known of the tales of animals who acte and thought like human beings; works intended for the amus ment of the middle and lower classes of that era, but nowada read by children.

Even today it is easy to contemplate the use of the terms f these creatures as nicknames. Depending on their attitude towa United States policy concerning escalation of the war in Vietna congressmen were dubbed Hawks or Doves. Those who thoug that the war efforts should be increased and pushed vigorous were Hawks. Senator Eugene McCarthy in his criticism of th Johnson administration policy became a leading Dove. Vic President Humphrey was a Hawk. Richard M. Nixon was a Haw

Thus in European countries there are various surnames co sisting of terms for animals, birds, fish, and insects. The deriv tions are chiefly two: (1) a real or fancied resemblance to th animal or wild life, and (2) from house, shop, or inn signs. He are mentioned those very likely to have been derived from son characteristic or appearance. Not so many English or Germa ames are in this class. Perhaps English SPARLING or SPARR and German SPATZ indicate some characteristic of a little sparrow. ARUNDEL is from French *arondel* "little swallow." Certainly some named FOX, HOGG, and BIRD or BYRD are in this class. It is not surprising that BYRD is such a common name when it is remembered that in Middle English *bird* originally meant "young bird, fledgling, and the young of animals in general, also a child or young man." CRANE, HERON, and STORK provide nicknames for all men with long legs. Spanish VELEZ must have been thought to have exhibited the qualities of a crow or raven. English CROWE and CROW were frequently used as nicknames, sometimes with the sense of blackness. Some such names are offensive, as PIGG, PIGGOTT, and HOGG, often used in the same perjorative manner as these words are employed today. HOGG originally referred to the wild boar more than to the farmyard pig; it was the most exciting animal to hunt and was admired because of its ferocity at bay.

Numerous other animal names such as English goat and goose have been changed or altered in spellings so as to be unrecognizable today. German forms for goose are GANS and GAUSS. Practically every species of wild and domestic life, common in any locality, has had some prominent attribute or characteristic applied to men, as LEO, LEON, and LYON "fierce," BULL and OX "strength," HARE and Czechoslovakian ZAJICEK and KRALIK "speed, timidity," NIGHTINGALE "melodious voice," PFAU, PEACOCK, and the Czechoslovakian PAV "gorgeous coloring, pride," DOVE and Czechoslovakian HRDLICKA "gentle," OWL "wisdom," and CRABBE and German KREB "ill-tempered, or one who walked like a crab." Small or baby animals, birds, and insects have been used as terms of endearment with children and have clung to them throughout life.

The Italians with their copious use of coarse or blunt nicknames have many such family names that have come down to modern times as family names. An ancestor of the late, unlamented dictator, Benito MUSSOLINI, must have reminded his neighbors of a gnat. MUSCARELLO also has the meaning of "gnat." Likewise, Mr. MARINELLO comes by his name because the early bearer had some quality of a lady bug. It is easy to guess what characteristic prompted neighbors to nickname Messrs. IZZO and Loizzo "the snail." One who strutted about like a rooster became GALLO or GAGLIANO. As a pheasant in Italy is a term for a dullard, this would explain FASANO "pheasant." Larklike characteristics would produce CALIENDO.

In the Slavic countries the inhabitants were also very free with sobriquets derived from life other than human. Polish names referring to birds and animals terminating in -*ski* are more likely to be nicknames than sign names because this ending has the same significance as English -*like*. There are SKOWRONSKI "like a lark" and RAKOWSKI "like a crab." Insects had qualities which they professed to find in their neighbors. That unlovable old Russian dictator, KHRUSHCHEV, undoubtedly had a paternal ancestor with some attribute of a cockchafer or large beetle. Other Slavic names from insects are ZHUKOV and ZUKOV "beetle," BLOXIN "flea," MUCHA "fly," BONK "horsefly," and PAJAK "spider." In Czechoslovakia BLECHA "flea" became a family name. These insect names which became surnames were often used by a man's neighbors to call attention to small size or significance. The Polish SIKORA in the surname period must have had some resemblance to a titmouse. In Czechoslovakia the fat or mustachioed man who looked like a walrus would be named MROZ, or the diminutive MROZEK if he were a small man. The Polish KUSEK descended from little KUS, a nickname meaning "short tail," probably referring to a dog. Russian ORLOFF or ORLOV had eaglelike characteristics. Ukrainian HOROBENKO had sparrowlike qualities.

The numerous pageants and festivals of importance in the otherwise drab life of the people in the cities and small towns during the Middle Ages tended to nickname the actors who often played the same part year after year. A common character was the KING, also found as REX, REYES, or ROY in England, CORONA in Italy, KAISER and KOENIG in Germany, KRAL in Czechoslovakia, KROLL in Poland, LE ROY in France, KIRALY in Hungary, and RIGAS in Greece. KAISER is sometimes simplified to KYSER and KISER. These names were also applied because of actual or assumed kingly qualities or appearance. The king's consort was played by a man and QUEEN came down as a surname. PROFFITT was the Prophet in the religious plays. POSTLE, an aphetic form of Apostle, named the man who played one of the Saviour's apostles in the pageant. POSTLE is also from Old French *apostle* "pope." POSTLETHWAITE designates the man residing at the apostle's meadow.

In the early mystery plays the abstract virtues and vices were personalized and PRIDE played the part of one of the seven deadly sins, but it is curious to note that the other capital sins, with the possible exception of LUST, did not appear to survive as family names. PRIDE, however, has two other derivations, a nickname for the exceedingly proud man and a name designating the dear, beloved man, from Welsh *prid* "dear, beloved." WINSHIP enacted the quality of friendship, although a contributory source of this name was residence in a wine valley. BLESSING was the personified blessing. English PARADIS and Italian PARADISO played the part of Paradise. VIRGIN played the part of the Virgin Mary. Polish POTEMPA enacted the part of a martyr in the early drama. There was competition for the important part of the devil and the name would not always be considered as derogatory as it has become today. The name is now often assimilated into the French DE VILLE "of town," sometimes into the elegant DE EYVILLE.

Quite a few surnames indicate family relationship. German VEDDER and VETTER signify the father's brother, later a male cousin. Germanic and English NEAVE and NEFF mean "nephew" while German OHM means "uncle." English EAMES and Dutch OOMS point out the "son of the uncle or cousin." Words meaning "uncle" have, in the Middle Ages as well as at the present time, been used as an affectionate term for another, especially an older man, and the terminal *s* on these last two names may not refer to the uncle's son, but merely serves as an easy pronunciation of the name. The German MUTTER and Yugoslavic-Bulgarian MAJKA refer to the mother's son, generally meant to designate the widow's son, the same as the English name WIDDOWSON. WIDDOW and WIDOE are not very common although the word was also used to include a widower. The German DOPPELT and the Norwegian GEMMELL record the man born at the same time as another, a twin. Triplets are uncommon but such an Englishman, associated with his brothers, would easily become known as TRIPLETT, and the surname is not a particularly rare one today. The French PARENT and the Italian PARENTI are nicknames for a father or possibly one who stood in the place of a male parent, or one known to have fathered an illegitimate child. FOSTER was sometimes a name applied to a foster parent, one who raised another's child. The English NABORS and NEIGHBORS and the Russian PRITIKIN signify the one who dwelt adjacent to another, the nearby farmer.

There are such simple names as BROTHERS and COUSINS which may have originated with the same meaning given them today. Here the terminal s is only an aid to pronunciation. However, in Middle English all of them also had the connotation of "kinsman," and loosely designated a relative by blood or marriage, or even a fellow member of a guild. EAMES "uncle" also sometimes connoted "kinsman." KINSMAN has also survived as a surname. The termination -magh "brother-in-law" seen in such names as WATMOUGH and HITCHMOUGH, each with several variant spellings, may also have meant "father-in-law" or "brother-in-law" of Walter or Richard. All of these names are well classified as nicknames.

Many Irish nicknames now have or formerly had the patronymic Mac or O prefix so that they could be classed either in this chapter on nicknames or in the chapter on patronymics. Indeed, many that could be mentioned here have been covered in Chapter II. DELANEY descends from one known as the challenger. GLEASON had an ancestor known as the little green man, probably from the color of his coat. KEATING descends from the reasonable or calm, urbane man. McCABE is the son of the hooded man. McCOLLUM is both Irish and Scottish and refers to a tender one, a person with the characteristics of a dove. McDOWELL is the son of the swarthy foreigner. McGUIRE on the other hand is the son of the light-complexioned man. NOONAN is the grandson of the small beloved man. QUIGLEY is the grandson of the friend or companion. One cannot be sure that these names did not originate from a font name, especially when some early forms are found with a prefix.

Many surnames which are derived from nicknames consist of a verb plus a noun and refer to some action or occupation. The author who was born and brought up in a small town remembers vividly one of the town characters known by all as *Chewtobacco*. It would not be difficult to visualize his outstanding habit. Many of these names might be classified as occupational. WAGSTAFF is a term for an official who carried a wand or staff such as the parish beadle. MAKEPEACE acted as a peacemaker or mediator. The name is most familiar as the middle name of William Makepeace Thackeray. One of Mr. Shakespeare's ancestors was a soldier or blusterer, who wielded a spear and thus earned that nickname. There has been much senseless controversy over the meaning of this name, and some respectable authorities contend that it refers to the man who lived on the *schalkesboer* "knave's farm or peasant farm." Possibly the name may have had some sort of connotation of "troublemaker," as evidenced by Hugh SHAKESPEARE who, upon enrolling at Oxford in 1487, changed his name to Saunder, giving as his reason that his surname was "of low repute." Mrs. Shakespeare's son William gave no hint of this but quickly made it one of the most honored of surnames throughout the world.

It would be easy to explain the name HANDSHAKER as a nickname for one so friendly as to be in the habit of frequently shaking the hands of those he met, and one writer on onomastics has hazarded that interpretation. However, it is a place name from Handsacre "Hana's field" in Staffordshire. Likewise, TOOTHAKER might be mentioned as one with pain in his dental parts, but it would be wrong even though one can find a dentist bearing that cognomen in Iowa. Old English *tote* "lookout" makes the origin clear as the "lookout field." TURNBULL may be a nickname for a man strong enough and brave enough to "turn a bull." The family has a legend that one of its members saved Robert de Bruce from being gored by a bull by seizing its horns and turning it about

As nicknames arose from every conceivable action, it is impossible to explain fully the many which originated from some habit or act which occurred long enough ago to become a settled hereditary surname. These can only be translated and their origin imagined. The Polish SLADEK means "footprint." Was it applied to one who made a large footprint? Or did the word footprint at the time in Poland have a colloquial meaning or slang connotation which is not remembered today? Polish GROMEK means "little thunderbolt"; what act produced the name? Slavic SMETANA translates to "sour cream"; probably some mental aberration is meant. Polish POCIASK means "cannon fire"; perhaps it referred in some vague way to the action or habit of a soldier. Polish

SWIATEK indicates one from the demimonde, one with an un
savory reputation.

LAWLESS was the man deprived of the protection of the law
an outlaw. OUTLAW is a curious surname which may be observed
in America. The term refers to one deprived of the benefit and
protection of the law, and in early times in England it was lawfu
for anyone to kill such a person. A fugitive from justice or one
who contemptuously refused to appear in court when called wa
an outlaw and might acquire the epithet. Just how such a tern
could become an hereditary name is hard to conceive except fo
the admiration often expressed even today for the man clever in
romantic defiance of law and order.

WIECZOREK was the Pole in the habit of engaging in some ac
tivity in the early evening. What it was probably has been long
forgotten. The Englishman who gave an unusual or unduly elabo
rate gift to his bride in pledge of marriage might acquire the
name WEDLOCK or WEDLAKE. GAGE denominates one who acted
as pledge for another in the courts. In early English law a man
might be forced to give pledges for his future good behavio
even after he was acquitted of crime through a trial by ordeal
In medieval times trials by ordeal or combat were frequently
used in the belief that the deity would see that the truth was dis
closed, but our early forefathers did not always place great con
fidence in the outcome. French HAZARD undoubtedly delighted
in games of chance, a gambler.

While not exactly a nickname or an occupational name "serv
ant" is the connotation of many family names in the sense of a
follower of a deity or of ecclesiastical personages. ABDULLAH witl
its various spellings is the servant of Allah, the Mohammedar
term for God. The French L'HOMMEDIEU designates "the man o
God," that is, the servant of God. The German cognate name i:
GOTTSCHALK "God's servant." GILDEA is the Irish disciple of God
while GILLIS is the servant of Jesus. The holy or sanctified man in
Spain may be nicknamed DE SANTIS or DE SANTO (except in some
cases where the man came from Dos Santos, the name of places
in Spain and Portugal).

The chronically sick or infirm man was likely to be referred to
by the French as MALONSON or MELANSON. The termination i:

not a patronymic but is the Old French suffix -*çon* used to make a noun. The invalid in Germany and Holland tends to acquire the name CRONKHITE. The German who was disgustingly healthy and robust could become HEILMAN. Italian LO BELLO was blessed with an attractive physique.

KNICKERBOCKER is a "Dutch" name not found in Holland today, although it may be observed in our modern American directories as a family name—a good "American" surname. A Knickerbocker family came from Holland and settled in this country about 1674. The name signifies the "clay marble baker." Washington Irving wrote *A History of New York*, published in 1809, under the pseudonym of Diedrich Knickerbocker. Various writers of columns concerning New York have used the pseudonym, Knickerbocker, and New Yorkers have become known as Knickerbockers. Some suggest that the name alludes to the wide breeches worn by the early Dutch settlers in New Amsterdam, the former name of New York.

GUERRA is a nickname for a man engaged in military operations. Such activity by Count Pedro Fernandez de Castro caused him to become known as Don Pedro de la Guerra. English FELLOWS and Polish SOUKUP designate one who was a business partner or associate of another. The name QUARTERMAIN from the Norman-French *quatremayns* "four hands," meaning mail-fisted, the extra hands being mailed, now may sometimes be contracted to QUARTERMAN and QUARTEMAN. It may in some cases be a nickname for a very dexterous or very busy person. Or, as one with tongue in cheek has conjectured, is it from a man in the habit of complaining, "Wha' da ya think I have—four hands?"

Some nicknames arise because the man is thought to have the character or attribute ascribed to a well-known mythical or historical person famous for such attainment or virtue. Thus SOLOMON may be a descendant of one so-called because he was thought to be "as wise as Solomon." JOB or JOBE might have had an ancestor who was "as patient as Job." LAZARUS might have descended from one who was "poorer than Lazarus." A successful hunter might become a NIMROD. APOLLO might have been a popular musician. CASS could be abbreviated from Cassandra, the prophetess who could accurately predict dire events but was doomed never to be believed. Every name, no matter what the obvious interpretation, may have arisen from a nickname casually applied at the time of some act or habit observed by others.

Many of these odd or unusual nicknames can be explained only by wild guesswork, although many of them can be translated correctly and, when properly interpreted, lose some of their exotic flavor. But let us wade in boldly and mention a few nicknames found in our current directories, although it must be admitted that the colorful ones are quite uncommon. BUTTERMILK, from German Buttermilch, is the man who sold buttermilk. De VILBISS, in many different spellings, is an American variant from German TEUFELBEISS "devil bite" and undoubtedly was first applied to one thought to be bold enough to bite the devil. An Italian with an eccentric imagination would be likely to be nicknamed FANTASIA.

We cannot forget that FORGET is a good French name for the dweller or worker at the little forge, that is, little in comparison to another. Or the diminutive might be a reference to the son of the worker. English GRUBB is a less than pleasant-sounding name for the short, dwarfish individual. Comparable to the Shakespeare type of name are HURLBURT and HURLBUTT (when not descendants of Hurlbert "army, bright") designating one proficient with a hurle-batte in the medieval game of hurling, or one in the habit of whirling the hurlbat around his head in combat.

HURTADO is a very old and honorable name in Spain, the name of several soldiers and men of letters which refers to the kidnapped man or the escaped one. The Portuguese FURTADO refers to a robber or thief; several are listed in the Lisbon directory. One can picture the happy-go-lucky German nicknamed IMMERGLUCK "always happy or ever lucky." The author was reminded of the meaning of this name upon noting it in the list of the victims of an explosion accident. In Spain the left-handed man might be called IZQUIERDO "left-handed." The anomaly is also frequently observed in other countries. Italy with its predilection for nicknames, surnames them MANCINI, MANCINELLI, and MANCUSO; German and Dutch LINK and LINKE also denominate the left-handed men; KITTO in Ireland used his left hand better than his right. KETCHUM sounds as if it might be a nickname but it merely signifies one who previously resided in Caecca's homestead in England. MAGGIORE is Italian, the descendant of the eldest son. The English surname MAIDEN was undoubtedly originally applied in a derogatory sense to an effeminate man. The term also served to describe a man who had always remained continent.

MOONSHINE is a translation from the German MONDSCHEIN, a name possibly bestowed on one who had committed some act in the moonlight. The Germans also had names referring to the new moon, half moon, full moon, and good moon. Many of these names may be better interpreted as patronymics, from names originally bestowed at the font indicating lunar conditions at the time of birth. A stumpy man, one with a clubfoot or perhaps a pot-bellied man might acquire the English name PUDDIFOOT. The Englishman unduly generous with his personal wealth might be dubbed SCATTERGOOD, with the connotation either of a philanthropist or a spendthrift. Thomas Scattergood was a famous itinerant Quaker minister traveling in the American colonies in the eighteenth century. The name did not prevent Harold Francis Scattergood from becoming a successful investment broker in Philadelphia. Clarence Budington Kelland, the American short-story writer, used the name, Scattergood Baines, with telling effect in many of his stories. The German given to the habit of joking might be nicknamed SCHIMPF; later the name came to have the meaning of insulting behavior. Alfred Schimpf is a banker in New York and Charles Schimpff is a mutual fund executive in Los Angeles. SHUNK is one with an unusual or deformed leg. Francis Rawn Shunk was governor of Pennsylvania, 1844–48.

Another name with a comic sound to American ears is the German SCHMUCK "the neat, elegant man." SUPERFINE surely was thought to surpass all others in elegant qualities, possibly a proud, haughty individual. SWINDLE did not denote the Englishman engaged in fraudulent transactions, as one might suppose, but is merely a respelling of SWINDELL "dweller in valley where swine were bred," or a corruption of Swindale "pig valley," a village in Westmorland. Polish SZCZESNY designates the man who became the recipient of some good fortune. VORMITTAG nicknamed a German who completed all his work or did some act regularly "before midday." WEINWORM is the carouser or tippler from Germany.

APPLESEED is the peculiarly American surname given John Chapman, the pioneer folk hero, who traveled throughout the Ohio River Valley in the first part of the nineteenth century planting appleseeds. BIRDSEYE is not a nickname for one with a small eye; it denotes the dweller on an island frequented by birds. It is from the name of Clarence Birdseye, the American inventor who developed a quick freezing process for foods, that the trade-mark "Birds Eye," so familiar to the housewife, is derived MOCKLER, although it has another explanation as mentioned elsewhere, is sometimes a corruption of Old French *mauclerc* "the bad clergyman or clerk." Dauzat gives this interpretation to the French surname MAUCLERC and mentions Pierre de Bretagne with this surname who, he says, was defrocked.

One could go on for many pages listing nicknames that have become uncommon surnames in America and guessing as to the circumstances leading to their bestowal, but to do so would just bore the reader and no useful purpose would be served. Only a few have been mentioned to give those interested an understanding of the matter.

It seems to be a universal principle that a nickname or any name with an obnoxious or disagreeable meaning quickly tends to become obsolete or is so altered in spelling and pronunciation as to be unrecognizable. For example, the adjectives "silly" and "moody" were used in early surnames. As explained earlier, these words have changed in meaning to the connotation given them today and many of the surnames derived from them have consequently been altered in spelling or have become obsolete. One outstanding exception to this rule occurs to everyone, although it may well succumb in the future. COWARD, a name from the occupation of the forefather whose daily work consisted in taking care of cows, has persisted as a respected family name, and several important families have borne it, such as that of Noel Coward, the English playwright, actor, and composer, and Edward Coward, the American playwright, with his son, Thomas R Coward, late president of the publishing firm, Coward-McCann, Inc.

5

SURNAMES FROM PLACES

Landscape names: With prepositions—Terminal s—Hill—Streams—Ford—Bridge — Woods — Heath — Trees — Clearing — Fields — Marsh — Island — Valley — Stones — Boundary — Corner — Buildings — Fortifications — Cross — Enclosures—Farms—Roads—Directions—Miscellaneous—Combinations -er and -man; Sign names: Objects—Animals—Birds; Town names: Men named after towns—English village suffixes: -ton, -ley, -ham, -burg, -burn, -by, -comb, -cot, -don, -land, -field, -ford, -well, -thorpe, -wick, -worth, -wood, -ey, -ington —Surnames from many English villages with same name—Villages in English counties—Norman villages—French towns—Scottish places—German towns—Russian villages—Italian towns—Spanish places—Dutch towns—Swiss cities—Polish towns—Names designating directions—From names of English counties —Names indicating nationality—From big cities.

F AMILIES ACQUIRED a place name as a surname under three different sets of circumstances: (1) the man lived or worked in, on, by, or near some topographic formation or landscape feature, either natural or artificial, (2) he formerly lived in a village, town, or city and acquired the reputation of being from that place, or (3) he owned or was lord of the village or manor designated. In the overwhelming majority of cases it is impossible to say whether a remote ancestor owned the manor or had merely once lived in that place. However, it is safe to say that in most cases a manor or village name merely identifies the place where the original bearer of the name formerly resided.

187

In this chapter will be discussed the names that disclose where the original bearer lives or formerly lived. Designation of the precise place where the original bearer lived might be called a toponymical, landscape, or location name, an address name. People in bygone times were observant; they had a much more varied vocabulary for natural features with which they were familiar than people of a later era. One who lived or worked on, by, or near a specific landscape feature easily acquired it as a surname. In countries where most people derived their living from the land there were common words for every formation of the landscape small or large. Today in America address names are just addresses, and consist usually of the name of the street with the number of the house and are not in any way personal names of people.

One of the easiest ways of identifying another was by reference to some natural or artificial feature in the proximity of which the person lived or worked. As early workshops or stores were generally in the man's home, the place where he lived and the place where he worked were usually the same. In a thinly populated region, description by reference to landscape features would be the natural thing. Almost every object, natural or man-made, or contour of the land, has become a family name now common in America, especially the short descriptions, such as hill, ridge, slope, valley, dale, pit, rock, spring, stream, lake, pool, well, bank, bottom, island, ford, gate, corner, bend, bridge, wood, grove, shaw, heath, tree, bush, house, hall, field, meadow, way, and road. Many of these are among the most prevalent family names.

These common words often have different meanings in different places. The generic name PLACE could designate a dweller at a country mansion, near a market square, or on a particular plot of land. Or the name could specify one who came from Plash or Plaish "marshy pool," names of towns in Somerset and Shropshire. Or it could be the man from Place "town or fortress" in France. Lest one think that our early forebears had difficulty in describing accurately a landscape feature or were confused about what constituted one, it must be remembered that no two topographical contours are exactly the same in appearance or look the same from different angles so shades or differences of meaning easily developed. An indefinite surname is the Dutch VAN BUREN which merely calls attention to one "from the neighborhood." French VOISIN is the man who came from an adjoining area, and the English NAYBORS and NEIGHBORS which have been mentioned in Chapter IV express the same concept. The English dweller in a village or town might be surnamed BYNUM.

In the earliest documents these topographic words or names were always preceded by a preposition and, generally, the definite article. The most common English prepositions that have survived as name adjuncts are *at, by, over, under,* and *up.* In a few cases both the preposition and the article have survived in modern family names, such as ATTERBURY "at the stronghold," ATHERSMITH "at the smooth or level field," and UPCHURCH "higher or farther church." Some descriptions such as *atten oakes, atten ash, atten hall, atten elm,* and *atten ea* "stream" condensed to the modern names NOAKES or NOKES, NASH, NALL, NELMS, and NYE respectively. The dative of the definite article in the masculine or neuter singular became in Middle English *then* and in colloquial speech the *n* left the article and attached to the noun. In the same way the *r* of the feminine singular *ther* went over to the noun to form such a name as RASH "at the ash." Sometimes the *t* of *at* transferred to the noun to form TASH "at ash." In other instances the entire definite article coalesced into the noun as when the resident "at the inn" collapsed into THINN.

In many other instances the article dropped out to leave only the preposition, especially in later surnames. The most commonly used preposition in English place names was *at,* and such names as ATWELL, ATWATER, and ATTRIDGE have become recognized American surnames. Atwell by aphesis has become the uncommon TWELL. *At* sometimes contracted into *a,* as in Thomas à Becket "at the becket or little stream" and Allan-a-Dale "at the valley," and it sometimes adhered to the noun as in AGATE "at the gate," AHERNE "at the corner," and AMORE "at the marsh." Other names that have retained the preposition are UNDERHILL "at the foot of the hill," UNDERWOOD "beneath the wood," OVERSTREET "beyond the Roman road," BYWATER "by pool or stream," BYFIELD "by the field," UPHAM and UPTON "the higher homesteads," and UPSHAW "the upper grove or thicket."

The French and Norman-French prepositions *de la, del,* and *du* have survived in such names as DELAFIELD "of the field," DELOREY "of granary," and DUPRE "of the meadow." The name of the great American ornithologist and artist, AUDUBON, translates from the French to "of the good," shortened from a longer name, the noun having been dropped. Spanish *de el* or *del* has been preserved in many names such as DELMAR "of the sea" and DEL RIO "of the river." Italian *del* and *della* are seen in DEL CORSO "of the high-way" and DELLACQUA "of the water." Dutch VANDENBERG "of the mountain," VANDERBILT "of the mound," VANDERWOUDE "near a wood," and TEN EYCK "at the oak tree" are further examples. Dutch *Van* and *Ten* are often separate from the rest of the name. In America it is merely a matter of personal preference with each family. German BIEDENWEG "by the way" is an unusual name. Other such direction names may be observed elsewhere in this work.

Some names that appear to be derived from residence on, in, or near a certain landscape feature are really metonyms for occupational surnames. We may speak of a man "at the post office" when we mean to designate the postal clerk. Names like KITCHEN and SHIPP, even though preceded by *atte* or *de la*, often do not refer to the man who lived in or by the kitchen or ship but to the kitchener who worked there and to the seaman manning the ship. Some names may denote either residence or occupation, as BRIDGE, PONT, and BOAT. HALL "manor house or principal room in the manor house" sometimes refers to the servant at the hall; MILL sometimes designates the millward; PARK, the park keeper; and MALTHUS, the worker in the house where malt was prepared or stored.

It may be noted that many short landscape or address names have the plural form with a terminal -*s*. This final -*s* is not a possessive form. It is not common with nicknames such as BLACK, YOUNG, or BULL or with patronymical names. This excrescent -*s* is frequently found in such short names from nouns as BROOKS, HAYES, BURNS, WELLS, WOODS, HOLMES, and MILLS where its use, if any, seems to be as an indefinite aid to pronunciation, if not the sign of the plural.

The most popular landscape name is HILL. Hills large and small were everywhere and cottages were found on top of them, at the foot of them, and at various places on the slope. If a number of people lived on the hill, none acquired the word as a surname, but the man in the lone cottage would almost certainly be so described. Other common English names from words referring to hills or mounds of various sizes and shapes are BERRY, DOWNING, DOWNS, HEAP, HIGH, HOY (when not Irish or Chinese), HOWLAND, HULL, KNOWLAND, KNOWLES, LAW, LOWE, and PENN, the last one sometimes designating the dweller near a pen or sheepfold. LAW and LOWE may also have the more definite connotation of burial mound. HOGUE dwelt on or near a hillock or barrow except in those cases where the name is only a fancy respelling of HOGG to conceal the origin from Old English *hogg* "pig," metonymic for a caretaker of pigs. The man who lived on or at a pointed hill became PEAK, PECK, PEEK, PIKE, or PILL. At the top of the hill would be found COPP, KNAPP, KNOLL, and KNOTT. Some terms for hill or mound served as nicknames for large, fat men. COPP is often a respelling of German Kopf "head." COPLEY and COPPINGER originally dwelt at the hilltop meadow. FOOTE dwelt at the lower part of the hill. CLINTON lived in the hill enclosure.

The Germans who resided on or near a hill acquired BESLER, BUEHLER, BUHL, KNORR, and PIEHL as family names, while if the hill was pointed, the name might be SPITZER. NIERMAN dwelt in the lower location, such as farther down the hill. Dutch cognate names are HOGER and HOOGLAND. French common names are DEPEW and DUMONT, sometimes with the initial of the second element capitalized. Italian names are COSTA, COLLETTI, and ZOLA. The Hungarian form is HEGY, and the Irish, BRYANT. The Finns are acquainted with MAKI. Slavic names are KOPECK and KOPECKY (Czechoslovakian), PAGOREK (Polish), and KOPEC (Ukrainian). Polish ZAGORSKI dwelt beyond the hill or mountain. The common Scandinavian names for hill or mountain are BERG and BERGEN. BAKKE is Norwegian, as are HAUG and HAUGEN.

Names which tend to designate a mountain rather than a hill (although the distinction in many instances is nebulous) are the English FELL, the Finnish WUORI, the Norwegian BERGE, the Spanish SERRANO, the Polish GORA, GORSKI, and GORECKI, and the Danish AMBERG. German EIFEL, BERGMAN, and HALDEMANN were mountain dwellers. Czechoslovakian HORWITZ, HURWITZ, and HORWICH lived in or near a mountainous place. Russian GORIN

191

was the mountain dweller. Polish PODGORSKI lived at the base of the mountain.

Many English names familiar to everyone consist of adjectives preceding a word meaning hill. CHURCHILL refers to the man living on or near the hill where there was a church. Some Churchills, however, derive from various settlements in England with this name. Sir Winston Churchill, the Mr. England of World War II, certainly had an early ancestor living by the church on the hill whether the entire settlement was so called or not. BURCHILL lived on the hill of birch trees. BIGELOW did not necessarily live on a big hill, but on a barley hill. BROWNLOW lived by a brown hill or burial mound. In Spain, ALVARADO dwelt on or near the white hill or on dry terrain. German and Dutch BRINKMAN dwelt on a grassy hill. BELDEN must have occupied a nice place on the beautiful hill. Italian MONTEFIORI lived on the hill covered by flowers.

Closely related to the hill residents are those who lived on the slope or incline or cliff, whether the side of a hill or not. Such residents were named BRINK, DOANE, HEALD, HELD, and ORCUTT in England. BUSHELL dwelt on the slope overgrown with bushes. Germans on a steep incline would become ECKER or STECK. Steeper slopes or cliffs would tend to name residents CLEAVES, CLIFF, CLIVE, or STACK in England, while HINCHCLIFFE resided near the overhanging cliff. STACK also derives from Stack "cliff or isolated rock" in Scotland. Italian ROCCA was originally located near a cliff, although in some cases the name refers to a fortress. SUTCLIFFE resided by the south cliff (or south of the cliff) in England while YARNALL was located at the slope or cliff where eagles were observed. German KRAMP was found near the brim or edge.

RIDGE, RIGGS, and RUGE dwelt at a ridge or range of hills. All three of these surnames also derive from small settlements with these names in the British Isles. Residents living near a dike or embankment would acquire such surnames as BANGS, BANKS, DAMM, or DYKE in England, DYKSTRA in Holland, and DIECKMANN in Germany. KAMM dwelt on a ridge or crest of a mountain in Germany. English LINK and LYNCH would be found at a ridge or bank separating strips of arable land, often on a slope or rising ground, while SHEDD would denominate one who resided at the division separating lands sloping in different directions. As an element, ridge is often found preceded by an adjective. In England, EUBANKS dwelt on a ridge where yew trees grew; WRIGLEY dwelt at the ridge meadow; FAIRBANKS would be found where bulls and sheep were confined by a ridge or embankment (when not referring to a beautiful ridge); SELFRIDGE would be on or near the rocky ridge; and WHITTREDGE would call a white ridge his home. RIGDALE dwelt in the valley by the ridge. Slavic MESIROW dwelt on a strip of land between ditches.

Where there were hills there were, of course, many streams, and the lone cottage on the banks of a small brook housed men who were known as BURNS, BROOKS, BOURNE, BORN, BECK, BECKETT, BAK, and BACK in England. LEAKE also designated the dweller by a stream; however, many with this name came from Leake "stream," the name of several places in England. BECK is also a German name for the dweller by the stream as are BACHMAN and BACKMAN. STROHM, when not from Strohm "stream" in Germany, dwelt near a watercourse, and ZUBER dwelt near a stream, the latter also being a Swiss surname. The Dutch cognate forms are BEEKS and BEEKMAN, the Polish, POTOCKI, and the Spanish, RIVERA and ARROYO. Norwegian and Swedish names are SUNDE and STROM, respectively. The Swedes also use SUNDSTROM, both elements meaning "stream," but it is an artificial name, and so does not refer to the place where the original bearer dwelt. The French OUELLETTE and OUELLET refer to the source or eye of a little stream. English FALLS refers to a waterfall, as does French DUSSAULT.

Dwellers near a river or some stream larger than a brook or creek, and here again the differences in meaning are not clear cut, might be denominated RIO in Spain, JOKI in Finland, BREGER in Germany. There was the pious friar who called his hearers to note that Providence always caused a river to run through a large town for the benefit of its inhabitants without thinking that the river might have been there before the town. Surnames referring to an artificial watercourse such as a ditch or drainage sluice are VOSE, FOSS, and MOTT "moat" in England and ZYLSTRA in Holland. Other stream names are KOSKI from Finland and RHEA from Wales, both referring to a dweller near the rapids. The English RYNNE and SYKES designate the man by the water channel on the moor and the mountain stream, respectively. German KLING and Dutch KLINK originally dwelt near a rushing mountain stream English FLOOD, when not referring to a descendant of Floyd, and Polish ZALEWSKI were dwellers near the stream that often overflowed.

Men who lived near an important, named river were sometimes surnamed with the name of the stream. Some English river names that became surnames are: ASHBURN "ash tree brook," BAIN "straight," BOLLIN (etymology obscure), CALDER "violent stream," CHEW "river of the chickens," ELLEN "white," KYLE "narrow," LEACH "muddy ditch," LEMON "elm," LOUD "the noisy one," REA "stream," THAMES "dark river," TILL "stream," WILEY "tricky river," and WYE "running water." It will be noted that many river names mean simply "water, river, stream, brook." This is true of river names in all countries. Other river names with this meaning in England are the Avon, Dover, Esk, Don, and Ouse; there are the Danube in Austria and the Don in Russia. River names in Europe are usually very ancient names, often very old Celtic names. For this reason their exact interpretation is consequently often obscure and the onomastic authorities frequently disagree as to the correct explanation.

As will be observed in the preceding paragraph, the meaning of river names is usually descriptive of the river, often different from the common meaning ascribed to the words. The common Scottish name MONROE or MUNRO refers to the Irishman who came from near the Roe river in Derry, Ireland. James Monroe the fifth president of the United States, made the name a great American one through his enunciation of the Monroe Doctrine which profoundly influenced the foreign policy of this country for such a long period. Some with this surname dwelt in or near a reddish swamp. Some surnamed ALLEN originally dwelt near the Allen "green plain," the name of several rivers in England. Other European river names that have surnamed families are EDER and HAVEL in Germany (the etymology of both of them is obscure) KOCHAN "beloved" in the Ukraine, and Dutch MAAS "from the Meuse" in Western Europe.

Where the emphasis was residence on the river bank, the following names arose in England: ORR, OVERMAN, STRAND, and SELF, the last referring to a shelf or ledge, such as a riverbank

194

A sojourner at the riverbank in France might acquire LARRABEE as a surname. WINDSOR in England designated "a landing place with a windlass." This name, adopted by King George V during World War I, because the original Saxe-Coburg-Gotha sounded too Germanic, has been perpetuated by Queen Elizabeth as the permanent family name of Britain's royal house. Norwegian AAGARD dwelt in the yard or enclosure by the river.

Where there are streams or running water, people must cross them either by a bridge, a ferry, or by a ford, the latter being the usual way during the period surnames were becoming stabilized. The man who lived by the ford would be known as FORD, and as almost every river or stream could be crossed at a shallow place, the name became quite common. WADE has the same meaning, as does RAYFORD. FORTNER is the German form. The Russian cognate form is BRODNY. LUNSFORD was the dweller near the crossing of the Lune "white water," a river in England. CLIFFORD dwelt at the shallow river crossing with the steep bank. If the crossing were wide, the name might become BRADFORD. STANFORD would be "the stony ford" or possibly the river crossing by means of stepping stones. REXFORD lived near the king's river crossing. WEATHERFORD would be found near the ford used by wethers, that is, castrated rams. FORD later came to mean a way or road and so not all fords were passages across a river.

Even in very early times when the stream was too deep to ford, a bridge had to be constructed. In the country there were few bridges during the Middle Ages, and the dweller near one was likely to be so described. The great deficiency of bridges is impressed upon us when we note the number of places terminating in -*ford* compared to the number with the suffix -*bridge*. The famous stone London Bridge which took over thirty years to build at the end of the twelfth century was so extraordinary that it became a part of a children's game expressing the fear that it would collapse. The common name is BRIDGES in England and BRIGGS in Scotland. PUNCH, from Latin *pontis* "bridge," also designated the dweller near a bridge in England, and BEAM and BAMBRICK dwelt at the crossing formed by a single log across a narrow stream. BRIDGEMAN and BRICKMAN named both the resident near a bridge and the keeper of the bridge who exacted a toll from each passerby. In Germany the bridge dweller was BRUCKNER, or STEGER if the bridge were narrow. The common French name is DUPONT; if the bridge were made of stone, the name might become PIERPONT. The Dutch bridge address names are VAN BRUGGE and VERBRUGGE, each found in several different spellings. POMFRET is derived from Latin *ponte fracto* "broken bridge," probably the ruins of an old Roman bridge.

Lone residents near a lake, pond, pool, or quiet, deep water were very likely to be surnamed with reference to their address. Since most peasants, who seldom strayed far from home, knew of only one lake, pond, or pool, it was natural to refer to it. Men who spent their whole lives by such a natural feature would speak of it as "the lake" or "the pool," not referring to it by its formal name. In England the various surnames for the nearby resident are LAKE, LINN, LUMPP, LYNN, MEARS, PELL, POLWHELE "in a field," POOLE, POND, and PULLMAN, names mostly obvious. SOULE dwelt near a muddy pool, and STANGE near a stagnant pool or, if German, near a pole. The German cognates are KUHL, KUHLMAN, KUNKEL, LACHMAN, POHL, and TEICHMAN. Dutch forms are VANDERPOOL and VANDERMEER. The Scottish form of lake is LOCH, and the Finnish name is JARVI. Polish RYBICKI originally resided near a fish pond. English people with POLAND as a surname derive from the residence of the early ancestor who lived on the homestead on which there was a pool, or through which a stream flowed. POLLARD named the dweller near the head or end of the lake.

Ancestors who originally lived near a spring or well were termed WELLS in England, or MAXWELL if it were desired to refer to it as the big spring. A well was originally a natural source of water, a place where water springs up or issues from the ground, not a man-made shaft sunk in the ground as we know it today. A spring of pure water might be worshiped and the place referred to as HOLLOWELL "holy well." In some cases both HOLLOWELL and HALLOWELL originally lived in Haliwell in Middlesex or HALLIWELL in Lancashire, both meaning "holy spring." French forms are DUPUIS, FONTAINE, and FOUNTAINE; Italian, is FONTANA; and Spanish, is FUENTES. A German cognate surname is PUTZ, which also derives from the town of that name in Germany. BRUNER and BRUNNER were diggers of wells in Germany, as well as dwellers near a spring. Some with the name BRUNER descend from Brunheri "brown, army."

Surnames from Places

Sojourners at the boat-landing place would be known as HUTH or KAY in England, KEYES and KEYS in England and Scotland, and STEIGER in Holland. KAY and KEYS derive from Old French *kay* "quay" and Middle English *key* "quay." In the Netherlands, dikes were a common feature of the landscape and many families living near them acquired such surnames as OPDYCK, VAN DAM, VAN DYKE, and UPDYCK. In England a dweller on a dike where thorn bushes grew might become known as THORNDIKE. WARE was a dweller near a dam, also one who came from a town with that name. Persons living near a deserted seacoast would be surnamed SEA, SEAY, SEE, or SHORE in England, DEMAREE in France, DELMAR and ACOSTA in Spain, and DACOSTA in Portugal. LAHTI in Finland originally resided near the bay.

Family names referring to watercourses are often differentiated by an adjective which clings to the name. BLACKWELL and BLACK-LEDGE "black pool" (from Old English *læcc* "pool") in England call attention to the dark nature of the water as does DOUGLAS in Scotland. Reddish pools would originate RUTLEDGE. STILLWELL, contrary to the ordinary meaning of the word, would indicate a spring where the water flowed constantly, from Old English *stille* "constant." Swedish STREADBECK dwelt near a rapid brook. ROCK-WELL in England and STEINBECK and BORNSTEIN in Germany would call attention to the stony stream. HONEYWELL was the spring near which honey was found. English LIGHTBOURNE and German LOUDERBACK were the dwellers near the clear stream. THORNBURN lived near a stream where thorn bushes grew, and DEARBORN was found near the stream frequented by wild animals, from Old English *deor* "wild animals." WATERHOUSE lived in the building by the lake or stream, if not in a house surrounded by a moat.

In feudal times the population per square mile was thin and much land was covered with forest. Everywhere there were small woods or groves and the men living in or near them were so described by their neighbors. The distinction between a forest and a small wood or shaw, grove, or clump of trees or bushes or underbrush is not always clear at the present time in family names, but one may be very sure that it was quite clear in the minds of those in the immediate neighborhood who first used the names. Names referring to a group of trees are among the most common in all

197

European countries. English PARK or PARKS was the dweller in the enclosed wood stocked with game for the use of the lord or king. French DUBREUIL lived in or near a damp wood or similar enclosed park.

In even the most populous countries there were many small woods or shaws. The three common English names are WOOD, WOODS, and SHAW in that order, the last being also quite common in Scotland. The terminal -s in WOODS is probably just an aid to easy pronunciation. SMALLWOOD is also from Scotland. Other English surnames are ATWOOD, BEERS (from Old English *bearu* "grove"), BOSS, BUSSELL, BYSSHE, COADY, GROVE, HEARST, HOLT, HURST, LUNT, and PRESS. German cognates are HARDT, HOLTZ, LACH, STRAUCH, and STRUCK. A Dutch form is BOS. Common French names are BOIS, BOYCE, BUSSE, and DuBOIS. Note that several of the English names for a wood come from Old French and Old German roots. Polish surnames are BORK, BOROWSKI, and GAJEWSKI. HAJEK is Czechoslovakian, BOSCO is Italian, and DA SILVA is Portuguese. SILVA is very common in both Spain and Portugal. The Swedish name LUND "grove" does not necessarily indicate a dweller by a grove, being frequently a nature name deliberately adopted (see page 268).

Woods largely composed of a certain kind of tree are often so designated and so surname the lone residents in or near them. In England there are EMSLEY (elm), HAZLETT (hazel), and ASH-CRAFT (ash). A clump of rushes or bent grass provides RUSH in England and RUSCH in Germany and Switzerland. Other groups of trees are BROUSSARD "brushwood" in France; BUCHHOLZ and LAFAYETTE "beech grove" in Germany and France, respectively; DOZIER "willow grove" and BESSIE "birch tree grove" in France; LESZCZYNSKI "hazel bushes" in Poland; DABROWSKI "oak grove" in Poland; SILVEIRA "brier trees" in Portugal; OLIVIER "olive grove" in France; and PARADISO "fruit or flower grove" in Italy. A dweller near a small group of trees might be identified as TWELVETREES. SNOOKS, as clearly recorded in a series of deeds concerning a family of Snooks, is a contraction of Sevenoaks, although it is true that there are very early forms of the name derived from Old English *snoc* "projecting point of land."

Woods frequented by certain animals are often so denominated. In England, HENSLEY, HENSHAW, and COAKLEY are woods frequented by wild birds such as moor hens and partridges. Other English surnames of this kind are GRISWOLD "pigs," GATEWOOD "goats," ROSCOE "roes," and WHELPLEY "young animals." PETTI-GREW in Scotland and England is the grove frequented by cranes. In Holland, QUACKENBUSH is the wood or marsh where there are many frogs. Irish KILGORE dwelt in or near the wood where goats were kept. CHASE refers to the woods particularly suitable for hunting, and the name is also a metonym for a hunter, from Old French *chaceur* "hunter."

The dweller in or near the big woods or forest would be FOR-REST, LONGWOOD, or WOLD in England; FORST, HOLST, HOLTZMAN, and WALD in Germany; LASKO, LESNIAK, or ZALESKI in Poland; and SKOOG in Sweden. The word *forest* included land reserved for game whether wooded or not. GREENLEE and GREENWOOD in England and GREENWALD and GRUNEWALD in Germany are the verdant or green woods. SOUTHARD dwelt at or in the south wood.

In northern England and in Scotland there are many large tracts of open, uncultivated ground overgrown with heather and brushwood called a "heath," distinct from woodland, often a moor connoting a wasteland not a marsh. In England this begot such surnames as BENT and BRUSH, HEATH and HETH, and in Scotland, MUIR. A Norwegian name is MOE and the Finnish name is KANGAS. English SKIDMORE is "Skyti's wasteland." PENROSE dwelt at the head or upper end of the heath.

When a family lives near a single outstanding tree, its neighbors can call attention to its precise residence by reference to the tree. In some surnames it is impossible to tell whether a single tree is meant or whether a small grove of trees is indicated—to the neighbors who used the term the meaning was clear. TREES (usually with the plural *s*) has served to identify a few English families. BAUM connotes the German who lived by a tree. BEAM "tree," an obsolete Anglo-Saxon word, survived long enough to produce a surname. Even when the tree has been cut and only the stump remains, there is sufficient left to produce a family name. STOCK in England, STAMM and STUCKER in Germany, DUBUC in France, and KARCZEWSKI in Poland all refer to an unusual or prominent tree stump.

It is the stately oak that has brought about the most tree names: English OAKES and CASH; French CHEYNE, CASS, and DUCHESNE;

German Eich; Polish Demski and Dublinski; Czechoslovakian Doubek and Dub; Russian Dubin; and Dutch Ten Eyck. In addition, English and Dutch Tryder connotes the oak hamlet. English Holyoke "sacred oak" and Womack "hollow, or crooked, oak" are other surnames frequently observed.

The linden tree produced Lind, Lindh, Linden, and Lindner in Sweden, the first of which is also an English form; Lindenmann in Germany; Lipsky in Russia; and Lipinski in Poland. Beech trees are responsible for Beach and Beecher in England; Buchman, Buckner, and Hester in Germany; and Bukowski in Poland. Birch trees are responsible for the family names Birch, Bercher and Burch in England, Brzezinski in Poland, Ducharme in France, and Bereskin in the Ukraine. Men living by a willow tree are named Sass and Withee in England; Wyeth in Scotland; Sali in Germany; Wierzbicki and Vrba in Poland; and Urba in Czechoslovakia. The elm tree is referred to in English as Elms and Helms, in German by Rushing, in French by Delorme, and in Dutch by Olmsted, while the wych-elm tree in England yields such names as Wich, Witcher, and Wyche. The holly tree in England names men Hollins, Hollis, Hollister, and Holly. Spanish Acevedo dwelt near the holly tree. The alder tree produces Else and Eller in Germany, Fern in Scotland, Aune in France, and Olszewski in Poland. German fir trees originate Danner, Ficht, and Tannenbaum. Pine trees or pine woods are responsible for Pine and Pyne in England, Hojnacki and Sosnowski in Poland, and Bohren in Germany.

Other tree names are: English Trimble and Polish Osowsk "aspen"; German Ascher, English Ash, Rountree, and Rowan "ash or mountain ash"; Slavic Kalina "snowball"; Dutch Hagedorn "hawthorn"; German Hassel "hazel"; English Thorn and Thorner "thorn bush"; English Maple, Box, Hazel, Noyes "walnut"; and Crabtree "crab apple"; French Cormier "sorb" and Dufresne "ash"; German Nusbaum "nut"; Norwegian Gran "spruce"; Ukrainian Yalowitz "juniper"; Irish Quaile "hazel tree"; German and Polish Topel and Topol "poplar tree"; and Czechoslovakian Javor "maple." The Polish form for the dweller by the maple tree was Javorski. Yew trees were important because of their elastic wood used in the archer's bow, and a dweller near one could acquire the surname Yule in England.

Surnames from Places

Fruit trees engendered numerous surnames. There are German APPEL and APPLEBAUM, Polish JABLONSKI, and Czechoslovakian ABLON "apple tree"; English CHERRY and German KIRSCHBAUM "cherry tree"; and German PERSHING "peach." German BIRNBAUM, Czechoslovakian HRUSKA, and Portuguese PEREIRA all mean "pear tree"; German FEIGENBAUM "fig"; and Polish SLIWA and Czechoslovakian SLIVA "plum." Fruit tree appellations often indicated a group of trees, an orchard. The English and Scottish ORCHARD refers to a fruit garden as does the Polish SADOWSKI. English APPLEYARD and English and French POMEROY derive from the apple orchard; APPLEGATE is the entrance to the apple orchard, although in some instances -gate is just a corruption of -garth "enclosed place." English PLANT designates the dweller where bushes and young trees are started for transplanting; LA PLANTE is the cognate French name. English and German BUSH and BUSCH and Swedish STRUDER "bush" were men who dwelt near a particular bush. German LEIGHLY dwelt near a small clump of low trees or bushes, or in some cases on ground recently cleared. This name looks very English but the final element is the German diminutive suffix -le.

In connection with woods or forests the very popular LEE must be considered. It is derived from Old English *lēah* which has many meanings, of which the most common are "a wood and a clearing in a wood." Other exact interpretations of the word are "meadow, clearing, open land, woodland, rough clearing in a wood, piece of open land, woodland glade, and pasture land," and the exact meaning in any particular name is most difficult to ascertain. Other spellings of the name are LEIGH and LAY. LAIN is the dweller by certain tracts of arable land at the foot of the Sussex Downs, when not a respelling of LANE "country road."

Often when a clearing or small open place was made in a forest, the man who lived in or near the place would be so described by his neighbors. English surnames designating the sojourner in or by such a clearing are REDFIELD, RODE, RHODES, RHOADS, SNEED (from Old English *snad* "clearing"), and WOODING. A light place or clearing in a dark forest might originate the descriptive names, LIGHT in England and LICHT in Germany. Sometimes LIGHT, however, is a nickname indicating the active, bright, gay person. A newly cleared piece of land would name the resident NEWLAND.

201

An exotic sounding Italian name with the same meaning which is easily recognized by the casual student of Latin is TERRANOVA. Woods were often cleared by burning and the place might then be BRAND in England or BRANDT in Germany. English ACKROY is the clearing by oak trees and AXELROD is by the ash trees.

The difference between a clearing in a wood and a small meadow is often nebulous in medieval landscape words. With the decreased attention to natural topographic features the word "meadow" has all but dropped out of our modern vocabulary except in poetry. To our forefathers in the Middle Ages a meadow was a grassy, pasture land kept for mowing. The family name ENGLAND does not directly refer to the nation but designates the dweller at the *ing-land,* an Old English term for meadow land. From residence in or near the grassy field the following surnames have arisen in England: ENG, GARFIELD, LONGLEY, MAITLAND, MEAD, MEADOWS, PRATT, PRAY, TYE, and WINN. Other English meadow names refer to the identifying use or location, as FAIRLESS "bull," HENNING "wild birds," BROWNLEE "brown," SMEDLEY "smooth or flat," and TOPPING "upper." German names indicating the uncultivated or wild land or meadow are HEIDEMANN, HEIDEN, HEISER, and WIESE. Norwegian forms are HAUG and SATHER, the latter referring to the mountain pasture. French cognates are DUPREE and BEAUPRE, the latter a "beautiful meadow." The Polish name is MURAWSKI and the Spanish name is VEGA.

Closely related to terms for meadow lands are names indicating residence in or near a field, usually a large tract of open country free of trees. The modern sense of field as "an enclosed or fenced in plot of land" did not arise in England until the large-scale enclosure of open pasture lands which occurred after the Black Death epidemic of 1349. For the dweller in or near the ordinary open land the surname FIELD arose along with the more easily mouthed form, FIELDS, the latter being more than three times as common in America. Other English names are CAMP, FELD, FIELDING, FILES, PRINDLE, PYTEL, and VILES. The Polish name PYTEL, however, connotes a babbler or senseless chatterer. German forms for the dweller in a field or open country are FELT and FLACK. Italian names are CAMPO and CAMPAGNA, while the Spanish form is CAMPOS. French forms are GAST and CHAMP; a Dutch form is

VAN CAMP; there are Norwegian MORK, Polish POLINSKI, Russian
GOLENPAUL, and Scottish BLAIR.

Many family names indicate the use to which the particular
field is put. PLAISTED is the playing field in England. A millet field
in France is MILLARD and MILLION, the former also being English
for a miller. PANICO and PANOZZO in Italy also connote a field of
millet or forage grass cultivated for its grain. A rye field in Holland produced the now famous American name ROCKEFELLER and
a like field in Czechoslovakia named its dweller ZITO. German
and English BERLAND connotes the barley field. PEASLEY "peas"
and FILIP "hay" are English surnames, the latter name sometimes
being a corruption of Philip "lover of horses." Norwegian LILAND
is the field where flax was cultivated. French HAVILAND is the
oat field, German GERSTEIN is the barley field, and KORNFELD connotes a field of grain, not just what Americans call corn. English
names identifying the fields are BUTTERFIELD "good pasture for
cows," GREENFIELD, HYLAND "high," LITTLEFIELD, OLDFIELD, STUB-
BLEFIELD "recently cleared land where stumps are still evident,"
SUMMERFIELD "used by sheep or cattle in the summer," and WHIT-
AKER and WHITTAKER "white field or wheat field." English dwellers
in a hut in open country would be called BOTHFIELD or SATTER-
FIELD. Swedish WALLIN and German BRACH denote the fallow
field.

Everywhere there are marshes, swamps, fens, bogs, low muddy
lands often covered with luxuriant vegetation, but too highly sat-
urated with water to be fit for agricultural or pastoral purposes.
The exact shades of meaning ascribed to a bog, a marsh, or a
swamp are frequently interchanged in popular and international
usage. The man who lived in or near such a place would be easily
and definitely described. Simple English and Scottish names referring to low, wet ground or wasteland are BOGGS, CARR, FENN,
FENNELL, ING, KERMAN, KERR, MARS, MARSH, MOORE, MORSE,
MUDD, MUDGE, MUDGETT, SLAUGHTER, STRODE, STROTHER, STROUD,
TRASK, VANCE, VANN, WAGG, WISH, and WISHER. Two other Scottish names in this category are CARSON and STRUTHERS. When one
remembers that a fen is a low, swampy ground, the explanation
of Finland, the country, comes clear. MOOR, originally "barren
wasteland," was often used to mean wet wasteland.

Men who resided in or near a marsh in Germany would acquire

such names as AUER, EBNER, MOHR, MOSHER, and MUHR. Frenc
names are BERUBE, DESMARAIS, and MARAIS. DELANO refers to th
dweller in or near a marsh, although some came from the villag
of Delanoe "of the wet land," a town in France. The name i
familiar to Americans because of Franklin Roosevelt's middl
name, the maiden surname of his mother. Dutch surnames for
dweller in a marsh are VANDERVEEN and TEN BROECK. Other name
found in America are BOLOTIN and BRODY (Russian), MARF
(Czechoslovakian), NEVA (Finnish), PADULA (Italian), and TA
NAKA (Japanese). Sometimes the marsh is more particularly de
scribed as in the English names HINDMARSH "marsh where th
female of the red deer were found," WHITMARSH "white marsh,
MOREHOUSE "house in the moor," MORROW "row of houses in th
moor," and LANGEMORE "large moor."

The permanent resident on the small island in England woul
be ELAND, ENNIS, HUME, or HOMER. Sometimes, as in the latte
name, the island referred to might be only a piece of land pai
tially surrounded by a stream or even be only a spot of dry lan
in a marsh. SHOREY would be the island near the shore and SKERR
would designate the rocky isle. Other surnames indicating th
island address of the resident are OLANDER (Swedish), SAA
(Finnish), HOLMAN (Norwegian), and DELISLE and LYLI
(French). Danish NYHOLM is the sojourner on the new rive
island. English ALMY is "elm island" and ESTEY is "east island."

Everywhere in the world except in the unusual flat lands (
tablelands are valleys, large and small. A lone resident in a valle
would be so described by his neighbors. English dwellers in
valley, dale, glen, deep hollow, pit, ravine, or bottom land woul
acquire such surnames as BOTTOMS (the delicate, fastidious pe
son may spell it BOTHAM), CLEW, CLOUGH, CLOW, COMBS, DAL
DEAN, DELL, HELLMAN, HOLE, HOPE, HOYLE, PITTMAN, PITT
PUTMAN, SLADE, and VAIL, VALE, or VALLEY. Valley, howeve
came into the language too late to produce many surnames. HOF
is from Old English *hop* with various connotations such as "raise
or enclosed land in the midst of a swamp or wasteland, sma
enclosed valley, hollow among hills, or small bay or inlet." Frenc
names signifying a valley, hollow, or pit are DEVEAUX, DUVA
La VALLE, and VALLE. German cognates are DOBLER and GRUN
Other such names are COREY (Irish), COWAN (Irish and Scottish

DAHL (Norwegian and German), DAHLIN and DAHLMAN Swedish), SIMA (Spanish), GLAB (Polish), GLENN and GLYNN Welsh), and SERRITELLA (Italian).

The romantic French insist on pointing out the beauty of the ale, as in BELLIVEAU. Many English valley names have significant lements added, as BARKSDALE, "birch tree valley," HAZELTINE where hazel trees grew," HIGGINBOTHAM "Richard's valley," LOB-ELL "valley infested with spiders," PETTIS "house in the deep avine," SELDEN "willow tree valley," SLOCUM "blackthorn or sloe ree valley," SWINDELL "valley where swine were bred," and WIN-ERBOTTOM "hollow used by shepherds in the winter." Wide val-ys are WIDEN and SIDEBOTHAM. German names are FELSENTHAL rocky valley" and LILIENTHAL "lily valley," this latter being also he name of several villages in Germany.

Rocks and stones, especially unusual ones often used as bound-ry marks, are prominent features that serve to describe the earby householder. At various places in England and on the con-nent great stones have been erected by prehistoric peoples, as ritness Stonehenge, possibly the best known in England. All the ountries where ancient civilizations flourished have large build-g stones standing here and there, the remaining ruins of temples nd forgotten holy places. Primitive man erected large stones or haped rocks to keep in memory the exact place where a certain vent occurred or to mark a route or call attention to a burial site, specially in parts of the world where wood was not plentiful, nd rocks were readily available. Heaps of stones or boulders vere used to mark off the lands of a particular family or tribe. ireat menhirs or rough stones remained long after their signifi-ance was forgotten and became so sacred that men feared to move them. FEATHERSTONE is the man from Featherstone, the ame of places in Northumberland and Yorkshire, a name from n Old English word *fether* "four" which refers to a tetralith, onsisting of three upright stones capped by a headstone or lintel, our stones in all. Solemn oaths could be sworn on a great stone. he stone itself might become invested with a sacred character nd become the object of elaborate propitiatory rites. Defacing memorial or moving a boundary stone was an act believed sure bring retribution to early man.

The common names are STONE in England and STEIN in Ger-

many, the latter sometimes Anglicized to STINE in America. Th
Dutch forms are STEEN and VANDERSTEEN. Other English name
are CARNES, FLINT, RING, and ROCK. CAIRNS, CLOUD, and CRA
are both English and Scottish. French names are LAFFITE, M
LIERE, ROCHE, DEROCHE, and DUROCHER. Irish forms are CLOUGH
ERTY and ROACH. Slavic forms are KAMEN and KAMIEN, wit
KAMINSKI in Poland and KAMINSKY in Russia. KAMIN is also
Russian and Ukrainian name for a dweller in a hut with a fir
place. SKALA is both Polish and German for the dweller near
rock or for one who came from Skala "rock" in Germany. Finnis
dwellers in the environs of stone are KALLIO and KIVI. The Italia
TUFO lived near soft sandy stone. Numerous German names i
clude modifying elements. BRONSTEIN and the partially Anglicize
BROWNSTEIN designate the brown stone usually a boundary mar.
HARTSTONE is the hard stone, probably in distinction to nearb
softer material; ROTHSTEIN is the red stone. German ZAHN dwe
near a pointed rock. Spanish CANTU resided near a circular ston
  MARCH and MARKS dwelt in England at the division of land
boundary mark, as did DOLE and DOLL. POST lived near a signi
cant post or marker, as did German STENGEL and STOLL, the latt
sometimes near a mine shaft. When a new marker was erecte
the resident nearby might become NEUMARK in Germany or NE
MARK in England. Swedish NEWMARK might be translated to "ne
field." Spanish TREVINO dwelt near the place where three boun
ary lines came together. English HEAD dwelt at the upper end
some natural feature such as a wood, field, valley, or the lik
HEMMER dwelt near the border. Others who lived at the edge
outskirts of the town are English TOWNSEND, French DESCARTE
and Polish KONIECZNY and KRAJEWSKI. Hedge fences were ve
common boundary marks in medieval times and some village
owe their surnames to them. English HEDGES, Irish HAGEN, a
Dutch SCHUTT are examples. German PLOTKE refers to a sm
fence, although in some cases it denominates the dweller near t
quicksand. BRAXTON dwelt at or near Bracca's stone or bounda
mark.
  If one lived in or near a spur, point, corner, nook, pocket, ang
of land, projection, or curve or bend in a river, the situation w
duly noted by his neighbors in locating his address. Such Engli
names are ANGLE, BEY, BYERS, CORNER, CROKE, CROOKER, HEAR

HERNDON, HOKE, HOOKER, HOOKS, HORN, SHEETS, SHORTALL, VHAM, and YALE. All these names have to be mentioned together because the exact meanings overlap. Dutch cognates are HAACK, HOEKSTRA, and VAN HOEK. German names are ECK, ECKMAN, and ZIFF. The Slavic corner dweller was KALATA. A Polish name is the short, distinctive ROG. The ancestor of THACKERAY originally lived at the corner where thatch grew or was stored. The thatched roofs found everywhere in medieval times required immense quantities of the material.

Heretofore we have been dealing with natural features not generally manmade with the exception of bridges and prehistoric remains. Following are mentioned objects seen on the land which have been constructed by the inhabitants. The most prominent are, of course, buildings, the principal ones in medieval times being the HALL and the CHURCH which, being found in every village, served to name numerous families. In some cases HALL was merely the servant in the hall, and in other cases he dwelt at the rock or stone, generally a boundary marker, from Old English *eall* "rock." Likewise, in some instances the surname CHURCH designated the church official. HALLER dwelt in or near the hall. However, the German with that name originally lived in Halle "salt-works" in Prussia. The Spanish surname for the hall is CAMERO. The great hall, a barnlike structure at the time surnames arose, consisted of one large room, the living, sleeping, dining parts all in one. From it developed the homes we know today. Other dwellers in or near the most important house in the English village might be named HOUSE, SALE, SAYLES, SEALS, or TREVORE. French LACOUR also dwelt in or near a house, although this name has several other derivations.

If the home were more modest, a cottage or a hut, the names might be BOARD, BOOTH, BOTH, BOWERS, COTE, LODGE, or SELL, the latter from Old English *gesell* meaning a shelter for animals or a herdsman's hut. BOWERS also named the man from Bower "house" in Peeblesshire. BOARD also designated the dweller on a small farm. COTTON had nothing to do with the soft, white, fluffy material, but designated the dweller in a small cottage, from Old English *cot* plus the diminutive ending *-on*, when not from a village name. The booth or circular hut is still built all over Europe by shepherds and others for temporary use. It is constructed of

207

stakes driven into the ground and forked or tied together at th
top. When a man lived in a dwelling markedly more simple o
unpretentious than his neighbors, the fact would be noted by hi
associates not squeamish about commenting on another's misfor
tune. The English dweller in the hut or shed in the field woul
be SCHOFIELD. STADEL and STADLER are the German dwellers nea
the barn or shed when not metonymic for one who was oversee
of the barn for the lord, or a place name for one who came fror
Stadel "barn" in Germany.

An Englishman who had built his home on a promontory o
neck of land might be surnamed NESS, ROSSMAN, STURT, or eve
NOSEWORTHY. If Scottish, the form would be ROSS, if Finnisl
NIEMI, and if Danish, HOEGH. TALCOTT resided in front of th
cottage or in the cottage in the valley.

ENDICOTT located the man in the end cottage; LIPPINCOT
would be in the cottage at the edge or on the bank of a strean
if not one who lived in Lippa's cottage. BERRA is the Italian an
HUTTER is the German living in a hut or hovel. The Spanish res
dent on a large estate could become known as VILLA. Englis
BLANTON dwelt at the horse farm, GRAHAM at the gray home
stead, and STEAD at the dairy farm. German HAUSER lived in
house for which a money rent was paid; IMHOF dwelt in the cour
German DORFMAN and BUERGER, English TOWNE and TOWNE
and French La VELLE all dwelt in the town or village. Englis
PARRISH resided within the parish, an area originally in the car
of a single priest, except where the man came from Paris.

If the English house were recently built, the name might be
come NEWHALL, NEWHOUSE, or NEWELL, or, if German, NEUHAU
Old houses produced the surnames OLDS or ALDIS and ALCOT
Particular houses were BARKHOUSE and BARKUS "house made o
birchwood, or a tannery," MALTHUS "malt house," LOFTUS "hou:
with an upper story," NORCOTT "northern cottage," WAINHOUS
"house where wagons were made," and WHITEHOUSE. The bak
house became BACKUS and BACCUS in England and BACKHAUS i
Germany. As a name, BACKHOUSE quickly became obsolete, or ver
rare, in the United States because of its reference to the littl
place in back formerly so familiar to the residents in rural Ame
ica. STACKHOUSE lived in a habitation by a steep rock or hill.

DOOLITTLE, when not a nickname for an idler, is from th

French *de l'hôtel,* referring to one who lived in or near the mansion house or palace. Spanish PACHECO resided in or near a country palace. French DEMAS and DUMAS dwelt in or near the house, sometimes the connotation being more particularly "little farm." PITTAL is the Englishman who lived or worked in or near the hospital, a house for travelers, usually a religious house, which later developed into a place for residence or care of the needy and infirm. SPITTAL was also the name of several small places in Scotland.

Other surnames that indicate the ancestor's residence near a church or religious house are the English and Scottish ECCLES and ECHOLS, English CHAPPELL, Scottish KIRK, German KIRCH, Italian CHIESA, and Polish KOSCIELNIAK. TEMPLE brings to mind the religious house of the Knights Templars. HARKNESS refers to a heathen temple, when not to a dweller on or near the cape or headland. The recently constructed church in Scotland would be NEWKIRK. KAPPEL was the German and Hungarian dweller near a chapel. Dwellers in or near a monastery or other holy place would be called STOCKS or STOWE in England and MENCKEN in Germany. Italian CELLA resided in a cell, probably in some religious house. German KIRCHHOFF dwelt in or near the churchyard. Scottish KIRKLAND would be found adjacent to the land belonging to the church, often the village cemetery.

The third most important building in the village would be the mill, and the family adjacent thereto would be MILLS, MULL, MILNE, or TREVELYAN if British, and DESMOULINS, MULLINS, or MOULINS if French. German KOERNER dwelt or worked near a mill. WINDMILLER is the Anglicized form of the German or Dutch name for one who dwelt by the windmill, or in some cases it merely meant one who owned such a contrivance. A dweller near a tall tower or spire would be the English HIGHTOWER, TOWER, and TARR, and the Spanish TORRES. Residents near the smithy would be described as SMIDDY or SMITHERS. Dutch VAN WINKLE lived near a shop or store, as did German WINKLER and WINKLEMAN. German SCHOBER passed his life near an outstanding haystack.

Fortified castles were naturally large imposing structures and the peasant living nearby would be so described. The principal English surnames referring to residence in or near the stronghold or fortified place are BORROWS, BURG, BURGE, BURKS, BURR, BURRI: (all from Old English *burg* "fort"), CASTLE, CORWIN, PEALE, and WORK, while NEWBERG describes the more recently erected forti-fication. Norman Vincent PEALE, the New York clergyman and author, may have had an early forebear who came from Pee "fortress" on the Isle of Man or who dwelt near a fortress in Eng land. CHESTER, when not from a place name, designated the dweller near an old Roman fort. Irish forms of the name are the common BURKE and BOURKE. BURK is from the common Englisl pronunciation of Burgh, an uncommon form although several vil lages have this name in England. BORG is a Swedish, Norwegian and German cognate. An especially strong castle in Germany is BURKHARDT. An Italian form is La ROCCO. Spanish names are CASTILLO and CASTRO for a castle or fortress, the latter also being Portuguese.

In many places throughout medieval Europe a Christian cros. was set up at a roadside often dedicated to some saint and fre quently serving as a marker or guidepost. Edward I of England put up twelve crosses, one at each place where the funeral party of Eleanor, his queen, had stopped on its way from Nottingham shire to Westminster Abbey in the fourteenth century. Where there was no church, a cross might designate a preaching or meet ing place. Men residing nearby would be surnamed CROSS, CRUSE CREWS, CROUCH, CRUTCH, or ROOD in England; if by a cross ir the glade or meadow or by the north cross, it would produce the name CROSSLEY or NORCROSS, respectively. Popular French name are La CROSSE, La CROIX, and DELACROIX. German forms are KREUTZ, KRIZ, KRITZ, and KROSS, the latter also being Scottish CRUZ is a Spanish and Portuguese form. Sometimes a medieva image of the Virgin Mary was set up near the roadside and a resident nearby might be surnamed VIRGIN. However, this name more often arose from playing the part in a pageant. Some o these names meaning "cross" refer to one who dwelt at the plac where two roads crossed.

Many men were identified by reference to some sort of en closure in or near which they resided or worked. French LACOU was the man who dwelt in or near the court. His compatriot whe lived near the gardens might be called DESJARDINS. JARDINE and JARDEN are French and Scottish names designating the dwelle

n, or near, a garden. There are a number of English words, not
ll of them in common use today, which describe enclosures of
various types. Modern urban life has faded them from the con-
ciousness of the ordinary man. English dwellers in or near a
mall, simple, enclosed or fenced yard of some sort might become
nown by such diverse names as CLOSE, CRAFT, CROFT, GARTH,
GLADNEY, HAMM, LOCKE, LOCKETT, TAFT, TOFT, TUFTS, and
WOODY. PICKELL and PICKLES lived in or near a pightle, a small
nclosed piece of land, sometimes with a cottage on it. England
s pre-eminently a land of enclosures. Englishmen craved privacy,
ossibly developed by a need for protection from intruding colo-
ists in early Britain.

A common German cognate is HOFF "a courtyard or fenced-in
lace." If the place were fenced with a hedge in England, the
ame might become HAWES, HEGG, or the common HAYES. The
requency of these names gives us a hint that hedge fences were
bundant. HAAG is a Dutch cognate form. Enclosures designed to
estrict animals are PENN, PENNER, and POUNDS. WEATHERSPOON
nd WITHERSPOON dwelt at or near the sheep enclosure. Enclo-
ures on a hill might serve to name men HILLIARD or, if on a
wooded hill, PARKHURST. Dwellers near the village green, gen-
rally unenclosed, would be known as GREEN, a very common
ame, or MEANS. This latter name is from Anglo-French *mesne,*
nd also has the connotation of "home farm." An Italian cognate
s LO VERDE. WHITTY is the dweller at the white enclosure.

Men who could be addressed by the particularly well-known
arm or piece of land on or near which they lived would be
nown by such names. Size or shape of the plot of land would be
bserved. Spanish QUINONES worked a small plot. On a triangular
iece of land the farmer would be GORE or GORHAM in England
r KEIL or ZWICK in Germany. A dweller at or near an area
ectangular in shape and as long as the distance the plow went
without turning might be named SHOTT or FURLONG in England;
n a plot of one acre the names AKERS and ACKER would be used;
PLATT merely designated a small piece of ground. HEADLAND
would be found at the area set apart at the end of the field for the
urning of the plows and for access by the villagers to their indi-
idual plots. An English resident near a cultivated field would
e LAND or LANDIS; or if newly broken up for cultivation, BRICK-

211

LEY; or if near rough or uncultivated land, ROWE. LELAND was t
be found in or near the fallow or untilled field. The Italian o
or near the plowed land would be known as ARVIA. VANN wa
often the English dweller near the place where grain was threshe

Although in the Middle Ages most wines consumed in Englan
were imported from southern France, there were a few vines c
vineyards, and dwellers near them might become known as VINE
or WINGARD. The wine trade in England was active and the ave
age price in the thirteenth century had risen to a penny a gallo
The price is still rising! The French dwellers near the numerou
vineyards acquired such names as LA VIGNE, DELAVIGNE, an
DUCLOS. German cognate forms are TRAUB and WEINSTOCK, whil
WEINTRAUB grew or handled grapes.

Particularly in a country destined for commerce, roads or stree
were of necessity prominent features of the landscape. Englis
STREET and STREETER, also LONGSTREET, surnamed one who live
near the early paved highway, that is, the ancient Roman roac
The four principal Roman roads in Britain were Ermine Stree
Dere or the more modern Watling Street, the Fosse Way, an
Akeman Street. Icknield Way was a prehistoric trackway. Thes
street names, however, did not become English family name
Spanish ESTRADA lived near a paved road. An English resider
near a narrow passageway, rural road, or narrow way betwee
fences might receive such surnames as ALLEY, LANE, MUSE, PAS
MAN, PATHE, TWITCHELL, WAY, and WIND, the latter referring t
a winding path or ascent.

Ernest HEMINGWAY, the famous American novelist, must hav
had an early ancestor who dwelt at the road to Heming's estat
Names describing passages to a particular large or important far
or homestead are not common as surnames.

TRAVIS and TRAVERS dwelt at the crossroads. If the way was u
a hill or over a fence or wall, STILES, STILLMAN, and STYLES woul
be the names. Dwellers in a gate, gap, or passage through a chai
of hills or entrance of some kind would be GATES, PORT, SLACK
or YATES. HYATT dwelt at the high gate. The word "gate" ir
cludes both what we call a street and what we call a gate or ba
rier. One who lived at the gate or entrance to a park or fore:
would acquire such names as HACK, HATCH, HATCHER, and HECK

Wynn is a Scottish and Welsh surname for one on a wynd or narrow street.

Many surnames refer to a road or passage of a certain kind and an adjective or noun is one element of the name. There is Cole-gate, the cool gap in a chain of hills. Hathaway is the road by the heath; Gatewood, the road to the wood; Passmore, by the moor; Treadwell, by the stream; Withrow, through the willow trees; Ridgway, along the ridge; Holloway, between two ridges; Haley, the way leading to the hall; and Ledford, the path leading across a stream. Few people were named after a named city street, clear evidence that city street names did not have the importance that they do today. Small villages usually had only one street, so it was not necessary to give it a name. Ferry designated the man near such a water crossing when not a metonym for the ferryman. Vanderveer is the Dutch cognate.

A German living near a country road would be surnamed Strass, or Zweigler if near a branching road; Gass lived on a narrow passageway; Bergstresser resided on the mountain road; and Steinweg on the stony road. Dutch Steege lived on the alley or lane. French residents on an important street were often called LaRue, or La Porte if near the city gate. Finnish Sola dwelt at the pass or gorge. Irish Stritch lived on the paved road. One who resided on or near the town square in Italy would carry the surname Piazza.

The four cardinal directions, North, South, East, and West, served to surname men who had come to a new residence from an indefinite place in the direction named. West and North are also short forms designating men who came from the English counties of Westmorland and Northumberland. Norris is a common surname for a man from the north country, Southern for one from the south, and Eastman and Westman for one from the east and west, respectively. These directions frequently modify other landscape words and produce self-explanatory names, such as Estabrook, Northbrook, Northway, Northlake, West-lake, and Westcott "western cottage." The meaning of many of these names is somewhat vague. For example, Westlake could mean either the man who lived at the west lake or who lived west of the lake, and in many cases it is impossible to decide which meaning is the correct one. Westervelt is the Dutchman

who lived in or near the west field. OSTER is a Swedish name fo
one from the east. Many other surnames of this type will be ob
served and the explanation will be obvious, except in a few case
where they are from a place name.

Dwellers on or near land which produced certain crops ac
quired distinctive names. English BANCROFT, BENFIELD, and BAN
FIELD lived on or near fields where beans grew. Honey was th
only available source of sugar during medieval times and bee
were important in the life of that time. BEEBE would be foun
near the bee farm or apiary while BEASLEY would be located nea
the meadow or wood where bees were found. WEATHERLEY dwe
in the meadow or wood where sheep were kept. HARLAN woul
be found in the land infested with hares. English ARMITAGE an
ARMISTEAD lived near the hermit's place. The residence of Spanis
MERCADO and MEDINA was adjacent to the market place.

Many landscape or address names describe the place wher
plants, herbs, or flowers grew. Italian FIORE "flowers," GIGLI
"lilies," and GAROFALO "soapwort," together with Spanish FLORE
"flowers," are examples. German BLAUVELT "blue field or fla
field," ROHR "reeds," RUBINCAM "turnips," and Dutch ROOSEVEL
"rose field" are further examples. The Poles have many such sur
names: LUBIN "lupine, herbs of the pea family," MAKOWSKI "pop
pies," PAPROCKI "ferns," RUCINSKI and RUTKOWSKI "rue, a medic
nal herb," and SZAFRANSKI "saffron or crocus." The Ukrainia
BURIAN dwelt at a place overgrown by weeds.

Many small villages in the British Isles and in Europe hav
acquired as names the words for simple landscape features. Whe
men bear these as family names, it is impossible to say wheth
an early ancestor originally lived in one of such towns or wheth
he merely resided in or near such a landscape feature. Some c
these English names are CROFT "enclosure," DEAL "valley
DINGLE "deep dell," HAIGHT from *haigh* "enclosure," MINSTE
"monastery," NANCE "valley," RIVERS, SCALES "hut or temporar
shelter," SHELL "bank," SHUTE "park," STAPLES "post or pillar
STOKES "monastery, cell, place, or outlying farm," and WELD, fro
Old English *weald* "woodland." These small villages or cluste
of houses may have names composed of only one topograph
element, with or without a modifying adjective, or a combinatio
of such terms.

Surnames from Places

Names combining two or more different landscape features are quite common and are quite easily recognized. Many English names consist of a landscape word coupled with a word referring to a wood or clump of trees. There are MARKLEY "wood near the boundary," ROCKWOOD "rocky wood," STANWOOD "stony wood," WINDLEHURST "wooded valley where swine were kept," WOODHOUSE "house in the wood," WOODLOCK "enclosure in the wood," WOODRICK "wood on a ridge," and WOODWORTH "homestead in the wood." Others refer to a marsh as BARRYMORE "woodland marsh," HISLOP "hazel tree marsh," KERSHAW "boggy wood," and the French BROUILLET "swampy wood." There are numerous other such names, among them ASPINWALL "aspen tree stream," LINCOTT "cottage by linden trees," OGDEN "oak valley," PRIESTLEY "priest's meadow," and RAYFIELD "river field." German STEINFELD is "stony field" and WESEBAUM is "meadow tree." WHITESIDE originally resided on the "white side (of a tree, valley, etc.)." Scottish KIRKWOOD dwelt in the wood belonging to the church.

The English dweller at, on, or near a wall such as the old Roman wall would be surnamed WALL or WALLER, sometimes spelled WOLL and WOLLER. WAUGH is a Scottish cognate. It must be remembered that many medieval towns depended for protection on the thick walls surrounding them. WALL and WALLER also designate the men who built or repaired walls. The ancient English city of York is an excellent example of a walled city, enclosed by walls dating in part from Norman times.

English WEIR and WYER were found at or near a dam or fish trap. German SCHACHT lived near a mine and Italian FERRO near an iron mine. German KLEIMAN and English CLAY dwelt on clay ground; Polish PIASECKI dwelt on sandy soil; German LAUSCHE resided near quicksand.

Usually surnames ending in -er or -man denote the occupation of the original bearer. But there are many toponymical or landscape surnames that have these terminations which in no way suggest the occupation of the early bearer. They occur frequently in both England and Germany and there are even a few in France. Gustav Fransson calls them toponymical surnames. English examples in -er are BECKER "brook," BROKER "brook," GROVER, HILLER, LINDER, "lime tree," SPRINGER, WELLER, and WILDER "forest," and in -man are BECKMAN "stream," BROCKMAN "brook,"

HILLMAN, and WELLMAN. Some with the names MILLER and MILNER undoubtedly acquired their family names from residenc near the mill rather than from their occupation. A French ex ample is ROCHER "dweller by the rock." German examples ar BACHER "brook," GASSER "alley," KREUTZER "cross," STRASSE "country road," BUSCHMAN "bush," and GASSMAN "alley." The ter mination -man can be added to a place name, the best know example possibly being the Dutch GELDERMAN, one who cam from Gelders, a province in the Netherlands. These names endin in -er and -man have exactly the same meanings as the simila name without these terminations. WILDER has two other cor tributory sources: a descendant of Wealdhere "powerful, army, and from Old English *wildeor* "wild animal."

Certain final place name elements are weakened when ur stressed and are altered in spelling in such a way as to disguis their correct origin. For example, SANDHILL can be reduced t SANDELL, TOOTHILL to TUTTLE, and CALDWELL to CAUDLE. Name terminating in -house are often slurred or contracted into -us c similar syllables, as BACKHOUSE "bake house" to BACKUS, HILL HOUSE to HILLIS, and MALTHOUSE to MALTHUS. The common enc ing -ham sometimes becomes -um, as when BARNHAM collapse into BARNUM. SMITHTHWAITE "the smith's clearing, or small clear ing" may become SMITHWHITE. To mention all the changes tha naturally come about through quick, slurring pronunciation c variant spelling would enlarge this work to the size and shape c a large metropolitan telephone directory.

• • •

At a time when the ordinary man and most of the wealthy nc bility could not read and even the village priest and other clerg had little more education than a child now receives before he i more than halfway through grammar school, the business sign a we know it today listing the name and the business or occupatio was unknown, and would have been quite useless in attractin customers. Tradesmen had no large shop windows in which t display their goods. Thus there developed signboards displayin a picture or even just the article offered for sale, erected outsid shops. Inns also attracted attention through their signboard. The picture might be of a dragon, and DRAKE, the archaic form would in the natural course of events become the surname of the man who lived or worked there. English GRIFFIN is the resident at the sign of the griffin, a fabulous monster half lion and half eagle. English STARR, Spanish LUCERO, Polish GWIAZDA, and Russian ZORIN designate the dweller at the sign of the star. Star and Zorin are also baptismal names, so STARR and ZORIN could indicate descent from one so named—Polish ZORICH does designate the son of Zorya "star." STARNS and STARNES are plural and name one residing at the sign of the stars, a pictorial signboard.

It is often easy to explain a difficult name by saying that it emanates from a signboard, but to do so would be an error in many instances. Very little has been written recording facts about the early medieval signs, and the soft material of which they were fashioned made their preservation over the centuries unlikely. They were placed before small inns and craftsmen's homes and places of work and thus seemed unimportant to the people at the time. Also we know that in the Middle Ages they were quite simple and had not developed into the elaborate signboards pictured in the street scenes of the seventeenth and eighteenth centuries. The earliest signboards were used by the ancient Egyptians, early Greeks, and particularly by the Romans. More family names can be explained from signs in Germany where fixed surnames evolved later than in England and France.

Sign names are closely related to occupational names because the sign often denoted the occupation. The German who hung up a shoe or a pair of shears might become known as SCHUCH "shoe" or SCHEER "shears." Passersby would know that the first was a shoemaker, and that the man who hung up the shears was a tailor. The name would come from the sign. Dutch SCHAAF, "a carpenter's plane," designated the carpenter who became so known. Spanish PADILLA "frying pan" would designate the cook at such a sign. Polish BOCHENEK "loaf of bread" would be one who worked where an actual loaf of bread was hung, or at a signboard depicting a loaf of bread. English WAYNE was the resident at the sign of the wagon, usually a wagonmaker. It must be remembered that in medieval times a man usually had his shop at his place of residence. The shop was on the ground floor and the family lived on the floor above, or behind the shop.

The most common English family name from a sign is BELL.

217

AMERICAN SURNAMES

Chaucer gathered his pilgrims to Canterbury "in Southwark, at this gentil hostelrie, that highte, the Tabard, faste by the Belle." A tabard was a sleeveless jacket worn by knights. Not all in America with the name of BELL derive it from a sign. Sometimes, from French *bel*, it refers to the handsome man. Italian CAMPANELLA and CAMPANA lived at the sign of the bell or bell tower A bush, a bunch of ivy or evergreen tied to the end of a pole hung outside a shop, designated a wine merchant and English BUSH and German BUSCH were wine merchants. These tavern ale-stakes sometimes projected over the king's highway so as to impede travelers, and laws were promulgated to regulate their length. The old English proverb tells us: Good wine needs no bush. French and Italian proverbs are similar. French DUBUISSON was originally found at the sign of the bush. French FEUILLET would be at the sign of the leaf which also represented a wine merchant. German FLASCH "a flask or bottle" generally denoted a tavern. Russian DRELL resided at the sign of the arrow. The rose either a picture or a crude drawing, served to name many who lived under it, and we have English, Scottish, and German ROSE Spanish and Italian ROSA, English ROYCE and ROOS, Finnish RUUSU, and Czechoslovakian RUZICKA. German ROSENSCHMIDT is the smith at the sign of the rose.

German BLOCH and English BLOCK lived at the sign of the block, although in some cases the short, stumpy, or stupid man was meant, in the same manner in which we use the term "blockhead" today. HAND would be found at the sign of a hand; if the hand was closed, the name could be POINDEXTER "right fist." English, Scottish, and French PENNY dwelt at the sign of the feather, as did German FEDER. PENNY is also a nickname from the coin and a patronymic from the personal name, Penny. BALANCE lived and worked at the sign of the balance, a scale-maker. Polish KULA and MOTEL lived at the sign of the ball and butterfly, respectively. This latter name is also a French surname for a dweller at the small *motte* "hillock." The modern word *motel* is a telescoping of motorists' hotel. German HERTZ would be at the sign of the heart, although the name was sometimes applied to a particularly courageous man. English GREENMAN was sometimes active at the sign of the green man; because of present-day insistent advertising he might be known as the "Jolly Green Giant."

The nobility often noted on their houses their crest or heraldic sign. When the owner was away, the house was sometimes operated by his servants as an inn for the convenience of travelers. KRONE was the German at the sign of the crest. English CROWN dwelt at the sign of the crown. CROWNINSHIELD would be found at the sign of the crown and shield. Some families with this name in New England pronounce it *Crunchell.*

Animals, domesticated and wild, have been commonly employed as inn signs. While it is certain that many men acquired their surnames from the signs in front of their houses or inns, as mentioned before, there is little direct documentary evidence of the fact. Camden in his *Remaines* (London, 1605) wrote, "Neither is it improbable, but that many names that seeme unfitting for men, as of brutish beasts, &c. came from the very signes of the houses where they inhabited; for I have heard of them which said they spake of knowledge, that some in late time dwelling at the sign of the Dolphin, Bull, White-horse, Racket, Peacocke, &c. were commonly called *Thomas* at the *Dolphin, Will* at the *Bull, George* at the *White horse, Robin* at the *Racket,* which names as many other of like sort, with omitting *At,* became afterward hereditarie to their children."

While the vast majority of surnames referring to animals have other explanations, many are undoubtedly from early signs. Fox is a sign name as well as a nickname for a shrewd or crafty man. Reynard has the same reputation for cunningness throughout Europe that is ascribed to him in this country. In the north of England TODD was the common name for the fox. Another English name is COLFAX "black fox." Scottish GUPTILL, German FUCHS, Finnish KETTUNEN, Czechoslovakian LISKA, Polish LISS, Italian VOLPE, and Dutch and German VOSS and VOS all refer to the crafty animal of the chase. TALBOT dwelt at the sign of the talbot, a white sporting dog. Even the elephant was used as a sign and the names OLIPHANT and OLIVANT from Middle English *olifant* are occasionally observed, although some authorities deny this and contend that OLIPHANT and OLIVANT derive from Olifard "olive branch."

Throughout all of Europe the wolf was one of the animals most revered and feared in medieval times. Lycanthropy, the transformation of men into wolves, was widely believed in during the

219

Middle Ages. The majority with the name WOLF derive from the element in Old Germanic given names. But that there are some with this name that are derived from inn signs is not open to question. Another English name is LOWELL, from Old French *lou* "wolf" plus the diminutive termination. German forms are WOLFE, WOLFF, WOLK, WOOLF, WULF, and WALK, the last being also Polish. Another Polish form is WILK, and a diminutive form is WILCZAK. Italian forms are LUPO and LUPINO; the Russian name is VOLKOV; Ukrainian, VOVCENKO; Hungarian, FARKAS; Greek, LYCOS; and Czechoslovakian, VLK.

Surnames referring to the deer family in one way or another are common and many arose from residence of an ancestor at a tavern sign. English names, many referring to the red deer, are BUCK (male), HART and HURT (adult male), PRITCHETT (a buck in his second year), ROE, ROEBUCK, and DOE (female). German names are HERSH and HIRSCH. The French name is CERF, the Spanish, RENO, the Polish, SARNA, and the Czechoslovakian, JELINEK. The bear was a popular tavern sign in Germany and there are the following family names: BAER, BARTZ, BEHNKE, BEHR, BEHRENS, and BENZ. The Italian cognate is URSO and the Ukrainian, VEDMEDENKO. English BEAR and BEER derive from tavern signs in a few cases, but these names mostly originate from residence in a grove from Old English *bearu* "grove." Among many north European peoples the bear was a sacred animal, and so favored in song and story.

Other animals that served as signs and consequently developed into family names in England are BRACKETT "little hunting dog" and OTTER. However, this last name is also derived from the personal name, Otthar "terrible army" in Norway. The Swedish form of the name is UTTER. German MARDER dwelt at the sign of the marten or in a field infested by those animals. Russian SUSLOV would be found near the sign of the gopher. German EICHHORN would have a likeness of a squirrel at his place. That fabulous animal resembling a horse with one horn, the unicorn, provided the family name EINHORN in Germany.

When the inn sign emphasized a lion, the proprietor might become LYONS or LYON in England and Scotland. German names are LAU, LEIB, LOEWE, LOEWY, and LOWE. LEON is a Greek and Spanish form; LEV is the Polish name. The bull was also a popular sign and there are English BULL, BULLOCK, and FARR. The Ukrainian form is BUHAJENKO.

English sign names referring to the pig family are FARROW, HOGG, HOGUE, PURCELL, and SUGGS. The rabbit family produces such sign names as COONEY and HARE in England, HAAS in Holland and Germany, ZAJICKA in Czechoslovakia, and ZAJAC in Poland and the Ukraine. The horse family is responsible for STOTT in England, CHEVALLO and CAVALLO in Italy, and SIWEK in Poland. The names meaning "horse" in Italy are more likely to be nicknames than sign names. SCHECK, SCHELL, and SCHIMMEL in Germany refer to the roan horse, the stallion, and the gray or white horse, respectively.

Surnames relating to the goat are CHEEVER, KIDD, and HAVER in England, CAPRA in Italy, BOCK in Germany, and CHEVROLET "little goat" in France. Few people riding in a Chevrolet regard it as a little goat. From sheep we have AGNEW, LAMB, and WITHERS in England. GATTO resided at the sign of the cat or tomcat in Italy and KOCOUREK did the same in Czechoslovakia. The sable gives us ZOBEL in Germany and SOBEL and ZABEL in Poland and Czechoslovakia. German OCHS and English STEERE dwelt at the sign of the ox. English BEAVER owes his name to that animal, except when his ancestor came from Beauvoir "fair view" in western France. Czechoslovakian BOBER also dwelt at the sign of the beaver. Polish WYDRA and Italian RAGO dwelt at the signs of the otter and frog, respectively. With no particular animal in mind there might be mentioned English BEST, the dweller at the sign of the beast, in those cases where the name was not applied to one assumed to have the qualities of a beast, sometimes not in an uncomplimentary sense.

Birds of all sorts made popular signs. For the general feathered tribe the English popular spellings are, of course, BYRD and BIRD from Old English *bridd* "bird"; FOWLE was a game bird. German and Dutch forms are FOGEL and VOGEL. FINKEL is a German diminutive form, which is also interpreted as a descendant of Finkel "little bird," a popular woman's name in the Middle Ages. Czechoslovakian forms for bird are KAFKA and PTACEK, while the Poles spell it PTAK. The Spanish name is GARZA, probably from the Arabic, possibly more particularly signifying a dove or heron. The domestic chicken family, especially the male, is well known.

221

An English name is Cox, a name that has other forms and subject to several different interpretations without any agreement among onomastic authorities. German names are HAHN and KALLEN, while the Dutch use HAAN and DE HAAN. The Poles say KUREK as do the Czechoslovakians who also use KOHOUT, the latter being moreover a Ukrainian name. The Italian GALLINA refers to the hen. A very popular sign name is the princely EAGLE, with the Dutch form being AHRENS, the German, ADLER, the Spanish, AGUILA, and the Swedish, ORNE.

The pigeon and dove are represented in the English surnames of PIDGEON, CULVER, and DOVE. The dove has taken a large part in legend, folklore, and religious symbolism. It is frequently seen in early Christian art, often as the symbol of the Holy Spirit. From the French there are COLOMB, COULON, and DUBE. German names are HOLLEB and TAUBER. Italian forms are COLOMBO and PALUMBO. From Czechoslovakia comes HRDLICKA and from Russia, GOLUB. Different finches give us the English FINK, FINCH, and PINK "chaffinch," Polish ZIEMBA "bullfinch," Italian CARDELLA "goldfinch," and German GIMBEL "red finch." The magpie produces English PYE, Swiss AGASSIZ, and Polish SROKA. Besides English SWAN and the diminutive form SINNETT, there are German SCHWAN, Dutch SWEM, and Ukrainian LEBEDENKO, all with the same connotation.

From the hawk on an inn sign come the English surnames HAVOC and KITE, the Italian FALCO and FALCONE, the Polish KANIA and SOKOL, the latter being also Czechoslovakian. English SPARKS is a contraction from the sparrow hawk. Also common in signs is the RAVEN. English and French names for this bird are CORBETT and CORBIN. The Czechoslovakian CAPEK translates to raven. The crow is CROWE and CROW in English, KRACKE and KRAHE in German, and WRONA in Poland. HERRON in English and CAPLENKO in Ukrainian represent the heron sign. The lowly sparrow is SPARROW and SPURR in English, SPERLING in German, and WROBEL in Polish. POE, PEABODY, and PEACOCK dwelt in England at the sign of the peacock as did PFAU in Germany. The original name of the family of the American poet and writer, Edgar Allan Poe, is said, however, to have been POER "poor (possibly poverty as the result of a vow)." The crane is common in England and the surnames are CRANE and CRAIN. The woodpecker is represented by German SPECHT and English SPECK. English SNITE and Russian KULIK designate the snipe. ROOK and WREN are English surnames representing these familiar birds.

A few additional miscellaneous bird names from signs are German GEIER and GEYER "vulture," Czechoslovakian KOS and Polish KOSIEK "blackbird," English COE "jackdaw," Spanish ORTEGA "grouse," and German NACHTIGALL and Polish SLAWIK "nightingale." From Germany come GANS, GAUSS, and HUSS, all deriving from the sign of the goose, as does the Czechoslovakian HUSAK. English TEELE would be found at the sign of the teal, a small duck; MALLARD at the sign of the wild drake or common wild duck; and PARTRIDGE at the sign of the partridge.

The Slavic nations frequently used small birds as signs, although it must not be forgotten that in many cases the meaning was as a dealer in such birds used for food. Polish CZAJA designated the large lapwing or gull while CZAJKA was the small lapwing or gull in both Poland and Russia. Czechoslovakian CERMAK dwelt at the sign of the robin. Polish SOWA would be found at the sign of the owl except in those instances where the name was applied because of assumed owlish characteristics. Also from Poland come DROZD "thrush" and SKOWRON "lark."

It cannot be too strongly emphasized that while these animal and bird names sometimes come from shop or inn signs, many also have other derivations such as nicknames from a real or fancied resemblance to the creature depicted. Some fish names derive from signs but most of them probably denote the fisher or seller of the particular kind of fish. Examples are the English SPRATT "spratt" and SHATTUCK "shad"; the German DORSCH "codfish," FISCHL "little fish," HECHT "pike," KREBS "crab"; the Dutch KARP "carp"; the Russian PLOTKIN "plotka"; and Czechoslovakian and Polish RYBA "fish."

Extreme caution must be exercised in interpreting surnames as sign names. It is easy to explain them as house or inn signs but, as has been mentioned, the evidence is scanty and most of them have other more common derivations. Even apparent sign names like BALL "residence near a ball-like mound," ROSE from Rosmund "horse, protection," and SWAN "servant" thus have other and more likely explanations.

● ● ●

So far, the names discussed in this chapter tend to disclose the exact place where the original bearer lived. When a man moved from one town or city to another, his neighbors would be likely first to inquire from the newcomer whence he came and would refer to him as of or from that place. In an age when every man was suspicious of strangers, the knowledge of the place a man hailed from helped to establish a friendly relation. Many English, Scottish, German, French, Polish, Russian, Italian, Spanish, and Portuguese persons derive their family names from the town or village where their remote ancestors first saw the light of day and from which they later moved. Most of the people lived in small villages or settlements. Even the houses outside a village were not separate. They were grouped together in small clusters and might have names even though not true villages.

If one was lord of a manor or large estate, he would become known by its name. The nobles who came at the time of William's invasion of England, in 1066, brought with them the names of their castles and estates in Normandy and Brittany. Not many Irish have family names derived from places, although there is the common DEVLIN from an early spelling of Dublin "black pool." Almost every village, town, or city in England has been used as a surname by some English family.

A few—a very few—family names derived from place names designate ownership of the village or manor so named. Most of them merely indicate that an ancestor originally came from that place. Some have thought that *de* before the name indicated possession of landed property, but this is not true; it merely means "of" or "from." But the place names that did become surnames because the man owned the place were the first surnames in Western countries, and they were the first to become hereditary family names.

A curious name is UNTHANK "ingratitude," the name of several villages in England. It indicates a place settled without leave of the lord, originally with the meaning "squatter's farm." The name is also found in Scotland referring to a farm on barren soil. Many unusual names are from names of places. BOWES denominates one from Bowes "bow" in the North Riding of Yorkshire, probably in the sense of an arched bridge. CHIONIS is the Greek from Chios "snow" an island, also its chief town, in the Aegean Sea.

Surnames from Places

One careless writer explained WATERBURY as one "drowned in the sea"—how did he get the name before his untimely end? The name refers to one who came from Waterperry "pear trees by a stream," in Oxfordshire. English and German place names are essentially prosaic. Isaac Taylor, writing of place names in his *Names and Their Histories,* London, 1896, has well remarked, "In English names hardly a trace of imagination, or of any perception of natural beauty, can be discovered; they record in the most prosaic manner the name of the earliest settler, or some fact as to the nature or situation of the place." French place names are more romantic as evidenced by the frequent use of *bon* "good" and *beau* "beautiful."

Names are employed as simply sounds. While place names all originally have a meaning, sometimes the meaning is lost in antiquity. There is Brindon Hill, in Somerset. The Celts called it *Bryn* "hill." To this was added *-dun* "hill," a Saxonized Celtic word, and later the English word *hill* was added when neither *bryn* nor *dun* were any longer significant words. Pendle Hill, in Lancashire, is similarly compounded of three almost synonymous words each meaning "hill." An extreme example is the spot named Torpenhow Hill, from Celtic *tor,* Welsh *pen,* Cumbrian or Saxon *how,* and English *hill,* so it may be translated as Hillhillhill Hill. If the author had known of these examples in his student days, it would have been less embarrassing when he spoke of seeing the beautiful Dom Cathedral in Cologne, Germany, not knowing that *Dom* was just the German word for cathedral.

In America and in other parts of the globe newly inhabited by civilized peoples there is sometimes a conscious effort to attach an appropriate name, but mostly places here are named after towns in the Old World or after early settlers. Men are named after places in the Old World because surnames developed later; in the new, places are named after men. Even America was named after a man, Amerigo Vespucci. The Italian form Amerigo (Latinized Americus) is from the Old Germanic Amalricus "work, rule" or Haimirik "home, rule," or perhaps a combination of the two names.

In the United States, when men did not name places after the familiar names in Europe, they often named them after famous statesmen. All prominent early American officials have had numerous towns, cities, and counties named in their honor. Washington, Jefferson, Madison, Jackson, and Lincoln have been the eponym of so many places as to cause much confusion. Many small places have been named after local heroes and prominent inhabitants. Columbus "dove" is honored all over the Americas. The assassination of President Kennedy, like that of President Lincoln, brought forth such a surge of affection for him as to cause his name to be attached to places all over the world.

In Europe, place names were short descriptions of the places. Occasionally a man's name is included to indicate original ownership of a small settlement. The name arose when near neighbors in speaking of the place identified it by some outstanding feature, location, time of origin, or as owned or occupied by some man. The names of most villages were not given by the inhabitants but by their neighbors. To the inhabitants it was simply "the village"; to the people of neighboring villages it was Weston "the settlement to the west," or Milton "that place with the mill," just some name to distinguish it from their own village.

NUTALL is derived from Nuthall "place where nuts grew," in Nottinghamshire. The spelling of the place name is found as Notehala in the Pipe Roll of 1194. In the three succeeding years the scribe varied the name each time, an excellent example of the spelling problems encountered in old records. In the 1195 Roll he spelled it Nuchala. Then in the next year he misread the *c* for an *e* and wrote it Nuehala. A year later, in the Roll for 1197, the clerk thought that the first element was the word "new" and spelled the name Niewehale. What is the correct early spelling of the name? No one knows. NEWHALL "new hall" could be confused with the latter spelling of the name, although this surname is from several places of that name in England (spelled Newehale in Leicestershire in 1284).

Surnames from town names started with the same spelling as the town name. As the spelling of the village name changed, the spelling of the surname might or might not change with it. For example, early spellings of Bristol, the Gloucestershire city, were Brycgstow and Bristow "place by the bridge," and family names derived from the place are BRISTOW, BRISTO, and BRISTOL. HONEYCUTT designates one who came from Huncoat or Huncote "Huna's cottage" in Lancashire and Leicestershire, respectively; early

pellings are Hunnecotes and Hunecote. Modern HAMILTON "bare
r treeless hill" had earlier place name forms of Hameldon, Ham-
ledon, and Hambleton. SWEETNAM derives from Swettenham
Sweta's homestead" in Cheshire. Names with suffix -*ham* were
ometimes slurred in speech and spelling. BARNUM, the name of
he famous circus magnate, is from Barham "homestead on the
ill," the name of several towns in England.

The place names of Europe are all descriptive of the localities
n one way or another. If the name of a village is Stanford, you
an be sure that it is located at a stony river crossing. Most town
ames in America were consciously and deliberately adopted from
notives other than a desire to describe the place. In Europe, poplar descriptions gradually became fixed by common consent of
he people in the neighboring localities. Unless the interpretation
scribed to an old European place name is descriptive in some
nanner of the place, there is serious question as to whether the
explanation is the correct one. These names therefore usually
contain words and elements denoting landscape features, often
ccompanied by an adjective or word making the description
nore precise. Many of the words designating landscape features
vithout modification came to be also the names of many small
ettlements or villages.

A recently founded homestead or settlement in England might
e appropriately named NEWTON "recent settlement" and this is
robably the most common English place name and so it has
roduced a common surname; also Newton is a common town
ame in Scotland. Likewise the aristocratic NEVILLE from Neuvelle
"new town" is a very common place name in France. A cognate
German form is NEUDORF, not particularly common as an Ameri-
an surname, although it is the name of many small places in
Germany. More common are the German names NEUBERG and
NEUBERGER from Neuburg "new town," often altered in America
o NEWBERG and NEWBERGER.

Some apparent Christian names in their unaltered form are
place names and as such are one source of such family names.
For example, ARNOLD "corner frequented by eagles" is the name
f villages in Nottinghamshire and in the East Riding of York-
hire; CHARLES "rock court" (from the Celtic words *carn* "rock"
nd *lis, les* "court") is in Devonshire; FLORENCE "flourishing" is

the cultural city in Italy; HARROLD "stone woods" (from Old Eng
lish *haer* "stone" and *wald* "woods") is in Bedfordshire; Lesli
"garden of hollies" is in Scotland; MARK "boundary house" is i
Somerset; PAUL "church of St. Paulinus" is in Cornwall; ROWLAN
"roe wood" is in Derbyshire; and SAUL (from Old English *salh*
leah) "sallow wood" is in Gloucestershire. None of these name:
with the exception of Florence, has the connotation generall
given to the font names.

Some names of birds and animals in their unaltered form ar
place names, and as such are one source of the family name
derived from them. CRANE is found in Kent and Middlesex; it is {
back formation of such names as CRANBORNE and CRANBROO}
"cranes' stream," and CRANFORD "cranes' river crossing." HAR'
"stag island" is in Durham and ROE "clearing or boundary" is i
Hertfordshire.

Although in most European countries men were named afte
towns, many names of very small places do contain the Old Ger
manic or Celtic name of the early possessor of the place, but al
most none of them can be identified at the present time. Th{
personal name is now usually so corrupted that the exact spelling
can only be approximated. If any would proudly affirm that the
gave their names to such towns as Leffrington, Lancaster, Leices
ter, or Shordich, that courteous old gentleman, William Camden
in 1603, attacked their veracity, saying, "I would humbly, with
out preiudice, crave respite for a further day before I beleeve{
them." Isn't that a gentle but telling way of calling a man a pre
varicator, a downright liar?

In this discussion of surnames from place names it must b{
understood that the surname is from a place name with approxi
mately that spelling (sometimes the termination *-er* is ignored)
and only a short translation or explanation of the original mean
ing of the place name is given. Once the common suffixes are ex
plained, the interpretation cannot be repeated continuously.

Richard Verstegan in 1605 quoted the old couplet:

> In ford, in ham, in ley, and ton
> The most of English surnames run.

Mark Antony Lower in his work *Essays on English Surnames*
did not think the proverb sufficiently comprehensive and added:

Ing, Hurst and Wood, Wick, Sted and Field,
Full many English surnames yield.

Still not being satisfied he appended the following, saying that
here were several other terminations only second to the others in
requency:

With Thorpe and Bourne, Cote, Caster, Oke,
Combe, Bury, Don and Stowe, and Stoke;
With Ey and Port, Shaw, Worth, and Wade,
Hill, Gate, Well, Stone, are many made;
Cliff, Marsh, and Mouth, and Down, and Sand,
And Beck and Sea with numbers stand.

To understand better the many English surnames which are
derived from place names it might be advisable to scrutinize the
most common terminations of English place names. The ending
ton, from Old English *tūn* and Old Norse *tún,* is by far the commonest element in English place names. Originally it meant "an
enclosure, a farmstead or single dwelling, an estate or manor, a
village or collection of houses," the precise meaning at any one
time or place being difficult to determine. This is also true of all
the other similar terminations such as *-by, -burgh, -ham, -thorp,*
and *-worth.* The form of a name or some circumstance will often
give a hint as to which meaning is the right explanation for a particular place. At the present time *ton* and most of these other
terminations have grown into towns and that is the connotation
they now have.

Examples of surnames containing this element from village
names with the first part translated are ASHTON "ash tree," BURTON
"fortified," CARLTON "free men," CLAYTON "clayey soil," CLIFTON
"hill slope," COMPTON "hollow," DALTON and DENTON "valley,"
EATON "river or island," FELTON "open country," FENTON "marsh,"
HILTON "hill," HORTON "muddy," KINGSTON "king's," LANGTON
"long," LAWTON "hill," LAYTON "leeks," MELTON "mill," MORTON
"marsh," OVERTON "riverbank," PRESTON "priest's," STANTON
"stony," STAPLETON "post," STRATTON "Roman road," TEMPLETON
"Knights Templars," THORNTON "thorn bushes," and WALTON "wall
or wood." TOWNE, a not uncommon family name, derives from
the simple element, *tun.*

The next most common English termination is *-ley* from the

229

dative of Old English *leah*, "a wood or a clearing in a wood," and in later times, "a meadow." This element is especially common in districts that were once heavily forested and in well wooded areas. Here also the word attained so many different meanings that it is difficult in many instances to determine the exact one. (See page 201.) Examples of surnames with this ending are: ASHLEY "ash tree," BENTLEY "bent grass," BRADLEY "wide," BRANTLEY "broom," FARLEY "fern," HARLEY "hare," HARTLEY "stag," HAWLEY "hall," HURLEY "corner," KINGSLEY "king's," LANGLEY "long," MOSELEY and MOSLEY "Moll's or mice," OAKLEY "oak tree," ROWLEY "rough," SHIPLEY "sheep," SHIRLEY "shire," STANLEY "stony," TINSLEY "Tynne's," UTLEY "outer," and WHITLEY "white." Sometimes this termination is spelled *-leigh*, as in RAWLEIGH "rye," SHAPLEIGH "sheep," and WADLEIGH "Wada's," or *-lee*, as in PARLEE "pears." The simple names LEA, LEE, and LEY serve to identify many minor settlements, and have been used to surname many families.

The third most popular termination is *-ham* from Old English *hamm* "a village, a manor, a homestead," and some instances are BERNHAM and BURNHAM "stream," DENHAM "valley," DUNHAM "hill," FARNHAM "fern," INGHAM "Inga's," LATHAM "barn," PARHAM "pear," and WAREHAM "fish trap." It may be observed that most of the surnames terminating in *-ton* are also found terminating in *-ley* and *-ham*. The meanings are practically the same.

There are two surnames terminating in *-ham* that when pronounced in the ordinary easy manner can give cause for some raising of the eyebrows. One is CHEATHAM, often observed in several different spellings. The family so named had an ancestor who came from Cheetham "homestead by a forest" in Lancashire. Cheating is bad but killing is worse, and there is KILHAM spelled Killum in the twelfth century. The name comes from former residence at Kilham "kiln for drying or burning," the name of places in Northumberland and the East Riding of Yorkshire. Children with these names have to steel themselves to withstand the ridicule of their playmates and the tired witticisms of others.

Other terminations are the *-burg* endings, from Old English *beorg* and Old Norse *berg*, often spelled *-brough*, *-borough*, *-bury*, even *-berry*, usually meaning "a fortified place," later "a town," as in YARBROUGH "earth," SCARBOROUGH "Skarthi's," KINGSBURY "king's," SALISBURY "Searu's," NEWBERRY "new," and HENNEBERRY "high." There are many with the suffix -*bury*, the same names often being also with the suffix -*berry*, which contain a man's name as the first element, as BAMBURY "Bebbe's fort or Bana's fort," DEWBERRY "David's fort," GOLDSBURY "Godhelm's fort or Golda's fort," LOUNSBURY "Lothen's fort," MAYBURY "Maerec's fort," PILLSBURY "Pil's fort," and SEABOROUGH "seven hills fort." Names which indicate the material used in building the fort are BRADBURY "boards," STANSBURY "stone," and WOODBURY "wood." Many small settlements were simply called BURROWS or BUR-ROUGHS and so became surnames.

There is -*burn* from Old English *burna* "a spring, a stream," as in KILBORN "kiln," MILBURN "mill," SHERBOURNE "bright," and WASHBURN "fuller's." Others are COBURN "cool," HEPBURN "high," RATHBUN "reeds," RAYBURN "fierce," and WILBURN "brook coming from a spring." Similar to -*burn* is -*brook* "a stream," as in HOL-BROOK "deep ravine," and WESTBROOK.

In the north of England is the Scandinavian -*by* "a homestead, a village," as in ASHBY "ashtree," BARNABY "Beornwald's," BUSBY "shrub," and CROSBY "village at the cross. " Crosby has been said to name Sir John Crosby, London alderman in the year 1470, because he was found by a cross, but this is just a legend; the preposition *by* never appears after the noun. There are KIRBY "with a church," NEWBY, SELBY "sallow copse," WEATHERSBY and WETHERBY "sheep," and WILLOUGHBY "willows." The spelling is sometimes altered to -*bee*, as in BISBEE "Besy's," and KIBBEE "Keti's." Other -*by* names are APPLEBY, BOOTHBY "huts," CLASBY "Klepp's," COLBY "Koli's," FRISBIE "Frisians'," OGLESBY "Odkell's," ORMSBY "Orm's," RIGBY and RIGSBY "ridge," and SHELBY "willows." OVERBY, however, is a contraction of Overbury "upper earthwork or fort" in Worcestershire.

Frequently found in the southwest of England is -*comb* from Old English *cumb* "a hollow or a valley." Examples are HOLCOMB from Holcombe "deep ravine," LIPSCOMB from Letcombe "ledge," WHITCOMB from Whitcombe "wide," and WITHYCOMBE "willow." Other -*comb* names are BALCOM from Balcombe "Baegloc's," BRANSCOMB from Branscombe "Branoc's," LARCOM "Lar's," and WIDDICOMB from Widdicombe "willow." It will be noted that sur-

names from town names ending in *-combe*, more often than no
dropped the final *-e*.

Ending many surnames is *-cot* "a cottage, a shelter, a hut," a
in PRESCOTT "priest's," WALCOTT "serf's," WOLCOTT "Wulfsige's,
and WESTCOTT "western." In these names the usual tendency i
to double the final *t*. COTTON is from various English place name
referring to a dweller at the cottages. COATS and COATES ar
sometimes the man who moved from Coates or Cotes "cottag
or shelter for animals," the names of several places in England.

A common ending is *-don* from Old English *dūn*, sometime
spelled *-dun, -den,* or *-down* "hill," as in BRANDON "broom,
BLODEN "blue," CONGDON "king's," GLENNON "clean," HARNDE
"thorns," LOWDEN "flame," MARSDEN "boundary," RAMSDE
"ram's," WALDEN "Britons'," WEEDEN "temple," and WHEDO
"wheat." Sometimes the element begins the name, as in DUNTO
"village on a hill." There is also the termination *-den* or *-don* wit
the signification of "valley," as in BARDEN "barley," BRADE
"broad," HARDEN "hare," HAYDEN "hay," HOLDEN "deep," WALDE
"Britons'," WHEDON "wheat," and WORDEN "weir or dam." It wi
be noted that WALDEN and WHEDON both terminate with the sens
of hill in certain localities, and in other instances refer to a valle
Some surnames derive from several villages in England with th
same name but with different meanings or in instances where th
exact signification cannot be determined, as BURDEN "valley wit
a cow barn or hill with a fort," and WHIDDEN "wheat hill or va
ley." Both of these surnames are also found with the ending *-do*
—BURDON and WHIDDON.

Old English *-land* "estate or landed property" terminates sev
eral American surnames. Land can also mean "lane" as in ACLAN
from Acland "Acca's lane." MARLAND derives from Marland "lan
on the lake," TOLAND comes from Tolland "land on Tone river,
and WOODLAND formerly dwelt in Woodland "wooded land." NEW
LAND in some cases came from Newland "newly cleared land," th
name of several villages in England.

BROMFIELD "broom-covered," FAIRFIELD "beautiful, or hog,
FIFIELD "five hides," HATFIELD "heather," MAYFIELD "madder,
SHEFFIELD "sheep," WAKEFIELD "festival plays," and WHITFIEL
"white" are well-known examples using the ending *-field* "ope
country." Others are BARFIELD from Bardfield "border," BRANS

ELD from Bramfield "steep," CANFIELD "Cana's," CRUTCHFIELD
om Cruchfield "hill," LITCHFIELD "hill slope," LONGFIELD, WAR-
ELD "on the Wearne river," and WINFIELD and WINGFIELD from
'ingfield "grazing ground, or field of Wiga's people."

Settlements near a river crossing tend to add -*ford* to a descrip-
ve word, as in ASHFORD "ash tree," BRELSFORD "burial place,"
RADFORD "wide," BUFORD from Beeford "bee," HALFORD "narrow
lley," LANGFORD "long," LANSFORD from Landford "lane," SAN-
RD from Sandford "sandy," and STANFORD "stony." Other names
ith the common -*ford* as a suffix are: BERESFORD from Barford
arley," BICKFORD "Bica's," BLATCHFORD from Blackford "black,"
OTSFORD from Bottesford "house," COMERFORD from Comberford
Combra's," GUILFORD "marigolds growing," HANNAFORD from
anford "cock's," HARTFORD "stag," HUNGERFORD "where people
arved," LATCHFORD "stream," LYFORD "flax," MEDFORD from Mea-
rd "junction of streams," MILFORD "mill," MUMFORD from
undford "Munda's," RADFORD "red," RAINSFORD from Rainford
Regna's," RUSHFORD "where rushes grew," SHACKELFORD and
HACKFORD from Shackleford "Shackel's," STRATFORD "Roman
ad," TILFORD "convenient," WALLINGFORD "of Wealh's people,"
d WOODFORD "by a wood."

Sometimes -*ford* corrupts into -*fork,* as WOODFORK from Wood-
rd. It might be observed here as elsewhere that an unusual
ame has been twisted into a common word. Thus WATERFORD
as nothing to do with a crossing over the water; it refers to a
an from Watford which does not mean Wat's or Walter's ford,
ut merely names the ford where woad grew. GIFFORD does not
dicate a river crossing but surnames one who had an ancestor
lled Giffard "give, bold." LEDFORD is the man from Lydford
ord over the torrent" in Somerset. Ford sometimes was corrupted
-*forth,* as in BRIDGEFORTH "ford with a footbridge," and DAN-
RTH "valley ford." A footbridge near a ford would bring about
e name BAMFORD, designating a log across a stream. The expla-
ations for family names given in this chapter are from the earliest
rms and spellings of the place names and, of course, do not
ecessarily agree with meanings of the words into which the
ames have been compressed by the vagaries of uneducated clerks
by dialectal pronunciation.

A few names have -*bridge* as the termination, as in BAINBRIDGE

233

"across the river Bain," WOODBRIDGE "wooden," and STOCKBRIDG
"monastery cell." BRIDGEWATER in Somerset merely translates t
"the bridge." As a suffix -*bridge* sometimes alters into -*brick*, as i
PHILBRICK "bridge by a field."

Surnames with the termination -*well* "a spring, a stream" ar
BRADWELL "wide," CALDWELL "cold," CASWELL and CRISWEL
"watercress," CORNWELL "crane's," RODWELL "red," SHERRIL
"clear," TIDWELL "Tidi's," and WARDWELL "winding." Other name
which terminate in -*ll* usually end in a corruption of a wor
meaning "valley" or a word meaning "hill" or one meaning "cor
ner." Some that refer to a valley are: DOWDELL "frequented b
doves or does," GASKELL "wild goose," IREDELL "Aire river," LIN
DELL "lime tree," RAMSDELL "ram," and UDELL "yew." Such name
where the final element refers to a hill are: AVERILL "oats," BARN
HILL "Beorn's," COGSWELL "Cogg's," GRINNELL "green," HEMPHIL
and HEMPEL "Hemede's," PEARSALL "Per's," THORNEHILL "thor
bushes," and WARDELL "watch." Names referring to a corner ar
BRAMHALL "broom" and GOODALL "marigold."

The Old Danish termination -*thorpe* "an outlying farmstead,
hamlet," usually altered to -*throp*, is found in LATHROP an
LOTHROP "Logi's," NORTHROP "north," and WINTHROP "Wina's c
Wigmund's." There are many small settlements in England simpl
called THORPE.

The ending -*wick* "a dwelling, a farm, a dairy farm" is found i
such names as BARWICK "barley," BUTTRICK "butter," HARDWIC
"sheep," RENWICK "ravens," SEDGWICK "Siggi's," SOUTHWICK "soutl
ern," WARRICK, WARWICK, and WORRICK "dam or weir." There i
also WICKHAM "homestead with a dairy farm." Several settlement
that grew from a dairy farm have been called WICK, and me
who left such places have been so named. BOSTWICK, however, i
a corruption of the place name Bostock "Bota's cell."

The ending -*worth* "enclosure, homestead" may be noted i
FARNSWORTH "where ferns grew," HAWORTH "hawthorn," RUSF
WORTH "rushes," ILLINGSWORTH "of Illa's people," SHUTTLEWORT
"bars," and WHITWORTH "Hwita's." Other -*worth* surnames ar
AINSWORTH "Aegen's," BUTTERWORTH "butter farm," DILWORT
"where dill grew," DUCKWORTH "Ducca's," LONGWORTH "large,
WADSWORTH "Wada's," and WIGGLESWORTH "Wincel's." Som
small places in England became known simply as Worth an

ormer inhabitants acquired the family names WORTH and WIRTH.
There being woods all over England, the ending *-wood* is observed in HAYWOOD and HEYWOOD "high or enclosed," HARWOOD "hare's," HAZELWOOD "hazel bushes," LOCKWOOD "enclosed," and WEDGEWOOD "guarded." WOODALL does not contain "wood" as an element. It designates the man from Woodale "wolves' valley" in Yorkshire, although it is possible that some with the name derive it from dwelling in the hall or manor house by the wood. WOODSIDE identifies the man from Woodside "side of the wood" in Ayrshire, or in some cases just one who dwelt at the side of the wood.

Places on islands are likely to have that fact included in the name. Such names often end in *-ey,* such as KELSEY "Cenel's island" in Lincolnshire, KERSEY "cress island" in Suffolk, MAXEY "Maccu's island" in Northamptonshire, OLNEY "Olla's island" in both Buckinghamshire and Northamptonshire, PITNEY "Pytta's island" in Somerset, STICKNEY "stick island" in Lincolnshire, and TANSEY "island in the branch of a river" in Somerset.

There is a group of place names which has given rise to surnames terminating in *-ington,* the most famous of which is Washington, a name that has become quite common in America. The meaning of *ton* has already been explained. The meaning of the element *-ing* is quite complicated and obscure, but in many instances has a patronymic connotation, a clan name rather than one restricted to a single person. The surname of the father of our country may be explained as "the homestead of Wassa's people or manor of the Wessyng family." BARRINGTON refers to Bara's or Beorn's people, PENNINGTON to Pinna's people, WHITTINGTON to Hwita's people, WADDINGTON to Wada's people, WIGGINTON to Wicga's people, CARRINGTON to Curra's people, ADDINGTON to Cadda's people, and WILLINGTON to Wifel's people.

Many names of this type end in *-ham* instead of *-tun.* BIRMINGHAM is from Birmingham "the homestead of Beormund's people," and BUCKINGHAM is from Buckingham "the homestead of Bucca's people in Buckinghamshire." DILLINGHAM comes from Dullingham "the settlement of Dulla's people" in Cambridgeshire. BURLINGAME is a corruption of Burlingham "village of Baerla's people" in Norfolk. BILLINGS contains no reference to William but refers to Billa's people or one from Billinge "sword" in Lancashire. These

235

personal names contained in the place names of this type are usually of Saxon origin. With the Saxons the sense of kinship was highly developed, distant cousins being regarded as family members for whose welfare and conduct the family was responsible Living in a hostile country, they resided in large family groups in a *tun* or *ham* they founded.

There are many place name elements, as the late Professor A. H. Smith found when he filled volumes XXV and XXVI of the English Place-Name Society publications to describe them, in 1956, under the title *English Place-Name Elements*. And to list fully the German, French, Spanish, Scandinavian, and Slavic place name elements would fill many more volumes. A selected list is set out and discussed in Christina Blackie's *A Dictionary of Place Names*, Third Edition, London, 1887. Place name elements in most European languages consist chiefly of words descriptive of the landscape just like the English place name elements.

Because many villages in England could be described and thus named using the same descriptive words, some designations stood for many villages and many of these names gave rise to surnames Some of the most common are ALFORD "alder ford, or ford of Ealdgyth," ALSTON "Al's village," BACH "stream valley," BAGLEY "ram's or pig's woodland," BARLOW "barley hill or clearing," BARROW "wood or hill," BARTON "grain farm," BEAL "bee hill, or Beaga's corner," BICKLEY "Bicca's homestead," BLAKEMORE "black wasteland," BOLES "tree trunk, or wood where bows were obtained," BOWDEN "Bucge's pasture," BRISCOE "birch wood," BUCKLAND "land held by charter," BUCKLES "Bucca's corner or hill," CHESTER "walled town," CHILTON "noble youth's town," CLIFFORD "ford at a cliff," CRANSHAW "grove frequented by cranes," CROOK "hill, or bend of a river," CROWLES "winding, or meadow by the bends," DARBY "place frequented by wild animals," DENNY "wet land, or Dane's island," FENWICK "farm by a marsh," HADLEY "heather-covered clearing," HALE "corner, nook, or secret place," HAM "meadow on a stream," HAMPTON "enclosure in a village or high village," HARGROVE "hare's grove," HAYNE "hedges," HEATH "wasteland with low shrubs," HELTON "homestead by the slope," HENLEY "high wood or clearing, or one frequented by wild birds," and HINTON "homestead on high land, or the monk's homestead." Two different translations are given in instances where two or more villages with exactly the same names have been derived from different words; usually these are not just differences between onomastic authorities.

Others are HOLLAND "land on a projecting ridge," HOLLINGSWORTH "holly enclosure," HUTTON "village on the spur of a hill," IVY "from St. IVES (yew)," LANGSTON "long stone," LAUGHTON "homestead where leeks were grown, or enclosed homestead," LEIGHTON "place where leeks were grown," LINDLEY "glade where flax was grown," MIMS possibly from Mimmas, the origin of which is obscure, NEWSOME from places now called NEWSHAM, NEWHOUSE, NEWSAM, and NEWSHOLME, all formerly spelled Neusum and meaning "new houses," PUTNAM "Putta's homestead," RAMSAY "ram's isle or wild garlic island," RATCLIFFE and RATLIFF "red cliff," REDDING "clearing, or red meadow, or Read's people," SHELTON "homestead on the ledge," SHIELDS "shepherd's summer hut," SKELTON "hill manor," STAFFORD "stony ford or ford by a landing place," STALEY "wood where staves were obtained," STEELE "stile or steep ascent," STRICKLAND "pasture for cattle," TUTTLE "lookout hill," WEEKS "dairy farm," WESTGATE "west gate," WHALEY "meadow by a road or hill," WHITTEN "Hwita's homestead, or white homestead," WHITTLE "white hill," WINSTON "Wine's or Winec's homestead," WOTTEN "homestead in, or by, a wood," and WRAY "isolated place." All of these surnames served to denominate several villages throughout England and thus many families.

Here will be listed some of the more common family names derived from towns in various counties in England. Here, as elsewhere in this chapter, when the surname has the same spelling as the place name from which it was derived, the place name is usually not given.

Bedfordshire: BEDFORD "Beda's ford," BIDWELL "stream in a valley," BILLINGTON "Billa's hill," BLEDSOE from Bletsoe "Blaecci's hill," HAINES and HAYNES from Haynes "enclosures," ODELL "woad hill."
Berkshire: EARLY from Earley "eagle wood," HANEY from Hanney "island frequented by wild cocks," ILLSLEY from Ilsley "Hild's meadow," LITTLEWOOD from Littleworth "small homestead," NEWBERRY and NEWBURY from Newbury "new fort or castle," PUSEY "pea island," READING "Read's people."
Buckinghamshire: CHESLEY from Chearsley "Ceolred's meadow," CRACKSTON from Crafton "place where wild caffron grew," KIMBALL

and KIMBLE from Kimble "royal hill," MARLOWE from Marlow "lak remains," WINSLOW "Wine's burial mound."

Cambridgeshire: ARRINGTON "homestead of Erna's people," ELLSWORT from Elsworth "Elli's homestead," ELY "eel district," HEYDEN froi Heydon "hay valley."

Cheshire: BOSTIC and BOSTICK from Bostock "Bota's place," BUCKLE from Bulkeley "bullock pasture," CARDON from Carden "rock enclc sure," DAVENPORT "town on the Dane river," DUTTON "Dudda homestead," HOUGH "spur of hill," HULL "hollow," MANLEY "commo wood," MOBLEY from Mobberley "glade with an assembly mound."

Cornwall: LANYON "John's church," TREMAINE "stone village," TREVO "great house."

Cumberland: BLENNERHASSETT "hay hut on a hill," CARLISLE "wall c the god Lugus," COPELAND "bought land," LIDDELL from Liddel "lou river valley," TINDALL from Tindale "fort in fertile upland region."

Derbyshire: ALPERT from Alport "old town," BEARD "bank," BRADSHAW "broad grove," DERBY "homestead frequented by wild animals. FLAGG "sod or turf," SMALLEY "narrow wood."

Devonshire: COMSTOCK "monastery in a narrow valley," GOLDSWORTH from Galsworthy "slope where bog myrtle grew," ODOM from Odc ham "Ode's homestead," RALEIGH "red meadow," SATTERLEE froi Satterleigh "robber's wood," WHITFORD "white ford."

Dorsetshire: BLANDFORD "ford where gudgeons abound," BOWDITC "arched bridge ditch," BRITT from Brit "Bredy's borough," CAN "deep valley," ELWELL "the wishing spring," STOCKWOOD "monastei by a wood," TRENT "trespasser."

Durham: BOLDEN from Boldon "hill with a homestead," DURHAI "island with a hill," HAWTHORNE from Hawthorn "hawthorn tree STANHOPE "stony valley," TISDALE from Teesdale "surging river va ley," WINGATE "pass where wind blows."

Essex: EASTER "sheepfold," LISTON "Leofsige's homestead," SHELLE "wood on a slope," STEBBINS from Stebbing "clearing," WICKS froi Wix "dairy farms."

Gloucestershire: ELMORE "shore where elms grew," HUNTLEY "woo of the huntsmen," ROWELL "roe stream," STOWELL "stony stream TEWKSBURY from Tewkesbury "Teodec's fort."

Hampshire: CRANDALL from Crondall "a hollow," FULLERTON "villag of the birdcatchers," WINCHESTER "Wintan's Roman fort," WORTH "enclosed homestead."

Herefordshire: DULLES from Dulas "dark river," FOY "the church of S Moi or Mwy," GOODRICH "Godric's castle," WHITNEY "Hwita's islan or white island."

Hertfordshire: LILLY from Lilley "meadow where flax grew," PELHAM "Peola's homestead," RIDGE "field on a range of hills," WARE "dam or fish trap."

Huntingtonshire: COVINGTON "homestead of Cufa's people," ELLINGTON "homestead of Ella's people," OFFORD "upper ford."

Kent: BORDEN "swine pasture hill," ELDRIDGE from Elbridge "plank bridge," HAMILL from Hammill "Hamela's wood," SNOOKS from Sevenoaks "seven oaks."

Lancashire: BLAKELY from Blackley "the black wood or clearing," BOLAND "land by the river bend," HANNA and HANNAH from Hannah "Hanna's island," LANCASTER "Roman settlement on Lune river," LOOMIS from Lomax "flat alluvial land by a pool," PARR "enclosure or district," PENDLETON "hill hill village," TATUM from Tatham "Tata's homestead," WORTHINGTON "village of the Wurthingas."

Leicestershire: BOSWORTH "Bar's or Bosa's homestead," CHARLEY "rock woods," KILBY "Cilda's homestead," LESTER and LEISTER from Leicester "dwellers on Legra river," QUIMBY from Quenby "queen's manor," SKIFFINGTON from Skeffington "homestead of Sceaft's people."

Lincolnshire: BIXBY from Bigby "Bekki's homestead," BOSTON "St. Botulf's stone," LINCOLN "lake colony," SPAULDING from Spalding "tribe of Spaldas," WELBY "settlement by a stream."

Middlesex: HELLIWELL from Haliwell "holy spring," HOLLOWAY "sunken road," KENNISTON from Kensington "homestead of Cynesige's people," NORWOOD "north of the wood."

Norfolk: ALBEE from Alby "Ali's homestead," BYNUM from Binham "Bynna's homestead," CHATFIELD from Catfield "place frequented by wild cats," GRESHAM "grazing farm," QUARLES "circles," STANFIELD "stony field."

Northamptonshire: BLACKSLEY from Blakesley "black wolf wood," HARRINGTON "heath-dwellers' enclosure," ISHAM "village on the Ise river," WEEKLEY "wych elm wood," WELDON "hill by a stream."

Northumberland: BENTON "place where bent grass grew," BLANKENSHIP from Blenkinsopp "top valley," ELSDON "Ellis' valley," EWERT from Ewart "homestead by a stream," LYMAN from Lyham "homestead by a wood," RUGGLES from Rugley "woodcock glade."

Nottinghamshire: BINGHAM "Bynna's estate," CROMWELL "winding stream," HOLEBECK from Holbeck "deep stream," MANSFIELD "open land by Mam hill," SHERWOOD "wood belonging to the shire."

Oxfordshire: BENSON "Benesa's homestead," CROWELL "crow's stream," OXFORD "ford used by oxen," STANLAKE from Standlake "stony stream."

Shropshire: CRITTENDEN from Criddon "Cridela's hill," FITCH from Fitz "Fita's spur of land," HARCOURT "hawker's cottage," MINTON "mountain village," PICKFORD from Pitchford "ford where pitch is found," TILLEY "branch," or from Tilly "lime tree."

Somerset: BATH "referring to Roman bath," BURNETT "place cleared by burning," COKER "water," CRANDON "crane's hill," FARRINGTON "homestead where ferns grew," PYLE from Pylle "creek," WORLEY from Worle "woodgrouse wood."

Staffordshire: ALDRIDGE "village among alders," FARWELL from Farewell "beautiful stream," HANLEY "high meadow," TIPTON "Tibba's homestead," WHITMORE "white waste ground."

Suffolk: COOLIDGE from Cowlinge "Cul's or Cula's people," PAYTON from Peyton "Paega's homestead," THURLOW "assembly hill," THURSTON "Thori's homestead," WESTERFIELD "westerly open land," WORTHAM "enclosed homestead."

Surrey: HANSCOM from Hascomb "witches' valley," MITCHAM "great homestead," SANDS from Send "sandy place," SHERE "bright," STOCKWELL "footbridge across the stream," TILDEN from Tillingdown "Tilmund's hill."

Sussex: BARNHAM "Beorna's homestead," COOMBS from Coombes "valleys," HARTFIELD "open land frequented by stags," HASTINGS "Haesta's people," PERHAM from Parham "homestead where peas grew," WALDRON "house in a wood."

Warwickshire: CHADWICK "Ceadda's farm," MERRIFIELD from Merevale "pleasant valley," PARTLOW from Pathlow "path by a sepulchral mound," SANBORN from Sambourn "sandy stream," WOLFORD "enclosure protected from wolves."

Westmorland: BURNSIDE "Brunwulf's headland," FAWCETT "multi-colored hillside," KENDALL from Kendal "Kent river valley," MORELAND from Morland "grove by wasteland," MUSGRAVE "grove overrun with mice."

Wiltshire: BASCOM from Boscombe "box tree valley," CHUTE "forest," TITCOMB from Tidcombe "Titta's valley," TROWBRIDGE "wooden bridge."

Worcestershire: DUDLEY "Dudda's meadow," COOKSEY "Cucu's island," ROCHFORD "river crossing used by hunting dogs," REDDICK from Redditch "reedy ditch."

Yorkshire: BLAND "windy place," BOWLING "dip in ground by a hill," BRACKEN "fern," BURRELL from Burrill "hill of the fort," CLEVELAND "hilly district," COLBURN "cool stream," CRAVEN "garlic," DARNELL from Darnall "hidden nook," HUDDLESTON "Huda's homestead," PICKERING "people at the edge of the hill," REMINGTON from Rimington "village on the rim or border," STALLINGS from Stalling "stallion," WOODSON from Woodsome "houses in a wood," YORK "place of yew trees."

Some other interesting English surnames derived from names of English towns at the forefront in America are APPLEWHITE from Applethwaite "clearing with apple trees" in Cumberland and Westmorland. BLAISDELL from Bleasdale "bare spot on a hillside" in Lancashire, and BRADDOCK, the name of a village in Cornwall meaning "wide oak." That broom grew throughout England is evidenced by the several place names referring to it from which such surnames as BROMLEY, BROMS, and BRUMFIELD are derived. Today broom is seen only in those old-fashioned brooms which were formerly so much in evidence used to sweep out our homes each day. LYNG is from Lyng "hill," the name of settlements in Norfolk and Somerset.

OLDHAM is a curious and difficult name; it refers not to the older village, but to the older island since it is derived from Old-ham, the early spelling of which was Aldholm. It could, nevertheless, refer to some now unknown older settlement after a more recent one was founded. A French onomatologist, deficient in his knowledge of Old English, carelessly defined it as "ancient pork." RADCLIFFE is from Radcliffe "red cliff." SHANKLIN is from a town of that name in Wight meaning "leg hill"; shank was the early and more common term for leg. SPINNEY originally came from Spinney in Cambridgeshire meaning "a thicket." STANSFIELD "stony field" and WENTWORTH "Wintra's homestead" each are derived from two different places in England. WASS, when not a German name referring to a descendant of Was "sharp" or of Vad "strife," designates one from Wass "swamp" in Yorkshire.

CAREW "fort" is a surname from the place of that name in Pembrokeshire, the pronunciation sometimes softened into CAREY, although the name in this latter spelling is usually considered to be Irish "grandson of the dark-complexioned man." Two members of the widely separated family are said to have disputed the correct pronunciation of the name before the first Queen Elizabeth of England. With Solomonic wisdom she settled the matter by turning to one and decreeing, "Carey you shall be, and what care I?" and to the other, "Carew you shall be, and what care you?"

241

The names are sometimes found as CARRIE in the United States Places in Somerset derived from a British river name have been spelled both CAREW and CAREY.

Some miscellaneous surnames derived from English place names are: ALLERTON from Allerton "the alder settlement, or Ælfweard's estate"; BERKLEY from Berkeley "birch wood" in Gloucestershire; BOSLEY from Bosley "Bosa's wood" in Cheshire BRAITHWAITE "broad clearing," the name of places in Cumberland and Yorkshire; BRENT "high place" in Devonshire; BROOME from Broome or Broom "place where broom grew," the name of several villages; DENT from Dent "hill" in Yorkshire; DINSMORE from Dinmore "great hill" in Herefordshire; GREENOUGH from Greenhaugh "green enclosure" in Northumberland; and HALSTEAD "place of shelter for cattle," the name of several villages.

Others are HORWICH from Horwich "gray wych-elms" in Lancashire; LIGGETT from Lidgate "swing-gate" in Suffolk; REDDISH "reed ditch" in Lancashire; SALTONSTALL from Salternstall "salt works place" in Kent; SATTERTHWAITE "clearing by a hut" in Lancashire; STARBUCK from Starbeck "stream near where swamp grass grew" in Yorkshire; WIGMORE "Wicga's wasteland" in Herefordshire; WILDE from Wild or Wyld "trick" in Berkshire; WOODROW "row of trees," places found in Wiltshire and Worcestershire WOODY from Woodhay "enclosure in a wood," villages located in Berkshire and Hampshire; and WORCESTER, WOOSTER, and WURSTER from Worcester "Wigoran tribe's Roman fort" in Worcestershire.

William Camden, in his *Remaines*, published in the early part of the seventeenth century, declared, "Neither is there any village in Normandy that gave not denomination to some family in England." To name a few English, Welsh, and Scottish names from across the channel, there is BEAUMONT from Beaumont "beautiful mountain," the name of five places in Normandy; BEMIS is from Beaumetz "good cultivation." BOSWELL and BUSWELL are from Bosville "wood town." BRANCH is from Branche "bow." BUSSEY is from Bussy "little wood." Scottish BRUCE is from Braose, now Brieuse, "enclosed wood."

Others are COVELL from Colleville "Kolli's manor"; CHAUNCY from Chancey or Chançay "oak grove"; DISNEY from Isigny "Isi-

ius' estate"; HARRELL from Harel; HERSEY from Herse "railed
place"; HUSSEY from Houssay "holly grove"; IVORY from Ivry
"Eburius' estate"; LACEY and LACY from Lassy or Lessay "Latius'
estate"; LEVITT from Livet "little yew tree"; LINDSAY from Linde-
ay or Limesay "Limetius' dwelling"; LUCEY from Lucé "Lucius'
possession"; MASSEY from Massy or Macey "Mathieu's farm"; and
Scottish MENZIES is from Mesnieres "residence or castle." Welsh
MONTGOMERY originally came from the ancient castle of Saint Foi
le Montgomery "hill of Gomeric" or from Saint Germain de Montgomery, two places in Normandy. Roger de Montgomery accompanied the Conqueror to England. MORTIMER derives from Mor-
emer "stagnant water," MONTAGUE from Montaigu "peaked hill,"
PECHE from Peche "rounded hill," and PERCY from Perci "Percius'
estate." William de Percy, a Norman chieftain, accompanied the
Conqueror. PERCIVAL, however, is from the French place name of
Percheval or Perceval "valley-piercer." ROCKETT is from La Roc-
quette "little rock," SCOVILLE is from Escoville "Scot's estate,"
SOMERVILLE and SUMMERVILLE are from Sommerville "Sumar's
estate," and STAMPS is from Estampes "warehouse."

Many Englishmen have names derived from French villages;
most of them emigrated to England with the Conqueror or soon
thereafter. AVERY came from Evreux "on the waters," BELLOWS
is the Englished form for the Frenchman who formerly resided
in Bellou or Belleau "beautiful water"; BOONE hailed from Bohon.
There are several places in France called Bray "marsh or knoll,"
and BRAY became the surname of several emigrants. CASE originally knew the village of Case "country house" as home. CHANEY,
CHENEY, and CHEYNE came from such towns as Quesney, Cheney,
or Chenay all meaning "oak grove" in France. FAY is derived
from Fay "beech tree." GOULET is the man from Goulet "mouth of
small stream," the name of several villages in France. IVEY is from
Ivoy "place of the yew trees." MOON came from Mohon "houses,
or Muoto's place."

MOLINE came from Moline "mill." ORANGE moved from Orange
"from Arausione on River Araise" (the river name is quite difficult, having nothing to do with the popular citrus fruit). POSEY
comes from Pace "Paccius' dwelling" and PRINDIVILLE from Fer-
manville "Faramann's domain." QUINCY, the middle name of an
early American president, is a surname for the man from Quinçay

"Quintus' estate" in Maine. RICHMOND is from Richemont "lofty mountain."

St. CLAIR, St. GEORGE, and St. JOHN are the English versions of these several villages in France. These and other surnames beginning *St.* are from villages in France known by the dedication of their churches. Many of these have been telescoped into one word in some families. Thus some St. Clairs are contracted to SINCLAIR, St. Denys to SIDNEY, St. Maur to SEYMOUR, St. Pierre to SEMPER, and St. Paul to SEMPLE or SAMPLE.

SAVILLE moved out of Sauville "refuge." SMILEY is derived from Semilly or Semily "Similius' estate," and STOVALL from Esteville "east settlement." TRACY came from Tracy "terrace." TROY owes his name to Troyes "from Gaulish tribe, the Tricassii," and VERNON came from Vernon "alder grove," the name of several small French places. VARNEY came from Vernay or Verney "alder grove." VENABLES moved to Wales from Venables or Vignoles "vineyard" in France. VERRY and VERY came from Very or Verrie "glass works or Verrius' farm," the names of several French places. Jones Very was an eminent American poet extravagantly praised by Bryant, Emerson, and others. VESEY originally lived in Vessey "Vitius' estate," the name of places in Normandy and Burgundy. VICK is from Vicq "village," the name of several small places in France.

Of course, many Frenchmen in the United States never lived in England but came directly from France having there acquired their surname from a small village. Some of them are BEAUCHAMP and BELLMONTE signifying "beautiful field" and "beautiful hill," respectively. BELANGER is a contraction of "beautiful Anger," which is an ancient town name combining *Ans* "a divinity" and *gari* "spear." CASSELL came from Cassell "chateau or castle" and COURTNEY from Courtenay "Curtenus' estate." DELORME came from Lorme "elm tree," and DUMELLE came from Melle "ring." DE LONG retained the early preposition signifying his original residence at Long "large place." FONTENOT, FONTENAY, and FONTENEAU came from one of the many villages in France with similar spellings meaning "small springs." GORNEY and GURNEY came from Gournay "Gornus' estate." GRASS came from Grasse or Gras "Crassus' town" in France. NUGENT was from Nogent "fair wet meadow," the name of several villages in France. Coming to

England with William the Conqueror, some Nugents settled in Ireland and the name is completely Hibernicized today.

Since numerous Scottish names are much like those south of the border, one finds many popular American surnames derived from the towns in Scotland in which the original bearer was a resident. Here is a list of some of the most common: ABERNATHY and ABERNETHY from Abernethy "narrow opening"; BARR "height"; BARRY "hill on the isle"; BILLY from Billie or Bellie "village farm" (not a derivative of William); BLACKBURN "dark stream"; BLACKSTONE "dark boundary stone" (sometimes, however, a descendant of Blaecstan "black stone"); BLACKWOOD "dark wood"; BUCHANAN from Both-Chanain "the Canon's seat"; CARMICHAEL "castle of St. Michael"; CARNEGIE "fort at the gap" (Andrew of that name was a Scotsman who helped to found libraries all over the United States, and set up charitable foundations in this country and the United Kingdom); CLYNE when not a translation of German Klein "little" is from Clyne "slope"; CRAWFORD "crow's river crossing"; CUNNINGHAM "rabbit farm"; CURLEY "bend or turn in the road"; DOWNEY from Downie "little hill"; DRUMMOND "ridge"; DUNBAR "fort on the hill"; DUNLAP "hill at the bend"; FINLEY from Findlay "white calf"; FORBES "field place"; FORSYTH probably from FORSYTH, or it may be derived from the old Germanic personal name Fearsithe "man of peace"; FULTON "fowl enclosure"; GORDON "spacious hill"; GUTHRIE "windy place"; HOUSTON "Hugh's town"; and IRVINE "green river."

Continuing Scottish names from places, there is JOHNSTON "John's manor," often confused with the patronymic JOHNSON. Others are KEITH "wood," KINCAID "head of the pass," KIRKPATRICK "church of St. Patrick," KNOX from Knock "hill," LIVINGSTON "Leofwine's town," LOGAN "little hollow," SNODGRASS from Snodgrasse "smooth grassy place," MURRAY from Moray "beside the sea," NESBITT from Nesbit "projecting site," PEOPLES and PEEBLES from Peebles "assembly place," POLK and POLLOCK from Pollock "little pool," PRESLEY from Preslie "priest's wood," REDDEN "raven valley," RENFRO "flowing stream," RUTHERFORD "ford used by cattle," STERLING and STIRLING from Stirling "Velyn's dwelling," SYMINGTON "Symond's stone," and WADDELL from Waddel "woad valley." CUMMINGS or CUMMINS denominates the man who went to Scotland from Comines in Flanders or from Bosc-Benard

Commin in France. MELVILLE came from Maleville "bad town
in Normandy. MELVIN is a corruption of Melville.

Many Scottish names that have become familiar American sur
names are interesting and colorful, reminiscent of the hones
frugal sons of Caledonia. There are ABERCROMBIE "crooke
marsh," ANSTRUTHER "marshy meadow," ARBUCKLE "shepherd
height," ATHERTON "Ethelhere's homestead," BALFOUR "pasture
land place," BALLANTINE from Ballindean "village by the hill,
BANKHEAD "end of the ridge," BOTHWELL "booth by the fish pool,
BRECKENRIDGE from Brackenrig "ridge overgrown with bracken,
CAULFIELD from Cauldfield "cold open country," CHISHOLM fror
Cheseholm "meadow where cheese was made," CLENDENNIN
and GLENDENNING from Glendinning "glen of the beautiful hill
(it is easy to note that *Glen* can be pronounced *Clen* withou
putting the tongue into a permanent s-curve), COLQUHOUN "nar
row corner or wood," COWIE "wood," CRAIGIE "rock," DALRYMPL
"field on the winding stream," DALLAS "place on the plain,
DEWAR "dark plowed land," DINWIDDIE from Dinwoodie "hill wit
shrubs," DRYDEN "dry valley," DRYSDALE from Dryfesdale "Dryf
river valley," DUNMORE "big hill," DUNNING "little hill or fort,
ERSKINE "green ascent," GALLOWAY from Galloway "white hill
face," GLADSTONE from Gledstanes "kite's rock," GLASGOW "grey
hound, or green hollows," GREENLAW "verdant hill," HALIBURTO
from Halyburton "holy enclosure village," INNES "island," KELS
"chalk height," KILBRIDE "church of St. Brigit," LITHGOW fror
Linlithgow "dear large lake," and LOWES "lake."

MOONLIGHT is from Munlochy "at the foot of the lake." Thoma
Moonlight was a territorial governor of Wyoming in the latte
part of the nineteenth century. Then there are MOFFET fror
Moffat "long plain," MOREHEAD and MUIRHEAD from Muirhea
"end of the moor," OGILVIE "high hill," OXNAM "oxen farm,
PAISLEY "pasture slope," PRENDERGAST "priest's deep glen,
PRINGLE from Hoppringle "peg valley," RATTRAY "fort or moun
dwelling," SHERRICK "clear bay," SKENE "bush," STARRETT fror
Stairaird, now Stirie, "path over a bog," STOCKING "enclose
place," TORREY from Torrie "little hill," TULLY from Tullo o
Tully "small hill," UREY from Urie "abounding in yews," UR
QUHART "on a wood," WEEMS from Wemyss "caves." Now let u

eave these true sons of the old sod and turn our attention else-
vhere.

Numerous Germans in the United States have family names
lerived from German, Swiss, and Austrian towns and cities, many
·f them Jewish names. There are BIEBER "beaver's place"; BIEL
rom Buhl or Buhler "small hill"; BRANDENBURG "forest fortress";
3URGER from Burg "stronghold," the name of various small places
n Germany and Switzerland; DREYFUS from Treves or Trier
place of the Treviri tribe"; EISENBERG and ISENBERG from Eisen-
·erg "iron mountain"; EISENSTADT from Eisenstaedt "iron place"
n Austria; ELSEN, ELSER, and ELSNER from Elsen "alder"; EPSTEIN
rom Eppstein "Eppo's stone"; FRANK from Franken or Franconia
of the Franks," an old duchy of south central Germany; GREEN-
·ERG from Grünberg "green mountain." HASSEL came from Hassel
place of hazel trees" in Germany, while English HASSELL came
rom Hassall "witches' corner" in Cheshire. HELLER came from
Halle "the house, or salt house"; KESSLER from Kessel "castle," the
iame of many places in Germany; LAHR "empty, deserted" (also
rom Lahr, a pet form of Hilarius "cheerful"); LAUTERBACH from
he place of that name meaning "clear brook"; LOOS and LOOSE
·ame from Loos, Loose, or Loosen in Germany; MANNHEIMER
rom Mannheim "servant's home"; MIDDENDORF "middle village";
)BERLIN from Oberlind "upper linden tree"; OPPENHEIMER from
)ppenheim "Oppo's place"; ROHR and ROHRER from Rohr or
Rohrau "reedy place"; RUBENSTEIN "ruby stone"; RUBIN from
Rubyn or Ruben "ruby stone"; SCHOENFELD from Schönfeld
beautiful field," the name of more than fifty places in Germany;
iCHWAB from Swabia "place of the Suevi tribe," a duchy in medi-
·val Germany; SCHNEEBERGER from Schneeberg "snow mountain";
iOMMERFELD and SOMMERFIELD from Sommerfeld "summer field,"
he name of several towns in Germany. Sometimes SUMMERFELD
vas the dweller at, or near, the field used in the summer.

To continue with German names: STAUFFER is from Staufen
fort on a rock"; STEINBERG "stone mountain," the name of many
)laces in Germany; STOVER, from Stove; STUCK "plot of land";
NALLACH "foreigners' place"; WEINBERG "grape mountain," the
iame of many places in Germany and Switzerland; WERTHEIMER
rom Wertheim "river island place," the name of several towns in
3ermany; WEISS is from Weiss or Weis, these names translating

either to "white or village"; and WEISBERG is from Weisserberg "white mountain." It will be noted that family names from place names in Germany often are composed of the place name plus *-er* Many are found in both forms. There are BERLIN and BERLINER HAMBURG and HAMBURGER, and WIEN and WIENER, to note a few that are best known. The suffix does not add anything to the meaning, other than to emphasize the fact that the name designates the man from that town or city.

Other German names from towns and cities in Germany and Poland that might be mentioned are: BAMBERGER "Bab's hill," BREMER from Bremen "by the seashore," BUCHLER from Buche "beechnuts," BUCHWALD "beech wood," DANZIGER from Danzig "Dane's town," ELLEN and ELLER from Ellen "elbow," FRIED-LANDER "peaceful country," GOMBERG from Homberg "high fortified place," GRONER from Grone "green," LANDAU "meadow land," LANGNER from Langen "long place," MAHLER from Mahlau, MUTZIGER from Mutzig, NURNBERG "fortress of the Noricii," POSNER from Posen (now Poznan in Poland), ROHRBACHER "reedy stream," SALTZBERG "salt fortress," SCHLESINGER from Schleusingen, STEINBACH "stony brook," STEINHAUS "stone homestead," STERNBERG "star mountain," STETTER from Stetten "place of green grain," STRAUBINGER from Straubing "place of Strubo's people," WALLNER from Wallen "forest," WENDORF "village of the Wends," WEISER from Weis "village," WESTPHAL and WESTFALL from Westphalen "western plain," WISNER from Wissen "white sand," WITTENBERG "white mountain," ZORN "anger," and ZWICKER from Zwickau "market town."

Continuing with the German names from towns, one comes across EHRENSPERGER from Ehrensperg "hill of honor," HERZBERG and HIRSCHBERG both being "red deer mountain," HORNBURG "horn fortress," KRONENBERG "crown mountain," OLDENBURG "old fortification," and SILVERBERG "silver mountain." The hills and mountains in Germany were responsible for many place names that were the eponyms of numerous family names. *Berg* "mountain" and *burg* "fortification" are frequently confused in German names. WEIL and WEILER are from Weil and Weiler "house," the names of many small places in Germany.

In Russia many families acquired their name from the place where the original bearer was born. LUSK came from Luck "river bend or winding river," a place in medieval Volhynia. PINSKY arrived from Pinsk "foam," and MINSKY from Minsk, both in Byelorussia. POLISCHUK is from Polissia "woody and marshy land." RUDNYCKYJ in its various spellings derives from birth in Rudnyk, Rudnyky, or Rudnyca "red," the names of various places in the Ukraine. SLUTSKY derives from Slutsk "crooked river" in Byelorussia. TCHAIKOVSKY had an ancestor who removed from Czajkowo "place of sea gulls," the name of many small places in Russia and Poland. Americans probably have more trouble with the spelling and pronunciation of the Russian composer's name than any other—Chaikovski, Tchaikowsky, Tschaikovsky, Tschaikowsky— you pay your money and you take your choice. UMANSKY came from Uman "wise one's settlement" in the Ukraine.

Many Italians received their family names from the city or province they left. Some of the more common ones are ALBANO "white," CAIRO "victorious" (in Italy, not from Cairo in Egypt), GENOVESE from Genova "head of the water," FERRARA "forum Allieni," LA GUARDIA "outpost," LOMBARD, LOMBARDI, and LOMBARDO from Lombardy "the longbearded men," LURIE from Luria "sorrowful," MESSINA from Messina "sickle," SERRANO from Serrano "saw-shaped mountain," and SORRENTINO is from Sorrento. NAPOLEON as a family name usually refers to the man from Neapolis "new city." NAPOLI is from Naples "new city." SANTANGELO came from Sant'Angelo "saint angel." SICILIANO originally lived in Sicily or Sicilia "tribe of the Siculi." VINCI came from Vinci "enclosed place."

Spanish and Portuguese people were fond of bestowing family names from the town or city from which the first bearer moved. Examples of the most commonly observed of such surnames are: ACOSTA "long coast"; ALVARA from Alvarado "whitened place"; AGUILAR from Aguilas "place of eagles"; AVILA, and the slightly more common DAVILA, from Avila, a very ancient proper name of obscure meaning, possibly Phoenician; AYALA "grassy slope"; CARDOZA from Cardoso "place where thistles grew"; CASTELLO from Castillo "fortress"; CONTRERAS from Contreras "contradiction" (the place was originally called Cuevas Contrarias "opposed caves"); CORTEZ from Cortes "court or town"; ESPINOSA "thorny thicket"; ESTRADA "paved road"; FIGUEROA "place of fig trees"; FRANCO "free"; LEON "lion," an ancient kingdom or region in Spain; LUGO "light or woods (probably sacred to a deity)"; MENDOZA "cold or high mountains"; MERCADO "market place"; MIRANDA "admired place"; MOLINA "mill"; MONTOYA, a Basque surname, is from Montoya "pasture (for horses)"; MORALES "mulberry tree"; and NAVARRO "the plain among hills."

To continue, there are NOGALES "walnut tree," PENA "large rock," QUINTANA from Quintana or Quinta "village," RAMOS "branch," ROBLES "oak tree grove," SALAZAR "manor house," SALINAS "salt mine," SANDOVAL, originally the Latin Saltus Novalis, "fallow ravine," SANTIAGO "St. James," SANTOS from Dos Santos or Los Santos "of the saints," SILVA "thicket of briars, or woods," SOTO "wooded place on bank of river," SOUZA and SOUSA from Sousa or Souza "salty place," TOVAR "quarry of soft, sandy stone," TRUJILLO "citadel of Julian," VALDEZ from Valdes, VARGAS "steep hill," VILLANUEVA "recently founded settlement," VILLARREAL from Villareal "royal estate," and XAVIER from Xaberri or Xaverri "new house," this last name from the Basque section in northern Spain where the language is a remnant from an older civilization. XIMENA came from Ximena "place of Jimena or Simon."

The suffix -eira, sometimes -eiro, is an ending with diverse uses derived from the Latin -ariu and -aria. It is used in the formation of nouns and is found with some adjectives in the sense of "derived from" or "related to." Many place and location names have this suffix. The Portuguese surname FERREIRA denominates one from Ferreira "iron mine or workshop," the name of numerous small places in Portugal. Teixeira "place of yew trees," also the name of several places in Portugal, produced the surname TEIXEIRA.

Dutchmen who have surnames from towns, cities, or districts are mostly distinguished by the prefix Van as VAN CLEAVE "cliff," VAN DEVANTER "from Deventer," VAN GELDER "from the county of Gelder," VAN HORN "from Hoorn (promontory)," VAN NESS "from Nes (headland)," VAN PATTEN "from Putten (well or pool)." VAN PELT "from Pelt (marshy place)," VAN RENSSELAER "from Renselaer," and VANSITTART "from Sittard." In the United States the use of capital initial letters and spaces is optional with the particular family, and little thought is given to the matter by others. Two other well-known names are STUYVESANT "quicksand," and Voorhees "in front of Hess." Then there is the family name Onderdonk, the sort of sound a fat man makes by falling down stairs, but to the Hollander merely indicating the man who came from below Donk "mound surrounded by a marsh" in Brabant. Braband came from Brabant "the ploughed district." Terwilliger designates one who came from Willige "Wille's settlement" in Holland.

Some family names from Swiss towns are Bollinger from Bollingen, Breitenbach from Breitenbach "wide brook," D'Entremont from Entremont "between the mountains," Detweiler from Datweil, Geis from Geiss "place where goats graze," Longenecker from Longenegg, Oberdorf "high village," Oberlander and Overland from Oberland "high land," Zeller from Zell "monastic cell," and Zug "place where nets might be drawn ashore."

Many from Poland have ancestors who acquired their hereditary surnames by reason of former residence in a town or village. Some of them are: Baranowski from Baranow "Baran's settlement," Bielski from Bielsk "white," Budzinski from Budzyn "the huts," Czajkowski from Czajkowo "place of sea gulls," Czarnecki from Czarne "black," Czarnik from Czarnik "black," Czerniak from Czernia "black," Czerwinski from Czerwien "red dye," Dombrowski from Dabrova "oak grove," Grabowski from Grabowo "birch tree," Janiszewski from Janiszewo "Jan's place," Jaworski from Jaworow "maple tree," Kalinowski from Kalinow "guelder-rose or snowball," Kosinski from Kosino "scythe," Krakow "the town of Duke Krak," Kuta "corner," Lapinski from Lapy "claws," Laskowski from Laskowo "forest," Lesniewski from Lesniewo "forest," Lewandowski from Lewandow "Lewand's settlement," Lisowski from Lisowo "fox," Malkowski from Malkowo "little," Milewski from Milew "dear," Nowak "new," Nowakowski from Nowakowo "new place," Orzechowski from Orzechowo "hazel bushes," Rogowski from Rogow "horn," Smolinski from Smolensk "pitch, or pine forest," Wisniewski from Wisznia "cherry tree," Wolin from Volhynia "the plain," Wolski from Wola "liberty," Wroblewski from Wroblewsk "sparrow," Zielinski from Zielinsk "green," Ziolkowski from Ziolkow "herbs," Zukowski from Zukow "place infested by beetles," and Zurawski from Zuraw "cranes."

AMERICAN SURNAMES

Other polish surnames derived from place names are: BORUCKI from Boruty "Boruta's place," Kosowski from Kosow "scythe," Kostecki from Kostki "bone," Kulikowski from Kulikow "Kulik's settlement," Kurowski from Kurowo "cock," Kwiatkowski from Kwiatkowo "flower place," Madej "Madey's settlement," Markowski from Markowo "Marek's place," Maslankowski from Maslankowo "buttermilk," Muszynski from Muszyn "place where flies were troublesome," Ostrowski from Ostrow "river island," Plucinski from Plucice "settlement of Plut's descendants," Pluta from Pluty "settlement of the Pluty family," Pruszynski from Pruszyn "Pruch's village," Rosinski from Rosiho "dew," Sikorski from Sikora or Sikory "titmouse," Sobieski "Sobiech's village," Sowinski from Sowa or Sowin "owl," Swiatkowski from Swiatkowka or Swiatkowo "world village," Sypniewski from Sypniewo "Sypien's village," Trojanowski "three brothers village," Wachowski from Wachow "guard," Walkowiak from Walkow "battle site," Wysocki from Wysock "high settlement," Zawacki from Zawada "troublemaker."

The most common descriptive place terms naturally describe many villages in a given country. For example, it would be natural to signify a village by reference to its situation. Middleton and its contraction, Milton, are both very common surnames derived from numerous town names in England which designated the village between two others. Milton also in many cases refers to the town with a mill. The towns surrounding the middle town might be Weston, Norton, Sutton, or Easton, all indicating the direction in which they were situated. Wesley and Easley are similar surnames, as are Norbury, Northam, Norwich, Westberg, and Southworth. These popular descriptions are each found in many counties in England and all served to name innumerable families not related to each other. Nordby is the north village in Norway.

A small place might be named Littleton, Littlewick, or Littleworth, and many were so called, and these names became permanent family names. Large places might have the adjective *Long-* or *Grand-* as a prefix. It is said that a dispute once arose in England between two families, one named Littleton and the other Grandville, as to which was the older. Lord Littleton produced the convincing argument when he pointed out that his family was the more ancient since the *little-town* must have existed before the *grand-ville*. In Italy a similar dispute arose between the Ponti and the Canali, the latter asserting that "bridges" were over "canals" so that the Canali were necessarily in existence before the Ponti. The dispute waged so furiously that the town fathers were compelled to remind the families that they had both the power to pull down bridges and fill up canals.

There is a group of names mostly referring to counties such as KENTISH, CORNISH, CORNWALLIS, and DEVONISH which may be interpreted as "the Kentish (man)," "the Cornish (man)," etc. Other names for the man from Cornwall are CORNWALISH, CORNWALEYS, and the plain CORNWALL, all of which names might be used interchangeably for the same person until one was later frozen into permanency. The most common county surname is KENT "border land." Some Kents derive from Old Welsh *cant* "border," or from Old Welsh *caint* "open country." Several other interpretations of the name have been advanced and there is no agreement among the authorities. YORK "yew" sometimes refers to the man from Yorkshire. DORSETT refers to Dorset "bright place" and PEMBROKE to that county in Wales. Several other surnames are sometimes shortened forms of county names, such as BEDFORD "Bieda's ford," BUCKINGHAM "place of Bucca's people," DERBY "homestead frequented by wild animals," DEVON "men of Defnas," HAMP "town on river land," HEREFORD "army ford," LINCOLN "lake colony," OXFORD "ford for oxen," and WARWICK "farm by a fish trap." The termination *-shire* was often dropped. Men from WESTMORLAND "land of the Westmoringas or people west of the Yorkshire moors" have usually kept the full name of the county as illustrated by General William C. Westmoreland, former commander of our troops in Viet Nam, who includes even the medial *e*. CLARE "a plank" often refers to the man who came from that county in Ireland; the surname and the Christian name are not related. MOYNIHAN designates the descendant of the Munsterman. MANN and MAN sometimes designate the person from the Isle of Man, a Manxman.

When a man came from a different province or country and his speech and appearance were different from those of his neighbors, he was a stranger in the true sense of the word, and he would be referred to as from that country, often in the contemptuous manner people are wont to affect toward one who is different. In England a man from Wales would be called WALSH, WALLACE, WELCH, or WELSH, that is, "the foreigner" or "stranger," also GALES, this last name with the initial G instead of W, influenced by the French. Those from Ireland were called IRELAND or IRISH. Irish McNULTY refers to the "son of the Ulidian "native of East Ulster." Owen Patrick McNulty, the radio singing star, legally changed his name to Dennis Day, but appeared in court a few years later to change back because of the disappointment of his family. The man from Scotland was called SCOTT. The word originally indicated the Irish but this had narrowed to Scottish Gael by the time surnames became common. As a border name SCOTT is common in Scotland. ENGLISH was a name sometimes used in England after the Conquest to distinguish the defeated English from the Norman followers of William. ENGLAND and ENGLANDER are also found in England.

In the same way NORMAN arose to distinguish the arrivals from Normandy, although before the Conquest it was a given name referring to a Northerner as mentioned elsewhere. NORRIS sometimes designated a Norwegian; in other cases it identifies the man in or near the north house. Those from Flanders were dubbed FLANDERS or FLEMING. From Gascony the names became GASTON or GASKIN, from Brittany they were BRETT, BRITTON, and BRITTAIN, and from Burgundy the surname was BURGOYNE. Arrivals from Germany were called GERMAN and JERMAN. From Saxony came SAX and SAXON. From Portugal the name PETTENGILL, in various spellings, was used. SWEETSER came from Switzerland. FRENCH and SPAIN designated a Frenchman and Spaniard, respectively, in both England and Scotland. The common term for a Frenchman in England was FRANCIS, and this is the usual meaning of the name although it looks like a patronymic. St. Francis of Assisi came upon the scene too late to influence many surnames. Also in Scotland, FRANCE was used for a Frenchman. The Frenchman in Italy would acquire such names as FRANCO, FRANCIA, FRANZESE, and FRANCESCO. The surname SCOTLAND in Scotland merely designates one who came from the village of Scotland "cut place." The Englishman in Scottish territory was referred to as INGLIS. The man from Friesland was denominated FRAZIER.

The question naturally arises, why are so many men in England named ENGLISH or ENGLAND, so many named FRANCE in France, and so many in Scotland named SCOTT? Such names easily arise when a man goes from his native country into another country and stays long enough to acquire the surname and then moves back to the country of his birth keeping the surname he has acquired. SCOTT thus became a popular name in Scotland as men moved back and forth across the border between the two countries. Sometimes in Scotland the name refers to an Irishman from Old English *Scott* "Irishman." SCOTT is also derived from the Old English personal name Scott, particularly those from the south of England.

Numerous German surnames are in this class. The Englishman was called ENGEL or ENGELMAN; the Spaniard, SPANIER; the Swiss, SCHWEITZER and SWEITZER; the Hungarian, UNGER; and the Pole, POLLACK. The man from Bohemia was called BEHM, BOEHM, BOHMANN, or CZECH. HESS was from Hesse, and WENDT designated one who came from the Wends, a Slavic tribe in eastern Germany. BAYER and BEYER came from Bavaria. DEUTSCH is the German and Dutch term for a German. A Moroccan or Saracen was MOHR. The Dutch called a Frisian DE VRIES, and a man from Cortlandt, VAN CORTLANDT.

The Englishman in France was called l'Anglais or LANGLOIS but when he returned to England his name, from ease in pronunciation, slid into the spelling, LANGLEY. Some Englishmen in France acquired the name YANCEY. The French called the German, or anyone from the Baltic states or from Holland, ALLEMAND or ALLEMAN. The Spaniard became DESPAGNE. The French name for the man from Normandy was LENORMAND, from Picardy, PICARD, and from Champagne, CHAMPAGNE. Italian names for the Greek are GRECO and GRIECO.

In Poland, Czechoslovakia, and Russia, the German who could not speak the language remained mute, and the words and names for one who could not speak were NEMITZ, NEMETZ, and NIEMIEC, which became the appellations for a German. The Hungarian cognate is NEMETH. Poland had various names for arrivals from most neighboring states or countries. One from Russia was surnamed RUSSO or ROSSOW, while RUSIN was from Rus, now known as the Ukraine. The Hungarian became WEGRZYN; the

Slovenian, SLOWINSKI; and the Lithuanian, LITWIN. This last is also English referring to a descendant of Old English Leohtwine "bright, friend," an unrecorded personal name. The man from Muscovy (west central Russia) was called MOSKAL and the man from Turkey, OSMANSKI. MAZUR was the name given to the arrival from Mazury, a former East Prussian province. Czechoslovakians, Ukrainians, and others called one from Turkey, TURK or TUREK. SLEZAK from Silesia; VLACH from Italy; and MORAVEC from Moravia made their homes in Czechoslovakia. Ukrainians termed a man from Italy, VOLOSCENKO and from Lithuania, LYTVYNENKO. Some Ukrainians acquired the family name of RUSNAK, from Rus, now Ukraine. Hungarians called a stranger from Croatia, HORVATH. The general Slavic name for the man from Poland was POLAK. A gypsy, one of a wandering Caucasian race, would be surnamed CYGAN in Poland.

Surnames derived from the larger cities are not so common in proportion to size as those from smaller places for two reasons: (a) movement of the population was always from country to town, and (b) men gravitated to the important cities rather than away from them. The name of a large city would not be so likely to serve the purpose of explicit identification since there would generally be several from the larger place. LONDON "Londinos' place, or hill over the pool" and PARIS "marshy land or bright land of the Parisii (a Celtic tribe)" are not common surnames as one might assume from the size of their populations. The exact etymology of very ancient settlements is often most obscure. Paris was the *Lutetia Parisiorum* of the Romans. Matthew Paris, the English chronicler of the early part of the thirteenth century, acquired his name from his study at the University of Paris. Paris sometimes has an added *h* to make it PARISH or PARRISH, although these names also have other explanations.

German and Swiss BASSLER hailed from Basel "Basilus' town" in Switzerland. German BRESSLER moved from Breslau "King Vratislaw's town," now Wroclaw in Poland. Italian LA BUDA and Hungarian BUDA were from Buda "Buda's town," now a part of Budapest in Hungary. FRANKFORT "ford of the Franks" and HAMBURG "forest fortress" came from those cities in Germany; sometimes the termination -*er* became a part of these surnames, both well known as the popular sandwich meats of America. An inquiring newspaper reporter in Chicago once questioned six people surnamed HAMBURGER as to what it was like to be a hamburger. Some mentioned teasing as a child, but most of them found the name an asset not easily forgotten. Felix FRANKFURTER (the German spelling of the second syllable was always *furt*), who was born in Vienna, made a most able and dignified associate justice of the Supreme Court of the United States despite the association of his name with the sausage, a favorite food with the young people. Italian MILANO came from Milan "middle of the plain." Swedish FALKENBERG came from Falkenberg "falcon mountain" and LUNDIN from Lund "grove," both cities in Sweden. Some with the name LUND derive their name from various small towns named Lund or from residence near a small wood. Russian MOSKOVSKY, MOSKVIN, and MOSKWA are from Moscow "mossy water" in Russia, and NOVGORODCEV is from Novgorod "new village." German PRAGER and Czechoslovakian PRAZAC are from Prague "the threshold" in Czechoslovakia. Belgian WATERLOO "settlement near water" is from that place in Belgium where Napoleon met his nemesis. Russian WARSHAWSKY and Polish WARSAW, WARSHAW, and WARSHAUER derive from Warsaw "the fortified place," the capital of Poland. German and Austrian WIENER and WINER came from a former residence in Wien "the Wends' town, or torrential stream," the Austrian city the English call Vienna. It must be kept in mind that these large Old World cities were founded in the remote past and there is often no agreement among authorities as to their exact interpretation.

DUBLIN is a simple name and sometimes it does refer to the Irishman from Dublin "black pool." It is usually, however, a Slavic surname designating one from Dublin "oak tree" in the Ukraine or Byelorussia or one who dwelt near an oak tree. DUBLINSKI is the Pole from Slavic Dublin. The Ukrainian form is DUBLINSKY.

6

SURNAMES NOT PROPERLY
INCLUDED ELSEWHERE

*Change of names—Jewish surnames—Norwegian farm names—Swedish man-
ufactured combinations—Soldier names—Chinese family names—Japanese surnames—Negro surnames—Indian names—Foundlings' names—Masters' names
—Married women—Juniors—Surnames from periods of time—Garbled names—
Comic or odd names—Names spelled same as common English words—Hyphenated names—Relative position of the surname in the United States—
Pronunciation—Common surnames—Two thousand most common American
surnames.*

Governmental decrees have not influenced surnames in
America except for a few cases among Indians on the res-
ervations. However, naturalization laws have provided that the
immigrant could formally adopt a new name through his petition
for citizenship. Moreover, in all states there are laws which provide means by which one may make the change of name a matter
of record if no fraud, infringement of trade names, or unfair competition is involved, but no one is required to invoke the benefit
of such laws. In all the states in the United States, with the possible exception of Pennsylvania, a man may change his family
name freely without court authorization if he is willing to go

258

hrough all the trouble of communicating the change so that busy people will use the new name. In most other countries changes nay be made only with governmental sanction. Some states in his country have adopted laws preventing the use of fictitious names in certain circumstances such as registration at hotels or notels, obtaining employment, or practicing certain professions.

In America many family names are changed at the insistence of the young people who find the names of their foreign-born parents a burden, and are not inhibited by emotional attachments o the Old Country. Often their teachers have suggested the hange, and the children returning from school have demanded t. Spiro T. Agnew, Vice President of the United States in 1969, had a Greek father, Theofrastos Anagnostopoulos "son of Anag-osto" who left the Peloponnese township of Gargalianoi for this ountry in 1895. Would Spiro ever have succeeded even in reach-ng for the high office if his name had not been changed to the Inglish Agnew, a name Americans could pronounce and spell easily? ANAGNOSTIS may be translated as "reader" or more exactly ecclesiastical acolyte," a boy consecrated by the bishop or the bbot in a monastery church to read the epistles and assist both he priest and the cantor. When Nixon disclosed his choice for he vice-presidency some with a smattering of Greek quickly ex-plained the name as "son of the unknown" which is, of course, bsurd, but newspapers carried this interpretation. The full sur-name is often shortened to ANAGNOST and ANAGNOS, even to AGNOS, rom which AGNEW is an easy adaptation.

The place where changed names are accepted as a matter of ourse is the motion picture capital, Hollywood, and, indeed, in he whole entertainment industry. Performers from all over the vorld with the faculty and the personality to amuse and hold the ttention of an audience find that they can more easily worm hemselves into the affections of the people in America through a familiar and easily remembered name. Thus Benjamin Kubelsky becomes Jack Benny, Lucille Le Sueur becomes Joan Crawford, nd Irving Lahrheim changes to Bert Lahr. Rodolpho d'Anton-uolla, the young actor from Castellaneta, Italy, changed to Ru-lolph Valentino to become a legend after his early death at thirty-ne. On the other hand some, especially musicians, find it profit-ble to become known through an exotic foreign name. The

American dramatic soprano, Lillian Norton, attained internationa fame as Lillian Nordica.

It would be easy to compile an enormous list of prominen foreigners who have altered their names in America. Actually since all except possibly the Indians in America are "foreigners," it can be confidently asserted that every family has changed it: surname since all spellings have been altered from time to tim in early America, and also in the Old Country. And the peopl who affirm that the only names not foreign in this country ar those of the American Indian should be apprised of the fact tha most experts agree that the Indians came here from Asia.

There are several names that are unusual yet are merely Ger manic personal names altered to common syllables. RAINBIRD is corruption of Rambert "raven, bright," RAINBOW is from Reginbal "might, bold," and STARBIRD is altered from Storbeorht "strong bright." Another origin of many unusual or odd names is th change in spelling of a place name to a common word. SHAKELAD is from Shackerley "robber's wood" in Lancashire. TOOTLE is fron Toothill "lookout hill," the name of several lookout hills through out England. A name does not have to be a corruption; IDLE i from Idle "shining bright, or uncultivated land," in the Wes Riding of Yorkshire.

Some names were changed by immigrants while on the boa heading for America. These transformations were usually to name thought by the immigrant to be more respected in his native lanc than the one he bore. As an example, many Poles added -ski t their names to attain a higher social status since such names wer accorded more respect from people of Polish extraction. Thus larger proportion of Polish names carry this termination in Amer ica than in Poland. For the same reason some Swedes adoptec names in America which exuded a higher social status among thei countrymen. Certain terminations such as -berg, -gren, -in, -lund -man, -quist, and -strom enabled them to look down on their les fortunate compatriots in a country without fixed class distinctions

Since the first World War family names in the United State have become much more stabilized. This is due not only to th increase in education among the people at large and especiall among the clerks who keep the vital statistics, but to the necessit for a fixed identity felt by the veterans returning from the war i order to share in the pension payments and other privileges accorded them. The advent of Social Security laws and regulations, in 1935, with the requirement for exhibition of birth certificates in order to receive benefits made definite, fixed family names an absolute necessity. Various other laws and retirement schemes also promoted the use of fixed, unchangeable names, such as automobile registrations, driver's license requirements, industrial pension and profit-sharing plans, and the great expansion of life insurance. Now machine tabulation and the wide use of identification numbers have made change of names of little value in the evasion of debts and income or other taxes.

America is a nation of nations, where many are intensely proud of the Old Country, ever alert to protest when countrymen are shown in a bad light. Cinema and television writers run into trouble when they try to select a name for the villain. Italian organizations protested when gangsters in a television series were given Italian names. In an earlier generation, movie studios were deluged with complaints from national and religious groups and even from foreign governments. One studio issued orders that all villains must be white, Protestant Americans of Anglo-Saxon descent. And so on the screen, to the accompaniment of sinister music, appears the boss of the south side mob: Percival Courtenay Hathaway, the Third! One broadcasting network directed its staff to give names of towns and cities to fictional characters to avoid lawsuits.

Not sufficiently discussed previously are those surnames with that distinctive flavor used by Jews. Many names regarded as distinctly Jewish are Biblical names adopted frequently by Ashkenazim (middle and northern European Jews). Familiar surnames are AARON "lofty mountain"; ABRAMS, ABRAMSON, and ABRAMOWICZ "high father"; ABRAHAM and ABRAHAMSON "father of multitudes"; BARUCH "blessed"; BENJAMIN "son of my right hand"; ISAAC, ISAACSON, and ISAACS "he who laughs"; ISRAEL "champion of God"; JACOBS and JACOBSON "the supplanter, or may God protect"; JOSEPH "He shall add"; MOSES, MOSS, and MOSKOVITZ "child, or drawer of water"; NATHAN "gift"; RUBIN "behold, a son"; SAMUELS "God hath heard"; SIMON "gracious hearing"; and SOLOMON "peaceful." In the different languages there are many variants of these names. SACKS, for instance, is a French

261

name from Sack, a pet form of Isaac while Zisook is a Polish cor
ruption from Isaac.

Cohen is the most common Jewish name. Originally meaning
"prince or priest," it came to mean simply "priest," and was a
first restricted to descendants of Aaron, the high priest. Since the
spelling of the name and its pronunciation have been affected by
transliteration from the Hebrew which has no vowels and by the
differences arising from the various European languages, many
other forms have developed, of which the most often seen are
Cahn, Cain, Cohan, Cohn, Cone, Cowan, Kahan, Kahn, Kohen
Kohn, and Kohnen. Because of the uniform prevalence of the
name among Jews, counts of the name have been employed as an
accurate test to estimate the number of Jews in a given area
Another very Jewish name is Levy derived from the tribe of
Levites, descendants of Levi "united," a family whose function
it was to assist the priests and serve the congregation. Common
variants of the name are Lee, Levey, Levi, Levin, Levine, Levinson, Lewis, and the definitive Halevy "the Levite." A few other
common Jewish names may be noted by examining the list of the
twenty names in New York (page 299). In New York, use of
many of the English names has been augmented by Jewish adop
tion.

Other distinctive Jewish names from occupations might be men
tioned. Perlman and Perlmutter were probably dealers in pearl
or mother of pearl. Karfunkel and Garfinkel were dealers in
carbuncle, a red semi-precious stone. Dayan was a rabbinic judge
Chazin was a cantor, Chalfen a money-changer, and Lehrer, a
teacher. Ackerman was sometimes a Jewish name for a farmer
Singer was the soloist or officiating minister in the synagogue
Einstein, the great German-Jewish theoretical physicist who was
one of those who fled to the freedom of America, may have had
an ancestor who was skilful in stone construction. Rappaport in
dicates both the occupation and place of origin of its bearer: a
certain physician of Porto, Italy, was honored and admired–
known as Rofa di Porto "doctor of Porto," which in America
coalesced into the well-known Rappaport.

The Rosen "roses" names were favorites with the German Jews
most of them arbitrarily formed by combining two pleasant words
but some of them were derived from names of places. There are

ROSENBACH "brook," ROSENBAND "token," ROSENBAUM "tree,"
ROSENBERG "mountain," ROSENBLATT "leaf," ROSENBLOOM "flower,"
ROSENBLUM "flower," ROSENBLUTH "blossom," ROSENBUSCH "wood,"
ROSENCRANZ "wreath," ROSENDALE "valley," ROSENFELD "field,"
ROSENGARD "garden," ROSENHEIM "home," ROSENHOLTZ "wood,"
ROSENKRANZ "wreath," ROSENMAYER "farmer," ROSENSTADT "city,"
ROSENSTEIN "stone," ROSENSTOCK "trunk (of tree)," ROSENTHAL
"valley," ROSENWALD "forest," ROSENZWEIG "branch," to mention
only the best known, the most common, some of which have been
shortened to ROSEN and ROSE, or ROSS. There are some Swedish
"Rosen" names with the meaning in the first element of "rose,"
such as ROSENGREN "branch," ROSENQUIST "twig," and ROSENDAHL
"valley." Some of these names are shared by both Swedes and
Jews. ROSEMAN is both German and English but is usually interpreted as a descendant of Rosmund "horse, protection." Some
Jews have shortened their names, and such names as BLATT,
BLUM or BLOOM, and ZWEIG, shortened from the above and other
names, are not uncommon. Other terminations of the above
"Rosen" names are found generally among Germans.

Also favorites with the Jews are the "Gold" names. GOLD itself
is quite common, often being a short form of an earlier longer
name. A favorite occupation of medieval Jews was the lending of
money at interest and this being combined with other work of
the goldsmith made the German GOLDSCHMIDT a well-known
name. Some "Gold" names used by Jews are from place names as
GOLDBERG, the name of five places in Germany, GOLDBERGER,
GOLDENBERG, GOLDENSTEIN (GOLDEN may be a short form), and
GOLDSTEIN (often translated to GOLDSTONE). GOLDSTEIN in some
cases may be derived from the use of a goldstein, a touchstone
used by a goldsmith to test gold; or it may be handed down as a
surname for the dweller at the sign of the gollstein, a topaz em-
blematic of the goldsmith's shop. Other "Gold" names were
formed by linking another word to Gold, chiefly German names,
as GOLDBAUM "tree," GOLDBLATT "leaf," GOLDFARB "color," GOLD-
FINE, GOLDFINGER, and GOLDMAN.

A feature of German-Jewish surnames in America which tends
to distinguish them from ordinary German family names is the
scenic-geographical name-endings such as -*bach* "brook," -*baum*
"tree," -*berg* "mountain," -*blatt* "leaf," -*blum* "flower," -*burg* "forti-

fication," -*dorf* "town," -*heim* "home," -*stadt* "city," -*stein* "stone,
-*thal* "valley," and -*wald* "forest." Most of these elements may als
have the toponymic -*er* added which usually indicated derivatio
from a place name. Jews with these names resisted change mor
than any other Jewish group except for the Sephardic Jews wh
came to America many years earlier.

There are many other German-Jewish names which are merel
the results of florid fancy or the vindictive thoughts of petty of
ficials, adopted when the Jews in Europe were compelled to tak
surnames in the early part of the nineteenth century. Some o
the most familiar are: BLITZSTEIN and BLITSTEIN "lightning stone,
EDELSTEIN "precious stone," FEINGOLD "fine gold," FEINSTEIN "fin
stone," FEINBERG "fine mountain," FELDSTEIN "field stone," FINKEL
STEIN "little bird stone," GLICKSTEIN and GLUCKSTEIN "luck
stone," GOTTLIEB "God, love," GREENBAUM "green tree," HIMMEL
BLAU "heaven blue," LOWENTHAL "lions' valley," LUSTGARTEI
"pleasure garden," SILVERSTEIN "silver stone," SISKIND "swee
child," SONNENSCHEIN "sunshine," and WEINSTEIN "wine stone."

Many who adopted names with pleasant connotations had t
pay handsomely to the money-grabbing official for the privilege
Other names may be attributed either to capricious manufactur
or to German towns such as BURNSTEIN and BERNSTEIN "amber,
BLUMENTHAL "flower valley" the name of seven towns, GREENBER
"green mountain," RUBENSTEIN "ruby stone," and RUTTENBERG "re
mountain." BLUMBERG "flower mountain" is the name of two place
in Germany, and MONTEFIORE with the same meaning is the nam
of a place in Italy. It must be admitted that the Jews have ende
up with a very pleasant set of names, although some are too com
mon for exact and easy identification.

Many names generally regarded as Jewish are from names o
German towns and cities, and, of course, are sometimes borne b
others than Jews. EISENSTEIN came from Eisenstein "iron stone,
GINSBERG from Gunzburg in Bavaria, LICHTENSTEIN from Lichten
stein "light stone," LIPSCHULTZ from Lippschutz or Liebschit
LOEB from Löbau "dear meadow," LOWENSTEIN from Lowenstei
"lions' stone," SEELIG from Seelig "prosperous place," STRASSBURGE
from Strassburg "fortified place on a highway," and WEINGART an
WEINGARTEN from Weingarten "vineyard." It is not always easy t

etermine whether a Jewish surname stems from a place, as many
at look like town names are really just arbitrary inventions,
metimes even a combination of Hebrew and German, such as
RONSTEIN and LEVINTHAL.

Some Jews in America have shortened their names and FEIN
nd FINE "fine," GLICK "luck," GOLD, GREEN, GROSS "fat," KLEIN
mall," ROTH "red," SCHWARTZ "black," SILVER, STEIN "stone,"
TERN "star," and WEISS "white" are quite common family names
mong them. MEYER when borne by Jews is sometimes from He-
rew *meir* "wise or scholarly." Not all common German names
ave been adopted by Jews with the same interpretations as the
arlier Germans put on their names. JONAS is sometimes from the
lebrew word for "pigeon," a house name with no relation to John
r Jonas. ALTSCHULER refers to the Jew near the old synagogue in
rague, and other places. Although *schule* translates to "school,"
he meaning here is transferred to "synagogue."

Several Jewish names contain oblique references to Biblical
assages. BENJAMIN is favored as lucky because of Genesis 49:27
here it says, "Benjamin shall ravin as a wolf: in the morning he
hall devour the prey, and at night he shall divide the spoil." For
he same reason the symbolical WOLF is also regarded favorably.
rench CERF and German HIRSCH both meaning "hind" are fa-
ored because they are compared to Naphtali in Genesis 49:21,
Naphtali is a hind let loose: he giveth goodly words." A contribu-
ry source of HIRSCH is from a house sign. LEO, LEON, and LYON
ere esteemed because in Genesis 49:9 the tribe of Judah and its
ings were compared to the lion by Jacob saying, "Judah is a
on's whelp: from the prey, my son, thou art gone up: he stooped
own, he couched as a lion, and as an old lion: who shall rouse
im up?" TEITELBAUM "date palm tree" was a name selected be-
ause of the assertion in Psalm 92:12, "The righteous shall flourish
ke the palm tree."

Some common Jewish names have more of a story connected
ith them. KANN designated a Jew who dwelt at the sign of the
g, an emblem sometimes carved on the homes of Levites since
was their duty to pour water over the hands of priests about
bless the congregation. ROTHSCHILD refers to the famous red
ield the great banking family swung before their shop door in
rankfort, Germany. Rothschilds as successful resident merchants

265

are found all over America. SCHWARZSCHILD dwelt at the sign (
the black shield.

From the sixteenth century on many Jewish family names wer
derived from the house or shop signs in the Jewish quarter (
Frankfort and elsewhere. House signs were particularly favore
by Jews, and they were reluctant to give them up. When the cit
council, in 1776, ordered the houses in Frankfort's Judengasse t
be numbered, there was such determined resistance that the
fined the whole Jewish community. Some signs originated fro
the names of the owners. Thus BAER "bear" and GANS "goos
were originally surnames whose owners put pictures before the
homes. A family in Frankfort known as CAHN put the picture (
a boat at the entrance to their home since Kahn is German f
"boat." Others used SCHIFF "ship." From Psalm 103:5 the eag
was regarded as the symbol of Jewish survival and German ADLI
"eagle" became a popular house name which served as a Jewis
family name for those living in the house. Some other Jewis
family names derived from house signs are APFEL "apple," BU
BAUM "box tree," ENGEL "angel," FINK "finch," FISCH "fish," FISHE
"little fish," HECHT "pike," HERZ "hart," RAPP "black horse'
STRAUSS "ostrich, or bouquet of flowers," and TAUB "dove."

SACKS, besides referring to one from Saxony, is a surnam
adopted by Jewish refugees from Stendal in memory of the ma
tyrdom of their people, from the Hebrew initials for "The Ho
Seed of Stendal." SHAPIRO, SPERO, SPIRA, and SPEYER refer to th
Jew from Speyer, called by Jews in the Middle Ages, Shapira, i
Bavaria. SPECTOR is a Russian name meaning "inspector," use
by Hebrew teachers in old Russia which enabled them to live i
zones forbidden to Jews when they registered with the authoritie
FRIEDMAN, also spelled FREEDMAN, is sometimes a translatic
from Hebrew *chalom* "peace" or from Solomon "peaceful."

A curious feature of Jewish nomenclature is the acronym
name, consisting of an abbreviation formed from the initial lette
or syllables of separate Hebrew or Aramaic words and name
found mostly among the Jews of eastern Europe and their d
scendants. Some are shortened forms of the full name and title
In understanding the abbreviations it must be remembered th:
Hebrew words and names consist entirely of consonants; th
vowels are usually indicated in print by points or diacritical mar

above or below the consonants. In the acronymic names vowels are inserted for popular use in pronunciation in Western countries.

The Hebrew KATZ is an abbreviation or contraction of *kohen tzedek* "priest of righteousness," and consequently a member of the priestly clan with special functions and duties in Jewish religious practices. SEGAL, also spelled SIEGEL, is a shortened form of *segan leviyyah* "member of the Levites," literally assistant priest or rabbi, a name frequently used by Levites. SHUB is from *shohet ubodek* "slaughterer and examiner," that is, one who killed animals for food and inspected for ritual purity. SHATZ abbreviates *shaliach tzibbur* literally "representative of the congregation," a leader in congregational prayers.

BARASH stands for Ben Rabbi Shemuel, the ancestor from whom the surname is derived. BARON or BARAN in some cases commemorates Ben Rabbi Nachman. BROCK is sometimes an abbreviation of Ben Rabbi Kalman. CHABAD is a combination of three words *chochma, binah, deah* "wisdom, understanding, knowledge," the motto of a Chassidic sect active in the latter part of the eighteenth century. ZAK is used as an abbreviation of *zera kedoshim* "the seed of martyrs." This name and Czechoslovakian ZAK "schoolboy" through variant spellings are sometimes altered to the Jewish SACK or SACHS. ZATZ derives from *zera tzadikim* "the seed of righteous men." All of these names being short also have other derivations.

Many other rare Jewish surnames have similar derivations. Joshua H. Neumann in his article, "Some Acronymic Surnames," published in the December, 1965, issue of *Revue Internationale d'Onomastique,* says that E. S. Rabinovitz in Reshumot (Tel-Aviv, 1927–8) lists some 170 acronymic family names including variants. There is no doubt that acronymic formation of surnames is used in Israel where names of immigrants have often been altered to give them a Hebrew cast. The influence of Hebrew on other languages and place names, especially German, has produced many complicated Jewish family names, difficult to trace, and most Jews today are not aware of the correct interpretation of their names.

An unusual feature of many Norwegian names is the farm name. The farms were large and important centers of family life in Old Norway, some running from seacoast to mountain top. People

267

lived on farms rather than in villages, as in other countries. Each
farm was known by name often continuing the same over centuries. Some farm names have even been traced back to the Early
Iron Age, B.C. Probably Oslo and Bergen were originally farm
names. Farm names have been called the Norwegian "titles of
nobility." Before the Norwegian immigration to America many of
the large farms had been broken up into smaller units. Since the
name was well known and of greater importance than any byname of the owner or occupant, it was only natural for the resident on the farm to be known by the farm name. If a man removed to another farm, his farm name changed. The name did
not belong to the family but to the farm.

Nearly every natural object became part of some farm name
but the most common elements of farm names are the many terms
simply meaning "farm," the most important of which are *bo, by,
gardr, heimr, land, rud, setr, stad,* and *vin.* When one considers
that farms have been commonly named in Norway for more than
1100 years, it is apparent that the words used must vary in different dialects and in different times. The earliest names are probably *vin, bo,* and *setr,* the first two having been found on ancient
rune stones in the sense of "farm." The latter, often corrupted to
set or *sett,* has a connotation of dwelling. A later word is *stad* or
stadir but older than *land, rud, heimr,* or *gardr. Land* possibly
designates a sub farm, one cut off from a parent farm. *Rud,* originally "clearing" came to mean "farm" after the clearing was occupied, buildings built, and the ground cultivated. *Gardr* originally referred to a yard or enclosure. All of these words are sometimes contracted or altered in spelling so that they are difficult to
recognize.

The more important of the patriarchal family farm names commanded the most respect and dignity in Norway and to a lesser
extent in America. Typical farm names embodying the above
"farm" elements are: HOLLAND "rounded hill farm," SUDBO "south-
farm," HUSBY "house farm," ODEGARD "abandoned farm," SEIM
"seaside farm," ASKELAND "ash tree farm," EGGERUD "ridge farm,"
SATERLUND "farm grove," BJORNSTAD "Bjorn's farm," and VINJI
"farms." LAND and BOE are sometimes Norwegian farm name
with the simple meaning of "farm."

The Swedes have in recent times combined two words together

to manufacture family names to take the place of their common patronymics terminating in -*son*. This has been similar to the Jewish practice. These words are not just any words but are usually nature words combined for easy pronunciation without reference to meaning. Some of the most common are *alm* "elm," *äng* (eng) "meadow," *asp* "aspen," *berg* "mountain," *björk* "birch," *blad* "leaf," *blom* "flower," *bro* "bridge," *ceder* "cedar," *dahl* "valley," *ek* "oak," *fors* "waterfall," *gran* "pine," *gren* "branch," *hag* "pasture," *hall* "boulder," *hed* "meadow," *holm* "river island," *hult* "copse," *kvist* (quist) "twig," *lind* "linden tree," *ljung* (sometimes Englished to young) "heather," *löf* "leaf," *lund* "grove," *mark* "field," *mo* "heath," *ö* "island," *palm* "palm tree," *ros* "rose," *sand* "sand," *sjö* "sea," *skog* "forest," *sol* "sun," *strand* "shore," *ström* "stream," *sund* "sound," *wahl* or *vall* "field," and *wick* "bay." Some of these names have been included elsewhere in this work with their meanings, but most of them have no onomastic explanation other than as pleasant nature words. This custom has been actively encouraged by the Swedish government. In its latest list of recommended names the *Släktnamnskommitté* or Family Name Committee included some 56,000 combinations.

Common names found in America with these elements are: ALMQUIST, ASPLUND, BERGGREN, BERGLUND, BERGQUIST, BERGSTROM, BJORKLUND, BLOMBERT, BLOMGREN, BLOMQUIST, BROBERG, CEDERHOLM, DAHLBERG, DAHLGREN, DAHLQUIST, DAHLSTROM, ECKLUND, EKLUND, EKSTROM, ENBERG, ENGSTROM, FORSBERG, GRANQUIST, HAGSTROM, HALLBERG, HELLSTROM, HILLSTROM, HEDBERG, HEDLUND and EDLUND, HEDSTROM, HOLMBERG, HOLMGREN, HOLMQUIST, HULTGREN, LINDAHL, LINDBERG, LINDENBERG, LINDGREN, LINDHOLM, LINDQUIST, LINDSTROM, LUNDBERG, LUNDELL, LUNDGREN, LUNDMARK, LUNDQUIST, LUNDSTROM, MOBERG, OBERG, PALMQUIST, ROSENQUIST, SANDBERG, SANDQUIST, SANDSTROM, SJOBLAD, SKOGLUND, SKOOGLUND, SKOGSBERG, SOLBERG, STRANDBERG, STROMBERG, STROMQUIST, SUNDBERG, WAHLGREN, WAHLSTROM, WICKLUND, WICKSTROM, YOUNGBERG, YOUNGDAHL, YOUNGLOVE (löf), and YOUNGQUIST. It will be noted that some elements are used usually at the beginning, others generally at the end, and many in either position. Sometimes only one word is used, as ALM, BJORK, BLOM, BLOOM, HALL, HULT, LIND, LUND, NORD, PALM, QUIST, WAHL, and WICK, all of which have been translated in preceding paragraphs.

AMERICAN SURNAMES

The cardinal directions, *nord, soder, ost,* and *west,* are used with these name words to produce the common names, NORDBERG NORDGREN, NORDQUIST, NORDSTROM, SODERBERG, SODERLUND, SODERSTROM, OSTERBERG, OSTRAND, OSTROM, WESTERBERG, and WESTLUND. The word *ny* "new" is often found, as in NYBERG and NYSTROM, and *hog* "high" as in HOGLUND.

In Sweden some of these nature, manufactured names hinted at a higher status for those bearing them than those known by the old patronymical family names such as Petersson and Andersson, but not in democratic America where one man is as good as another, or, as the Irish affirm, "a whole lot better." Thus in Sweden those with such earlier nature names as LJUNGLUND, BERGSTROM, PALMQVIST, and HAMMARSKJOLD "hammer-shield" were considered to be socially superior and became the officers in the Swedish regiments and held most of the important governmental offices. Another type of status name is the "priest name" easily recognized by the classical terminations *-ius* and *-ander* "man," as in AURELIUS, SEBELIUS, OLANDER, and THELANDER. Not all men with such names were clergymen even in Sweden, and far fewer in America where some adopted the name to attain personal distinction. People everywhere eagerly display status symbols of one kind or another in a calculated effort to show that they are of purer or nobler breed than others, usually forgetting that the honor, if any, lies with the ancestor not with themselves.

Since the start of the twentieth century the Swedish government has given considerable attention to the question of common surnames and has encouraged its people with the profuse name terminating in *-son* to choose and adopt another not used by others, usually a combination of two familiar nature words or elements such as listed previously. No other country has officially regarded the surname as such a matter of importance to both the nation and the individual. Strict regulations were issued by the Swedish Name Committee concerning the adopted name. It must be consistent with Swedish linguistic usage in construction, pronunciation, and spelling, and different from others in use by more than a few persons. Applications for change must be made to the Family Name Committee which would not approve any new name that was in any way offensive or likely to cause trouble, pain, or embarrassment to present or future bearers.

If a name could be given an obnoxious connotation in any way, it was rejected. Even if a slight difference in syllabic division could give rise to an odious meaning, the Committee refused to allow it to be used. Hence such a name as Horsäng with the innocent meaning "horse meadow" would not be approved because it might be viewed as Hor-säng "whore bed." If the initial of the given name might attach to the surname to produce a ludicrous meaning, the governmental agency would not approve the change. A man with a given name commencing with S, for instance, should not petition to adopt a surname in which the first element was Vin as S. Vinbacken might coalesce into Svinbacken "swine hill."

Thus Swedes may have common names but not the odd, unusual, offensive, or ludicrous names that may be observed in America among all other peoples. And to understand fully the flavor of American names it is necessary to look at some of the odd names, some of which are noted later on in this chapter. Mostly, however, in this work the emphasis has been placed on the common names known to everyone in America.

When a Swede was conscripted into the army, he usually took, or was often forced to take, a soldier name or *tillnamn* for his period of service—a short, military or warlike name such as Fisk "fisherman," Freed "peace," Kula "bullet," Rapp "fast" (not to be confused with German Rapp mentioned elsewhere in this chapter), Raske "daring," Sward "sword," Tapper "courageous," and Varg "wolf." Several others are mentioned in Chapter I. Indeed, many short names with other interpretations have also been adopted for temporary use as soldier names. Later, the ex-soldier finding that his old family name was too common to be a proper identification, especially if in the meantime he had decided to seek his fortune in America, might drop it and resume his old soldier name, if it exuded a pleasant aura, as a permanent family name. Too many soldier names conferred by the commanding officer evinced a certain malicious, poetic fancy and were consequently shelved as soon as the soldier was discharged. Norwegians also used soldier names to some extent.

Chinese names are in a class by themselves. There are only about a thousand different Chinese surnames, of which only about sixty are at all common. They are short and easy to pronounce

271

and Americans have no trouble with them. Few are changed in America. Some of the more common are CHAN "old," CHANG "draw-bow, or open, or mountain," CHEW from the province of that name, CHIN from the dynasty of that name, FU "teacher," GEE "well mannered," HONG from dynasty of that name, LEE "pear tree," LI "plum tree," MOY "plum flower," WANG "prince or yellow," WING "warm," WONG "field or wide (sea or ocean)," and YEE "first person singular pronoun." However, a few unusual English names are similar to those of the Chinese and may be mistaken for them. For example, WING is also English, naming one who came from Wing "Weohthun's people or field," the name of towns in Buckinghamshire and Rutland, or a descendant of Winge "protector"; CHEW is the man from Chew "chicken," the name of several places on the river of that name in Somerset; CHIN is a nickname for one with a prominent lower jaw; and of course LEE is a common English name for the dweller at the meadow or for one from Lee, the name of several small places in England.

The Japanese in America have names that are easily recognized as they seem to have a definite flavor which stamps them as Nipponese. Some seem to have a reference to the place where the family originally lived but most of them are composed of two words, usually taken from nature, but not necessarily related, a practice observed in many Swedish and Jewish surnames. For example, ITO "only, wisteria," KATO "add, wisteria," SATO "help, wisteria," and SAITO "festival, wisteria" are all common family names. As Kanji words have two pronunciations and wisteria is highly favored by the Japanese, it may be noted that other common Japanese surnames are FUJII "wisteria, well," FUJIMOTO "wisteria, origin," and FUJIKAWA "wisteria, river." Other Japanese family names are HAYAKAWA "early, river," INOUE "well, above," NAKAGAWA "middle river," NAKAMURA "middle village," ONO "small field," TAKAHASHI "high bridge," TANAKA "ricefield, middle," SUZUKI "bell, trees," YAMASHITA "mountain, below," YAMAMOTO "mountain, origin," and MATSUMOTO "pine, origin."

The two large groups who have acquired their family names in the United States are the Negroes and the American Indians. The Negro when brought to this country by the slave traders had nothing corresponding to a family name. Even the simple name by which he was known in the African tribe did not survive except possibly for a short while among some of his fellow workers. The white masters completely ignored all African designations and alluded to the slave usually by some short, simple form such as Sam or Bob or Joe, sometimes preceded by an additional, careless epithet such as Big, Fat, or Old.

Although some able studies, of minor importance, have been made of Negro family names in America the field is still open to the young Ph.D. who wishes to make an important contribution to onomastics in this country, by giving the attention, drudgery, and effort that the matter deserves. A Black could do the necessary research better than others in the light of racial unrest at the present time since innumerable and tedious interviews to learn family tradition about the names will be required. Knowledge concerning the adoption of particular family names is not in writing and often reposes only in the memory of the older people. Even now through the lapse of several generations most Negroes do not know anything about the circumstances attending the origin of their family names. Consequently few authoritative observations may be made now concerning Negro names. The group as a whole cannot even decide what name they want for the race —Negro, Black, Colored, Afro-American?

While still slaves few Negroes needed or had family names. When the Negro became free in America, the thing he wanted most was status—to be like the white men around him, the only measure of status he knew. A second name would, he thought, lend that dignity he so devoutly desired. One of the first acts of the freed slave thus was to adopt a byname. The only surnames the freed slaves had from which to select were the names of the whites they knew. According to estimates which have been made the white blood in the South was two-thirds English and Welsh with about thirteen percent Scottish and about the same percentage Irish. The English, Scottish, and Welsh names were often patronymics, and consequently Negro family names are, in large part, patronymics.

The development of family names among the colored people in the United States has been in four stages according to that eminent authority, Howard F. Barker. They are (1) before emancipation, which became effective January 1, 1863; (2) during the last half of the War and Reconstruction, 1863–1877; (3) during the quiet period, 1877–1914; and (4) from the migration north, beginning about the start of the first World War in 1914.

Before emancipation only the free Negroes in the North had surnames. These were similar to those of their neighbors. A slave who desired to adopt a family name found that he had no way of inducing the whites to recognize it. Indeed, particularly in the South, even after the slaves were freed the whites persistently attempted to ignore the Black's surname, insisting on referring to him only by his given name. During the Civil War regiments of former slaves were enrolled with second names more or less arbitrarily imposed. It was only after the beginning of the Reconstruction period that the Negroes first really felt the need for definite identification. Names were adopted and casually changed when a better or more dignified-sounding one came along. Not having the money to defray the expense of a change approved by court proceedings, the Negro changed his name rather informally but none the less effectively. Registration in the early Negro schools required a surname, and usually the surname of the mother rather than the father was used. In slavery, descent through the mother was recognized; the father often was unknown. The new colleges for Negroes influenced better naming. Negro churches grew during this period and registration of baptisms required a full name. But throughout this period schools and churches failed to reach a great number of the illiterate colored people who lived by themselves in the South, and hereditary family names were an insignificant part of their lives.

Although it has been asserted that the freed Negro generally took the surname of his former master, this was clearly not the customary practice. Everything that reminded him of his former condition was anathema to him. The names of the great slave owners in the South were little used as Negro family names. Benefactors were naturally more influential in the choice of family names, although the famous abolitionists were ignored by them when choosing surnames, except possibly for John Brown. General Oliver Otis Howard, head of the Freedman's Bureau, 1865–1874, was a hero to them, influencing many to take HOWARD as their family name.

It is curious to note that the name WASHINGTON was adopted

by many ex-slaves, so that four-fifths of those now bearing that name are black. In the first schools they learned of the father of his country and many, like Booker T. Washington, the great colored educator, thus selected the name so that it is one of the more popular Negro family names in the country. Little attention was paid by the Negroes to the names of northern statesmen and generals. The names of Lincoln, Sherman, and Grant were largely ignored. Most of the Negroes thus merely adopted the common English and Welsh surnames frequently observed in the South after the Civil War. Numerous Blacks bear the name SPIVEY "askew or boggy" although no outstanding man of that name was known. None are listed in *Who Was Who in America,* Historical Volume 1607–1896. Negro family names now are generally indistinguishable from those of southern whites. Negroes in French Louisiana acquired French names. Some Spanish Negro names have come in from the West Indies.

Few Negroes adopted place names; there is little record of any who took the names of towns or cities where they lived or where they were born. There are no Mountvernons or Monticellos. Many first saw the light of day on the southern plantations but this had no effect on the names they selected; hills, woods, and fields did not influence their nomenclature very much. Occupational names with the exception of Smith were not popular. Most nicknames, except the color names of BROWN, BLACK, REID, and GRAY, were generally rejected. African names tended to remind them of their former bondage and were not used as family names. Today the growing desire for an African name reflects the developing sense of race consciousness and an awareness of cultural heritage.

The most popular Negro surname is JOHNSON which could be regarded as a white man's name, but it is a little difficult to understand the exact reasons that caused it to lead all other names. Andrew Johnson, President of the United States, succeeding Lincoln, 1865–1869, did little to attract Negro affection. He believed that Negro suffrage was a matter for decision by each state, and in 1866 vetoed the act extending the Freedman's Bureau and the Civil Rights Act passed by Congress. BROWN is the second most popular Negro surname. Without regard to the Confederate President, Jefferson Davis, who was conspicuous as a defender of the South and of the institution of slavery, many

Negroes adopted the surnames JEFFERSON and DAVIS. Other common Negro patronymics are HARRIS, JACKSON, JONES, ROBINSON, WILLIAMS, and THOMAS.

With the upheaval caused by the first World War the demand for labor in the North provided openings for great numbers of Negroes who moved to the large cities there. Employers required full names. Conscripts in the army had to settle on a permanent surname which, upon marriage, became a hereditary family name. Social Security laws were most effective in stabilizing the colored man's name.

Indian names in America have presented a most confused pattern. Among the Indians prominent in early American history were Osceola, Powhatan, Shabonee, Shikellamy, Squanto, Tecumseh, Tiyanoga, and Washakie; names of this type did not become family names. Others were better known by the English translation of their native names, as Black Hawk, Kicking Bird, Red Wing, Sitting Bull, and Spotted Tail. Before the coming of the white man they did not have, and did not need, family names. It was only when the government, through the Indian agents, started to number the Indians on a reservation or the Indian off the reservation mingled with the English and French that the need for a surname arose.

In the eastern part of our country the early settlers gave European names to many of the Indians with whom they came into contact. Then the Indian might be assigned a recognized English surname or might use as his surname the last word of the phrase used to translate his Indian name. Charley Goodnurse, Tall Singer, and Black Cattle produced such surnames as GOODNURSE, SINGER, and CATTLE. Others used the full phrase as the surname especially those still living on the reservation. Among the Indians protesting a decision of the United States Supreme Court in Washington in 1968 were the Dakota chief, George Crows Fly High, and George Yellow Wolf. The widow of Geronimo, the Apache chief, was Kate Cross-Eyes.

In many cases the Indian when requested to select a permanent family name picked that of a white man he knew or perhaps selected a word from a sign or even a label on a package. Over the years the Indians have gradually conformed to European naming practices; many crude names have in time been changed for recognized surnames. The old Indian names have had no influence on Indian family names in America. Although Indian place names are common, most refer to a tribe or consist of a description of the place in an Indian tongue, and very few are taken from the personal name of an Indian. Still, there are some well-known names, such as Keokuk (Iowa), Seattle (Washington), and Sequoyah (Sequoia National Park, California), the names of prominent Indians given to these places by the white settlers. The whites have not driven the Indians out of America; they have smothered their names.

A group of surnames which came into existence since the surname period are those given to foundlings. Most foundlings were illegitimate and our ancestors had few compunctions against so labeling them. The blunt speech of our rude forefathers involved "calling a spade a spade." Bastard was freely used. William the Conqueror did not hesitate about referring to himself as "the Bastard." The word in earlier times did not emit the same stigma it does today in English-speaking countries.

TEMPLE was commonly given as a surname for foundlings left at the Temple in London. In Italy there is a group of names recognized by educated people as originally given to illegitimates left at the church door. Some of these names are ESPOSITO "exposed," DE BENEDICTIS, DEI BENEDETTI, DEI ANGELLI, DE ANGELIS, DEI SANTI, DE SANTIS, DELLA CHIESA, and DELLA CROCE. In later times the first element was often dropped. FORTUNA "good fortune" was sometimes given to foundlings. The names selected were often due to the momentary whim of the priest or director of the asylum. In Spain a name often given to the poor unfortunates was EXPOSITA. Now, modern compassionate laws in both Italy and Spain provide for names common in the locality to be given to illegitimate children with unknown parents.

Young men who were bound apprentices often acquired the surname of their masters. When a boy at an age when he was just becoming an individual was apprenticed to a craft or trade, he left his father's home and lived in the home of the master. Previously he had little need for a surname. His importance in the life of the community was small and he might be casually referred to by neighbors as the master's man or servant. It was quite usual in the thirteenth and fourteenth centuries in London and Paris for the family name of the master to be transferred to the apprentice. After the apprentice had become a journeyman or master himself, he might revert to his former surname or might continue to use the master's name by which he was better known. In some instances both surnames were used. Servants sometimes adopted and were known by the surnames of their masters in the same way as apprentices. In the same manner many wards acquired the names of the guardians with whom they resided. A husband sometimes adopted the wife's maiden name in cases where she came from a family with more prestige.

At marriage in America and elsewhere the wife by custom loses her maiden surname and thereafter her name consists of her own first name and her husband's surname, and this style continues as a matter of custom after she is widowed. For a middle name or initial, society has quite generally recognized the use of the wife's own middle name or initial or the name or initial of her maiden surname. *Mrs.* is a title and is not part of the name of a married woman. The law, in most states, however, does not compel a wife to use her husband's name; she may continue using her maiden name, and many women do this in business and in the professions where the husband has no connection with that business or profession, even though socially she is known by her husband's surname.

That a woman generally loses her maiden name upon marriage is emphasized by a professor of psychology in Brooklyn who found that not one out of fifty Americans can remember what mother was called before she met father without racking their brains for at least sixty seconds.

Several state courts have held that upon marriage a woman's surname by custom and law changes to that of her husband and she cannot continue to use her former surname in certain cases where there is an apparent conflict with a statute. For example a Massachusetts court (*Bacon* v. *Boston Elev. Railway Co.* 256 Mass. 30) held that when a married woman registered her car under her maiden name and was injured in an automobile accident, she could not recover damages due to the negligence of the other party because her car was not legally registered, since it was not registered in the name of its owner as the law required and was thus a nuisance on the highway.

Surnames Not Properly Included Elsewhere

The use of *Junior* or *Jr.*, affixed to the name of a man who has the same name as his father, is a typical American practice which began about the middle of the eighteenth century and is not normally found in England or in any other English-speaking nation. Three signers of the Declaration of Independence, in 1776, attached *Jr.* to their names. The next few paragraphs represent a conglomerate of gleanings about this practice of using *Jr.*, peculiar to the United States.

The use of *Jr.* presents problems that psychologists have investigated. According to some a child is entitled to a name that is both dignified and individual. Making him subordinate to the father demeans him and does little more than feed the father's vanity. The able son of a famous father is especially handicapped. In view of some recent findings, when a father names his son after himself he is doing two things—flattering himself and placing a millstone around the neck of the baby. In some communities the use of *Jr.* attached to a name is considered pompous.

Giving a boy the same name as his father and calling him Junior can make it harder for a boy to grow up. This is the opinion of some psychologists. An informal poll by Joe Hyams, Jr., in 1958, disclosed that about fifty percent of the Juniors of famous or successful fathers were generally opposed to the practice, about twenty-five percent were in favor, and the remaining twenty-five percent saw both good and bad features in the situation. Those who were in favor of the practice were close to and proud of their parent and happy to bear his name. Those opposed said that people expect one to exhibit the same kind of talent as the father and exploit the father's reputation without being a separate individual. They also cited the irritation of constant mix-ups. Harold Lloyd, Jr., son of the famous motion picture comedian, changed his name to Duke Lloyd to get away from the disadvantage of being a Junior.

Junior and *2nd* are masculine suffixes. There is little cause for confusion between mother and daughter with the same name because the mother uses her husband's name. When for professional reasons both mother and daughter are known by the same name, "the younger," the feminine equivalent of junior, may be used. Emily Post, the authority on etiquette, thought that this might be abbreviated to *Yr.*, but suggested that "younger" writ-

279

ten in full and not capitalized was much better. Quite evidently this advice has never instituted a national custom, perhaps for two reasons, (1) because most women solve the problem by marriage, and (2) what woman would ever let a grown daughter be "younger"?

A boy is "Jr." only if he has exactly the same name as his father. If his middle name is different, he is not correctly a Junior. If the name is the same, he is "Jr." whether he is the first or fifth son. Emily Post decreed that a boy was also Junior if he had exactly the same name as his grandfather even though not the same as his father as long as he had no uncle who was Jr. In other words, she contended that a junior is always a direct descendant of one with the same name.

One man queried Dr. Charles Funk, the eminent lexicographer, saying that since his father, grandfather, and great-grandfather all had the same name as his, was it proper to use the Roman numeral IV after his name or should he just use "Jr."? The Doctor replied that if the father used "III" or "3rd" after his name, then "IV" or "4th" should be used, otherwise the abbreviation "Jr." should be used.

According to Dr. Arthur A. Hartman, the well-known psychologist, writing in *The Journal of General Psychology,* the continued use of *Jr.* in later life after the death of the parent indicates immaturity and dependency. Attaching a numeral to the name, Dr. Hartman says, "suggests upper-class identification, awareness of status and tradition, or close family identification." It is interesting to note that many of the nation's most glamorous heroes, the Astronauts, are juniors, such as Charles Conrad, Jr., Gordon Cooper, Jr., John Glenn, Jr., James Lovell, Jr., Walter Shirra, Jr., Elliott Lee, Jr., and Alan Shepard, Jr. However, the use of *Jr.* has been definitely declining in popularity during recent years.

There are plenty of Springs, Summers, Falls, and Winters found both in the singular and the plural. SPRING refers to a dweller at or near a spring or well; SUMMER calls to mind the summoner, that is, the petty official who calls people to appear in court, although in a few cases it designates a descendant of Sumer "one born in summer." FALL or FALLS sometimes designates one from Fal, a river in Cornwall, but mostly the name is for one dwelling near a waterfall. WINTER names the son of Winter "one born during that season of the year," but in some cases it is the descendant of Winidhari "wind, army," or in other cases, it denotes the dealer in wine.

The names of months most commonly found as family names are March, May, June, and August. MARCH is the dweller at the boundary mark or one who lived on or near the swamp. JUNE is from the French *jeune* and refers to the young person. MAY and AUGUST are patronymics, the first descending from May, a hypocoristic form of Matthew "gift of Yahveh" and August being a descendant of August, short form of Augustus "venerable" and especially of the diminutive form Augustine. Some of the other months are occasionally noticed. They are all often derived from a given name selected because the child was born in that month.

WEEK or WEEKS from *wich* designates one who dwelt at a dairy farm. Earlier the word meant a dwelling place, then a village, but it was used of a dairy farm by the time surnames came into use. Some acquired the name because they came from Wich, the name of many places in southwestern England. Curiously, DAY or DAYS also referred to a dairy worker, originally a kneader of bread, a female servant, by the fourteenth century used of both men and women. In some cases DAY comes from Dai or Day, pet forms of the Welsh Dafydd and the English David.

The days of the week occasionally observed as surnames are Sunday, Monday, and Friday. German SUNDAY and FRIDAY are explained later in this chapter. MONDAY designates the holder of Mondayland, one who occupied land in an English manor for which he worked for the lord one day a week, on Mondays. The name also means the descendant of one named Monday because born on that day. Even parts of a day, as MIDDAY and MIDNIGHT, appear as family names being derived from birth at noon or in the middle of the night.

A small group of family names consists of those arbitrarily manufactured and adopted by their bearers. Since it is almost impossible to take any pronounceable group of letters and not find it to be a name somewhere, these cannot be identified except in those cases where the circumstances are known. Some take a word which they think indicates a quality they would like. Russian political figures have operated in this manner. There are, for example, MOLOTOV "hammer," and STALIN "steel." Writers have

281

selected pseudonyms or adaptations, such as Mark Twain (Samuel Clemens) and Anatole France (Jacques Anatole François Thibault).

Some people have the type of name that is automatically garbled in speech or misspelled in writing. For example, Hy Averback, the television director, has been reported to have such a name. People seem just naturally to insist on replacing the *k* with an *h,* and to use all sorts of variations, Averbach, Auerbach, Overback, Everbach, Avirbach, Eberback. Even his first name comes out as Hi, Hei, Hai, Si, Ty, and High. People with this type of name must face a lifetime of correcting others or give up and resign themselves to being known by a protean caricature of their real name. Some like Mr. Averback turn the name into a conversational advantage.

Names ending -*le* preceded by a consonant doubled have a slightly comic even plebian tinge, if one may credit the observations of those who have noted such names in the cartoons and comic strips. It was Lord Byron in his satire, "English Bards and Scotch Reviewers," who exclaimed, "Oh, Amos Cottle!—Phoebus! what a name!" (Basil Cottle, recent compiler of a *Dictionary of Surnames,* in retaliation carefully pointed out that Byron's name meant "at the cowsheds"). These names are subject to various interpretations. COTTLE, for example, is a cottager who tilled only five or ten acres and occupied a small cottage; or one who came from Cotleigh "Cotta's grove"; or from Cotehele "wood by the estuary" in Cornwall; or a nickname for the little cottager; or from Old French *cotel* "coat of mail," possibly a metonym for a maker or dealer in armor and daggers.

BITTLE is a perversion of Old English *bydel* "constable, crier or usher in a court." CUTTLE is a descendant of little Cutt, a pet form of Cuthbert "famous, bright." DIBBLE and DIPPLE are descendants of Dibald, a corruption of Theobald "folk, bold." DIPPLE is also from Dipple "dark stream" in Scotland. FIDDLE is probably a metonym for the man who played the fiddle, although it might refer to a descendant of Fitel, a variant of Vitalis "pertaining to life," a name found in the English Domesday Book, the compilation of the occupiers of land before 1086. HEBBLE dwelt near a hebble, that is, "a narrow plank bridge." HIPPLE and HEPPLE came from Hepple "corner where hips (fruit of the dog-rose or wild brier) grew" in Northumberland. KITTLE is a descendant of Old Norse Ketill "sacrificial cauldron." KIBBLE is a descendant of Cybbel "cudgel" or it may designate one who made and sold cudgels. KIDDLE does not refer to a little kid but surnames one who came from Kiddal "cow valley" in the West Riding of Yorkshire.

BATTLE, BIDDLE, LITTLE, POTTLE, RIDDLE, and SETTLE are explained elsewhere, and, with the exception of Pottle and Biddle, appear to be ordinary English words, although only Battle and Little have the meaning they appear to have. COPPLE is the man who came from Coppull "peaked hill" in Lancashire. TIPPLE is a descendant of little Tipp, a pet form of Theobald "folk, bold"; TITTLE is not a minute part, a jot, but is the man who left Titley "Titta's wood" in Herefordshire. TUGGLE is the man from Tughall "Tucga's corner" in Northumberland. TRIBBLE owes his name to an ancestor named Thrythbald "might, bold." TWADDLE, now there's a name, is the Scotsman who came from Tweedle "pasture dale" in Scotland. General Harry Lewis Twaddle of the United States Army did not disguise the pronunciation of his name. WADDLE, another Scotsman, is one who came from Waddel "valley where woad grows" in Midlothian near Edinburgh. WIGGLE is both an English and a German surname. As the former it is the man who came from Wighill "corner with a dairy-farm" in the West Riding of Yorkshire, and as a German name it denominates the descendant of Wincel "child" or of Wiggo, a short form of names beginning with Wig "fight," such as Wigberht, Wigbrand, Wighard, and Wigheri. Finally, WHITTLE is the one who came from Whittle "white hill," the name of several villages in England.

Other names that terminate in -*le* are of interest and some of them are here examined briefly. BEETLE does not relate to the insect but merely surnames the man who came from Beetley "wood where wooden mallets were obtained" in Norfolk. BIBLE does not call attention to the pious carrier of the good book; he is merely a descendant of little Bibb, a pet form of Isabel "oath to Baal or oath to God." BICKLE came from Bickley "Bicca's homestead," the name of several places in England. COCKLE dwelt in or near a field covered by Old English *coccel*, a common weed, or he was one who made and sold head coverings for women. CRUMBLE did not collapse but came from Cromwell "winding stream" in Nottinghamshire, GAMBLE is a respectable man, a descendant of Old Norse Gamall "old." GINGLE had an early ancestor named Gingold "ample, gold."

HUMBLE descends from Humbold "young bear, bold." MARBLE and MARPLE came from Marple "hill by the boundary valley" in Cheshire. RUMBLE is a descendant of Rumbeald "fame, bold," or of Rumwold "fame, forest." St. Rumwold was the infant prince of Northumbria who, upon being baptized, it is said, confessed himself a Christian, preached a sermon, and then died. TICKLE came from Tickhill "Tica's hill" in the West Riding of Yorkshire. TINDLE came from Tindale "Tyne valley" in Cumberland. TINGLE and TINKLE dwelt at or near the court or meeting place; in some cases TINGLE is a metonym for one who made Middle English *tingles* "small nails." TREMBLE was not timid; he and TRUMBLE descended from Trumbold "strong, bold." TWEEDLE does not derive from Tweedledum or Tweedledee, characters met by Alice in Wonderland, but designates the man who came from Tweedle "pasture dale" in Scotland.

Love enters into several English names. As a not uncommon family name LOVE has two distinct origins both from given names. It refers to a descendant of Love or Lufa, early English font names which mean "love." Or it may be interpreted to mean a descendant of Anglo-French Louve, feminine of *loup* "wolf." The principal diminutive forms of the name which became family names are LOVELL and LOVETT. FULLILOVE designates the man "full of love," a nickname for one with a passionate affection for one of the opposite sex.

LOVEJOY is simply the man who craved pleasure. LOVELESS was originally the man who was void of love or was unlovable, although in some cases it could mean one who loved a lass. The name did not prevent Herschel C. Loveless from becoming governor of Iowa in 1957. LOVELESS is often corrupted into LOVELACE. LOVELADY made love to, or flirted with, several women; the name may also denote a woman of easy virtue. Opposite of Lovelady are found both LOVEMAN and MANLOVE. The first has three interpretations, the servant of Love, the dear manor sweetheart, and the descendant of Leofman "beloved man." On the other hand MANLOVE is probably the philanthropic man, from Early English *mannlufe* "philanthropy."

284

Not all of these "loving" surnames are what they appear to be. LOVING names the man who came from Louvain "lions" in Belgium. FREELOVE is a descendant of Frithulaf "peace, survivor." LOVELY in medieval times had the sense of "loving, affectionate" and so denoted the loving or affectionate man. Others with the name dwelt at or near Lufa's clearing or wood, although another explanation is "one worthy to be praised." LOVELAND is not a name for one active in acquiring real estate, but is a place name, the man who came from Leaveland "Leofa's land" in Kent. LOVEMORE is a landscape name, the dweller in a moor infested by wolves. YOUNGLOVE when not a Swedish name refers to the young wolf or cub and is an animal or sign name. LOVERING designates the newcomer from Louvergny "Lovernios' estate" or Auvergni "Arvernus' estate," places in France. Finally, GODLOVE designates one addicted to the expression "God love (you)." Love does make the world go around.

With love such a part of life in the world it is not surprising to find a little hankey-pankey in the United States. Both Mr. Hankey and Mr. Pankey are found in some large telephone directories. HANKEY is a diminutive of Hank, a pet form of German Heinrich "home rule" and the more familiar form, Henry. A contributory origin is a sharpened form of Hane, a pet form of John. PANKEY is a German-Slavic name for a lordling or member of the minor nobility.

Fractions are always interesting. Would Halfmann be just a boy, half a man? Would he have to work a Doubleday to pull his weight? HALFMAN is from the German *haffman*, the worker at a seaport, a seaman. HALFPENNY may have been the man who held and farmed land for which he paid a yearly rental of half a penny. HALFHILL probably lived halfway up the hill. DOUBLEDAY has two meanings: first, the female servant of Dobb, a pet form of Robert "fame, bright," since day as a word sometimes has the connotation of "a female servant"; and second, the female servant of the twin, from Old French *double* "twin." WATMAN is a descendant of Hwaetman "bold, man," an Old English given name, when it is not used for a servant of Wat, the pet form of Walter "rule, army."

Some names have a pleasant aura from their relation to common English words. DANDY, for example, is not the fop who gives

AMERICAN SURNAMES

undue attention to elegant attire, or something that is particularly fine or first-rate. The name is derived from Scottish Dandy, a pet form of Andrew "man." GLAD is one who dwelt in the glade or descended from Glad, a short form of Gladwin "kind, friend." Mr. NICE descended from an ancestor who had lived in Nice "victory" in France. MARVEL is also French, a surname for one who came from Mereville "Merila's town" in France, except in those cases where it refers to the wonderful man, from Old French *merveille* "marvel." PEACE, so sorely needed in this world, is a variant of Pace, a name given to one born during the Passover festival or at Easter. In some cases it surnames a descendant of Pace, a pet form of Bonapace "good peace." PRETTY is the cunning, crafty man, from Old English *praettig* "a trick." TWEET dwelt in a forest clearing, a name derived from Old Norse *thveit* "a meadow." WHISTLER dwelt near the fork of a river, from Old English *twisla* "fork of a river." WISDOM came from Wisdom "knowledge," a hamlet in Devonshire.

But many more names appear in the form of words with unpleasant or derogatory connotations than with agreeable overtones. This is consistent with the tendency of nicknames to express a blunt, vulgar meaning. Both in nicknames and general slang usage, terms of disparagement loom far larger than those of encomium. There are said to be more slang synonyms for drunk than any other concept; there are numerous nicknames for ethnic groups, most of them derogatory; William Feather found fifty-two slang synonyms for wife, none of which expressed affection. Let us examine some American surnames found in this category.

As a surname BATTY does not have today's slang meaning of crazy, but designates little Batt, a pet form of Bartholomew "son of Talmai (furrow)." BELLY is the Frenchman who came from Bellay "wood of birch trees" in France. In Wales, BLOOD does not give one a gory sensation, but is derived from a coalescing of ap Lloyd, the son of Lloyd "gray." BONES is a nickname for one so thin that his bones protruded. BRAGG is the descendant of Brego "chief." BUGGIE and BUGGY descended from Buga "to stoop" or from an ancestor who came from Bugey in France. Because in England the word *bug* means a bedbug, there was quite a clacking of tongues when Joshua Bug announced that he was thereafter to be known as Norfolk Howard.

286

Surnames Not Properly Included Elsewhere

BUZZARD is a nickname from the buzzard, an inferior species of hawk useless for falconry, occasionally applied to a stupid, ignorant person. English CRUMB is the deformed, bent, stooping man, while Scottish CRUMMIE is the dweller on the lands of Crummy. DEADMAN, often spelled DEADMON or DEDMOND, is not a mimicry of Ed Sullivan by the comics of today, but is merely the man who came from Debenham "deep river homestead" in Suffolk. As a surname DRAGON is the dweller at the sign of the dragon or a nickname for one thought to possess features resembling the mythical monster. The name is also metonymic for Old French *dragonier* "standard-bearer."

DRUNKEN is a Swedish soldier name from Drucken "drunken," a name certain to make the news items when the bearer is picked up for you know what. DULL is the Scotsman who came from Dull "a plain," a village and parish in Perthshire, while English DULLARD is clearly a nickname for a dull or stupid person. DUMM, and DUMMER with the toponymic termination -*er*, dwelt on or near the *dun* "hill." DUST is a descendant of Dust, a pet form of Thurstan "Thor's stone," although in some cases it must be interpreted as one with a dust-colored complexion. FAKE derives from Fauke, variant of Fulco "people," a very common Old English given name spelled in several different ways. In the same way FLUKE is derived from other spellings of Fulco.

HUNGER need not be quickly fed; he came from Ongar "grazing land" in Essex. Some, however, interpret this name as a variant of Hungar "bear cub, army," an unrecorded given name. IDLER is the man from Idle "shining bright, or uncultivated land," the name of several villages in England. LOONEY is an Irish name for a warrior or soldier; it is also derived from Luinneach "merry or jovial." MORON is a diminutive form of the name More "swarthy." MULE is a German name from *mühle* "mill," the dweller near the mill. QUARRELLS came from Quarles "circles" in Norfolk. German SAPP cannot be interpreted from the current slang meaning, but is a descendant of Sabbe, a short form of names beginning with Sache "legal action," such as Sacbert and Sagebrecht.

SICK and SICKMAN are German family names with simple explanations. The first is a descendant of Sicco, a short form of names beginning with Sieg "victory," as Sigibold and Sigifrith. The second is a descendant of Sigmund "victory, protection." SMELLEY is the citizen who moved from Smalley "narrow wood" in Derbyshire. SWEAT is the "dear or beloved man," a descendant of Swet "agreeable," the name of a landholder mentioned in Domesday Book holding land in the time of King Edward the Confessor. TART came from Tarrant, the name of several places on the Tarrant "flooder," a river in England. TEUFEL, the German word for devil, as a family name usually designates the descendant of Tiefel, a pet form of Theudobald "people, bold," although in some cases it is a nickname. WORMS is a German family name for one from Worms "high plain," a city in Germany. WORST is metonymic for a maker or seller of sausages in Germany.

There are numerous family names that are spelled the same as ordinary English words but which have little or no relation to the English word. Several will be explained here. Most of them are far from common but everyone will know some people with these names. ASKEW is not crooked but is the person from Aiskew "oak wood" in Yorkshire. BODY is Hungarian, a man who came from Bod "meadow" in Hungary. BUTTERS descended from Botthar or Bothere "messenger, army." CASHMAN is an Irish surname, the grandson of Casan "little curly-haired one." Irish COFFEE is the grandson of Cobhthach "victorious." Scottish DOLLAR formerly lived in Dollar "dale of plowed land" in Clackmannanshire. Robert Dollar came to America to found a great shipping line where the canny Scotsman amassed many dollars.

DUDE, a name from Germany, may be interpreted as a descendant of Dudy "bagpipe," or as metonymic for a bagpiper. EVEN is a descendant of Even, a Swedish form of John. FIREMAN is a variant of Fairman "handsome man." German FURTHER designates one who came from Furth, a Jewish suburb of Nuremberg in Germany. FURY, from French *furet* figuratively "inquisitive," is a nickname for the inquisitive or nosy man. Such behavior can put one in a fury. GALLON is a descendant of little Gale "pleasant." HAMMER dwelt at the pasture ground or at the low, wet meadow, or if German, from Hamm "forest," a city in Germany. HOLY is a Czechoslovakian nickname for a bare man, one without clothing. HUMAN is the servant of Hugh "spirit."

Surnames Not Properly Included Elsewhere

JUSTICE, if not found elsewhere, can be observed in our telephone directories. The surname designates either a descendant of Justus "the just" or one who performed the functions of a judicial officer, a judge. German LUSH is the dweller in or near a marsh. English MANNERS is the man who came from Mesnieres "to remain (residence)" in France. METCALF, far from being an ironic substitution for Turnbull, is not a nickname at all. It is the dweller at or near the meadow where calves were kept. MONEY denotes the man whose ancestor came from Monnaie "mint" in France. MUCHMORE sounds lavish or even superabundant but it merely names the English dweller in the large marsh or extensive high wasteland.

OFFICER is a translation of the German *offizier* "the senior official." ONION is a descendant of Welsh Einion or Annion "anvil, or upright," names of several important early Welsh men. ONLY is the man who formerly lived in Onley "lonely glade" in Northamptonshire. OVERALL dwelt in or near the upper hall. RABBIT has little to do with hares, being only the descendant of little Rab, a short form of Raban "raven" or of Little Rabb, a Scottish pet form of Robert "fame, bright." READY is always Ready, a descendant of little Read "red," the nickname for a redhead, or of little Read or Red, pet forms of Redmond "counsel, protection," or, in some cases, the Scotsman from Reedie in Angus. RIDEOUT is a descendant of Ridwulf "horseman, wolf," although some authorities hold that it connotes a dweller near a fortification.

SELF is a contraction of Old English Saewulf "sea, wolf." SIX is a descendant of Sixte "sixth" or one who came from Sixte "sixth" in France. Sixte, the usual Latin form being Sixtus, was the name of three saints who occupied the papal throne before the end of the fifth century plus a pope with this name who died in 1484 and another a hundred years later. SPECK is one who came from Speke "brushwood" in Lancashire. STOREY and STORY are descendants of little Store or Stori "strong or powerful." SUCH was the dweller in the field newly cleared where the tree stumps still appeared, from Old French *souche* "tree stump." SWALLOW either dwelt in a deep hollow or came from Swallow "rushing river" in Lincolnshire. TRUMP descended from Trum, a pet form of names beginning with Trum "strong," as Trumbald and Trumwine. In some cases, however, it is metonymic for a trumpeter.

AMERICAN SURNAMES

Twist is from Old English *twisla* "fork of a river, or land in such a fork" and thus means one who dwelt near the fork of a river. Vinegar is a respelling of Winegar "friend, spear." Walkup does not refer to an apartment building of several floors, but designates the man who came from Wallop "valley of the stream" in Hampshire. Welcome is a pleasant name for one who came from Welcombe "valley with a stream" in Devonshire. Whisker is one who had Wiscard "wise, hard" for an ancestor. Whitecotton dwelt in one of the small white cottages.

All of these names spelled as ordinary English words are illustrations of the universal tendency to change the spelling of a name to that of a familiar word. It is this kind of corruption that produces so many names that are difficult of interpretation. In earlier times when spelling was more in the discretion of the user there was little to prevent this wholesale perversion of surnames.

Pancake is an English metonym for one who made and sold pancakes, although it could be a nickname for one referring to some unknown incident involving griddlecakes. In some cases the name is merely a translation of the German Pfannkuche, also found in our directories in several spellings. There is also the Polish Placek with the same meaning. Pancakes were enjoyed everywhere. These names remind one of the man who visited an insane asylum where a patient convinced him of his sanity saying that he was being detained merely because he liked pancakes.

"Why, that's no reason to keep you here. I like pancakes, too."

"Do you?" replied the inmate. "Come up to my room, I have a whole trunkful of them."

Some family names just seem to have a funny, curious, waggish, sometimes affectionate sound—a gentle breeze of whimsey—to them. German Bopp, which reminds one of a rap on the head in America, originated as an innocent descendant of Bube "lad," if not just a childish lall name. Cuddy is descendant of Cuddy, a pet form of Cuthbert "famous, bright." St. Cuthbert was a seventh-century English monk but Americans insist on regarding the name with a supercilious airiness. Curley came from Curley "turn in the road" in Scotland, or from Curley "Curilla's dwelling" in France, except in those cases where his name called attention to his curly hair. Dingus, a slang term for an indefinite object, is an English dweller in a house in a narrow valley. Duddy is both

rish and English, the grandson of Dubhda "black," or one whose
ncestor came from Duddy "Dudda's enclosure," a lost place
ame in Sussex.

FUZZEY is the Frenchman who made and sold steel used to
gnite combustibles, certainly not a common occupation even be-
ore friction matches were invented. Russian GOLUB is a small
mouthful for people in the United States; his ancestor dwelt at
he sign of the pigeon or dove if the name is not a metonym for
ne who raised and sold pigeons. Scottish KIDDIE is a son of Addie,
a double diminutive of Adam "red earth." KITTY is a descendant
f little Kitt, a pet form of Christopher "Christ-bearer" and of
Katherine "pure." TREMBLY came from Trimley "Trymma's
grove" in Suffolk. TRICK has two origins—the trusty true man,
rom Old Norse *tryggui* "trusty," and a metonymic name for one
who cheats or deceives.

TWEEDIE is the Scotsman who came from the lands of Tweedie
"hemming in," in the parish of Stonehouse, Lanarkshire. POPOFF,
often transliterated POPOV, is a very respectable, staid name re-
erring to "the descendant of the priest" in Russia. TWITTY is the
man who came from Thwaite "forest clearing," the name of places
n Norfolk and Suffolk. YELL is the Scotsman who came from Yell
"barren," one of the Shetland Islands. German YELLIN dwelt at
he sign of the red deer, one of the house names adopted by the
Ashkenazic Jews.

Finally some attention must be given to a few miscellaneous
odd names that should not be ignored. There is BACCHUS, a surname not related to Bacchus the Roman god of wine; it simply
refers to "the back house." And the back house referred to is not
he old-time back house so familiar to rural America, but nothing
more than the residence back of another. BARBEE is the Frenchman with the beard. BESSER is a Danish name from Besser "better
place" in Denmark, although it also designates the German who
collected fines. BOOZ, besides being a slang term for strong drink,
indicates as a personal name descent from Biblical Boaz "in Him
is strength," or it is from Old English *bothe* "hut or stall." BOYLAN
refers to one who came from Boyland "Boia's grove" in Norfolk.

BRANDY is a French family name designating a descendant of
Brand "sword," the more common form of which is BRANDON.
BROADFOOT is a Scottish family name of one whose ancestor came

291

from Bradford "wide river crossing," the name of several place
in England. The termination -foot is often a corruption of -ford
CATTENHEAD does not refer to a cat's head but is simply the mar
who had an ancestor who formerly lived in Cattenhall "Catta'
corner" in Cheshire. It may be readily observed that Old Englisl
halh "corner" can easily be changed to hall, and influence of the
first element causes it to alter further into head. CHILDERS is a
contraction of childer-house or children's house, that is, an or
phanage, and refers to one who operated such a place or who
resided nearby.

FEATHER was a dweller at the sign of the feather or one who
dealt in feathers. FURNESS, sometimes spelled FURNISH or FUR
NACE, is a place name referring to one who came from Furnes:
"podex headland" in Lancashire, or in some cases from Furneau:
"furnaces" in France. PICKLE came from Pickhill "Picca's nook, or
nook by the hills" in the North Riding of Yorkshire. GOINGS and
GOINS are French family names for descendants of Gudin "God's
friend." GRAMMER is not a child's term for his female grand
parent, but designates the grammarian or scholar. GUESS, a soft
ened form of Guest, is from Old English gast "the accepted
stranger, the newcomer or guest." The bearer of such a name
often carelessly replies with the enigmatic "guess" upon being
asked his name, which is likely to irritate the one who enquires
GUM is the man, from Old English guma "man," probably in the
sense of servant.

HANDLOSER had an early German forebear who occupied land
for which he paid a yearly rent in money rather than in work
Many strange men are addressed, "Hey! man," but German
HEYMAN has really accepted the name, probably having a me
dieval ancestor named Hagimar "hedged place, famous." In other
cases the name is derived from Hagen "hedged place" in Ger
many, or, if Jewish, one who descended from Hyam "life." Occasionally the newspapers call attention to a Chinese named I; this
is the first syllable of a Manchu's name which sometimes serves
as the family name. IRONS is an English and Scottish name referring to the immigrant from Airaines "brass" in France. English
JUMP possibly dwelt near a steep cliff or else came from the village of Jump "leap" in the West Riding of Yorkshire, although
there is no evidence of the town's existence in early times.

RIPLEY, believe it or not, is the man who formerly resided in Ripley "long narrow wood," the name of several villages in England. SHACKLEY is interesting in that it may refer to a very early criminal inclination from Old English *sceacere* "robber." The name derives from the village of Shackerley or the village of Shakerley, both in Lancashire, which translate as "wood of the robbers." REVERE is an English name meaning "robber," although as a French name it signifies one who came from Riviere "riverbank," villages in France and Belgium. The American patriot, Paul Revere, was of French extraction. Dutch SHY dwelt in or near the brushwood. SIDNEY, occasionally spelled SYDNEY, is a contraction of St. Denis which itself is a contraction of Dionysius, the Grecian god of wine. St. Denis is the name of several villages in France. English STORM is a descendant of Storm "tempest," although in some cases it is a nickname for the stormy, excitable man. TEACHOUT which reminds one of the modern extralegal "teach-ins" is merely a descendant of little Tache "spot or blemish."

VENUS has nothing to do with the Roman goddess of love and beauty. The name designates the immigrant from Venoix in France or from Venice "bluish" in Italy. WOODEN did not have a phlegmatic, wooden disposition necessarily, but did have a forefather who dwelt at the end of the wood, or who came from either Wooden "wolves' valley" in Northumberland or Woodend "end of the wood" in Northamptonshire. German WURM (the medieval mind allowed itself free expression) derives from Wurm, a short form of names beginning with Wurm "worm," as in Wurmhari.

Some names are of passing interest to people in the United States from familiarity with characters in the popular American comic strips. English GUMP, a name made famous by the late Sidney Smith, the *Chicago Tribune* cartoonist, is the man who dwelt on or near the flat place. A well-known comics character, Boob McNutt, a name schoolboys were fond of applying to their companions, cast a derogatory aroma on the Irish-Scottish family name McNUTT. Those with this name are sons of Nuadha "ancient sea divinity" or of Neachtan "pure one." BUMSTEAD is slightly sullied by the character portrayed by Chic Young in the comic strip *Blondie*, although it is a respectable, even dignified place name designating the man from Bumpstead "reedy place" in Essex. In line with the American comic strip characters is FRANK-

293

ENSTEIN, the name impaired by association with the monste created by Frankenstein in the tale by Mary W. Shelley. Thi surname is derived from Frankenstein "the Frank's stone," th name of several places in Germany. To the American motion pic ture industry Frankenstein was the monster.

A name curious to Americans of English ancestry is the no uncommon family name DeJESUS found among Spanish- and Por tuguese-speaking people. It is a religious name adopted by lay men to express devotion to Jesus, the idea being similar to, bu not identical to, the practice of nuns and other religious wh upon entering a Catholic order take a saint's name or the name o a mystery such as John of Jesus. DE CHRISTO is also found amon; the Portuguese, but is not nearly so common as DeJesus.

SONNTAG and FREITAG are two German family names whicl may be translated into English SUNDAY and FRIDAY, and many do The surnames originate from descendants of men with thes names which were sometimes given because of birth on thes days. Why Sunday and Friday were more used than the othe days is difficult to explain. Perhaps it was recognized that Sunda was different from other days—not a workday. Friday was a sac day, a solemn and gloomy day, thought to be unlucky in allusio to the crucifixion of the Savior and to the Roman Catholic insist ence on fasting on that day. FRIDAY may have been a nicknam applied to one who had a Friday-face, a dejected man. The othe days of the week, with the exception of Monday, explained else where, do not appear to have had any appreciable effect on th formation of surnames. There was nothing to set them apart.

Then there is the name FINK "finch," quite a respected nam until the labor unions commenced to use the term to describe strikebreaker or other man who labored contrary to the wishe of the union. It has been observed, perhaps facetiously, that re spectable families could change the spelling, if not the pronun ciation, by adopting the form Fynck or even Phynque. Peopl named Finch are sometimes careful to spell their name to avoic Fink as illustrated by the chief character in the play and motio picture *How to Succeed in Business Without Really Trying.*

Many more in proportion to the population are found with ex ceptional and rare names or spellings in early America, as show by the collections made by Bowditch in his *Suffolk Surnames* during the first half of the nineteenth century than at the present time. Far from poking fun at the curiosities of nomenclature is the thought of delving into the problem of how our names came about and how they became Americanized.

Some families, such as the ffrenches and the ffulkes, so write their names, not through snobbery but from ignorance of the fact that in seventeenth century documents the normal way of writing *F* was *ff,* a symbol almost indistinguishable from two f's. Then they find their names listed as Ffrench and Ffulke. Over the years many have changed or altered the names to escape the repeated witticisms that seem to amuse the empty-headed person who utters them. Almost any name can, by the alteration of a few letters, slide into a disguise where the meaning appears to be entirely different from the original form.

The British custom of hyphenated surnames is quite rare in America. The English practice usually indicates the merger through marriage of two important land-owning families. Wealthy American families often own little land. In the United States a few women, upon marriage, are reluctant to drop their maiden name entirely and thus hyphenate it with their husband's name. There is some reason for this if they have achieved a business or professional reputation, but most of them in this situation merely continue the use of their maiden surname alone. Aggressive, independent, masculine women sometimes use hyphenated names to indicate individuality according to some psychologists. In general, Americans tend to ridicule the practice.

These hyphenated names do present a problem to library cataloguers. Under which name do they list the author with an hyphenated name? The British Museum Library lists Edward George Earle Lytton Bulwer-Lytton under Bulwer while the Library of Congress includes him under Lytton. *Webster's Biographical Dictionary* lists him under Lytton while *The New Century Cyclopedia of Names* prefers Bulwer-Lytton. Both reference books, however, do include cross-references. Bulwer-Lytton's son, Edward Robert Bulwer-Lytton, is put under Lytton by the British Museum. *Webster's* follows, but the *Century Cyclopedia* lists him under his pseudonym of Owen Meredith.

Hungarians with Chinese, Japanese, and many other Asiatics put the surname first in their native countries, but in the United

States they quickly reverse the order to comply with usual West ern custom. Some famous travelers or musicians temporarily in this country have found it expedient to alter for a short time the order of their names. A man like Szigeti Joseph, the eminent Hun garian musician, while in the United States and other countrie outside of Hungary, is generally known as Joseph Szigeti. In the Social Security lists are found some persons with family name consisting of only a single letter, such as X, Y, and Z. In fact, o the entire alphabet, only Q was not found in 1964 in the Socia Security list. Most of these are, of course, artificial names, bu some are words in languages other than English.

When a terminal -s is added to a personal name as in Edward and Williams, or the diminutives as Hutchings and Philpotts, o pet forms as Gibbs, Hicks, and Watts it could refer to the son o descendant, or to the wife or widow or servant of the man desig nated. In these cases it must be regarded as the genitive or pos sessive form, except in cases where it was arbitrarily added at later date. The addition of -s as it developed later was doubtles just fashion or force of habit, a friendly but meaningless ending to a name. Such names as MASTERS, PARSONS, or NUNNS have the genitival -s and mean the servant at the master's house or the parson's or nunnery.

Americans seem to recognize clearly that certain surnames serve to denominate many families, and to aid identification there is a tendency to use the full first name together with the middle name or initial, while in Europe the popular practice seems to be to use initials only with the surname. For example, the martyred civil rights' leader is always called Martin Luther King, Jr., never M. L. King, Jr.

Americans are fond of poking fun at the English pronunciation of certain surnames, especially the families who pronounce BEAUCHAMP as Beecham, CHOLMONDELEY as Chumley, and St. JOHN as Sinjin. The pronunciation of St. CLAIR as Sinclair has made the latter spelling the common form in both England and America. In the current edition of Who's Who in America Paul E. Taliaferro lists the pronunciation of his name as Toliver. Topping these, however, is the famous Virginia family named Enroughty who pronounced it Darby, a story that has been rejected by many s too fantastic for belief. Although H. L. Mencken in the earlier ditions of his *The American Language* recounted the Enroughty-Darby tale, he explained it in Supplement Two to the Fourth Edition (1948) as two names. Charles Earle Funk in the Revised Edition of his *What's The Name, Please?* (1937) stated that he ad established beyond question that the story was not merely egendary. He quoted from an item in the Baltimore *Sun* of January 24, 1882, under a Richmond, Virginia, date line which chronled the death of Nathan Enroughty or Darby and then ex-lained: "Deceased was the oldest member of the family well-nown in this section, whose name by some remarkable perver-ion was called Darby instead of Enroughty, which continued for nore than half a century and is still kept up." The supposed ex-lanation is that the Darby family was promised a considerable nheritance if it would change its name to Enroughty. It met the ondition but continued the name as Darby in conversation.

In the United States the most common combination of fore-ame and surname is Mary Smith. For men it is William Smith, vho leads John Smith by about three percent. The Browns, oneses, Millers, and Wilsons have more sons named William than ny other name, while the Johnsons, Martins, and Andersons pre-er John. For the Williamses and the Davises James is the most opular forename. For girls all of these families prefer Mary.

The following list of the fifty commonest names in 1790 in this ountry is calculated from the census taken in that year. The ensus of 1790 is probably the only large census ever taken where tatistics were made of surnames. The list is taken from those ecords and the number set opposite each name includes various pellings of the name. Due to the invasion and burning of Wash-ngton by the British or the subsequent Patent Office fire, part of he records were destroyed or lost and the schedules are missing or the states and territories of New Jersey, Delaware, Virginia, Georgia, Kentucky, and the Southwest Territory (Tennessee). he records are complete for what is now Maine, New Hamp-hire, Vermont, Massachusetts, Rhode Island, Connecticut, New 'ork, Pennsylvania, Maryland, North Carolina, and South Caro-na. Partial returns are available from the state enumerations of 'irginia which are included. The total population of the states ncluded was 2,505,371. The total number of surnames was 27,337,

AMERICAN SURNAMES

Name	Number	Name	Number	Name	Numbe
1. Smith	33,245	18. Reed	6,897	35. Phillips	4,88
2. Brown	19,185	19. Baker	6,798	36. Stewart	4,87
3. Johnson	15,004	20. Green	6,764	37. Robinson	4,65
4. Jones	14,300	21. Lewis	6,699	38. Foster	4,60
5. Davis	14,300	22. Martin	6,678	39. Roberts	4,51
6. Clark	13,766	23. Thomas	6,516	40. Richardson	4,49
7. Williams	12,717	24. Stevens	6,352	41. Cole	4,45
8. Miller	12,694	25. Parker	6,339	42. Jackson	4,42
9. Wilson	9,797	26. Wright	6,306	43. Campbell	4,31
10. White	9,523	27. Rogers	5,975	44. Scott	4,31
11. Taylor	9,447	28. Young	5,847	45. Wheeler	4,22
12. Thompson	9,390	29. Cook	5,812	46. Turner	4,15
13. Allen	8,894	30. Harris	5,764	47. Russell	4,12
14. Moore	8,701	31. Walker	5,616	48. Stone	4,09
15. Hall	8,315	32. Pierce	5,440	49. Lee	4,07
16. Hill	7,162	33. Bailey	5,106	50. Bennett	4,04
17. Adams	6,958	34. King	4,972		

making an average of 16.2 families per name, and 91.6 perso
per name.

Today the twenty most common American family names in th
United States in order of frequency are: Smith, Johnson, William
Brown, Jones, Miller, Davis, Wilson, Anderson, Taylor, Moor
Thomas, Martin, Thompson, White, Harris, Jackson, Clark, Lewi
and Walker. Due to differences in ethnic groups and the influ
of peoples at different times speaking various languages and r
gional dialects this list differs in different cities in the countr
To determine the twenty most common surnames in certain re
resentative cities counts have been made in the telephone dire
tories of those cities. In New York counts had to be made in a
five boroughs since the differences were quite marked. It is rea
ized that some ethnic groups may have fewer telephones in pr
portion to their numbers, but it is not believed that this will alt
these proportions in any significant manner.

In this study the general explanation of common surnames
the assumption that they arose under the same or similar circum
stances in many different places or at many different times,
two or more names coalesced into a single accepted spelling. Th

Surnames Not Properly Included Elsewhere

SURNAMES IN CITIES IN ORDER OF FREQUENCY

Boston	Chicago	New York	Mil-waukee	Minne-apolis	San Francisco
Sullivan	Johnson	Smith	Johnson	Johnson	Smith
Smith	Smith	Cohen	Smith	Anderson	Johnson
Murphy	Williams	Brown	Miller	Nelson	Lee
Johnson	Brown	Williams	Schmidt	Peterson	Williams
Brown	Jones	Johnson	Anderson	Olson	Wong
Cohen	Anderson	Miller	Mueller	Larson	Brown
McCarthy	Miller	Schwartz	Brown	Carlson	Jones
White	Davis	Levine	Schultz	Smith	Anderson
Williams	Jackson	Davis	Williams	Miller	Miller
O'Brien	Harris	Friedman	Krueger	Thompson	Davis
Miller	Thomas	Goldstein	Meyer	Brown	Wilson
Davis	Wilson	Harris	Schneider	Williams	Taylor
Kelly	Nelson	Jones	Jones	Jones	Young
Jones	Taylor	Rodriguez	Peterson	Martin	White
MacDonald	White	Levy	Schroeder	Wilson	Thompson
Wilson	Moore	Goldberg	Davis	McDonald	Moore
Martin	Robinson	Murphy	Fischer	Lee	Martin
O'Connor	Thompson	White	Martin	Davis	Murphy
King	Martin	Martin	Thompson	White	Thomas
Harris	Lewis	Lewis	Wilson	Clark	Sullivan

kelihood that they became the names of many families by reason
f the extreme fecundity of a few early bearers of the name can-
ot be entirely ignored, but the laws of probability militate
gainst it.

In 1964, the United States Department of Health, Education,
nd Welfare, Social Security Administration made a report of the
Distribution of Surnames in the Social Security Account Number
"ile." The file contained 152,757,455 account numbers. By ma-
hine count covering the first six letters it was found that there
vere 1,091,522 different surnames in the file. Therefore, there is a
onsiderably larger number of family names in this country, since
uch names as Martin, Martina, Martinaga, Martinaitis, Martinak,
Martinat, Martincevic, Martinchuk, Martincic, Martindale, Mar-
ne, Martineau, Martinec, Martineck, Martinek, Martinel, Mar-
nelli, Martinello, Martinenas, Martiner, Martines, Martinesi,
Martinet, Martinez, Marting, Martingilio, Martini, Martiniak,

AMERICAN SURNAMES

Martinic, Martinich, Martinicky, Martinico, Martiniques, Mar
tinka, Martinkenas, Martinko, Martinkus, Martino, Martinott
Martinov, Martinovic, Martinovich, Martinowski, Martins, Mar
tinsen, Martinsesh, Martinski, Martinsky, Martinson, Martinu
Martinucci, Martinus, Martinussen, and Martiny, all to be foun
in the Chicago telephone directory, were listed as only one name
the first six letters being the same. Thus, the author calculate
that there must be upwards of 1,500,000 different surnames in th
United States. Some day, perhaps, an exact and complete machin
count of the Social Security lists will be made.

Besides the twenty-five surnames consisting of just one lette
mentioned earlier, the Department counted 253 names with onl
two letters, 3,634 with three letters, 31,255 with four letters, an
143,078 with five letters. The count disclosed that about eighty
four percent of all surnames in America had six or more letter

Following is a list of the two thousand most common surname
in America in order of frequency with estimated number of pe
sons in the United States with each name, roughly calculate
from the machine count in the Social Security Administratio
report above mentioned. The spelling of the names after the firs
six letters is the author's work, and the ranking position of suc
names in the list and their estimated number is consequently les
accurate than the short names which are dependent only on th
computer. In this day and age computers hold the reverence an
respect of the people that college graduates enjoyed at the tur
of the century. Even so, the work of the computer must b
checked carefully as it can dredge up misleading names. Fo
example, it lists the non-existent surname De La as 933rd in ran
and the equally non-existent Van De as 1357th in rank. Ther
may be such names, but the writer has never come across then
they are certainly not common. There are many names precede
by these prepositions and articles separated from the rest of th
name and they could become surnames where the last part c
the name is dropped through ignorance. It is easy to see how th
machine could go wrong and the explanation is the same as tha
given for the blunders of the famous mechanical man in the ol
comic strip: "Brains it has nix." An additional comment must b
made as to the accuracy of the estimates of the number of pe
sons bearing each name. Where it consists of five or fewer letter

300

Surnames Not Properly Included Elsewhere

ιe estimates are quite correct, but where a name consists of six
: more letters and the first six letters would stand for more than
ιe name, the estimates are consequently much less exact.

MOST COMMON SURNAMES IN THE UNITED STATES

ank	Surname	Estimated No. of Persons	Rank	Surname	Estimated No. of Persons
1	Smith	2,238,400	34	Roberts	350,300
2	Johnson	1,684,300	35	Mitchell	345,300
3	Williams	1,348,000	36	Campbell	339,000
4	Brown	1,268,400	37	Phillips	337,400
5	Jones	1,230,500	38	Carter	322,500
6	Miller	1,076,100	39	Evans	316,100
7	Davis	972,500	40	Turner	305,800
8	Wilson	737,300	41	Collins	301,700
9	Anderson	712,500	42	Parker	299,800
10	Taylor	648,400	43	Murphy	297,900
11	Moore	646,900	44	Rodriguez	292,600
12	Thomas	632,800	45	Edwards	289,900
13	Martin	603,400	46	Morris	285,530
14	Thompson	594,500	47	Peterson	282,300
15	White	592,200	48	Cook	279,800
16	Harris	587,800	49	Rogers	278,400
17	Jackson	576,500	50	Stewart	273,100
18	Clark	513,600	51	Morgan	254,800
19	Lewis	457,900	52	Cooper	251,100
20	Walker	450,900	53	Reed	249,200
21	Hall	437,600	54	Bell	248,400
22	Robinson	429,000	55	Kelly	246,400
23	Allen	426,700	56	Wood	245,600
24	Young	423,800	57	Bailey	245,300
25	King	404,900	58	Garcia	242,000
26	Nelson	401,400	59	Ward	241,300
27	Wright	401,000	60	Cox	239,300
28	Baker	388,000	61	Griffin	231,300
29	Hill	386,200	62	Howard	229,400
30	Scott	378,800	63	Bennett	228,500
31	Adams	378,700	64	Brooks	224,900
32	Green	375,800	65	Watson	224,100
33	Lee	361,300	66	Gray	223,500

AMERICAN SURNAMES

Rank	Surname	Estimated No. of Persons	Rank	Surname	Estimated No. of Persons
67	Sullivan	222,100	106	Snyder	165,400
68	Hughes	218,100	107	Ford	165,100
69	Myers	217,700	108	Martinez	164,600
70	Ross	217,300	109	Gibson	164,000
71	Long	216,400	110	Burns	160,100
72	Price	211,000	111	Bryant	159,600
73	Russell	207,800	112	Hernandez	159,100
74	Richardson	207,300	113	Wells	158,300
75	Fisher	207,000	114	Porter	156,100
76	Foster	206,400	115	Owens	153,700
77	Henderson	203,900	116	Wagner	153,500
78	Sanders	198,300	117	Gordon	150,000
79	Powell	197,700	118	Spencer	149,560
80	Perry	196,900	119	Tucker	149,550
81	Butler	196,200	120	Crawford	149,480
82	James	192,400	121	Webb	148,600
83	Jenkins	192,100	122	Stevens	148,550
84	Barnes	191,600	123	Meyer	148,550
85	Gonzalez	189,600	124	Perez	148,350
86	Reynolds	187,100	125	Woods	147,980
87	Patterson	185,400	126	Mason	147,750
88	Wallace	181,600	127	Shaw	147,550
89	Graham	181,500	128	Simpson	147,500
90	Simmons	180,200	129	Stone	146,400
91	Coleman	179,900	130	Freeman	146,200
92	Hamilton	179,400	131	Palmer	146,000
93	Lopez	178,500	132	Ryan	143,700
94	Rivera	176,500	133	Rice	143,300
95	Murray	175,500	134	Johnston	143,100
96	Cole	174,100	135	Fox	142,400
97	McDonald	173,900	136	Hunter	142,350
98	Alexander	172,900	137	Henry	142,220
99	West	172,700	138	Black	140,900
100	Hayes	172,500	139	Hunt	140,100
101	Ellis	167,800	140	Holmes	139,800
102	Marshall	166,700	141	Warren	139,300
103	Kennedy	166,500	142	Kelley	138,200
104	Jordan	166,100	143	Boyd	137,300
105	Olson	165,600	144	Hicks	137,000

Surnames Not Properly Included Elsewhere

Rank	Surname	Estimated No. of Persons	Rank	Surname	Estimated No. of Persons
145	Elliott	136,300	184	Perkins	119,900
146	Rose	136,000	185	Nichols	119,800
147	Carlson	135,350	186	Riley	119,500
148	Ferguson	135,300	187	Ray	119,200
149	Dunn	135,200	188	Greene	119,050
150	Mills	135,100	189	Grant	118,300
151	Hansen	134,500	190	Hudson	117,900
152	Andrews	134,100	191	Wheeler	117,500
153	Arnold	132,800	192	Chapman	116,600
154	Dixon	131,700	193	Willis	115,300
155	Schwartz	131,500	194	Oliver	114,400
156	Pierce	130,750	195	Lynch	113,800
157	Gardner	130,700	196	Richards	113,100
158	Little	130,550	197	Lawrence	112,700
159	Carroll	130,000	198	Gilbert	112,600
160	Cunningham	129,200	199	Watkins	112,100
161	Hart	128,800	200	Harrison	111,950
162	Hawkins	127,700	201	Schneider	111,900
163	Hoffman	127,550	202	Schultz	111,500
164	Weaver	127,500	203	Carr	110,700
165	Stephens	127,300	204	Walsh	110,500
166	Knight	126,300	205	Harper	110,400
167	Washington	126,200	206	Fullerton	109,900
168	Payne	125,800	207	George	108,500
169	Berry	124,500	208	Bishop	106,800
170	Lane	124,490	209	Weber	106,200
171	Armstrong	124,350	210	Peters	105,800
172	O'Brien	124,100	211	Holland	105,600
173	Burke	123,100	212	Hanson	105,500
174	Robertson	122,600	213	Montgomery	103,940
175	Duncan	121,500	214	Howell	103,800
176	Sanchez	121,100	215	Jensen	103,650
177	Carpenter	120,850	216	Harvey	103,500
178	Matthews	120,800	217	Austin	103,000
179	Cohen	120,660	218	Morrison	102,000
180	Bradley	120,640	219	Franklin	101,900
181	Larson	120,600	220	Keller	101,500
182	Daniels	120,500	221	Davids	100,100
183	Torres	120,100	222	Dean	99,900

AMERICAN SURNAMES

Rank	Surname	Estimated No. of Persons	Rank	Surname	Estimated No. of Persons
223	Welch	99,750	262	Jacobs	85,30
224	Newman	99,600	263	Caldwell	85,10
225	Douglas	99,580	264	Banks	85,00
226	Lawson	98,800	265	Wade	84,80
227	Garrett	98,600	266	McDaniels	83,40
228	Fowler	98,400	267	Benson	82,95
229	Day	97,900	268	Swanson	82,90
230	Reid	97,200	269	Winters	82,88
231	Barrett	96,800	270	Stanley	82,80
232	Curtis	96,700	271	Jennings	82,45
233	Pearson	96,550	272	Lowe	82,40
234	Bowman	96,100	273	Norris	82,00
235	May	95,800	274	McCormack	81,70
236	McCoy	95,300	275	Sutton	80,80
237	Burton	95,000	276	Rhodes	80,70
238	Becker	94,980	277	Chambers	80,35
239	Sims	94,600	278	Wolfe	80,30
240	Higgins	94,100	279	Erickson	80,20
241	Ortiz	93,700	280	Holt	80,00
242	Beck	93,600	281	Vandermeer	79,85
243	Leonard	93,400	282	Strickland	79,84
244	Barnett	92,900	283	Barker	79,80
245	Atkins	92,800	284	Warner	79,30
246	Hopkins	92,300	285	Steele	79,00
247	McCarthy	92,100	286	Parks	78,90
248	Williamson	91,900	287	Lyons	78,70
249	Lambert	91,800	288	Barber	78,30
250	McKinnon	90,400	289	Frazier	78,26
251	Lucas	89,100	290	O'Connor	78,13
252	Fields	88,600	291	Byrd	78,05
253	Powers	88,500	292	Neal	77,83
254	Hammond	88,400	293	Hale	77,82
255	Ramirez	87,800	294	Watts	77,65
256	Brewer	87,750	295	Gregory	77,52
257	Craig	86,950	296	Page	77,47
258	Cummings	86,500	297	Graves	77,15
259	Bates	85,900	298	Gross	77,00
260	Fleming	85,890	299	Shelton	76,80
261	Klein	85,800	300	Mann	76,78

Surnames Not Properly Included Elsewhere

Rank	Surname	Estimated No. of Persons	Rank	Surname	Estimated No. of Persons
301	Walters	76,680	340	Moss	70,380
302	Harding	76,510	341	Potter	70,200
303	Flores	76,500	342	Goodwin	70,140
304	McLaughlin	76,480	343	Chandler	70,030
305	Bush	76,360	344	Rodgers	69,920
306	Christensen	76,260	345	Ramsey	69,620
307	Fitzgerald	76,160	346	Zimmerman	69,530
308	Horton	75,950	347	Brady	69,210
309	Quinn	75,900	348	Hardy	69,200
310	Jacobson	75,840	349	Saunders	69,130
311	Doyle	75,540	350	Blair	69,070
312	Vaughn	75,530	351	Walter	69,010
313	Fischer	75,490	352	Cross	68,660
314	Ball	75,230	353	Cruz	68,590
315	Robbins	75,130	354	Love	68,400
316	Baldwin	74,800	355	Newton	67,830
317	Dawson	74,760	356	Reese	67,260
318	Ramos	74,410	357	Frank	67,140
319	Haynes	74,290	358	Burgess	66,950
320	Fletcher	74,170	359	Webster	66,580
321	Schroeder	73,810	360	Harmon	66,220
322	Parsons	73,740	361	Berger	66,010
323	Miles	73,660	362	Bowers	65,990
324	Thornton	73,490	363	Todd	65,850
325	Reeves	73,290	364	Bridges	65,840
326	Terry	72,730	365	Curry	65,830
327	Goodman	72,640	366	Waters	65,320
328	Morales	72,300	367	Gomez	65,240
329	Manning	72,290	368	Moran	65,200
330	Stevenson	72,240	369	Norman	64,960
331	Sherman	72,150	370	Rowe	64,810
332	Bowen	72,020	371	Walton	64,680
333	Sharp	71,700	372	Flynn	64,590
334	Wolf	71,680	373	McGee	64,570
335	Diaz	71,570	374	Simon	64,510
336	Gallagher	71,440	375	Mueller	64,480
337	McCullum	71,310	376	Barton	64,350
338	Petersen	70,500	377	Santiago	64,190
339	Hendricks	70,430	378	Harrington	64,140

Rank	Surname	Estimated No. of Persons	Rank	Surname	Estimated No. of Persons
379	Summers	64,130	418	Fernandez	60,275
380	Meyers	63,990	419	Marsh	60,270
381	Hubbard	63,920	420	Daniel	60,250
382	Weiss	63,910	421	Patton	60,180
383	Garner	63,890	422	Ingram	59,760
384	Wise	63,870	423	Single	59,550
385	Cannon	63,840	424	Mathews	59,540
386	Bauer	63,750	425	Gill	59,510
387	Mack	63,740	426	Hogan	59,290
388	Buchanan	63,700	427	Lang	58,820
389	Nicholson	63,640	428	Wilcox	58,080
390	Conner	63,500	429	Drake	57,980
391	Olsen	63,490	430	Hess	57,880
392	Norton	63,400	431	Adkinson	57,810
393	McGuire	63,240	432	Moody	57,720
394	Gonzales	63,200	433	Glover	57,530
395	Owen	63,190	434	Reyes	57,130
396	Casey	63,130	435	Pope	57,120
397	Townsend	63,110	436	Gibbs	57,050
398	Kramer	63,060	437	Pratt	56,890
399	French	63,020	438	Tate	56,850
400	Cochran	62,980	439	Farrell	56,680
401	Dennis	62,900	440	Richard	56,550
402	Hodges	62,870	441	Floyd	56,530
403	Farmer	62,660	442	Shaffer	56,440
404	Blake	62,460	443	McBride	56,390
405	Herman	62,440	444	MacDonald	56,220
406	Hines	61,970	445	Lamb	55,800
407	Maxwell	61,960	446	Tyler	55,700
408	Paul	61,610	447	Yates	55,580
409	Francis	61,460	448	Sparks	55,510
410	Andersen	61,420	449	Decker	55,420
411	Wilkins	60,980	450	Carson	55,400
412	Clarke	60,910	451	Burnett	55,380
413	Cobb	60,870	452	Lloyd	55,370
414	Logan	60,830	453	Cain	55,220
415	Roth	60,710	454	Mullins	55,200
416	Osborne	60,510	455	Garrison	55,070
417	Morton	60,460	456	Ballard	54,950

Surnames Not Properly Included Elsewhere

Rank	Surname	Estimated No. of Persons	Rank	Surname	Estimated No. of Persons
457	Carey	54,940	496	Patrick	51,230
458	Hampton	54,860	497	Randall	51,080
459	Herring	54,380	498	Stein	51,050
460	Larsen	54,320	499	Roberson	51,045
461	Hutchinson	54,180	500	Goldstein	50,970
462	Malone	54,170	501	Chase	50,870
463	Wall	53,600	502	Underwood	50,855
464	Briggs	53,590	503	Dickerson	50,680
465	Nash	53,550	504	Greer	50,520
466	Foley	53,530	505	Bass	50,360
467	Stokes	53,400	506	McNeil	50,270
468	Harrell	53,375	507	McMillan	50,210
469	Holloway	53,300	508	Huff	50,130
470	Lindsey	52,980	509	Hood	50,100
471	Sweeney	52,460	510	Skinner	49,970
472	Shepherd	52,450	511	Kirby	49,950
473	Hoover	52,400	512	Shield	49,870
474	Horn	52,360	513	Bruce	49,820
475	Jefferson	52,270	514	Davenport	49,780
476	Callahan	52,250	515	Colon	49,760
477	Collier	52,230	516	Kirk	49,760
478	Churchill	52,140	517	Mathis	49,755
479	Berg	52,110	518	Copeland	49,690
480	Humphrey	52,080	519	Goldberg	49,410
481	Morrow	52,030	520	Boyer	49,380
482	Brennan	52,010	521	Monroe	49,340
483	Kane	52,005	522	Parrish	49,180
484	Bryan	51,910	523	McClure	49,150
485	O'Neill	51,870	524	Poole	49,145
486	Clayton	51,860	525	Phelps	49,040
487	Abbott	51,720	526	Allison	48,990
488	Brock	51,700	527	Gates	48,975
489	Short	51,695	528	Levine	48,880
490	Golden	51,690	529	Whitehead	48,880
491	Camero	51,670	530	Schaefer	48,600
492	Silva	51,590	531	Booth	48,550
493	Sawyer	51,460	532	Hartman	48,475
494	McFarland	51,430	533	Friedman	48,290
495	Koch	51,420	534	Marks	48,270

AMERICAN SURNAMES

Rank	Surname	Estimated No. of Persons	Rank	Surname	Estimated No. of Persons
535	Mullen	48,090	574	Garza	45,480
536	Gutierrez	48,030	575	Eaton	45,270
537	Middleton	48,015	576	McDowell	45,260
538	Bond	47,810	577	Wiley	45,210
539	Bartlett	47,800	578	Dyer	45,205
540	McCall	47,780	579	Kerr	45,195
541	Whitaker	47,690	580	Kline	45,170
542	Ruiz	47,665	581	York	45,100
543	Massey	47,660	582	Levy	45,095
544	Kaufman	47,655	583	Boone	45,010
545	Springer	47,574	584	Buckley	45,000
546	Wiggins	47,510	585	Alvarez	44,980
547	Conley	47,350	586	Reilly	44,970
548	Huffman	47,290	587	Preston	44,940
549	Houston	47,090	588	Hensley	44,910
550	Blackwell	47,080	589	Pitts	44,900
551	Silverman	47,030	590	Combs	44,895
552	Heath	47,000	591	Flowers	44,795
553	Grimes	46,960	592	Rosenberg	44,790
554	Blanchard	46,720	593	Nolan	44,760
555	O'Donnell	46,670	594	Small	44,620
556	Russo	46,660	595	Roy	44,500
557	Baxter	46,550	596	McKenzie	44,490
558	Wyatt	46,460	597	McConnell	44,410
559	Vincent	46,380	598	Johns	44,300
560	Barry	46,310	599	Christian	44,280
561	Hancock	46,160	600	Anthony	44,230
562	Joseph	46,080	601	Beard	44,210
563	Glenn	46,050	602	Barr	44,175
564	Romero	45,940	603	Ware	44,170
565	Bradford	45,920	604	McKee	44,165
566	Rich	45,900	605	Chavez	44,110
567	Cline	45,860	606	Merritt	43,860
568	Gilmore	45,835	607	Gillespie	43,710
569	Savage	45,790	608	Shannon	43,670
570	Wilkinson	45,730	609	Conway	43,460
571	Dalton	45,680	610	Schoen	43,440
572	Dillon	45,610	611	Mayer	43,265
573	Hodge	45,550	612	Orr	43,260

Surnames Not Properly Included Elsewhere

Rank	Surname	Estimated No. of Persons	Rank	Surname	Estimated No. of Persons
613	English	43,240	652	Clay	40,870
614	Medina	43,200	653	Stout	40,720
615	Hobbs	42,910	654	Vaughan	40,700
616	Howe	42,890	655	Bernard	40,680
617	Stafford	42,880	656	Maloney	40,620
618	Leach	42,855	657	O'Neal	40,610
619	Roach	42,820	658	Wilkerson	40,550
620	Pittman	42,805	659	Pritchard	40,470
621	Donald	42,720	660	Browning	40,310
622	Keith	42,675	661	Glass	40,275
623	Kemp	42,660	662	Hahn	40,220
624	Livingston	42,650	663	Edmonds	40,160
625	Melton	42,600	664	Figueroa	40,110
626	Conrad	42,470	665	Hurst	39,960
627	Donnell	42,465	666	Vance	39,890
628	Morse	42,380	667	Dougherty	39,865
629	McIntyre	42,350	668	McClain	39,800
630	Snow	42,310	669	Griffith	39,765
631	Hendrickson	42,260	670	Nielsen	39,710
632	Knapp	42,130	671	Weeks	39,695
633	Castro	42,120	672	Everett	39,610
634	Solomon	41,840	673	Henson	39,580
635	Boyle	41,760	674	Fitzpatrick	39,490
636	Buck	41,740	675	Katz	39,200
637	Beasley	41,675	676	McLean	38,970
638	Gould	41,670	677	Prince	38,950
639	Hull	41,650	678	Billings	38,905
640	Donovan	41,610	679	Kaplan	38,890
641	Stark	41,550	680	Randolph	38,880
642	Tanner	41,500	681	Bullock	38,800
643	Strong	41,490	682	Gaines	38,710
644	Peck	41,460	683	Mahoney	38,700
645	Sloan	41,445	684	Lester	38,645
646	O'Connell	41,425	685	Bender	38,590
647	Duffy	41,340	686	Woodward	38,585
648	Vazquez	41,260	687	Woodard	38,490
649	Knox	41,160	688	Ellison	38,480
650	McMahon	41,070	689	Bradshaw	38,445
651	Kent	40,970	690	Dorsey	38,445

Rank	Surname	Estimated No. of Persons	Rank	Surname	Estimated No. of Persons
691	Dunlap	38,440	730	Brandt	36,320
692	Gentry	38,435	731	Haley	36,310
693	Frost	38,400	732	Novak	36,310
694	Noble	38,280	733	Rasmussen	36,250
695	Stephenson	38,190	734	Huber	36,220
696	Meadows	38,090	735	Whitney	36,205
697	Sellers	38,080	736	McGrath	36,200
698	Pennington	38,070	737	Rollins	36,160
699	Hurley	38,020	738	Davies	36,100
700	Moreno	38,015	739	McIntosh	36,030
701	Durham	37,990	740	Blackman	35,995
702	McKenna	37,860	741	Crosby	35,990
703	Shea	37,810	742	Stuart	35,760
704	Castillo	37,800	743	Alberts	35,720
705	Case	37,570	744	Roman	35,700
706	Pugh	37,485	745	Ritter	35,650
707	Werner	37,460	746	McDermott	35,600
708	Bright	37,405	747	Pruitt	35,550
709	Crane	37,260	748	Pace	35,545
710	Valentine	37,210	749	Jiminez	35,400
711	Hays	37,200	750	McGinnis	35,340
712	Hickman	37,195	751	Rush	35,260
713	Fry	37,190	752	Frederick	35,255
714	Calhoun	37,175	753	Greenberg	35,150
715	Shepard	37,165	754	Sexton	34,960
716	Krueger	37,140	755	Vasquez	34,880
717	Mooney	37,005	756	Dodson	34,850
718	Blackburn	37,000	757	Bentley	34,835
719	Maldonado	36,990	758	Costello	34,800
720	Moyer	36,910	759	Baird	34,795
721	McCann	36,840	760	Dudley	34,770
722	Krause	36,820	761	Giles	34,735
723	Irwin	36,795	762	Daugherty	34,670
724	Haas	36,770	763	Joyce	34,635
725	McKay	36,705	764	Ayers	34,630
726	Charles	36,540	765	Farley	34,620
727	Santos	36,535	766	Hayden	34,560
728	Potts	36,400	767	Delgado	34,555
729	Raymond	36,380	768	Moon	34,550

Surnames Not Properly Included Elsewhere

Rank	Surname	Estimated No. of Persons	Rank	Surname	Estimated No. of Persons
769	Lynn	34,535	808	Burch	32,930
770	Finley	34,465	809	Cowan	32,880
771	Sanford	34,455	810	Fritz	32,830
772	Shoemaker	34,410	811	Sampson	32,735
773	Schulz	34,330	812	Walls	32,730
774	Benton	34,305	813	Pollard	32,675
775	Soto	34,300	814	Holden	32,565
776	Waller	34,275	815	Horne	32,495
777	Frey	34,205	816	Mays	32,465
778	Holcomb	34,180	817	Crockett	32,455
779	Avery	34,170	818	McPherson	32,450
780	Mosley	34,135	819	Proctor	32,435
781	Hartley	34,055	820	Sheppard	32,420
782	Dickson	34,040	821	Kaiser	32,415
783	Faulkner	34,030	822	Richmond	32,380
784	Holder	33,955	823	Herrera	32,375
785	Nixon	33,930	824	Kuhn	32,310
786	Daly	33,850	825	Mercer	32,285
787	Gorman	33,840	826	Streeter	32,275
788	Madden	33,805	827	Branch	32,270
789	Bean	33,780	828	Clements	32,260
790	Lowery	33,780	829	Rowland	32,230
791	Cooke	33,750	830	Ewing	32,140
792	LeBlanc	33,745	831	Merrill	32,130
793	Stanton	33,740	832	Vargas	32,110
794	Estes	33,570	833	Carney	32,065
795	Coffey	33,565	834	Good	32,040
796	Best	33,430	835	Sorensen	31,995
797	Frye	33,420	836	Hebert	31,990
798	Lutz	33,375	837	Pedersen	31,940
799	Hooper	33,355	838	Lindsay	31,880
800	Connelly	33,235	839	Cherry	31,865
801	Shapiro	33,200	840	Riddle	31,860
802	Christiansen	33,190	841	Pearce	31,845
803	Gay	33,170	842	Moses	31,840
804	Duke	33,065	843	Fink	31,815
805	Compton	33,055	844	Crowley	31,785
806	Hester	33,030	845	Delaney	31,730
807	Maddox	32,955	846	Brownell	31,700

Rank	Surname	Estimated No. of Persons	Rank	Surname	Estimated No. of Persons
847	McGowan	31,675	886	Snider	30,665
848	Downs	31,650	887	Wilder	30,635
849	Ferrell	31,645	888	O'Neil	30,630
850	Braun	31,625	889	Landry	30,610
851	Guthrie	31,590	890	Kessler	30,600
852	McCollum	31,560	891	Cramer	30,575
853	Spears	31,510	892	Hanna	30,565
854	Gustafson	31,445	893	Mendoza	30,485
855	Donahue	31,440	894	Kinney	30,480
856	Barron	31,430	895	Feldman	30,460
857	Petty	31,410	896	Jarvis	30,435
858	Fulton	31,375	897	Castle	30,390
859	Hickey	31,370	898	Forbes	30,360
860	Flanagan	31,350	899	Rivers	30,360
861	Welsh	31,350	900	Rios	30,340
862	Galloway	31,345	901	Sutherland	30,330
863	Vogel	31,310	902	Vega	30,305
864	Mendez	31,275	903	Richter	30,275
865	Riggs	31,275	904	Padilla	30,260
866	Maynard	31,265	905	Osborn	30,250
867	Witt	31,115	906	Booker	30,240
868	Goldman	31,100	907	Rosen	30,215
869	Connolly	31,030	908	Velez	30,185
870	Bird	31,005	909	Travis	30,155
871	Wong	30,970	910	Chamberlain	30,130
872	Lange	30,935	911	Gamble	30,065
873	Slater	30,920	912	Terrell	30,060
874	Gibbons	30,905	913	Singer	30,055
875	McCabe	30,845	914	Bray	30,050
876	Haines	30,840	915	Marino	30,036
877	Muller	30,835	916	Schaffer	29,960
878	Schreiber	30,830	917	Odell	29,930
879	Archer	30,790	918	Cantrell	29,930
880	Newell	30,760	919	Byers	29,910
881	Sears	30,745	920	Haney	29,840
882	Swartz	30,715	921	Schmitt	29,790
883	Ashley	30,705	922	Dailey	29,745
884	Robison	30,705	923	Siegel	29,735
885	Gilliam	30,700	924	Cotton	29,670

Surnames Not Properly Included Elsewhere

Rank	Surname	Estimated No. of Persons	Rank	Surname	Estimated No. of Persons
925	Lyon	29,655	964	Bonner	28,560
926	Hinton	29,645	965	Herbert	28,530
927	Cooley	29,630	966	Woodruff	28,460
928	Goff	29,605	967	Hewitt	28,445
929	Steward	29,500	968	Kern	28,390
930	Lancaster	29,495	969	Waldron	28,315
931	Stern	29,485	970	Downing	28,305
932	Kenney	29,455	971	Pierson	28,300
933	Valdez	29,450	972	Cornell	28,280
934	Bolton	29,425	973	Blevins	28,260
935	Byrne	29,400	974	Sweet	28,185
936	Dolan	29,395	975	Chaney	28,175
937	Hatfield	29,345	976	Rubin	28,160
938	Bacon	29,335	977	Dickinson	28,130
939	Odom	29,320	978	Pickett	28,110
940	Holman	29,295	979	Doherty	28,080
941	Winkler	29,280	980	Nicholas	28,080
942	Michaels	29,260	981	Hastings	28,040
943	McLeod	29,145	982	Bernstein	28,015
944	Tracy	29,130	983	Park	27,995
945	Mackey	29,085	984	Sharpe	27,985
946	Dwyer	29,075	985	Hyde	27,975
947	Larkin	29,055	986	Kidd	27,965
948	Beach	29,050	987	Key	27,960
949	Dodd	29,020	988	Munoz	27,890
950	Mayo	29,010	989	Steiner	27,885
951	Emerson	29,005	990	Carver	27,840
952	Camp	28,995	991	Silver	27,835
953	Hoffmann	28,980	992	Moser	27,825
954	McKnight	28,845	993	Salazar	27,775
955	Benjamin	28,820	994	Hartmann	27,700
956	Starr	28,755	995	Cleveland	27,690
957	Abrams	28,750	996	Molina	27,685
958	Kendall	28,750	997	Chappell	27,680
959	Bloom	28,748	998	Barlow	27,670
960	Sheehan	28,740	999	Rutherford	27,650
961	Lake	28,710	1000	Tuttle	27,630
962	Finch	28,665	1001	Dale	27,610
963	Heller	28,590	1002	Elder	27,590

AMERICAN SURNAMES

Rank	Surname	Estimated No. of Persons	Rank	Surname	Estimated No. of Persons
1003	McFadden	27,575	1042	Connors	26,200
1004	Espinosa	27,550	1043	Cash	26,195
1005	McNamara	27,415	1044	Minor	26,160
1006	Whitten	27,290	1045	Godfrey	26,155
1007	Helms	27,270	1046	Bruno	26,095
1008	Field	27,210	1047	Talley	26,088
1009	Guzman	27,190	1048	Grady	26,060
1010	Hopper	27,160	1049	Pate	26,025
1011	Crowe	27,150	1050	David	26,015
1012	Ritchie	27,150	1051	Fraser	26,005
1013	Craft	27,090	1052	Connor	25,990
1014	Knowles	27,070	1053	Melendez	25,960
1015	Franks	27,050	1054	England	25,955
1016	Kirkpatrick	26,990	1055	Denton	25,915
1017	Farris	26,975	1056	Corbett	25,875
1018	Wills	26,970	1057	Mayfield	25,870
1019	Britt	26,875	1058	Thomson	25,868
1020	Alford	26,830	1059	Hoskins	25,860
1021	Britton	26,830	1060	Beatty	25,810
1022	Metcalf	26,800	1061	Courtney	25,790
1023	Slaughter	26,740	1062	Wooten	25,785
1024	Steinberg	26,720	1063	Ziegler	25,775
1025	Costa	26,700	1064	Gleason	25,765
1026	Downey	26,690	1065	Schiller	25,760
1027	Temple	26,685	1066	Brenner	25,680
1028	Head	26,680	1067	Pena	25,605
1029	Arthur	26,670	1068	Ott	25,520
1030	Currier	26,640	1069	Kirkland	25,515
1031	Dillard	26,630	1070	Rankin	25,495
1032	Domingo	26,625	1071	Pike	25,490
1033	Cassidy	26,590	1072	Emery	25,485
1034	Hilton	26,560	1073	Lowry	25,470
1035	Childers	26,510	1074	Webber	25,460
1036	Curran	26,505	1075	Dick	25,420
1037	Holley	26,360	1076	Wynn	25,405
1038	Dempsey	26,355	1077	Castello	25,400
1039	Conklin	26,345	1078	Locke	25,375
1040	Clemens	26,250	1079	Belcher	25,365
1041	Sargent	26,225	1080	Henning	25,295

Surnames Not Properly Included Elsewhere

Rank	Surname	Estimated No. of Persons	Rank	Surname	Estimated No. of Persons
1081	McGill	25,275	1120	Koenig	24,280
1082	Burt	25,270	1121	Tompkins	24,245
1083	McCauley	25,270	1122	Crow	24,240
1084	Whitfield	25,240	1123	Gillis	24,230
1085	Pryor	25,205	1124	Dotson	24,220
1086	Driscoll	25,200	1125	McManus	24,210
1087	Workman	25,185	1126	Boyce	24,205
1088	Rossi	25,125	1127	Tomlinson	24,195
1089	Hinkle	25,110	1128	Rosenthal	24,190
1090	Shafer	25,060	1129	Joyner	24,185
1091	Childs	25,045	1130	Padgett	24,170
1092	Gregg	25,030	1131	Ortega	24,160
1093	Albright	25,005	1132	Schumacher	24,157
1094	Lund	25,000	1133	Schell	24,155
1095	Justice	24,985	1134	Hollins	24,145
1096	Law	24,905	1135	Bergman	24,140
1097	Harden	24,895	1136	Burrows	24,115
1098	House	24,890	1137	Devine	24,110
1099	Whalen	24,860	1138	Cavanaugh	24,105
1100	Burris	24,840	1139	Kimball	24,097
1101	Fish	24,710	1140	Pollock	24,095
1102	Rutledge	24,615	1141	Simms	24,090
1103	Simons	24,600	1142	Hutchins	24,080
1104	Funk	24,590	1143	Whitley	24,070
1105	Langley	24,585	1144	Brandon	24,050
1106	Puckett	24,545	1145	Bland	24,025
1107	Wolff	24,495	1146	Block	24,020
1108	Stringer	24,485	1147	Tyson	24,005
1109	Tillman	24,480	1148	Foreman	23,980
1110	Grace	24,465	1149	Greenwald	23,940
1111	Crouch	24,460	1150	Plummer	23,935
1112	Lord	24,455	1151	Kitchen	23,920
1113	Kendrick	24,430	1152	Seymour	23,913
1114	McElroy	24,400	1153	Egan	23,910
1115	Miranda	24,385	1154	Meier	23,900
1116	Dye	24,370	1155	Corbin	23,820
1117	DeWitt	24,365	1156	Sinclair	23,790
1118	Childress	24,330	1157	Sykes	23,785
1119	Shirley	24,310	1158	Grossman	23,750

AMERICAN SURNAMES

Rank	Surname	Estimated No. of Persons	Rank	Surname	Estimated No. of Persons
1159	Magee	23,740	1198	Rucker	23,155
1160	Meeks	23,730	1199	McDonough	23,153
1161	Ratliff	23,700	1200	Crabtree	23,135
1162	Guy	23,690	1201	Healy	23,130
1163	Dunbar	23,660	1202	Kay	23,130
1164	Morin	23,645	1203	Rouse	23,130
1165	Mercado	23,635	1204	Horner	23,110
1166	Dickey	23,600	1205	Engel	23,085
1167	Navarro	23,590	1206	Purcell	23,085
1168	Groves	23,585	1207	Bowles	23,080
1169	Goss	23,580	1208	Neff	23,065
1170	Coffman	23,530	1209	Eubanks	23,050
1171	Boggs	23,525	1210	Schafer	23,025
1172	Mobley	23,520	1211	Lockhart	23,010
1173	Weinstein	23,505	1212	Jamison	23,005
1174	Garland	23,495	1213	Wilhelm	23,000
1175	Schmitz	23,490	1214	Beaver	22,990
1176	Forrest	23,479	1215	Manley	22,990
1177	Kurtz	23,465	1216	Swift	22,990
1178	Couch	23,460	1217	Weston	22,985
1179	Hollis	23,460	1218	Herron	22,965
1180	Maher	23,450	1219	Stover	22,950
1181	Ludwig	23,440	1220	Yeager	22,945
1182	Butts	23,425	1221	Neely	22,925
1183	Whitlock	23,405	1222	Leslie	22,910
1184	Rosario	23,390	1223	Covington	22,900
1185	Nieves	23,340	1224	O'Leary	22,898
1186	Aguilar	23,335	1225	Buckner	22,885
1187	Stinson	23,333	1226	Erwin	22,870
1188	Alston	23,320	1227	Hatch	22,855
1189	Roe	23,315	1228	Hamm	22,850
1190	Acosta	23,305	1229	Clifton	22,825
1191	Dooley	23,300	1230	Mead	22,820
1192	Post	23,290	1231	Waldon	22,815
1193	Madison	23,288	1232	Drew	22,805
1194	Sheridan	23,280	1233	Pacheco	22,770
1195	Dunham	23,240	1234	Dodge	22,730
1196	Barrow	23,210	1235	Talbot	22,725
1197	McKinley	23,170	1236	Meredith	22,720

Surnames Not Properly Included Elsewhere

Rank	Surname	Estimated No. of Persons	Rank	Surname	Estimated No. of Persons
1237	Hagen	22,710	1276	Eldridge	22,115
1238	Griggs	22,705	1277	Dubois	22,105
1239	Guerrera	22,700	1278	Elkins	22,095
1240	Sprague	22,690	1279	Sandoval	22,080
1241	Swenson	22,675	1280	Quick	22,070
1242	Polk	22,670	1281	Gabriel	22,065
1243	Regan	22,655	1282	Vinson	22,060
1244	Swain	22,655	1283	Clifford	22,055
1245	Levin	22,650	1284	Diamond	22,000
1246	Womack	22,620	1285	Ames	21,995
1247	Jorgensen	22,600	1286	Dahl	21,970
1248	Blankenship	22,590	1287	Lehman	21,960
1249	Trujillo	22,575	1288	Gore	21,885
1250	Yarbrough	22,545	1289	Clement	21,880
1251	Crowder	22,535	1290	Gold	21,860
1252	Stroud	22,473	1291	Villarreal	21,855
1253	Alvarado	22,470	1292	Swan	21,840
1254	Ferris	22,442	1293	Lombardo	21,820
1255	Elmore	22,435	1294	Dickens	21,785
1256	Babcock	22,425	1295	Hand	21,780
1257	Davison	22,405	1296	Geiger	21,775
1258	Worley	22,395	1297	Strauss	21,760
1259	Bowden	22,380	1298	Grove	21,755
1260	Redmond	22,355	1299	Gunter	21,740
1261	Ambrose	22,350	1300	O'Hara	21,735
1262	Stratton	22,345	1301	Craven	21,725
1263	Berman	22,330	1302	Barnhart	21,715
1264	Otto	22,315	1303	Nix	21,700
1265	Stahl	22,285	1304	Esposito	21,695
1266	Cullen	22,280	1305	Coates	21,690
1267	Hutcheson	22,260	1306	Hatcher	21,677
1268	McClellan	22,230	1307	Burks	21,675
1269	Weiner	22,185	1308	Duran	21,675
1270	Teague	22,180	1309	Murdock	21,670
1271	Gunn	22,170	1310	Dugan	21,655
1272	Tipton	22,170	1311	Blanton	21,650
1273	Goodrich	22,150	1312	Isaacs	21,585
1274	Willard	22,145	1313	Romano	21,580
1275	Daley	22,125	1314	Lacy	21,560

AMERICAN SURNAMES

Rank	Surname	Estimated No. of Persons	Rank	Surname	Estimated No. of Persons
1315	Quinones	21,530	1354	Washburn	20,860
1316	Snell	21,500	1355	Burrell	20,855
1317	Ackerman	21,480	1356	Estrada	20,845
1318	McCallum	21,480	1357	Winn	20,835
1319	Burger	21,445	1358	Sherwood	20,825
1320	Draper	21,440	1359	Piper	20,805
1321	Smart	21,410	1360	Stiles	20,781
1322	Finn	21,380	1361	Jewell	20,740
1323	Greenwood	21,375	1362	Gallegos	20,665
1324	Yoder	21,345	1363	Marcus	20,650
1325	Crews	21,333	1364	Peacock	20,648
1326	Holbrook	21,330	1365	Thurman	20,612
1327	Jeffries	21,325	1366	Coker	20,610
1328	Ervin	21,310	1367	Mayes	20,605
1329	Ayala	21,305	1368	Broussard	20,604
1330	Milligan	21,265	1369	Gagnon	20,595
1331	Akers	21,263	1370	Urban	20,595
1332	Lorenz	21,240	1371	Boucher	20,575
1333	Lott	21,225	1372	Martino	20,570
1334	Kowalski	21,220	1373	Poe	20,570
1335	Painter	21,215	1374	Whitman	20,550
1336	Metzger	21,145	1375	Goode	20,550
1337	Nance	21,125	1376	Noel	20,545
1338	Serrano	21,125	1377	Waddell	20,540
1339	Bullard	21,120	1378	Sewell	20,525
1340	Sterling	21,118	1379	Battle	20,520
1341	Cahill	21,070	1380	Boudreau	20,500
1342	Hutchison	21,070	1381	Miner	20,480
1343	Bingham	21,030	1382	Darling	20,470
1344	Grimm	21,025	1383	Platt	20,450
1345	Link	21,024	1384	Reece	20,442
1346	Hennessy	21,012	1385	Carmichael	20,440
1347	Kraft	21,010	1386	Metz	20,405
1348	Pendergast	20,990	1387	Koehler	20,385
1349	Biggs	20,960	1388	Whaley	20,383
1350	Toth	20,950	1389	Phipps	20,380
1351	Inman	20,940	1390	Hackett	20,360
1352	Clemons	20,935	1391	Hoyt	20,350
1353	Bower	20,895	1392	Baumann	20,340

Surnames Not Properly Included Elsewhere

Rank	Surname	Estimated No. of Persons	Rank	Surname	Estimated No. of Persons
1393	Weir	20,325	1432	Schwab	19,820
1394	Tatum	20,305	1433	Helton	19,815
1395	Priest	20,300	1434	Sheets	19,795
1396	Lockwood	20,295	1435	Shipley	19,750
1397	DeJesus	20,290	1436	Latham	19,730
1398	Samuels	20,290	1437	Robles	19,705
1399	Coyle	20,285	1438	Carlton	19,700
1400	Maurer	20,270	1439	Christopher	19,680
1401	Luna	20,220	1440	Messina	19,665
1402	Butcher	20,195	1441	Givens	19,650
1403	Masters	20,188	1442	Bragg	19,635
1404	Rosado	20,180	1443	Spangler	19,625
1405	Ivey	20,175	1444	Amos	19,605
1406	Cronin	20,173	1445	McHugh	19,570
1407	Cote	20,170	1446	Aldridge	19,560
1408	Root	20,160	1447	Lovell	19,540
1409	Keenan	20,140	1448	Sadler	19,525
1410	Newsome	20,140	1449	Paulson	19,515
1411	Kearney	20,135	1450	Blue	19,430
1412	Montoya	20,105	1451	Sheldon	19,425
1413	Boswell	20,085	1452	Bunch	19,420
1414	Danielson	20,084	1453	Bassett	19,415
1415	Godwin	20,080	1454	Barnard	19,410
1416	Irvin	20,078	1455	Marquez	19,405
1417	Cartwright	20,045	1456	Tobin	19,400
1418	Bowling	20,036	1457	Guerra	19,395
1419	Carlisle	20,030	1458	Pettit	19,390
1420	Zimmer	20,016	1459	Diehl	19,382
1421	Hurd	20,015	1460	Coulter	19,380
1422	Colbert	20,013	1461	Hildebrand	19,380
1423	Colvin	20,010	1462	Caruso	19,315
1424	Blum	19,975	1463	German	19,300
1425	Voss	19,965	1464	Hanley	19,290
1426	McCray	19,960	1465	Yost	19,270
1427	Weinberg	19,945	1466	Dietz	19,265
1428	McWilliams	19,926	1467	Nunez	19,260
1429	Rainey	19,925	1468	Self	19,260
1430	Houser	19,910	1469	Thorne	19,240
1431	McCracken	19,840	1470	North	19,215

AMERICAN SURNAMES

Rank	Surname	Estimated No. of Persons	Rank	Surname	Estimated No. of Persons
1471	Ash	19,210	1510	Schuster	18,655
1472	Ernst	19,205	1511	Southern	18,655
1473	Hager	19,190	1512	Pagan	18,645
1474	Benedict	19,185	1513	Landers	18,635
1475	Epstein	19,155	1514	Hirsch	18,630
1476	Eddy	19,150	1515	Crump	18,600
1477	Sample	19,145	1516	Eckert	18,595
1478	Land	19,120	1517	Burkett	18,590
1479	Gee	19,115	1518	McGraw	18,570
1480	Lovett	19,090	1519	Trevino	18,567
1481	Thorpe	19,075	1520	Shearer	18,565
1482	Norwood	19,065	1521	Moseley	18,552
1483	Pappas	19,060	1522	Ogden	18,550
1484	Kraus	19,055	1523	Hurt	18,535
1485	Heard	19,030	1524	Burroughs	18,525
1486	Corder	19,028	1525	Hawley	18,523
1487	Westbrook	19,005	1526	Reeder	18,505
1488	Huggins	19,000	1527	Dennison	18,500
1489	Meade	18,980	1528	Sylvester	18,465
1490	Jacobsen	18,960	1529	Huddleston	18,450
1491	Flaherty	18,942	1530	Goldsmith	18,440
1492	Hilliard	18,940	1531	Read	18,425
1493	Rudolph	18,915	1532	Sapp	18,420
1494	Mansfield	18,910	1533	Putnam	18,415
1495	Hagan	18,880	1534	Culver	18,405
1496	Michael	18,880	1535	Fitch	18,370
1497	Adler	18,870	1536	Kahn	18,355
1498	Lilly	18,845	1537	McGhee	18,350
1499	Winston	18,840	1538	Tripp	18,335
1500	Stanford	18,805	1539	Henley	18,325
1501	Herndon	18,780	1540	Tolbert	18,320
1502	Kruse	18,775	1541	Crowell	18,315
1503	Rosa	18,775	1542	McMullen	18,305
1504	Engle	18,770	1543	Lanier	18,300
1505	Contreas	18,757	1544	Lehmann	18,300
1506	Beal	18,720	1545	Roche	18,300
1507	Chappelle	18,680	1546	Laird	18,298
1508	Perrin	18,680	1547	McNeal	18,296
1509	Hadley	18,665	1548	Kilgore	18,290

Surnames Not Properly Included Elsewhere

Rank	Surname	Estimated No. of Persons	Rank	Surname	Estimated No. of Persons
1549	Vogt	18,275	1588	Deal	17,860
1550	Story	18,255	1589	Dill	17,835
1551	Payton	18,250	1590	Beyer	17,810
1552	Dietrich	18,243	1591	Keating	17,810
1553	Gifford	18,240	1592	Melvin	17,810
1554	Mohr	18,225	1593	Schrader	17,805
1555	O'Rourke	18,215	1594	Hinson	17,800
1556	Doty	18,205	1595	Penn	17,790
1557	Holliday	18,203	1596	Cortez	17,780
1558	Corcoran	18,200	1597	Cornelius	17,776
1559	Duvall	18,175	1598	McQueen	17,775
1560	Baer	18,170	1599	Stapleton	17,765
1561	Langford	18,125	1600	Mullin	17,760
1562	Manuel	18,115	1601	Wiseman	17,755
1563	Acevedo	18,110	1602	Maguire	17,745
1564	Busch	18,105	1603	Albrecht	17,735
1565	Wallin	18,100	1604	Hightower	17,725
1566	McNally	18,085	1605	Milton	17,723
1567	Ramey	18,080	1606	Gary	17,720
1568	Raines	18,070	1607	Betts	17,715
1569	Abel	18,068	1608	Brantley	17,705
1570	Nowak	18,062	1609	Goins	17,670
1571	Major	18,060	1610	Roper	17,667
1572	Langston	18,045	1611	Timmons	17,660
1573	McClendon	18,040	1612	Altman	17,645
1574	Jarrett	18,026	1613	Ulrich	17,623
1575	Vickers	18,015	1614	Wesley	17,620
1576	Sumner	18,000	1615	Coughlin	17,617
1577	Ledbetter	17,995	1616	Seaman	17,617
1578	Spaulding	17,935	1617	Tidwell	17,617
1579	Hutton	17,930	1618	Farr	17,612
1580	Shaver	17,930	1619	Brand	17,590
1581	Gerber	17,925	1620	Doran	17,577
1582	Layton	17,915	1621	Hathaway	17,550
1583	Munson	17,895	1622	McLain	17,548
1584	MacKenzie	17,890	1623	Shultz	17,546
1585	Shelley	17,880	1624	Dobson	17,540
1586	Landis	17,870	1625	Hamlin	17,493
1587	Baum	17,863	1626	Posey	17,491

Rank	Surname	Estimated No. of Persons	Rank	Surname	Estimated No. of Persons
1627	Nesbitt	17,487	1666	Hargrove	17,110
1628	Rock	17,455	1667	Monahan	17,110
1629	Aldrich	17,445	1668	O'Malley	17,106
1630	Lovelace	17,440	1669	Kohler	17,044
1631	Thayer	17,425	1670	Lind	17,041
1632	Stubbs	17,410	1671	Fair	17,017
1633	Leon	17,385	1672	Wilkes	16,990
1634	O'Keefe	17,375	1673	Cope	16,955
1635	Hay	17,363	1674	Salinas	16,946
1636	Quigley	17,361	1675	Cates	16,943
1637	Conroy	17,350	1676	Bryson	16,941
1638	Rhoades	17,328	1677	Dowling	16,935
1639	DeLong	17,320	1678	Sherrill	16,920
1640	Cummins	17,318	1679	Kyle	16,913
1641	Rizzo	17,315	1680	McClintock	16,896
1642	Sands	17,305	1681	Mott	16,889
1643	Cody	17,280	1682	Dukes	16,872
1644	Coe	17,250	1683	Hauser	16,861
1645	Horvath	17,238	1684	Thacker	16,861
1646	Gallo	17,228	1685	Hummel	16,858
1647	McCaffrey	17,223	1686	Stallings	16,856
1648	Hyatt	17,221	1687	Zimmermann	16,856
1649	McDougall	17,220	1688	Friend	16,848
1650	Bateman	17,217	1689	Arrington	16,793
1651	Adair	17,198	1690	Velazquez	16,776
1652	Julian	17,194	1691	Lackey	16,769
1653	McGovern	17,194	1692	Souza	16,762
1654	Fay	17,185	1693	Doss	16,710
1655	Huston	17,180	1694	Champion	16,701
1656	Suarez	17,180	1695	McRae	16,689
1657	Smiley	17,178	1696	Oakes	16,672
1658	Mattson	17,173	1697	McCord	16,645
1659	Overton	17,168	1698	Finney	16,643
1660	Flood	17,165	1699	Hoff	16,641
1661	Stoner	17,162	1700	Trotter	16,633
1662	Weller	17,155	1701	Brewster	16,625
1663	Spivey	17,150	1702	Capps	16,608
1664	Fagan	17,138	1703	Dobbs	16,605
1665	Sheffield	17,136	1704	Lacey	16,600

Surnames Not Properly Included Elsewhere

Rank	Surname	Estimated No. of Persons	Rank	Surname	Estimated No. of Persons
1705	Kenny	16,589	1744	Arroyo	16,202
1706	Meehan	16,582	1745	Drummond	16,201
1707	Rooney	16,570	1746	Crain	16,185
1708	Arnett	16,565	1747	Brunner	16,183
1709	Darby	16,560	1748	Hankins	16,182
1710	Whittaker	16,556	1749	Camacho	16,178
1711	Hannah	16,528	1750	Mosher	16,178
1712	Staley	16,523	1751	Gentile	16,174
1713	Brannon	16,486	1752	Cleary	16,148
1714	Spicer	16,486	1753	Herrmann	16,137
1715	Boykin	16,474	1754	Thrasher	16,136
1716	Connell	16,473	1755	Crum	16,102
1717	Kellogg	16,462	1756	Ennis	16,098
1718	Steinman	16,462	1757	Parr	16,094
1719	Crandall	16,461	1758	Whittington	16,072
1720	Napier	16,436	1759	Masterson	16,068
1721	Kiser	16,409	1760	Calvert	16,064
1722	Laughlin	16,407	1761	Hawk	16,054
1723	Oakley	16,407	1762	Schuler	16,045
1724	Richey	16,405	1763	Woodson	16,026
1725	Moreland	16,389	1764	Burnham	16,014
1726	McDonnell	16,385	1765	Judd	16,011
1727	Coon	16,358	1766	Denny	15,989
1728	Brothers	16,352	1767	Epps	15,984
1729	Pfeiffer	16,337	1768	Light	15,980
1730	Purdy	16,333	1769	Duff	15,974
1731	Weathersby	16,324	1770	Willett	15,972
1732	Cardenas	16,320	1771	Cutler	15,968
1733	Foote	16,317	1772	Eastman	15,965
1734	Giordano	16,285	1773	McCain	15,960
1735	Kasminski	16,274	1774	Atwood	15,953
1736	Bledsoe	16,256	1775	Bolden	15,951
1737	Gaston	16,244	1776	Feliciano	15,946
1738	Bagley	16,227	1777	Pyle	15,942
1739	Bain	16,227	1778	Malloy	15,934
1740	VanDyke	16,223	1779	Fountain	15,921
1741	Pickens	16,210	1780	Salmon	15,918
1742	Blount	16,206	1781	Bracken	15,912
1743	Keene	16,204	1782	Darnell	15,905

Rank	Surname	Estimated No. of Persons	Rank	Surname	Estimated No. of Persons
1783	Mallory	15,905	1822	Leary	15,558
1784	Nickerson	15,904	1823	Woody	15,542
1785	Pendleton	15,900	1824	Unger	15,538
1786	Faust	15,881	1825	Abernathy	15,529
1787	Greco	15,830	1826	Hooker	15,520
1788	Borden	15,817	1827	Whiting	15,510
1789	Mims	15,809	1828	DeMarco	15,506
1790	Waite	15,801	1829	Burk	15,482
1791	Whiteside	15,800	1830	Gage	15,481
1792	Pepper	15,785	1831	Kincaid	15,465
1793	Mulligan	15,781	1832	Varner	15,461
1794	Corley	15,778	1833	Hillman	15,434
1795	Lucero	15,772	1834	Trimble	15,434
1796	Chadwick	15,761	1835	Davila	15,425
1797	Helm	15,756	1836	Kearns	15,420
1798	Madsen	15,753	1837	Chester	15,414
1799	Frankel	15,750	1838	McGregor	15,410
1800	Wetzel	15,738	1839	Loomis	15,409
1801	Dobbins	15,720	1840	Harman	15,408
1802	Ferrara	15,714	1841	Baron	15,405
1803	VanHorn	15,712	1842	Klinger	15,400
1804	Carrillo	15,707	1843	Rushing	15,400
1805	Shook	15,705	1844	Collett	15,398
1806	Vernon	15,702	1845	Beckman	15,390
1807	DeLuca	15,700	1846	Hobson	15,380
1808	Naylor	15,690	1847	Montague	15,378
1809	Rader	15,680	1848	Hough	15,376
1810	Ledford	15,675	1849	Prescott	15,370
1811	Dutton	15,669	1850	Keen	15,365
1812	Haywood	15,668	1851	Farrar	15,364
1813	Smallwood	15,657	1852	Reardon	15,361
1814	Nagy	15,653	1853	Dow	15,360
1815	Abraham	15,648	1854	Sommer	15,355
1816	Kimble	15,646	1855	Cohn	15,352
1817	Comer	15,638	1856	Queen	15,337
1818	Keys	15,625	1857	Cagle	15,336
1819	Trent	15,592	1858	Ransom	15,334
1820	Donohue	15,584	1859	Gale	15,329
1821	Knutson	15,581	1860	Starks	15,320

Surnames Not Properly Included Elsewhere

Rank	Surname	Estimated No. of Persons	Rank	Surname	Estimated No. of Persons
1861	Grover	15,304	1900	Sommers	14,960
1862	Lincoln	15,304	1901	Hare	14,952
1863	Stovall	15,302	1902	Hayward	14,909
1864	Burr	15,284	1903	Lentz	14,901
1865	Maier	15,280	1904	Ireland	14,892
1866	Stauffer	15,273	1905	Humphries	14,880
1867	Sneed	15,272	1906	Baumgartner	14,868
1868	Rider	15,270	1907	Hope	14,865
1869	Wilburn	15,265	1908	Pool	14,863
1870	Beebe	15,248	1909	Ruth	14,862
1871	Whitmore	15,245	1910	Bliss	14,857
1872	Skaggs	15,234	1911	Negron	14,857
1873	Tinsley	15,234	1912	Ladd	14,848
1874	Ashby	15,232	1913	Reagan	14,840
1875	McClelland	15,210	1914	Rodriquez	14,838
1876	Sauer	15,206	1915	Willoughby	14,838
1877	Thurston	15,188	1916	Power	14,809
1878	Triplett	15,178	1917	Meek	14,796
1879	Starnes	15,172	1918	Adamson	14,790
1880	Barth	15,168	1919	Cheek	14,776
1881	Alberts	15,165	1920	Paris	14,775
1882	Nugent	15,150	1921	Moeller	14,765
1883	Worthington	15,137	1922	Goddard	14,762
1884	Jacob	15,117	1923	Nagel	14,762
1885	Salter	15,112	1924	Paige	14,762
1886	Saylor	15,109	1925	John	14,761
1887	Crenshaw	15,106	1926	Christ	14,760
1888	Gipson	15,105	1927	Ham	14,756
1889	Newcomb	15,102	1928	Bruner	14,752
1890	McMurray	15,066	1929	Mock	14,748
1891	Wisniewski	15,057	1930	Flint	14,737
1892	Gruber	15,041	1931	Lawler	14,730
1893	Rapp	15,039	1932	Benoit	14,720
1894	Prather	15,037	1933	Stacy	14,718
1895	Lieberman	15,010	1934	Scruggs	14,709
1896	Means	15,004	1935	Bartley	14,700
1897	Hawthorne	14,996	1936	Hollen	14,693
1898	Watt	14,996	1937	Peoples	14,681
1899	Fenton	14,985	1938	Grubbs	14,676

AMERICAN SURNAMES

Rank	Surname	Estimated No. of Persons	Rank	Surname	Estimated No. of Persons
1939	Prater	14,675	1970	Hanks	14,457
1940	Waggoner	14,649	1971	Foss	14,449
1941	Brower	14,647	1972	Campos	14,445
1942	Beauchamp	14,642	1973	Fortner	14,433
1943	Calloway	14,632	1974	Fuchs	14,421
1944	Perdue	14,609	1975	Fuentes	14,416
1945	Schubert	14,605	1976	Presley	14,414
1946	St. John	14,598	1977	Sizemore	14,413
1947	Lunsford	14,596	1978	Grayson	14,412
1848	Hitchcock	14,590	1979	Akins	14,408
1949	Titus	14,578	1980	Parrott	14,408
1950	Fournier	14,573	1981	Tiller	14,386
1951	Tierney	14,573	1982	Barger	14,385
1952	Cantu	14,566	1983	Wray	14,369
1953	Conn	14,564	1984	Iverson	14,353
1954	Barbour	14,560	1985	Lay	14,328
1955	Ring	14,540	1986	Pack	14,318
1956	Corey	14,536	1987	Robins	14,310
1957	Stoddard	14,528	1988	Dumas	14,302
1958	Burdick	14,527	1989	Keyes	14,297
1959	Avila	14,513	1990	Rowell	14,281
1960	Cotter	14,511	1991	Gauthier	14,272
1961	Newmann	14,505	1992	Honeycutt	14,265
1962	Matheson	14,500	1993	Snodgrass	14,264
1963	Ryder	14,497	1994	Cottrell	14,246
1964	Hammer	14,490	1995	Skelton	14,240
1965	Hollingsworth	14,485	1996	Parkinson	14,238
1966	Eason	14,484	1997	Woodall	14,238
1967	Person	14,484	1998	Condon	14,230
1968	Gannon	14,461	1999	McNulty	14,201
1969	Purvis	14,458	2000	Ricks	14,201

Surely this list is a truly representative list of American surnames. Indeed, these are the American family names. This list contains English, Irish, Scottish, Welsh, German, French, Swedish, Norwegian, Danish, Italian, Spanish, Portuguese, Grecian, Polish, Hungarian, Russian, and Chinese names—all American names. Amen.

BIBLIOGRAPHY

For the reader whose interest in surnames has been heightened by his perusal of this work the following is a selective bibliography of the most useful books dealing in one way or another with family names, chosen from the author's private library of more than 1,200 works on personal names.

Adamic, Louis. *What's Your Name?* New York: 1942. Pp. xv, 248.

Bardsley, Charles Wareing. *A Dictionary of English and Welsh Surnames with Special American Instances.* London: 1901. Pp. xvi, 837.

――――. *English Surnames, Their Sources and Significations.* Ninth Impression, London: 1915. Pp. xxviii, 612.

Black, George Fraser. *The Surnames of Scotland.* New York: 1946. Pp. lxxii, 838.

Brown, Samuel L. *Surnames Are the Fossils of Speech.* Minneapolis: 1967. Pp. x, 350.

Carnoy, Albert. *Origin des Noms de Familles en Belgique.* Louvain: 1953. P. 408.

Chapuy, Paul. *Origine des Noms Patronymiques Français.* Paris: 1934. P. 351.

Constantinescu, N. A. *Dictionar Onomastic Romînescu.* Bucuresti: 1963. Pp. LXXVII, 470.

Cottle, Basil. *The Penguin Dictionary of Surnames.* Harmondsworth (England): 1967. P. 335.

Dauzat, Albert. *Dictionnaire Étymologique des Noms de Famille et Prenoms de France.* Paris: 1951. Pp. xxv, 604.

Ekwall, Eilert. *The Concise Oxford Dictionary of English Place-Names.* Fourth Edition. Oxford: 1960. Pp. li, 546.

Bibliography

Ewen, Cecil Henry L'Estrange. *A Guide to the Origin of British Surnames*. London: 1938. P. 206.

———. *A History of Surnames of the British Isles*. London: 1931. Pp. xx, 508.

Fransson, Gustav. *Middle English Surnames of Occupation 1100–1350 With an Excursus on Toponymical Surnames*. Lund: 1935. P. 217.

Fucilla, Joseph Guerin. *Our Italian Surnames*. Evanston: 1949. Pp. xi, 299.

Gottschald, Max. *Deutsche Namenkunde*. Dritte, Vermehrte Auflage. Berlin: 1954. P. 630.

Guppy, Henry Brougham. *Homes of Family Names in Great Britain*. London: 1890. Pp. lxvi, 601.

Harrison, Henry. *Surnames of the United Kingdom*. London: 1912–1918. 2 vols. Pp. iv, 290; viii, xvi, 332.

Hassall, W. O. *History Through Surnames*. Oxford: 1967. Pp. XV, 224.

Huizinga, A. *Encyclopedie Van Namen*. Amsterdam: 1955. P. 328.

Kneen, John Joseph. *The Personal Names of the Isle of Man*. London: 1937. Pp. lx, 295.

Lévy, Paul. *Les Noms des Israélites en France*. Paris: 1960. P. 210.

Linnartz, Kaspar. *Unsere Familiennamen*. Bonn: 1958. 2 vols. Pp. 280; 298.

Löfvenberg, Mattias Teodor. *Studies on Middle English Local Surnames*. Lund: 1942. Pp. XLVIII, 255.

MacLysaght, Edward. *A Guide to Irish Surnames*. Dublin: 1964. P. 248.

———. *Irish Families Their Names, Arms and Origins*. Dublin: 1957. P. 366.

———. *More Irish Families*. Galway & Dublin: 1960. P. 320.

———. *Supplement to Irish Families*. Dublin: 1964. P. 163.

Matthews, Constance Mary, *English Surnames*. London: 1966. P. 359; New York: 1967. P. 367.

Mencken, Henry Louis. *The American Language*. (Abridged edition by Raven I. McDavid). New York: 1963. Chapter X, pp. 572–701.

Names, Journal of the American Name Society. Vol. I, 1953, Continuing.

Pine, Leslie Gilbert. *The Story of Surnames*. London: 1965. P. 152.

Reaney, Percy Hide. *A Dictionary of British Surnames*. London: 1958. Pp. lxii, 366.

———. *The Origin of English Surnames*. London: 1967. Pp. xix, 415.

Redin, Mats. *Studies on Uncompounded Personal Names in Old English*. Uppsala: 1919. Pp. xlv, 195.

Rosenthal, Eric. *South African Surnames*. Cape Town: 1965. P. 262.

Bibliography

Smith, Elsdon Coles. *Dictionary of American Family Names.* New York: 1956. Pp. xxxvi, 244.

———. *Personal Names: A Bibliography.* New York Public Library. New York: 1952. Republished, Detroit, 1965. P. 226.

———. *The Story of Our Names.* New York: 1950. Pp. x, 296.

———. *Treasury of Name Lore.* New York: 1967. Pp. ix, 246.

Tengvik, Gösta. *Old English Bynames.* Uppsala: 1938. Pp. xxii, 407.

Thuresson, Bertil. *Middle English Occupational Terms.* Lund: 1950. P. 285.

Tibón, Gutierre. *Onomastica Hispano Americana.* Mexico: 1961. Pp. xi, 361.

Von Feilitzen, Olof. *The Pre-Conquest Personal Names of Domesday Book.* Uppsala: 1937. Pp. XXXI, 430.

Weekley, Ernest. *Surnames.* Third Edition, New York: 1937. Pp. xxii, 360.

———. *The Romance of Names.* Fourth Edition, London: 1928. Pp. xiii, 250.

Woulfe, Patrick. *Sloinnte Gaedheal is Gall. Irish Names and Surnames.* Dublin: 1923. Pp. XLVI, 696.

INDEX

330

Index

AMERICAN SURNAMES

Barnard, 55, 319
Barnas, 55
Barnes, 12, 302
Barnet, 55
Barnett, 55, 304
Barney, 84
Barnham, 216, 240
Barnhart, 317
Barnhill, 234
Barnum, 3, 216, 227
Baron, 174, 267, 324
Barr, 245, 308
Barrett, 76, 97, 304
Barrington, 235
Barron, 312
Barrow, 236, 316
Barry, 245, 308
Barrymore, 215
Bart, 67
Barta, 67
Bartels, 67
Barth, 154, 325
Bartholomew, 67
Bartlett, 45, 67, 308
Bartley, 325
Barto, 67
Bartok, 67
Barton, 236, 305
Bartos, 67
Bartz, 220
Baruch, 3, 98, 261
Barwick, 234
Bascom, 240
Basil, 72
Basile, 72
Bass, 156, 307
Bassett, 81, 156, 319
Bassler, 256
Basso, 156
Bastian, 83
Batchelor, 136
Bateman, 109, 322
Bates, 67, 304
Bateson, 67
Bath, 240
Batman, 109
Battaglia, 137
Battle, 67, 283, 318
Batts, 67
Batty, 67, 286
Bauer, 116, 306
Baughman, 116
Baum, 199, 321
Bauman, 116
Baumann, 318
Baumgartner, 325
Baxter, 111, 308
Bay, 151
Bayer, 255
Baylie, 139
Baylis, 139
Baynes, 149
Beach, 200, 313

Beadell, 138
Beal, 236, 320
Beam, 24, 195, 199
Bean, 24, 61, 311
Beane, 61
Bear, 8, 220
Beard, 153, 157, 238, 308
Bearse, 65
Beasley, 214, 309
Beaton, 67
Beatty, 67, 314
Beauchamp, 244, 296, 326
Beaumont, 242
Beaupre, 202
Beauregard, 161
Beaver, 221, 316
Bechtel, 79
Beck, 193, 304
Becker, 111, 215, 304
Beckett, 193
Beckman, 215, 324
Becvar, 114
Bedell, 138
Bedford, 237, 253
Bednarczyk, 114
Bednarek, 114
Bednarz, 114
Beebe, 214, 325
Beecham, 27
Beecher, 200
Beekman, 193
Beeks, 193
Been, 61
Beer, 220
Beers, 198
Beetle, 283
Beggs, 156
Begley, 126
Behm, 24, 255
Behn, 24
Behnke, 220
Behr, 220
Behrens, 220
Belanger, 244
Belcher, 160, 314
Belden, 192
Bell, 12, 217, 218, 301
Bellamy, 161
Beller, 141
Bellis, 70
Belliveau, 205
Bellman, 138
Bellmonte, 244
Bellows, 243
Belly, 286
Belohlav, 152
Bemis, 242
Benda, 61
Bender, 113, 309
Bendix, 61
Benedetto, 61
Benedict, 61, 170, 320

Benes, 61
Benfield, 214
Benjamin, 261, 265, 313
Benner, 120
Bennett, 4, 61, 298, 301
Benoit, 61, 325
Benson, 61, 239, 304
Bent, 199
Bentley, 230, 310
Benton, 239, 311
Benz, 220
Bercher, 200
Bercovitz, 83
Beresford, 233
Bereskin, 200
Berg, 191, 307
Berge, 191
Bergen, 191
Berger, 110, 305
Berggren, 269
Berglund, 269
Bergman, 191, 315
Bergquist, 269
Bergstresser, 213
Bergstrom, 269, 270
Berkley, 242
Berkowitz, 98
Berkson, 98
Berland, 203
Berlin, 248
Berliner, 248
Berman, 126, 317
Bernard, 55, 309
Bernardi, 55
Berner, 105
Bernham, 230
Bernhardt, 75
Bernstein, 264, 313
Berra, 208
Berry, 191, 303
Bertocco, 46
Bertram, 73
Bertrand, 92
Bertucci, 93
Berube, 204
Besler, 191
Besser, 291
Bessie, 198
Best, 221, 311
Betts, 321
Bevan, 43
Bevans, 43
Beveridge, 6
Bevilacqua, 166
Bewley, 27
Bey, 206
Beyer, 255, 321
Beynon, 43
Bialas, 150
Bialek, 150
Bialy, 150
Bianchi, 150
Bianco, 150

Index

Index

Index

Coleman, 13, 34, 74, 302
Coles, 56
Colfax, 146, 219
Colin, 56
Collett, 56, 324
Colletti, 191
Colley, 56
Collier, 105
Collins, 56, 301
Colomb, 98, 222
Colombo, 98, 222
Colon, 98, 307
Colonna, 56
Colquhoun, 246
Colson, 56
Colvin, 13, 319
Combs, 204, 308
Comer, 141, 324
Comerford, 233
Como, 64
Compton, 229
Comstock, 238
Conant, 87
Conboy, 87
Concannon, 87
Condit, 119
Condon, 85, 326
Cone, 262
Conforti, 163
Congdon, 232
Conklin, 74, 166, 314
Conkling, 74
Conley, 85, 308
Conn, 32, 326
Connell, 88, 323
Connelly, 87, 311
Conner, 306
Connery, 87
Connolly, 312
Connor, 44, 314
Connors, 85, 314
Conrad, 48, 309
Conroy, 87, 322
Considine, 72
Constable, 138
Constantine, 72
Conti, 175
Contreras, 249, 320
Converse, 134
Conway, 87, 308
Cook, 24, 101, 119, 298, 301
Cooke, 3, 311
Cooksey, 240
Cookson, 74
Cooley, 87, 313
Coolidge, 240
Coombs, 240
Coon, 162, 323
Cooney, 221
Coons, 5
Cooper, 101, 113, 301
Cooperman, 113

Coopersmith, 113
Coote, 163
Cope, 116, 171, 322
Copeland, 238, 307
Copley, 191
Copp, 191
Copper, 113
Coppersmith, 128
Coppinger, 191
Copple, 283
Corb, 87
Corbett, 222, 314
Corbin, 222, 315
Corcoran, 85, 321
Cordell, 130
Corder, 129, 320
Cordes, 130
Cordova, 33
Corey, 204, 326
Cork, 118
Corker, 118
Corley, 324
Corliss, 159
Cormac, 43, 87
Corman, 119
Cormier, 200
Cornelius, 321
Cornell, 72, 313
Corner, 206
Cornett, 125
Corney, 149
Cornish, 253
Cornwaleys, 253
Cornwalish, 253
Cornwall, 253
Cornwallis, 253
Cornwell, 234
Corona, 178
Corso, 82
Cortez, 249, 321
Corwin, 210
Costa, 33, 191, 314
Costain, 72
Costello, 86, 310
Coster, 135
Costin, 72
Cote, 115, 207, 319
Cotin, 83
Coton, 83
Cotot, 83
Cotter, 115, 326
Cottle, 115, 282
Cotton, 207, 232, 312
Cottrell, 115, 326
Couch, 316
Coughlin, 85, 321
Coulon, 222
Coulter, 110, 319
Courtney, 244, 314
Cousins, 47, 180
Coutts, 163
Covell, 242
Covier, 113

Covington, 239, 316
Cowan, 204, 262, 311
Coward, 110, 186
Cowherd, 110
Cowie, 246
Cowper, 113
Cox, 222, 301
Coyle, 86, 319
Coyne, 85
Cozzi, 82
Crabbe, 177
Crabtree, 200, 316
Crackston, 3, 237
Craft, 211, 314
Craig, 206, 304
Craigie, 246
Crain, 222, 323
Cramer, 125, 312
Cranborne, 228
Cranbrook, 228
Crandall, 238, 323
Crandon, 240
Crane, 177, 222, 228, 310
Cranford, 228
Crankright, 24
Cranshaw, 236
Craven, 240, 317
Crawford, 245, 302
Crebs, 24
Crenshaw, 38, 325
Crews, 162, 210, 318
Criss, 60
Crist, 60
Criswell, 234
Crittenden, 240
Crocker, 114
Crockett, 156, 311
Croft, 211, 214
Croke, 206
Cromwell, 239
Cronin, 46, 319
Cronkhite, 183
Crook, 156, 236
Crooker, 206
Crooks, 156
Crosby, 231, 310
Cross, 210, 305
Crossley, 210
Crotty, 156
Crouch, 210, 315
Crouse, 162
Crow, 177, 222, 315
Crowder, 125, 317
Crowe, 177, 222, 314
Crowell, 239, 320
Crowles, 236
Crowley, 86, 311
Crown, 219
Crowninshield, 219
Crozier, 135
Cruikshank, 158
Crum, 156, 323
Crumb, 287

337

Index

Ford, 195, 302
Foreman, 110, 315
Forester, 107
Forget, 184
Forman, 110
Forrest, 199, 316
Forristall, 107
Forsberg, 269
Forst, 199
Forster, 107
Forsyth, 245
Fort, 168
Fortner, 195, 326
Fortuna, 277
Fortunato, 160
Fortune, 160
Fosco, 149
Foss, 193, 326
Foster, 107, 180, 298, 302
Foulkes, 72
Fountain, 323
Fountaine, 196
Fournier, 111, 326
Fowle, 221
Fowler, 122, 304
Fox, 177, 219, 302
Foy, 238
France, 56, 254, 255
Francesco, 254
Francia, 254
Francis, 56, 254, 306
Francisco, 56
Francke, 56
Franco, 56, 249, 254
Francois, 56
Franczak, 56
Franczyk, 56
Frank, 56, 247, 305
Frankel, 14, 324
Frankenstein, 293–294
Frankfort, 256
Frankfurter, 257
Franklin, 3, 174, 303
Franks, 314
Franz, 56
Franzen, 56
Franzese, 254
Fraser, 314
Frazier, 254, 304
Frech, 162
Frederick, 76, 310
Fredrickson, 44
Freed, 271
Freedman, 266
Freeland, 174
Freelove, 285
Freeman, 9, 174, 302
Freitag, 294
Fremling, 172
French, 254, 306
Freund, 160
Frey, 311
Freyer, 134

Friar, 134
Frick, 162
Friday, 281, 294
Friedlander, 248
Friedman, 76, 266, 299, 307
Friedrich, 48
Friend, 159, 322
Frisbie, 231
Fritsch, 79
Fritz, 79, 311
Froehlich, 159
Fromm, 162
Frost, 107, 310
Fruehauf, 164
Fry, 174, 310
Frye, 311
Fryer, 134
Fu, 272
Fuchs, 219, 326
Fuentes, 196, 326
Fujii, 272
Fujikawa, 272
Fujimoto, 272
Fulk, 72
Fuller, 3, 118
Fullerton, 238, 303
Fullilove, 284
Fulton, 245, 312
Funk, 159, 315
Furlong, 211
Furman, 125
Furnace, 292
Furness, 292
Furnish, 292
Furr, 171
Furst, 175
Furtado, 184
Further, 288
Fury, 288
Fuzzey, 291

Gabel, 14
Gabler, 139
Gabor, 70
Gabriel, 70, 317
Gaffney, 85
Gage, 182, 324
Gagliano, 178
Gagnon, 116, 318
Gainer, 149
Gaines, 72, 309
Gajda, 170
Gajewski, 198
Galbraith, 171
Gale, 161, 324
Galer, 128
Gales, 254
Gall, 171
Gallagher, 88, 305
Gallant, 161
Gallas, 161
Gallegos, 318
Galligan, 149

Gallina, 222
Gallo, 178, 322
Gallon, 288
Galloway, 312
Gallup, 125
Galvin, 149
Gamble, 284, 312
Gannon, 152, 326
Gans, 177, 223, 266
Gant, 141
Garber, 78
Garcia, 27, 92, 301
Gardiner, 3, 111
Gardner, 97, 111, 303
Garfield, 202
Garfinkel, 262
Garland, 76, 318
Garner, 97, 306
Garnett, 81
Garofalo, 214
Garrett, 73, 304
Garrison, 306
Garth, 211
Gartner, 111
Gary, 87, 321
Garza, 221, 308
Gaskill, 234
Gaskin, 254
Gaspard, 71
Gasparo, 71
Gasper, 71
Gasperec, 71
Gass, 213
Gasser, 216
Gassmann, 216
Gast, 202
Gaston, 254, 323
Gates, 212, 307
Gatewood, 199, 213
Gatsch, 78
Gatto, 221
Gatz, 78
Gaul, 171
Gault, 171
Gauss, 177, 223
Gauthier, 53, 92, 326
Gay, 159, 311
Gaylord, 159
Gaynes, 72
Gaynor, 149
Geary, 87
Gee, 156, 272, 320
Gehrke, 45
Geier, 223
Geiger, 127, 317
Geis, 251
Geisler, 14
Gelb, 152
Gelbfisch, 5
Gelderman, 216
Gellatly, 165
Geller, 14
Gelman, 127

Index

AMERICAN SURNAMES

Index

Hammer, 288, 326
Hammett, 45
Hammock, 45
Hammond, 38, 45, 304
Hammonds, 38
Hamon, 45
Hamp, 253
Hampton, 236, 307
Hancock, 3, 50, 54, 82, 308
Hancox, 50
Hand, 54, 157, 218, 317
Handelman, 125
Handler, 125
Handloser, 292
Handshaker, 181
Handy, 54, 161
Haney, 237, 312
Hanke, 54
Hankes, 54
Hankey, 285
Hankin, 54, 82
Hankins, 50, 323
Hanks, 326
Hanley, 240, 319
Hanlon, 86
Hanna, 239, 312
Hannaford, 233
Hannah, 239, 323
Hanrahan, 86
Hans, 51
Hanscom, 240
Hansen, 51, 303
Hanson, 51, 54, 82, 303
Harcourt, 240
Harden, 232, 315
Harder, 110
Hardiman, 109
Hardin, 71
Harding, 43, 305
Hardt, 198
Hardwick, 234
Hardy, 92, 305
Hare, 177, 221, 325
Hargrove, 236, 322
Harker, 121, 124
Harkins, 54
Harkness, 209
Harlan, 214
Harley, 230
Harman, 48, 324
Harmon, 48, 305
Harnack, 161
Harold, 15
Harper, 125, 303
Harrell, 243, 307
Harriman, 109
Harrington, 239, 305
Harris, 38, 53, 276, 298, 299, 301
Harrison, 38, 53, 303
Harrod, 15
Harrold, 15, 228

Harry, 53
Hart, 220, 228, 303
Hartfield, 240
Hartford, 233
Hartig, 168
Hartley, 230, 311
Hartman, 76, 307
Hartmann, 313
Hartnett, 87
Hartstone, 206
Harvard, 42
Harvey, 48, 303
Harwood, 235
Haskins, 72
Hassel, 200, 247
Hastie, 163
Hastings, 240, 313
Hatch, 212, 316
Hatcher, 212, 317
Hatfield, 232, 313
Hathaway, 213, 321
Hatt, 117
Hatter, 117, 142
Hauck, 55
Haug, 191, 202
Haugen, 191
Hauke, 55
Haupt, 157
Hauser, 208, 322
Havel, 194
Haver, 221
Haviland, 203
Havlik, 70
Havoc, 222
Hawes, 211
Hawk, 8, 54, 323
Hawker, 8
Hawkes, 54
Hawkins, 54, 303
Hawkinson, 54
Hawley, 230, 320
Haworth, 234
Hawthorne, 3, 238, 325
Hay, 322
Hayakawa, 272
Hayden, 232, 310
Hayes, 88, 190, 211, 302
Hayman, 107
Hayne, 236
Haynes, 237, 305
Hays, 310
Hayward, 107, 325
Haywood, 235, 324
Hazard, 182
Hazel, 200
Hazeltine, 205
Hazelwood, 235
Hazen, 126
Hazlett, 198
Head, 157, 206, 314
Headland, 211
Heald, 192
Heaney, 87

Heap, 191
Heard, 110, 320
Hearn, 206
Hearst, 198
Heath, 199, 236, 308
Hebbard, 77
Hebble, 282
Hebert, 77, 311
Hecht, 223, 266
Heck, 212
Heckmann, 107
Hedberg, 269
Hedges, 206
Hedlund, 269
Hedrick, 78
Hedstrom, 269
Heffner, 114
Hegg, 211
Hegy, 191
Heidemann, 175, 202
Heiden, 202
Heider, 175
Heilman, 183
Heiman, 75
Heinemann, 107
Heinrich, 54
Heins, 54
Heintz, 54
Heintzleman, 107
Heinz, 54
Heiser, 202
Heisler, 106
Heitz, 79
Held, 137, 192
Heldt, 137
Heller, 247, 313
Helliwell, 239
Hellman, 204
Hellstrom, 269
Hellyer, 129
Helm, 14, 28, 324
Helms, 200, 314
Helton, 236, 319
Helwig, 15
Hemingway, 212
Hemmer, 206
Hempel, 234
Hemphill, 234
Henderson, 38, 54, 302
Hendricks, 54, 305
Hendrickson, 54, 309
Hendries, 54
Hendriks, 54
Hendrix, 54
Hendry, 38, 54
Henke, 46
Henley, 236, 320
Henneberry, 231
Hennessy, 85, 318
Henning, 202, 314
Henri, 54
Henrici, 54
Henriksen, 54

345

Index

Index

Index

McManus, 84, 315
McMillan, 307
MacMillan, 74
McMorrow, 86
McMullen, 88, 320
McMurray, 90, 325
McNabb, 132
McNair, 45
McNally, 172, 321
McNamara, 44, 314
McNamee, 87, 89
McNeal, 320
McNeil, 307
McNicholas, 56
McNiff, 87
McNulty, 254, 326
McNutt, 293
Macomber, 69
Macon, 123
MacPhail, 66
McPherson, 311
MacPherson, 74
McQueen, 90, 321
McRae, 90, 322
McRay, 88
McShane, 51
McTavish, 62
MacTavish, 69
McTigue, 126
MacWalters, 53
McWard, 74
McWilliam, 84
McWilliams, 49, 319
Madden, 67, 311
Maddocks, 91
Maddox, 91, 311
Mader, 16
Madej, 252
Madigan, 87
Madison, 67, 95, 316
Madox, 6
Madsen, 67, 324
Madura, 161
Magee, 88, 316
Mager, 156
Maggio, 97
Maggiore, 184
Maggs, 95
Magnus, 83
Magnuson, 83
Magoun, 74
Maguire, 321
Mahan, 89
Maher, 88, 316
Mahler, 248
Mahon, 89
Mahoney, 85, 89, 309
Maiden, 184
Maier, 102, 325
Maitland, 202
Majewski, 97
Majka, 179
Major, 154, 321

Makepeace, 181
Maki, 30, 191
Makowski, 214
Makris, 154
Malatesta, 157
Maldonado, 92, 172, 310
Malec, 156
Malecki, 156
Malek, 156
Malenkov, 45
Malkin, 94
Malkowski, 251
Mallard, 223
Mallett, 94
Mallin, 94
Mallory, 160, 324
Malloy, 87, 323
Malone, 87, 307
Maloney, 88, 309
Malonson, 182
Malthouse, 216
Malthus, 190, 208, 216
Maly, 156
Malyshev, 156
Man, 72, 253
Mancinelli, 184
Mancini, 184
Mancuso, 184
Mandel, 78
Manke, 156
Manley, 238, 316
Manlove, 284
Mann, 72, 78, 109, 253, 304
Manners, 106, 289
Mannheimer, 247
Manning, 45, 305
Manns, 84
Manos, 82
Mans, 84
Mansfield, 239, 320
Manson, 84
Mantel, 171
Mantell, 116
Manuel, 321
Manypenny, 172
Mapes, 95
Maple, 200
Mapp, 95
Marais, 204
Marangopoulos, 74
Marble, 284
March, 16, 97, 206, 281
Marchand, 124
Marchese, 175
Marchetti, 68
Marciniak, 68
Marciszewski, 168
Marckwardt, 128
Marco, 68
Marcus, 32, 68, 318
Marder, 220
Marek, 68

Mares, 204
Margeson, 3, 95
Margolis, 95
Marinello, 177
Marino, 312
Marion, 94
Marison, 94
Mark, 68, 228
Marker, 121
Markiewicz, 68
Markley, 215
Markowitz, 68
Markowski, 252
Marks, 32, 68, 206, 307
Markus, 68
Marland, 232
Marlowe, 238
Marquez, 92, 319
Marquis, 68
Marrero, 129
Marriott, 94
Mars, 203
Marsden, 232
Marsh, 203, 306
Marshall, 105, 302
Marsters, 136
Marszalek, 103
Martell, 105
Martello, 113
Martensen, 59
Marti, 59
Martikke, 59
Martin, 3, 59, 298, 299, 301
Martin- prefixes, 299–300
Martineau, 59
Martinek, 59
Martinelli, 59
Martinet, 59
Martinez, 59, 302
Martini, 59
Martino, 59, 318
Martinson, 59
Marvel, 286
Marx, 32, 68
Marzec, 97
Marzullo, 97
Masaryk, 112
Masek, 112
Maslankowski, 252
Mason, 123, 302
Mass, 69
Massa, 69
Massey, 69, 243, 308
Massie, 69
Masson, 69
Masters, 136, 296, 319
Masterson, 74, 323
Matheson, 67, 326
Mathews, 306
Mathiesen, 67
Mathieu, 67
Mathis, 307

Index

Moneysmith, 127
Monk, 134, 147
Monks, 135
Monroe, 194, 307
Montague, 243, 324
Montefiore, 264
Montefiori, 192
Montgomery, 243, 303
Montoya, 250, 319
Moody, 39, 162, 306
Moon, 243, 310
Mooney, 172, 310
Moonlight, 246
Moonshine, 185
Moor, 203
Moore, 3, 4, 203, 298,
  299, 301
Moorman, 107
Morales, 250, 305
Moralez, 92
Moran, 88, 305
Moravec, 256
Mordecai, 32
Moreau, 149
Morehead, 246
Morehouse, 204
Moreland, 240, 323
Morello, 46
Moreno, 149, 310
Moretti, 46
Morgan, 91, 301
Morin, 149, 316
Mork, 203
Moron, 287
Morrill, 148
Morris, 91, 301
Morrison, 42, 303
Morrow, 204, 307
Morse, 203, 309
Mortenson, 84
Mortimer, 243
Morton, 229, 306
Moseley, 230, 320
Moser, 119, 313
Moses, 69, 261, 311
Mosher, 204, 323
Moskal, 256
Moskovitz, 69
Moskovsky, 257
Moskowitz, 261
Moskvin, 257
Moskwa, 257
Mosley, 230, 311
Moss, 69, 261, 305
Motel, 218
Motley, 118
Mott, 193, 322
Moulin, 106
Moulinier, 106
Moulins, 209
Moy, 272
Moyer, 45, 310
Moynihan, 253

Mozart, 76
Mraz, 99
Mrazek, 83
Mroz, 178
Mrozek, 178
Much, 155
Mucha, 178
Muchmore, 289
Mudd, 203
Mudge, 203
Mudgett, 203
Mueller, 35, 106, 299,
  305
Muench, 134
Muhr, 204
Muir, 199
Muirhead, 246
Mulcahy, 87
Mulder, 106
Mule, 287
Mull, 209
Mullaney, 87
Mullen, 88, 308
Muller, 106, 312
Mulligan, 88, 324
Mullin, 321
Mullins, 3, 153, 209, 306
Mulvihill, 87
Mumford, 233
Munch, 134
Mundt, 80
Mundy, 97
Munger, 124
Munk, 134
Munn, 134
Munoz, 92, 313
Munro, 194
Munsen, 84
Munson, 84, 321
Murawski, 202
Murch, 156
Murdock, 73, 317
Murphy, 86, 299, 301
Murray, 159, 245, 302
Murrell, 148
Muscarello, 177
Muse, 212
Musgrave, 240
Muskie, 168
Mussolini, 93, 177
Mustanen, 149
Muszynski, 252
Mutch, 155
Muth, 80
Mutter, 179
Mutziger, 248
Myer, 102
Myers, 102, 302

Nabors, 180
Nachtigall, 223
Nadler, 128
Nagel, 128, 325
Nagy, 155, 324

Nakagawa, 272
Nakamura, 272
Nall, 189
Nance, 214, 318
Napier, 111, 323
Napoleon, 249
Napoli, 249
Nardi, 93
Nash, 189, 307
Nason, 158
Nathan, 261
Navarro, 250, 316
Naybors, 189
Naylor, 112, 128, 324
Naysmith, 112
Neal, 72, 304
Neat, 173
Neave, 179
Neely, 86, 316
Neff, 179, 316
Negron, 149, 325
Neighbors, 26, 180, 189
Neighbours, 26
Neil, 72
Neilson, 84
Neiman, 172
Nelms, 189
Nelson, 30, 299, 301
Nemec, 172
Nemecek, 172
Nemeth, 255
Nemetz, 255
Nemitz, 255
Neri, 82
Nesbitt, 245, 322
Nesmith, 128
Ness, 208
Nestor, 156
Neubauer, 172
Neuberg, 227
Neuberger, 227
Neudorf, 227
Neuhaus, 208
Neuman, 172
Neumark, 206
Neva, 204
Neville, 227
Newberg, 210, 227
Newberger, 227
Newberry, 231, 237
Newbury, 237
Newby, 231
Newcomb, 171, 325
Newcomer, 171
Newell, 208, 312
Newhall, 208, 226
Newhouse, 208, 237
Newkirk, 209
Newland, 201, 232
Newman, 171, 304
Newmann, 326
Newmark, 206
Newquist, 26

Index

Index

Reiff, 79
Reilly, 308
Reimer, 75
Reinecke, 45
Reiner, 75
Reinert, 75
Reinhardt, 75
Reinke, 78
Reisman, 137
Remington, 240
Renaud, 27, 93
Renault, 93
Renfro, 245
Renner, 108
Reno, 27, 220
Rentsch, 60
Rentz, 60
Renwick, 234
Repa, 120
Resnick, 112
Reuss, 116
Reuter, 116
Revere, 293
Rex, 178
Rexford, 195
Reyes, 178, 306
Reynolds, 76, 97, 302
Reznick, 112
Rhea, 193
Rhoades, 322
Rhoads, 201
Rhodes, 201, 304
Rhys, 91
Ricardo, 52
Ricci, 54
Riccio, 153
Rice, 92, 302
Rich, 51, 172, 308
Richard, 51, 306
Richards, 51, 303
Richardson, 51, 298, 302
Richer, 73
Richey, 51, 323
Richie, 51
Richman, 109, 172
Richmond, 244, 311
Richter, 138, 312
Rickard, 51
Rickert, 51
Ricketts, 51
Ricks, 51, 326
Rideout, 289
Rider, 107, 325
Riddle, 17, 283, 311
Ridge, 192
Ridgway, 213
Rieck, 79
Rieger, 75
Riemer, 123
Ries, 155
Rifkin, 83
Rigas, 178
Rigby, 231

Rigdale, 3, 193
Riggs, 192, 312
Rigsby, 231
Riha, 165
Riley, 85, 303
Rimkus, 83
Rindskopf, 157
Rinehard, 75
Rinehart, 75
Rinella, 93
Ring, 206, 326
Rio, 193
Riordan, 126
Rios, 312
Ripley, 293
Ritchie, 52, 314
Ritrovato, 164
Ritter, 136, 175, 310
Rivera, 193, 302
Rivers, 214, 312
Rix, 51
Rizzo, 153, 322
Roach, 206, 309
Roback, 109
Robb, 52
Robbie, 52
Robbins, 52, 305
Roberson, 52, 307
Roberts, 52, 298, 301
Robertson, 52, 303
Robeson, 52
Robie, 52
Robin, 52
Robins, 326
Robinson, 52, 276, 298, 299, 301
Robison, 52, 312
Robles, 250, 319
Robson, 52
Rocca, 192
Roche, 206, 320
Rocher, 216
Rochford, 240
Rock, 206, 322
Rockefeller, 3, 5, 203
Rockett, 243
Rockwell, 197
Rockwood, 215
Rode, 201
Rodgers, 53, 305
Rodin, 93
Rodriguez, 27, 92, 299, 301
Rodriques, 28
Rodriquez, 325
Rodwell, 234
Roe, 220, 228, 316
Roebuck, 220
Roelandts, 83
Rog, 207
Rogers, 3, 28, 52, 298, 301
Rogerson, 52

Roggenfelder, 5
Rogowski, 251
Rohr, 214, 247
Rohrbacker, 248
Rohrer, 247
Roland, 48
Roleau, 27
Roller, 130
Rollins, 82, 310
Roman, 167, 310
Romano, 167, 317
Rome, 167
Romero, 167, 308
Rood, 210
Rook, 223
Rooney, 87, 323
Roos, 218
Roosevelt, 3, 5, 23, 214
Root, 159, 319
Roper, 129, 321
Rosa, 218, 320
Rosado, 48, 319
Rosario, 136, 316
Roscoe, 199
Rose, 218, 223, 263, 303
Roseman, 263
Rosen, 98, 263, 312
Rosenbach, 263
Rosenband, 263
Rosenbaum, 263
Rosenberg, 263, 308
Rosenblatt, 263
Rosenbloom, 263
Rosenblum, 263
Rosenbluth, 263
Rosenbusch, 263
Rosencranz, 263
Rosendahl, 263
Rosendale, 263
Rosenfeld, 263
Rosengard, 263
Rosengren, 263
Rosenheim, 263
Rosenholtz, 263
Rosenkranz, 263
Rosenmayer, 263
Rosenquist, 263, 269
Rosenschmidt, 218
Rosenstadt, 263
Rosenstein, 263
Rosenstock, 263
Rosenthal, 263, 315
Rosenwald, 263
Rosenzweig, 263
Rosin, 93
Rosinski, 252
Rosner, 17
Ross, 208, 263, 302
Rosser, 53
Rossetti, 151
Rossi, 315
Rossini, 151
Rossman, 208

360

Index

Rossow, 255
Roth, 151, 265, 306
Rothbart, 154
Rothschild, 265
Rothstein, 206
Rotter, 126
Rounds, 154
Rountree, 200
Rouse, 151, 316
Rousseau, 151
Roux, 151
Rowan, 200
Rowe, 212, 305
Rowell, 82, 238, 326
Rowland, 91, 228, 311
Rowley, 230
Roy, 178, 308
Royce, 218
Royster, 163
Rubenstein, 247, 264
Rubin, 70, 247, 261, 313
Rubincam, 214
Ruby, 70
Rucinski, 214
Rucker, 78, 316
Rudd, 151
Ruddy, 151
Rudnick, 105
Rudnyckyj, 249
Rudolph, 75, 320
Rudy, 82
Ruebsamen, 34
Ruff, 151
Ruffin, 98
Ruge, 192
Ruggiero, 53
Ruggles, 239
Ruiz, 82, 308
Rulo, 27
Rumble, 284
Rund, 155
Rundlett, 155
Runyon, 163
Ruppert, 77
Rusch, 198
Rush, 198, 310
Rushford, 233
Rushforth, 234
Rushing, 200, 324
Rusin, 255
Ruskin, 81
Rusnak, 256
Russ, 151
Russel, 35
Russell, 35, 151, 298, 302
Russo, 255, 308
Rust, 151
Rutgers, 53
Ruth, 80, 325
Rutherford, 245, 313
Rutkowski, 214
Rutledge, 197, 315
Rutsen, 53

Ruttenberg, 264
Ruud, 151
Ruusu, 218
Ruzicka, 35, 218
Ryan, 88, 302
Ryba, 223
Rybak, 122
Rybar, 122
Rybarczyk, 44
Rybicki, 196
Ryder, 107, 326
Ryerson, 83
Rynne, 193
Rzepka, 120

Saari, 204
Sabo, 116
Sacco, 17
Sachs, 267
Sack, 267
Sackett, 81
Sacks, 261, 266
Sadd, 39
Saddler, 123
Sadler, 123, 319
Sadowski, 201
Sage, 161
Sailor, 126
St. Clair, 244, 296
Saint-Gaudens, 55
St. George, 244
St. John, 244, 296, 326
Saito, 272
Salazar, 250, 313
Sale, 207
Salinas, 250, 322
Salisbury, 231
Salk, 200
Salmon, 63, 323
Salter, 120, 126, 325
Saltonstall, 242
Saltzberg, 248
Salvage, 163
Salzman, 120
Sammons, 63
Samp, 63
Sample, 63, 244, 320
Sampson, 63, 311
Samson, 3, 63
Samuel, 63
Samuels, 63, 261, 319
Samuelson, 63
Sanborn, 240
Sanchez, 92, 303
Sandberg, 269
Sandell, 216
Sanders, 58, 302
Sanderson, 58
Sandhill, 216
Sandler, 108
Sandoval, 250, 317
Sandquist, 269
Sands, 240, 322

Sandstrom, 269
San Filippo, 68
Sanford, 233, 311
Sanger, 126
Sansone, 63
Santana, 92
Santangelo, 249
Santiago, 250, 305
Santoro, 136
Santos, 250, 310
Santucci, 46
Sapp, 287, 320
Sargent, 136, 314
Sargis, 128
Sarna, 220
Saroyan, 175
Sartori, 116
Sass, 200
Saterlund, 268
Sather, 202
Sato, 272
Sattelmacher, 123
Satterfield, 203
Satterlee, 238
Satterthwaite, 242
Sattler, 123
Sauer, 163, 325
Saul, 64, 228
Saulnier, 120
Saunders, 58, 305
Savage, 163, 308
Saville, 244
Sawa, 99
Sawicki, 99
Sawin, 99
Sawinski, 99
Sawyer, 113, 307
Sayce, 171
Sayers, 17
Sayles, 207
Saylor, 126, 325
Sayward, 125
Sax, 254
Saxon, 254
Sbarbaro, 172
Scales, 214
Scalzitti, 165
Scarborough, 231
Scardina, 52
Scarpelli, 117
Scattergood, 185
Schaaf, 217
Schacht, 215
Schachter, 112
Schaefer, 110, 307
Schafer, 316
Schaffer, 312
Schaffner, 102
Schalk, 109
Schall, 109
Schaller, 169
Scharf, 162
Schatz, 160

361

Index

Index

Stowell, 238
Strand, 194
Strandberg, 269
Strang, 29, 168
Strange, 171
Strass, 213
Strassburger, 264
Strasser, 216
Stratford, 233
Stratton, 229, 317
Straub, 18
Straubinger, 248
Strauch, 198
Strauss, 32, 266, 317
Streadbeck, 197
Streng, 168
Street, 212
Streeter, 212, 311
Strickland, 237, 304
Stringer, 137, 315
Stringfellow, 168
Stritch, 213
Strobel, 18
Strode, 203
Strohm, 193
Strom, 193
Stromberg, 269
Stromquist, 269
Strong, 168, 309
Strother, 203
Stroud, 203, 317
Strube, 153
Struck, 198
Struthers, 203
Stuart, 102, 310
Stubblefield, 203
Stubbs, 18, 322
Stuck, 247
Stucker, 199
Stuckey, 154
Studer, 201
Stumpf, 155
Sturm, 162
Sturman, 125
Sturt, 208
Sturtevant, 165
Stutz, 156
Stuyvesant, 23, 250
Styles, 212
Suarez, 92, 322
Such, 289
Sudbo, 268
Sugar, 116
Sugarman, 116
Suggs, 221
Sullivan, 85, 299, 302
Summer, 280
Summerfeld, 247
Summerfield, 203
Summers, 306
Summerville, 243
Sumner, 138, 321
Sunday, 24, 281, 294

Sundberg, 269
Sunde, 193
Sundstrom, 193
Superfine, 185
Suslov, 220
Sussman, 160
Sutcliffe, 192
Sutherland, 312
Sutor, 39, 142
Sutter, 116, 142
Sutton, 252, 304
Suzuki, 272
Svec, 117
Svoboda, 166
Swain, 109, 317
Swallow, 289
Swan, 18, 222, 223, 317
Swanson, 44, 304
Sward, 271
Swart, 149
Swartz, 149, 312
Sweat, 288
Sweeney, 162, 307
Sweet, 46, 159, 313
Sweetman, 74, 159
Sweetnam, 227
Sweetser, 254
Sweitzer, 255
Swem, 222
Swensen, 84
Swenson, 84, 317
Swett, 159
Swiatek, 182
Swiatkowski, 252
Swift, 165, 316
Swindell, 185, 205
Swindle, 185
Swindlehurst, 215
Swindler, 118
Swope, 5
Sydney, 293
Sydoruk, 99
Sykes, 193, 315
Sylvester, 48, 320
Symington, 245
Symmes, 64
Symons, 64
Sypniewski, 252
Szabo, 116
Szafranski, 214
Szczepaniak, 69
Szczepanik, 69
Szczepanski, 69
Szczesny, 185
Szewc, 117
Szewczyk, 116
Szymanski, 64
Szymczak, 64

Tabor, 126
Taff, 62
Taft, 211
Taggart, 133

Taglia, 128
Tagliaferro, 6, 128
Tague, 126
Taillandier, 104
Tailleur, 116
Takacs, 117
Takahashi, 272
Talbot, 73, 219, 316
Talcott, 208
Talley, 86, 314
Tallman, 5, 109
Tanaka, 204, 272
Tanis, 83
Tannenbaum, 200
Tanner, 122, 309
Tansey, 235
Tappan, 115
Tapper, 139, 271
Tarr, 209
Tart, 288
Tash, 189
Tasker, 115
Tate, 157, 306
Tatum, 239, 319
Taub, 266
Tauber, 222
Tavenner, 139, 143
Taylor, 38, 100, 116, 298,
    299, 301
Tchaikovsky, 249
Teachout, 293
Teague, 149, 317
Tebbetts, 81
Teele, 223
Tegge, 149
Tegtmeyer, 139
Teichman, 196
Teitlebaum, 265
Teixeira, 250
Telfer, 128
Teller, 118
Temple, 209, 277, 314
Templeton, 229
Templin, 69
Ten Broeck, 204
Ten Eyck, 190, 200
Tennant, 174
Tenny, 71
Tennyson, 71
Tepper, 137
Terhune, 6
Terhunen, 6
Terranova, 202
Terrell, 73, 312
Terry, 73, 305
Terwilliger, 251
Tesar, 113
Teslenko, 113
Testa, 157
Tester, 157
Teufel, 288
Teufelbeiss, 184
Tewksbury, 238

365

Index

AMERICAN SURNAMES

368

Index

ABOUT THE AUTHOR

Elsdon C. Smith, the author of many books on names, was born in Virginia, Illinois, on January 25, 1903, the son of Dr. George Walter Smith and Eva Coles Smith. He received his B.S. from the University of Illinois in 1925 and his LL.B. from Harvard in 1930. Since that date he has practiced law in Chicago.

In association with Professor Erwin G. Gudde he founded the American Name Society in 1951. He was president of the society from 1951 to 1954. He was Third Vice-President in 1967, Second Vice-President in 1968 and First Vice-President in 1969. He is also book review editor of *Names*, the Journal of the American Name Society. He is a member of the English Place-Name Society and of the International Committee of Onomastic Sciences, Louvain, Belgium.

Mr. Smith has a private library of more than twelve hundred books on names ranging from the earliest, dated 1575, down to the present time, together with dictionaries, word books, and various other works touching in one way or another upon names.

He is the author of *Naming Your Baby*, which Chilton published in 1943 and which is a standard work on the subject. He is also the author of *The Story of Our Names, Dictionary of American Family Names, Treasury of Name Lore,* and is the compiler of *Bibliography of Personal Names.*

Mr. Smith and his wife, the former Clare Irvette Hutchins, live in Skokie, Illinois.